ECONOMICS: A PERSONAL CONSUMER APPROACH

ECONOMICS: A PERSONAL CONSUMER APPROACH

MICHAEL R. BEHR, PH.D.

Associate Professor of Business and Economics
College of Business and Economics
University of Wisconsin—Superior

DENNIS L. NELSON, PH.D.

Associate Professor of Economics
Department of Economics
University of Minnesota—Duluth

RESTON PUBLISHING COMPANY, INC.
Reston, Virginia 22090
A Prentice-Hall Company

Library of Congress Cataloging in Publication Data

Behr, Michael R
  Economics, a personal consumer approach.

  Bibliography: p.
  Includes index.
  1. Economics. 2. Consumption (Economics).
3. Finance, Personal. I. Nelson, Dennis L.,
1929– joint author. II. Title.
HB171.B366   330   74–23841
ISBN 0–87909–238–6

© 1975 by
Reston Publishing Company, Inc.
A Prentice-Hall Company
Box 547
Reston, Virginia 22090

10   9   8   7   6   5   4   3   2   1

Printed in the United States of America.

❖❖

*To our wives and children, the consumers
we know best—if not the best consumers
we know.*

❖❖

CONTENTS

PREFACE

To Students—What do you want from your education? Some combination of personal and vocational skills and an understanding and appreciation of the world around you are common goals which overlap considerably within the field of economics—a fortunate circumstance at this point. Perhaps the most "practical" thing you can learn is to recognize problems, opportunities, and situations for what they are, to analyze alternative solutions and approaches to them, and to select the most plausible explanations and attractive courses of action. These "skills" are truly durable and practical. They are useful both in making good day-to-day decisions and in understanding the world around you. We hope to have written a book giving you the opportunity to develop those skills using a personal economic point of view. In Part I of the book we have developed a general framework within which economic choices are exercised; in Parts II and III we look directly at personal economic choices; in Part IV we have applied the tools of personal economic choice to some of the issues of public (or social) choice. Thus, we hope you will find the book worthwhile in your roles as a consumer, as a curious person, and as a citizen.

To Teachers—Clearly, economics taught exclusively from a personal stance is incomplete. Nevertheless, a personal orientation can be a powerful teaching lever, and one we may have set too far aside in face of the tide of modern macroeconomic theory. Fundamental issues of choice can certainly be developed within a personal framework; they can then be applied to a wide variety of nonpersonal and even noneconomic situations. We think our book may therefore be useful in introductory economics courses—consumer economics or otherwise.

Traditional consumer economics (as opposed to general economics) is a "case of the missing middle." On the one hand, abstract theory is pursued by a select group of professors and students. On the other hand, there is discussion of labels, laws, and procedures with little attention paid to decision-making frameworks and methods. The "missing middle" (which we hope to have buttressed) needs to deal more fully with fundamental preferences and the options available. The student must be led to generalize choices and reflect on preferences—their origin, modification, and means of satisfaction. The choice of a life-style is more important than the choice of a used car; but either choice is instructive in making the other if the question of choice is addressed at its root.

Many analytical tools and procedures are applicable beyond their customary narrow application. Present value must be dusted off as the core of the evaluation of time as an economic variable in the face of policies designed to let interest rates move more freely; the issue is broader than personal investment as usually defined. Elementary probability is useful in the evaluation of omnipresent risk; the issue is broader than insurance as such. Many subjects and tools often viewed as topical are, if developed more fully, actually guiding principles to the intelligent consumer. Thus, we see our book as a logical evolutionary step in the maturation of undergraduate consumer economics.

Although we did not set out to write an interdisciplinary book—and have not done so—it does contain a bit of interdisciplinary seasoning. We have expanded the issues of choice beyond the far fringes of the economic world into the edges of such fields as psychology, sociology, and political science. After all, choices (and therefore economic issues) are not exclusively economic!

This book may be used as a foundation for beginning economics courses with any of three different emphases: general introduction to economics; consumer economics; or personal finance. The following suggested sets of chapters will serve each of these emphases well and leave room in a one-semester course for supplemental problems, readings, activities, etc.

Introduction to Economics Emphasis

Consumer Economics Emphasis

Personal Finance Emphasis

To General Readers—The main object of personal economic activity is consumption. Personal satisfaction—the end consequence of consumption—is central to much of life itself. As a consumer you have developed a considerable store of common knowledge about consumer problems. In this book you will be exposed to a more formal problem-solving procedure which will lead to clearer understanding and wiser personal decisions. From time to time we need mirrors which reflect clearly the image we suspect is there but do not stop to recognize.

To Economists—Economics has traditionally dealt with the measurable—partly, we suspect, because much of the substance of economics *is* subject to measurement, and partly because we feel naked without a quantitative cover. The market is our refuge. Yet increasingly we find that social goods and direct personal consumption of resources in the form of increased leisure and related activity call for nonmarket decisions. Although the market does not address itself directly to many allocation questions, it remains central by providing a conceptual reference point from which we may work, relying on opportunity cost principles.

The market expresses itself in concepts, principles, forces, and relationships; these are the keys to the application of market economics to a wider variety of questions that extend into the interdisciplinary hinterland. Economists have developed a marvelous framework which they have too timidly applied. We are less inhibited—or more reckless—depending on one's point of view. Hence our occasional sidetrips.

In stretching the traditional market economics framework over a wider spectrum of applications we have taken a few liberties which we think most of you can live with. We are not incorrect—just mildly and expediently extraordinary!

MICHAEL R. BEHR, PH.D.
DENNIS L. NELSON, PH.D.

I

GENERAL ECONOMIC SYSTEMS AND DECISIONS

"Get organized."

"The world is too organized as it is," you say? Perhaps. But understanding, action, and a satisfying life require organization—of thought at least. How do the pieces fit together to complete a puzzle? Without organizing them you will never know.

Our puzzle happens to be economic, and you are the key piece. We must see how the puzzle is organized in order to find a strategy to accomplish desired goals. Although we do not dwell heavily on organization *as such* in Part I, it is perhaps the most adequate common foundation since words like *system, choice, alternative* and *decision* imply organization, either as a noun or in verb form; organization can be either a condition or a course of action.

The central organizational message in Part I deals with three related subjects: how *you* are constructed economically; how the economic *world* is constructed; and how you relate to the world wherein you are contained.

In Chapter 1 we discuss economics as a part of society—after deciding what we think economics is, of course. In Chapter 2 we look at your personal economic foundations followed by a procedure for decision making in Chapter 3. Chapters 4 through 7 develop the key features of economic systems that necessarily contain and influence you personally, and finally in Chapters 8 and 9, we explain how we think you need to look at yourself in your situation to make the most of it.

In Part I we are concerned mostly with background understanding—of you, the world, and your relationship to the world—all from an economic point of view. Having established these foundations you will be ready to look at more specific questions in Part II.

chapter
1

THE SCINTILLATING SCIENCE

The purpose of this chapter is to explain briefly what economics is, why it is important, and why its well-known nickname, "the dismal science," is totally misleading in the context of today's world. We will investigate the relationship between economic and noneconomic concerns and examine the overall position of the individual in his world. The range of choices available to you is broadening as time goes on; these are exciting times (if a bit confusing) in which to be alive, and it is our intent in this book to point out ways in which you can take advantage of the opportunities available to you.

► A BIT OF HISTORY ◄

"Economics is a dismal science," lamented the English writer Carlyle in 1849. He was referring to the apparent inability of mankind to provide even basic sustenance for itself. Carlyle based his conclusion on Thomas Malthus's dire predictions about population growth. Malthus maintained that the tendency of a population to propagate itself far outstripped a population's ability to increase the output of economic goods from available resources. The resulting outlook was grim indeed. Carlyle's intent is not of major interest at the outset of this book; however, it *is* of concern that economics may still be considered a dismal science. Too many students have been exposed to economics at some time in their formal education that was indeed pessimistic. Whatever the reason, or reasons, such an impression is all too prevalent.

Economics in the modern world is not at all a dismal science. On the contrary, it is precisely the opposite. Hence, we have taken the liberty of relabeling it the *scintillating science*. It is not that the problems of mankind, in a personal and societal sense, are less serious now than in Carlyle's day; in fact, our economic problems are more numerous and complex. Complexity, however, must not be confused with despair. The purpose of the discipline of economics is to provide knowledge and insights for us as individuals, and as a society, to better satisfy our many needs and wants for material things. Economics is people oriented—people centered. The purpose of economics is to aid man in the search for a more fulfilled, contented life.

Before dismissing Malthus and Carlyle as unduly pessimistic, it must be acknowledged that their case is not without merit. Certain parts of the world support Malthus' contention: Population expands so fast that perpetual poverty prevails. But other parts of the world provide an equally forceful refutation of his argument: Population rises slowly relative to economic capacity; thus the population enjoys a steadily rising level of economic well-being.

There is no point in debating whether Malthus was right or wrong relative to the time in which he lived. Clearly, he was a little of each. It is significant, however, that he is not *necessarily* right in today's world. Indeed, he is increasingly less right on the basis of present evidence. Mankind is learning to exercise control over both blades of Malthus' rampaging scissors—population and economic growth. This control opens new opportunities and prompts the substitution of *scintillating* for *dismal*. To be sure, all persons will not share equally in the expanding horizons. But it is reasonable to suppose that the economic future for the average world citizen will be considerably brighter than the past.

Consider the variety of activities available. It is an economic issue or concern whether man is

1 • Building an art gallery.
2 • Composing a musical score.
3 • Researching the causes of cancer.
4 • Working in a service station.
5 • Buying groceries.
6 • Voting on school-bond issues.
7 • Attending school.
8 • Fighting a war.
9 • Enjoying leisure.

Modern man can undertake a wide variety of activities because he can afford to; alternatives are available to him. In the world of Malthus, everyone's nose was to the grindstone to provide a subsistence level of food, clothing, and shelter. Short work weeks, long vacations, and mass exposure to the "good life" are evidence that most of us are really quite wealthy by historical standards. To conclude that economics is dismal is essentially to conclude that life has less meaning than it really does. We reject such cynicism. However, failing to recognize the reality of our economic problems, personal and societal, is like the proverbial ostrich sticking his head in the sand.

Furthermore economics is directly relevant to the desire that we all share—to lead a more meaningful, more satisfying, life. There are few things that you do in life that do not have real economic significance—for example,

1 • Where you work.
2 • What work you do.
3 • How you use your leisure.
4 • What you buy.
5 • How you vote, and why.
6 • Your attitudes on social problems.

All these, and more, are basically economic questions or have roots in economic reality.

The primary focus of this book is on you, the individual, and not the business, the state, the nation, or any other *group* of individuals. More specifically, the emphasis is on you as a **consumer** (user) of economic things rather than on you as a **producer** (maker) of economic things. Most of us spend a great deal of time as consumers and additional time as producers—so that we may be more abundant consumers. Yet there is evidence that many individuals do not think things through very carefully as consumers. Since a great deal is at stake, there would seem to be a

Reprinted by permission of Newspaper Enterprise Association.

strong incentive to proceed as consumers only after having carefully worked out a plan that assures us that we will be as well-off as possible in a given situation. The purpose of this book is to help you organize your thoughts, think things through, consider the alternatives, formulate a goal, and then proceed according to a plan that results in the most satisfactory outcome for you.

Our assignment will require that some new patterns of thought be developed that are slightly, though not entirely, unfamiliar. As an aid to this reorientation, we will look at your place as an individual in the over-all economic picture.

▶ ECONOMICS DEFINED ◀

What is this **economics** that is supposedly relevant to the consumer? Like most other things, it has been defined in a number of different ways. Most of the definitions suggest, directly or indirectly, that the central issue of economics is **scarcity**. Indeed, there is never enough to go around; not everyone can have everything he wants. This state of affairs dictates the necessity for choice. If we may not have everything, obviously a decision must be made as to which things to have and which things to forego. There are good decisions and bad decisions. **Good decisions** are decisions that lead to actions that take us toward a goal that has been previously selected. **Bad decisions** are all other decisions that either do not lead to the goal or lead there more slowly than could have otherwise been accomplished in the event of a better decision.

Choice permeates the economic world. Individuals decide between a car or a boat, a vacation or an education. Nations choose to support highways, schools, wars, or public housing. An individual or a nation may have any or all of the things that it wants to some degree, but it seems abundantly clear that neither individuals nor nations may have *all* they want of *everything*. Choices must therefore be made. In the pages that follow, an attempt will be made to help you make decisions that lead to positive results. Since the central issue will necessarily be choice, perhaps it could be said that this book is really a book on decision making that happens to use economic examples. In that event, if you are astute, you may use this framework to organize your thoughts about many noneconomic situations as well.

How, then, should economics be defined? There are a number of different ways, but to say simply that the central issue is **scarcity** is not sufficient. The purpose of a definition is to narrow a subject so that all parties to a discussion or investigation may know what every other person is talking about. The following will suffice as a starting point:

> **Economics is the study of the attempt to satisfy our material wants which are greater than our ability to satisfy them.**

The issue of scarcity is clear; we want more than we can have. Economics deals with material things (including intangible "things" such as services) as opposed to spiritual, emotional, social, psychological, philosophical, or other aspects of human existence. The fact that such noneconomic aspects of life may affect man's wants for material things is duly recognized. However, economics does not seek to analyze or explain them. The emphasis in economics is on the analysis and explanation of man's direct relationship to material "things."

––––––––––––––––––– **EXAMPLE 1–1** –––––––––––––––––––

The economist is concerned with whether or not you buy a new car and if so, in what price range, with what

options, and so on. He is not concerned with whether you want it to drive to work or to impress your neighbors. The psychologist may be interested in such a distinction; but the economic impact of your decision to buy the car will be the same whatever your motive.

Society's desire for things is satisfied by products and services that society creates by combining natural resources with labor, management, and capital. These means of production are in limited supply, so it follows that the products and services into which these resources are converted are also in limited supply. As we become more skillful (efficient) at converting resources into products, products become more abundant relative to resources. But the fact remains that our improving production techniques cannot provide sufficient products to give everyone everything he wants. Furthermore, such economic alchemy is not in prospect. It appears then that economists are reasonably assured that they will not be rendered obsolete by the march of technology. Consumers will need to continue to make the choices that the fact of scarcity requires.

It should be clear that the term "scarcity" is meant to convey the concept "limited," rather than the more common connotation of a critical shortage.

EXAMPLE 1–2

Textbooks are scarce if no one is *giving* them away. Anything not free is scarce. The fact that the bookstore has run out and you are in a panic about a course for which you do not have a text does not make them more scarce than if the bookstore had them in stock. In everyday conversation, scarcity may be relative; in basic economics scarcity is absolute.

A second definition of economics will serve to emphasize the point that economics is concerned with material things. The noted nineteenth-century economist Alfred Marshall observed that:

> *Political Economy or Economics is a study of mankind in the ordinary business of life; it examines that part of individual and social action which is most closely connected with the attainment and with the use of the material requisites of well-being.*[1]

Marshall's definition emphasizes an interesting dimension: the use of the term *ordinary*. In some respects, economics is rather grubby. Material things are indeed ordinary. This is probably one of the reasons that economics has been historically slower to gain academic respectability than many other disciplines unburdened by their ordinary character.

Economics as a discipline is generally considered to have begun with Adam Smith in 1776 upon the publication of his book *The Wealth of Nations*. Since man has spent so much of his history in the pursuit of "ordinary things," it seems odd that he should be so slow to systematically investigate how he chooses which ordinary things to have and which to forego. To this day, it is likely that the majority of consumers operate only on the basis of an ill-defined instinct in making choices that affect them profoundly.

It might be asked why attention to economic choice is urgent if the average person is reasonably well-off by historical standards and headed upward. Isn't economic choice more urgent for poor people, who must conserve their limited means? Not really. The "Malthusian subsister" has little latitude within which to operate and is forced in the only direction he can really go: nose to the wheel; little leisure; cheapest possible diet; and so on. But a person in a less confining economic condition has a bigger problem. He can abandon the rut to which he was originally confined; then he must decide among myriad alternatives previously unavailable. The opportunity for a higher level of living carries with it the risk of bigger blunders. Unless you are so well-off that you have no desire to be still better-off, you are interested in making better decisions. To be sure, you may know people who pay little attention to their consumer choices because they are wealthy enough to live well enough to suit them anyway. But many of these people probably act as they do out of ignorance rather than from a specific unwillingness to make better decisions. Since people display a distressing tendency to act in response to pressure, it is likely that a rising level of economic well-being throughout society will erode the quality of consumer choice, unless the consumer is aware of his situation and takes himself in hand. We think that the average consumer will wish to be more careful if he realizes more fully the losses from his carelessness.

► ECONOMICS VERSUS TOTAL ◄ HUMAN EXPERIENCE

It is perhaps necessary to develop some clearer idea of just what types of things are considered "ordinary" from the standpoint of economics. We have less of many "things" than we might like to have (love and affection, for example), yet even without further elaboration of the definition of economics, most people would probably assume that love and affection are not part of the world of economics. Why not? On what basis is a line drawn through human experience with the territory on one side labeled **economics** and the territory on the other side labeled **noneconomics?** A simple reference to scarcity is not sufficient. Noneconomic "things" are scarce, too.

As an aid to the discussion, we introduce the concept of **utility.** Anything—tangible, intangible, economic, or noneconomic—that has the **ability to satisfy** has **utility.** Cars, houses, haircuts, education, and friendships have utility. The car has the *ability* to satisfy, and as you use it, it *does* satisfy. Friendship has the ability to satisfy, and as you experience it, it does satisfy. Thus the ultimate concern of all human endeavor is to provide satisfaction, whether that satisfaction is derived from material things, from a feeling of harmony with a supreme being, or from something else. The acquisition of utility is obviously central to life itself. Since the major focus of this book is on the utility that derives from economic sources, it is worthwhile to try to gain some insights into the division between the economic world and the rest of human experience.

> **Put succinctly, the boundary between the economic world and the noneconomic world is wherever society says it is.**

Although that statement seems to dispose of the issue with dispatch, a nagging suspicion of evasiveness lingers, since there is much to be said about how society determines just where the boundary shall be. It might be said that economics encompasses all those things which can be bought and sold through socially sanctioned channels, that is, legal markets, in the case of the United States. In other words, if something can be legally bought and sold, society apparently considers it part of the economic world. Some things are obviously excluded because of an inability to transfer them in this way. A religious experience cannot be bought the same way a grapefruit is bought and, therefore, religious experience per se is excluded from the economic world. Aids to religious experience are another matter. The salary of the clergy, the use of supplies in the church are likewise economic. The spiritual experiences of the members of the church are excluded—or are noneconomic. However, there are other things that are capable of passage through markets, yet society disallows their passage. Why?

Consider a well-worn tale: One person asks a second whether a particular object is for sale, and receives the reply, "Everything is for sale at the right price." "Well," says the first, "everything except your spouse I suppose." "Make me an offer," answers the second drily.

A favorable relationship with a spouse has utility, yet spouses are not overtly obtained through economic channels—that is, by buying them in markets. They are therefore not directly economic in nature in the eyes of society. Yet society's position on the issue is not necessarily accepted by all individual members of society. Some individuals may abide by the law, and grumble about it or not, as their dispositions may dictate; or they may engage in illegal economic activity via black markets and the underground. In the story above, society says that spouses are not economic; the first person is apparently in agreement with this position (and perhaps assumes the same for everyone else, too); the second is in disagreement but abides by the law because it is the least painful alternative.

There are other subtle distinctions to be drawn from this story. Although spouses per se are not economic in nature, the acquisition of a spouse has an important economic dimension. In some cases the economic dimension may be the primary, and possibly the only, motivation in the acquisition of a spouse, although the persons involved will usually deny it and society may allow them to masquerade with splendid solemnity. Since society frowns on marriage for primarily economic reasons, it therefore does not provide organized markets for the purchase and sale of spouses. However, a case of cute-coed-marries-dirty-(and wealthy)-old-man may *in fact* be a matter of each making the best economic deal possible. He wants the satisfaction and prestige of a vivacious young coed, she wants his money; so they trade their "products." Each sees the other as a "best buy." Since the "transaction" has been tidied up through "private negotiation" by the parties rather than by purchase and sale in the open market, society concedes to view the "transaction" as noneconomic by stamping it *marriage*.

A number of important and far-reaching issues have been raised in this discussion.

1 • What is, and what appears to be, may be two different things.

A veneer of idealism associated with marriage may cover the less ideal reality of a grubby economic transaction taking place in an unorganized "market." Since society frowns on purely economic marriages, it fails to provide organized markets and marketplaces for marriage partners. Those persons desiring to enter into such "transactions" are left to make the best of it on their own. To assume that everything is what it appears to be is to be naïve. To assume that everything is different from what it appears to be is to be cynical. Since neither extreme is a very happy state, effort must be made to distinguish between appearances and reality and to determine when they are the same and when they are different. A good personal choice requires that distinction.

2 • **The bounds of economics are set by the society within which the economic system operates.**

These bounds are set by cultural, religious, philosophical, ethical, moral, and social values to which the economic system is subordinate. Public attitudes toward marriage seem to stem from the same source as public attitudes toward slavery. On whatever noneconomic grounds one may wish to cite, our society disapproves of the sale of persons as such. Persons are not considered to be economic objects. Now the sale of the *services* of persons is apparently another matter. The consensus is that the sale of labor is socially acceptable, and society thereby provides markets for labor transactions.

3 • **The distinction between economics and the rest of the world is a gray one.**

If it is unacceptable to sell *persons* but acceptable to sell personal *services,* where does this leave some activities? Prostitution seems to be neither fish nor fowl. Splinter political groups have even argued that labor is not an appropriate part of the economic world because of its personal nature.

4 • **The economic–noneconomic boundary will shift as social attitudes shift.**

The reasons for changes in attitudes on such matters as prostitution and slavery are complex. The entire spectrum of historical human experience and contemplation determine social policy. Perhaps attitudes on prostitution are becoming more liberal because of increased confidence that society can now better cope with some of the problems historically associated with it; perhaps it is because a general wave of "live and let live" is upon us; perhaps it is part of a wave of excessive permissiveness that is current; and on and on. No one knows the precise reason for any change in social policy. The only thing that is certain is that whatever social attitude prevails, it will surely change—sometimes slowly, sometimes rapidly—as the kaleidoscopic determinants of that policy continue to unfold with time.

It could be argued that the rejection of slavery was due to so fundamental an event as the redefinition of a person. It is difficult to conceive of the slavery of persons as *person* now seems to be defined. Those who were enslaved were perhaps considered to not quite measure up to the standard.

5 • **Society realizes the grayness of the boundary of economics and takes extra precautions when operating there.**

Social objection to the purchase and sale of persons apparently stems from a philosophical commitment to *individualism*. The individual is to be granted maximum discretion consistent with preservation of the choices available to all other persons. In other words, "I can do what I want as long as it does not interfere with your ability to do what you want." Legalized slavery is quite clearly inappropriate under such a philosophy.

But suppose that, for some strange reason, I wish to sell myself to someone and give him dominion over me. This does not infringe on anyone else's rights, yet society will not allow me to do this. Before you conclude (perhaps correctly) that no one in his right mind would wish to do this, bear in mind that marriages heavily dominated by one partner seem to constitute a de facto approximation of the sale of oneself into bondage. You might argue that no one in his right mind would enter into certain marriages any more than he would sell himself into bondage, yet persons do it every day with society's blessing. Perhaps it took women's liberation to articulate some of the more subtle inconsistencies we have become accustomed to accepting. A little heavy-handedness from time to time should not obscure the merits of the issues they raise from beneath the hazy surface.

Legislative care is taken to ensure that the selling of personal services does not degenerate into the selling of persons. Elaborate labor legislation is designed to ensure that the sale of personal services is voluntary and that the transactions take place under circumstances that do not put the personal service seller in a position that results in his exploitation. Child labor laws, nondiscrimination laws with respect to women and minorities, minimum wage laws, and so on are all efforts by society to assure individual rights in what society recognizes as a sensitive area in light of its own values. An occasionally misguided law does not alter the fundamental social motivation.

6 • **Social policy is the product of a consensus and will therefore find many individuals in disagreement with it at any point in time.**

Society takes some care to respect minority opinion. Some of the concessions to minority opinion are deliberate, others inadvertent, because of society's inability to make perfect decisions. Perhaps society allows cute-coed-dirty-old-man marriages simply because some of these marriages *are* based on what society considers valid grounds for marriage. Since the distinction between valid and invalid grounds is largely a matter of attitude or motivation, society concedes the case to individual prerogatives in circumstances of doubt. Some marriages then become inadvertent means of escape from social policy (that is, the prohibition of purchase and sale of persons or the selling of oneself into bondage).

In other situations, society is more deliberate in its provision for maximum individual liberty within the framework it has constructed. To return to the prohibition of transactions in persons but the sanction of transactions in personal services and the status of prostitution, we note that, in general, the attitude toward prostitution seems to be one of increasing tolerance. Some states and nations have legalized it; others are seriously considering doing so. The issue is talked of more openly than in the past. As it is increasingly sanctioned, there is, of course, no requirement that anyone *must* participate in this activity—only that you *may*. This observation would seem to augur for as liberal a social policy as possible. Why unnecessarily restrict anyone? Give everyone as much rope as possible. If he wants to hang himself with it, that's his business. The counterargument is that certain kinds of activities may be socially destructive. If prostitution aggravates medical, social, and psychological problems present in the land, perhaps it is socially destructive. Since social order is necessary for the exercise of individual freedom, there may be grounds for prohibiting prostitution. Thus short-run restrictions on individual action guarantee long-run preservation of individual action. Should the services of prostitutes therefore be included or excluded from the economic arena? The answer is obviously complex and depends on one's personal values and attitudes as well as on research findings as to the personal and social effects of prostitution.

If there is objection to prostitution as the sale of persons, then is there also objection to the sale of blood? In some states it is illegal, in others not. Some students (particularly those with rare blood types) have made a nice sideline of selling their blood to hospitals. Others view this as simply another form of prostitution. Selling the body is selling the body; why quibble over which part? Interestingly, there is little public debate about blood markets. Perhaps they are less "interesting" than other kinds of markets. More likely, there are fewer social ramifications. In the absence of social ramifications, let those who wish to participate do so and the remainder refrain from doing so. Under such conditions it seems likely that even though a majority might disapprove of the sale of blood, they might allow the minority to continue the activity as part of a philosophical commitment to a society allowing maximum individual choice. If so, this would constitute a deliberate implementation of individualism and would place blood within the economic arena that excludes prostitution.

As further evidence of the economic grayness of matters of the human person, blood is not viewed in the same light as other classes of property, even though it is occasionally bought and sold as other property. If the state wishes to put an "unnecessary" highway through your house, the state will legally take your house at a "fair market price." Period. However, even though someone is dying for lack of blood that you could supply, it is unlikely that you will be legally coerced to supply it. An interesting and, some would say, very incredible state of affairs. Perhaps; but the insights into the world of social and economic affairs are considerable.

Lest the issue seem confused at this point, recall that the main point is that there is utility in many "things" that lie outside the world of economics. The world of economics ends where society says it ends. The discussion that follows concentrates on those goods and services that *society* has concluded are a proper part of the economic world. In general, this *includes* all tangible property and physical human services voluntarily provided at the going market price. It *excludes* the utility of persons as provided in the course of all other interpersonal relationships—for example, love, affection, and friendship. Some economists would exclude these interpersonal relationships from the definition of utility entirely. If the discussion is to proceed only in terms of economics, this exclusion is perfectly legitimate. However, if you are trying to define the *realm* of economics, the exclusion of noneconomic utility will seem arbitrary, since utility is defined as the ability to provide satisfaction. Objects and persons, both inside and outside the economic world, possess this capability, so there may be some confusion as to why certain types of satisfaction are included in the world of economics and others excluded. The division lies wherever society wishes to place it. Figure 1–1 may help to illustrate

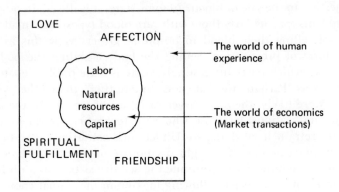

FIGURE 1–1 • The relationship between economics and noneconomics.

mainstream thought in modern American society concerning the relationship between economics and the rest of the world.

The economics versus noneconomics discussion is important because there is a considerable amount of substitutability across the economics–

noneconomics boundary. Failure to recognize the substitutability of economic for noneconomic ends, and vice versa, leads to disaster.

EXAMPLE 1–3

Utility may be gotten from economic goods purchased with money earned through gainful employment, or it may be gotten through contact with other persons in purely social situations. If the economic decision considers utility from only economic sources, the way to get the most satisfaction is to spend every waking minute at gainful employment. Obvious nonsense.

The reason that work weeks get shorter and vacations get longer is because most of us get substantial utility from noneconomic sources and are willing to give up utility from economic sources to get it. The difficult part of the decision is trying to measure the amounts of utility from various sources. Although we cannot measure it directly, we will be able to develop a means of getting useful insights into the amount of utility to be gotten from different alternatives available.

SUMMARY

1 • Economics was originally dubbed "the dismal science" because it was believed that it merely explained why mankind would always live in poverty. Economics has become particularly agreeable, however, as control over population and economic output has become more complete.

2 • Economics deals with mankind's conversion of resources into end products and services to satisfy his desire for material things. Since man's wants exceed the ability of available resources to satisfy them, the scarcity problem is central to economics.

3 • Scarcity dictates choice. Therefore, economics is centrally concerned with decision making.

4 • Good decisions lead to a goal as quickly and easily as possible.

5 • The goal of economics is satisfaction.

6 • A product or service has *utility* if it is capable of providing satisfaction.

7 • Almost all man's activities have an economic aspect, but few activities are uniquely economic. Therefore, economic analysis must acknowledge the noneconomic consequences of economic events and vice versa.

8 • The line between economic and noneconomic activity is where society says it is, although it is difficult to state precisely. A product or service is very possibly (though not necessarily) economic if

a. It is produced by converting resources into it.
b. It provides satisfaction.
c. It can be distributed.
d. It has a determinable market value.

9 • Historically, the emphasis in economics has been on production and distribution; consumption has received little attention. An increasing abundance of available products and services widens the range of consumer choice.

study materials

1 • Explain the reasons for Carlyle's conclusion that economics was "the dismal science."

2 • In summary, Malthus stated that population would grow faster than the ability to provide material goods and services for mankind. State evidence that supports Malthus' conclusion; that denies his conclusion.

3 • On the basis of your understanding at this point, list as many elements as you can which are economic in nature in the following activities:

a. Fighting a war.
b. Attending school.
c. Buying a car.

4 • Early economics (1700–1800) tended to emphasize production. State the probable reasons for this.

5 • Differentiate the term "scarcity" from the term "critical shortage."

6 • An understanding of the concept of scarcity is essential to an understanding of economic considerations in general. Using the concept
of scarcity, discuss the following items:
a. Coal.
b. Fresh water.
c. Gold.
d. Wood.
e. Wheat.
f. Land.

7 • Differentiate between good decisions and bad decisions.

8 • Using the concept of scarcity, indicate the necessity for choice in the
economic sense.

9 • Using the categories of economic, social, spiritual, psychological,
and philosophical, indicate to which one each of the following most
closely relates:
a. A religious belief or commitment.
b. Frustration over having failed an examination.
c. Purchasing your textbook at the bookstore.
d. Commitment to the concept of equality of men and women.
e. Relating to your roommate and friends.

10 • In question 9, indicate how each item could be considered part of
a category other than the one to which it most closely relates.

11 • State examples that support the contention that the boundary between the economic world and the noneconomic world is wherever
society says it is.

12 • Classify each of the following as economic or noneconomic; explain
your choices.
a. Selling heroin.
b. Fighting a war.
c. Prostitution.
d. Marriage.
e. Attending class.

13 • Define utility. Why is it important to understand utility when considering the subject of consumption?

14 • In each of the following cases give examples of when it might be
considered a good decision; a bad decision.
a. To buy a car.
b. To quit school.
c. To get a part-time job.

     d. To sell your car.
     e. To quit smoking.

15 • Indicate in what ways the economic activity of consumption has become easier in recent times (in relation to, say, 200 years ago). How has it become more difficult?

footnote

[1] Alfred Marshall, *Principles of Economics,* 9th ed., ed. by C. W. Guillebaud (New York: Macmillan Publishing Company, Inc., 1961), Vol. I, p. 1. (First edition, 1890.)

chapter 2

THE UNDERPINNINGS OF CONSUMER ECONOMICS

A person's value system leads to desires which, if nurtured, grow into needs from among which consumer choices are made. A "need," as it relates to economics, is a desire strong enough to prompt action and a conscious decision to satisfy or not to satisfy the need. Since these "needs" are a state of mind, consumer economics is underpinned by psychology, and consumer choice is heavily dependent on the consumer's experience and environment.

If you are to make good personal decisions, a moderate amount of introspection is required. The end result of a consumer choice is satisfaction. How is satisfaction generated? Why is one person satisfied by something from which another person receives no satisfaction whatsoever? The complete answers to these questions are probably unknown, and even the available answers are beyond the scope of this discussion.

But the opposite extreme—no thought whatsoever to the causes of satisfaction—is equally unacceptable. Many people bluster along through life keeping up with the Joneses like lemmings rushing to the sea. They might not be all that interested in the Joneses if they stopped to think about it, but they don't really know what else to do. It never occurs to them that there might be alternative courses. Other people get great satisfaction emulating the Joneses but feel guilty about it and so are not really satisfied after all.

Satisfaction is subjective. It cannot be readily measured and so it is difficult to grasp. Nevertheless, occasional glances at your inner self will keep you on course.

▶ VALUES ◀

The foundation on which satisfaction rests is very deep. A normally functioning person follows a broadly defined course based on his **value system.** For example, certain attitudes, relationships, and actions are acceptable to you; others are not; others are questionable. What is acceptable to one person is unacceptable to another. One person may be very selfless and receive great satisfaction from helping others succeed, from giving away money, from living an austere life, and so on. Another person lives by his own version of the Golden Rule: Do unto others before they do unto you. They have different value systems. But each provides the framework within which certain things provide satisfaction and other things do not. It does not necessarily follow that a person's actions are always in accord with his value system. Inner conflict results. You will fare much better if you identify approximately which kinds of actions are in conformance with your value system and which are not.

Your value system may undergo change of course. People occasionally make major changes in their life styles and stick with them because they finally took themselves in hand sufficiently to bring their actions out of the realm of habit and into alignment with what they really want. Either their value system underwent a change, or they discovered that one thing led to another and took them where they did not want to go, and they therefore made a correction.

Values involve a judgment of what is good or bad, right or wrong, just or unjust. The first step in consumer choice must be the attempt to determine for yourself your own present values. There is a strong possibility that you have never before seriously considered your own values; it is therefore difficult for you to determine and to state them. Perhaps the easiest way is to state for yourself what it is you want out of life. What do you desire or want? Then ask yourself *why* you want what you do. The answers will provide some insights into your values and may lead you to conclude that you do not really want what you thought you did after all.

EXAMPLE 2–1

- **Do you want to finish college? Why?**
- **Will you seek a job after graduation? Why?**
- **Do you want to work? Why?**
- **Do you want a new car? Why?**
- **Do you like new and fashionable clothes? Why?**
- **Do you relate well to your parents? Why?**
- **Do you like college? Why?**
- **Do you have many close friends? Why?**
- **Do you believe in religion? Why?**
- **Do you want to marry? Why?**
- **Do you work for grades? Why?**
- **Do you enjoy eating in "good" restaurants? Why?**
- **Do you think that pollution is a serious problem? Why?**
- **Do you plan to spend some money today? Why?**

Simple "yes" or "no" answers to these kinds of questions will provide little or no insight to your values. Serious reflection on the "whys" should provide some very meaningful starting points. Your answer may be "yes" to some of the questions simply because you want to get along with other people, be accepted, take care of yourself, help other people, be a success, or enjoy life. You may place high value on things that affect you personally; or you may find that you are very concerned about other people. Remember to be honest. You may want a new car because it will help your image with your peer group: You place high value on social acceptability from your peers. Digging out and scrutinizing values is not easy. Be patient and work at it. One cardinal rule can be stated in the words of Shakespeare: "Above all else, to thine own self be true." Nothing will be accomplished by deceiving yourself. (It is quite another matter to try to deceive someone else—and in some cases you may even consider it desirable. The same, however, cannot be said for deceiving yourself.) You must be honest with yourself and be willing to work at becoming even more so.

► DESIRES ◄

Values manifest themselves in desires. **Desires** are *what you want*. What you value determines what you want, although all your desires are not necessarily in complete agreement with your values at all times. Each of us comes "unstuck" occasionally. Looking at your desires says a great deal about your values. The questions in Example 2–1 ask about your desires and then reveal your values by asking the reason for your desire. Desires, of course, are basic to the quest for satisfaction. Although desires are based on values, your values may be loosely categorized as an aid to examining different kinds of desires. Within any value system, consider desires that have physiological, social, geographic, spiritual, or psychological roots. These categories are merely representative; you may wish to add others of your own.

▷ physiological ◁

You desire water because of your body's physical requirement for it. It is in accord with your value system because you value self-preservation.[1] The desire for water is present whether you are rich or poor, black or white, young or old, Russian or American.

▷ social ◁

Man is a social being. He wants to be around other people and to be accepted by his peer group. A major cause of personal discontent and mental anguish is rejection by one's peer group—whatever the group may be. The desire for acceptability is a major cause of "keeping up with the Joneses." Many people, if not most, would admit that they would prefer not to feel the pressure to "keep up" but that they fear rejection if they do not. Therefore, the people with whom we associate, whether rich or poor, intelligent or stupid, young or old, do have great influence in determining our desires. These desires are socially based.

The society we live in has a great bearing on our desires. "Society," in this sense, refers to the people with whom we live and associate. A student body within a school setting is a society. The city or community or neighborhood in which we live is another society. The family would be still another.

An individual born into and raised in a family society that has a great interest in music will be influenced by that fact. The family attends musical concerts, operas, and symphonies, and plays musical instruments in the home. A person raised in this society would be apt to have a desire for musical "goods and services" (or, depending on the circumstances, a particular aversion to these activities). Another family centers its interests in outdoor activities. Sports play an important part in the life of this family. Hunting, fishing, skiing, swimming, boating, hiking, and camping are popular family activities. A typical desire for a member of this society would be new or different sporting goods.

▷ geographic ◁

Your location affects your desires. If you live in the mountains of Colorado, you may have a desire for skiing and camping equipment. Probably few students in Florida have a desire for skis—at least not snow skis; their desire may be for a fast boat and water skis. A student who walks to classes in the winter in the state of Washington may desire an umbrella, whereas a student in Minnesota would desire a thermal-lined parka coat.

▷ spiritual ◁

Spiritual values affect our life styles profoundly and therefore our desires. There are people who would love to make a million dollars for the fun of doing it and then giving it away; other people would love to make a million dollars to undertake a life of ease and ostentation. Although such differences are not necessarily based on purely spiritual differences, a selfless person is probably quite spiritually different from a selfish person.

Some people get great satisfaction from religious objects and desire them above almost all else; other people think that they are worthless.

▷ psychological ◁

Perhaps all the categories of desires just discussed (with the possible exception of physiological desires) should actually be called "psychological"; that is, they arise out of a condition of the mind. We are conditioned to want what we want by the totality of our experience and environment. Our values are also necessarily based heavily on experience and conditioning; nothing exists in a vacuum in human affairs. Thus *the most immediate noneconomic foundation of consumer economics is probably psychological.*

Although desires are a foundation stone of consumer choice, you are obviously not going to choose to have everything you desire. Since you probably have at least a low level of desire for nearly everything, you would need unlimited capability to attain things and no choices would be required! Therefore, you have to sort out desires according to their desirability. As a beginning, ask yourself in a general way to distinguish between a "good" desire and a "bad" desire. You probably want some things that you are nonetheless disinclined to try to obtain. Why?

It is impossible to make a complete distinction between good and bad desires, but it might be valid to conclude that a desire is good if

1 • It is not in conflict with your basic values.

2 • It would provide real contentment and satisfaction if realized.

3 • It would not lead to great discontent if it were not realized.

4 • It is reasonably attainable.

5 • It would not interfere with the rights and contentment of other people (although this might depend on your values).

A desire is bad if

1 • It is in conflict with your basic values.

2 • It would not provide real contentment and satisfaction if realized.

3 • It would lead to great discontent if it were not realized.

4 • It is not reasonably attainable.

5 • It would interfere with the rights and contentment of other people (again, depending on your values).

In summary, "good" desires will normally lead to satisfaction and contentment; "bad" desires will not. The list of characteristics of good and bad desires is not necessarily complete, and a desire may be good or bad without meeting all five conditions listed. The point is that you will need some general means of sorting out those desires which you want to try to satisfy from those which should be dismissed early in the decision process.

▶ **NEEDS** ◀

Your desire for a product or service *leads* to its choice or selection but does not guarantee that you will actually choose or select it, since, as discussed earlier, there are surely many things you desire that you have not purchased and have no real intention of purchasing. Stated more formally, desire for something is a necessary, but not sufficient, condition for its acquisition.

Let us agree to define **needs** as *desires that have become strong enough to prompt you to consider action.* A need is a desire that has been nurtured to the point where you feel you must do something about it. Desires that call us to action are needs. In the act of consumption, we are generally responding to a need—a grown-up desire. Therefore, your "needs" prompt closer scrutiny than your desires. If the desire has grown to the point where you feel a need, it is difficult to be objective and rational in assessing it. It is too easy to make excuses for yourself by saying, "But I must have it because I need it." It is not easy to delineate between desires and needs; they are interrelated.

Note that a "need" does not imply a utilitarian necessity. It is too easy to dismiss something, especially for someone else, by saying, "You don't really need it." The "really" in this sense generally implies an absolute utilitarian necessity. If our consumption were concerned only with absolute, utilitarian needs, it would minimize the problems of consumption. In this absolute sense, the only needs would be for basic maintenance of life itself. In modern society we have progressed beyond merely sustaining life. Food, clothing, and shelter (at minimum levels) would be our only *absolute* needs. But we have *relative* needs that are just as important from the standpoint of consumer choice. Do not be trapped into thinking in *absolute* or extreme ways. Practically everything is *relative;* that is, everything has meaning only in relationship to something else.

EXAMPLE 2–2

Most of us would agree that food is a necessity. Must it then be argued that tenderloin steak is an absolute need? Certainly not. Boiled rice would keep us alive—at least for a long while. But if an individual has enjoyed tenderloin

steak all his life and has the income to acquire it, he might have developed a *relative* need for steak. That is, relative to his experience and environment he has nurtured his desire for tenderloin steak to the point of action; he has a need for steak. He *can* get it and he *will* get it. He needs it.

Is a telephone a necessity? Again, in an absolute sense it is not. But in a more practical and realistic way it is recognized as a necessity in our society. Most of us have allowed the desire for accessibility to friends, success in business, acceptability, and other personal satisfactions to grow to make the telephone a necessity. We have a *relative* need for it and proceed to action on that basis.

The problem you face in attempting to analyze a need is to place the need in proper perspective. Desires can be allowed to grow into needs when it should be apparent to you that you have little chance of satisfying the need. An unfulfilled desire is one thing—an unfulfilled need is quite another. Great unhappiness results from needs that you cannot fulfill.

EXAMPLE 2-3

If you allow the desire for a new luxury car to grow and grow—if you nurture it by visiting the dealer's showrooms, by browsing through the beautifully illustrated sales brochures and by dreaming endlessly about it—you will soon have the "need" for a $10,000 limousine. A Cadillac need on a Volkswagen income can be a pretty unhappy state of affairs. From this desire, which was allowed to run rampant, results a need which, if not satisfied, may lead to great unhappiness or, more likely, irrational consumer behavior. You may take virtually all your Volkswagen income and buy the Cadillac. At what expense? What of your other desires and needs?

Sensible, rational, intelligent consumers are going to have many identical desires. Each consumer must recognize them for what they are —wants and desires. Each consumer does not nurture all his desires to adulthood when he knows there is virtually no way of satisfying them.

EXAMPLE 2–4

Many people living in the northern states have a desire for a vacation in Hawaii in January or February. This is probably not a "bad" desire, yet the vast majority of these individuals do not develop a "need" for this vacation, simply because they know that they cannot afford it without making wholly unacceptable sacrifices. That is, they do not seriously consider it or entertain the thought.

Needs vary in intensity. Our common sense is telling us this when we say, "I need a new shirt, but I need shoes more, so I guess I'll buy the shoes." The choice between the shirt and the shoes is between two needs—each is seriously considered for action. A careful assessment of your needs and your ability to satisfy them is an important step in becoming an intelligent consumer. Do not be led to believe that if you are a sufficiently intelligent consumer, your income will stretch to cover everything you desire.

▶ **THE PROBLEM: CHOICE** ◀

These brief insights into values, desires, and needs point up the basic consumer problem—choice. Our desires may be virtually unlimited. Take time to list the things you would like to have or do; given enough time, and with honesty, your list would probably be very long. Now assume that you had all these things. Would you assume that you would have no new desires? Evidence points to the contrary. New desires always seem to emerge.

EXAMPLE 2–5

If you make available to the common man of Bangladesh all that is available to the common man of the United States, you might well assume that he would think he was in heaven. He would have all the material things he ever dreamed of and more. All his desires would be satisfied. However, does the common man in the United States have no unsatisfied desires? Certainly not. New desires continue to surface, and there is no end in sight.

Whereas our desires may be unlimited, our needs are limited to the degree that we have held our desires in check. We not only exercise choice over which of our needs we satisfy but we exercise substantial control over our needs. That is, to some extent, we decide what the alternatives will be from among which we make final choices; the alternatives we actually consider are not handed to us from above—we develop many of them ourselves. Needs are numerically fewer than desires but are felt more strongly. A need will force us to action; a desire will not. The consumer problem is basically the attempt of the individual to satisfy his needs. As previously recognized, needs are many and varied, depending on the individual.

As individuals our values differ; as our values differ, our desires differ; as our desires differ, our needs differ; as the strength of our needs differs, our consumer choices differ. We therefore recognize that we differ as individuals and thus face different consumer problems.

Although values, desires, needs, and choices differ among us, the *manner* in which the most desirable choice is selected is identical in every case. And therein lies the beauty of what follows. A choice is a choice. We will supply the procedure for making decisions and you supply your values, desires, and needs to plug into the problem.

► VALUES, DESIRES, NEEDS: ◄
REVERSIBILITY?

The relationships among values, desires, needs, and choices discussed in this chapter suggest the diagram in Figure 2–1. The division between

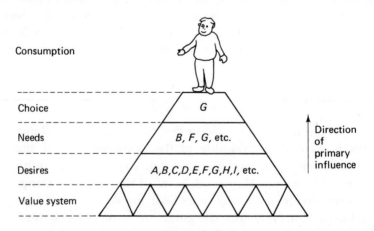

FIGURE 2–1 • The underpinnings of consumer economics.

each layer is not always clear-cut—particularly between desires and needs. Although the issue may be somewhat abstract for our purposes, it might be asked if there is any downward "flow" in the pyramid. Do desires affect values, for example? If we are not careful, the discussion can dissolve into questions of semantics—that is, into debates about primary versus secondary values or chicken versus egg questions. Nonetheless, it may be worthwhile to acknowledge that from some points of view there may indeed be downward "flows" in the pyramid. This should come as no great surprise, as we concluded earlier that value systems, as a part of human affairs, are developed in response to experience and environment. Consider the possible impact of desires on values.

EXAMPLE 2–6

Peter Plush places a high value on social esteem and believes that a new luxury automobile will raise his social esteem. He therefore has a strong desire for a new luxury automobile. His values affect his desires. But the strong desire for the automobile affects the value he places on his job (his source of money to buy the automobile). He places a high value on working and earning money so that he can buy that which will enhance his social esteem. His desires affect his values.

EXAMPLE 2–7

Conrad Conserver does not value social esteem in the same way. He views the luxury automobile as ostentatious and, in fact, yielding negative social esteem in the circle in which he travels. Conrad views the luxury automobile as a major source of pollution and his values are strongly negative on pollution. Conrad has no desire for a big car. His values affect his desires. Obviously, Conrad will place a lower value on money income than Peter Plush—if their other desires and values are the same.

Is it possible to need something that we do not desire? In a sense, perhaps. For example, physical checkups, polio shots, better nutrition, better grades, and so on may be needed but not particularly desired. That is, you may choose in favor of certain things because you know they "are good for you," even though you find their acquisition rather disagreeable. But in a larger sense, don't you choose this kind of need because you desire things that are "good for you"? The only honest answer that any of us could probably give would be, "Well, I suppose." Before you argue that people do not necessarily want what is good for them (since cigarette sales have not dropped to zero, for example), you must remember that "goodness" in consumer economics is an *amount of satisfaction,* and that is by no means to be equated with the longest possible physical human life or anything of that sort. Suppose that one pack of cigarettes a day will take five years (or whatever it may be) off your life. If you would rather have the enjoyment of the cigarettes than the extra five years, the cigarettes are good for you, are they not? Yes, of course, if we're talking about satisfaction.[2]

Thus, in a fairly narrow way, we may choose things that we need but do not particularly desire; in a broader sense, it would seem that no rational consumer would choose a need that he did not desire. After all, if you have no desire for something, why develop a need for it and ultimately choose it?

A more accurate view of the need-not-based-on-a-desire would probably be to recognize that the benefit (satisfaction) from some things is very general and long term in nature and that "need" and "desire" are more loosely defined in everyday usage. A more formal approach suggests that a need finally chosen would be based on a desire if you look deeply enough.

But the main point in this rather confusing discussion is yet to be made explicitly: What do you *really* want? Have you considered where you are headed? Is it where you want to go? Are all your consumer choices consistent with your overall choice of direction for your life? If you answer these questions with reasonable care, you will undoubtedly find that ultimately your choices are based on needs that developed from desires consistent with your value system. In other words, the predominant order of causality will be from the bottom of the pyramid toward the top. A surprising number of people would probably find that they would make substantially different consumer choices if they took more care in identifying their real preferences and the alternatives available.

SUMMARY

1 • The end result of consumer choice is *satisfaction* received from that which is chosen.

2 • A person's *value system* is the ultimate foundation upon which a consumer choice rests.

3 • *Desires* are wants that arise on the basis of physiological requirements or on the basis of a person's value system. Although desires (other than physiological) can be classified as stemming from social, geographic, spiritual, and other considerations, they are all highly psychological because they all represent a state of mind.

4 • *Needs* are desires that have grown strong enough to prompt a consumer to seriously consider satisfying them. A consumer has considerable discretion over which desires he cultivates into needs and which desires he squelches.

5 • Consumer *choices* are made from among a person's various needs.

study materials

1 • Considering values as an individual's basis for distinguishing right from wrong, good from bad, desirable from undesirable, just from unjust, fair from unfair, list five values that you have. Try to be specific.

2 • Analyze in detail why you are attending school. In what way do your values relate to this choice?

3 • List five things you desire. Why do you desire them? How strongly?

4 • Rank in order from 1 to 5 your desires listed in problem 3. What was the basis for your determining the rank of each?

5 • State at least two desires you have which relate primarily to each of the categories of physiological, social, geographic, spiritual, and psychological.

6 • Considering desires in the context of good or bad as defined in this chapter, list two examples that you believe *for you* would be (or could be) good or bad desires.

7 • Define the term *need*. Indicate under what circumstances each of the following would or would not be considered needs:
   a. New coat.
   b. New car.
   c. Food.
   d. Boat.
   e. Gasoline.

8 • Differentiate absolute needs from relative needs. Give examples of each.

9 • Discuss the idea that values determine consumption—that consumption determines values.

10 • Prepare as exhaustive a list as possible using the following categories:

    a. Do not have, but desire (want).

    b. Do not have, but need.

    c. Have, but do not need.

    d. Have, but do not desire (want).

footnotes

[1] You may wish to argue that self-preservation is instinctive and therefore not part of your value system. That is, you take the position that values relate to that part of your life which is purely discretionary. We have no quarrel with that except to point out that some persons' values apparently lead them to self-destruction. The "abnormality" of this condition of course leads to the question "What is normal?" Perhaps it is also normal to be consumed by a desire to "keep up with the Joneses." Identification of normality may be of interest from a psychological or philosophical point of view, but it doesn't lead very far in consumer economics; what is normal for you may not be normal for someone else. You are what you are—normal or otherwise—and we take it from there.

[2] Another dimension of this problem is satisfaction today versus satisfaction tomorrow, a question that will be considered in the chapters on investment. It might be asked why so many people want to quit smoking but do not do so if they would really feel better off quitting. Part of the answer lies in the fact that they will have to wait for the satisfaction from not smoking (the extra five years of life). As we shall see, there are substantial forces operating in favor of present satisfaction in place of future satisfaction. The person who attempts to quit smoking but doesn't succeed may acknowledge that he is attaching too much significance to the present and not enough to the future, but he lacks the discipline to make the adjustment in the face of the overwhelming force of the present.

appendix

MORE ON PSYCHOLOGY AND ECONOMICS

The text of Chapter 2 suggests that consumer behavior is psychologically based—with the possible exception of physiological requirements (although even physiological requirements are registered mentally and serve as an impetus to action—if with less reasoned discretion than when your consumer action is more truly voluntary). As a consumer, you steer yourself in the direction of viable alternatives and away from those options you clearly cannot obtain. That is, you tend to create, mentally, the *set* of choices you are willing to consider, and then you select the most satisfying *member* of the set. This is the essence of the statement made earlier that you exercise control over those desires that will be allowed to become needs. The satisfied consumer, therefore, must be master of himself "from the ground up."

Given the psychological roots of economics in general, and of consumer economics in particular, it is curious that both psychologists and economists have paid so little attention to the point of contact between the two fields. Interest is growing, however, particularly in the field of marketing, where decisions on advertising, product development, and so on are continuously being made. Much of the rest of the meeting ground between psychology and economics has related to consumption patterns and the implications of the forces behind them for society as a whole as opposed to a focus on the individual consumer. There are, however, many interesting personal insights to be drawn from these two approaches. Let us call the two approaches the *marketing approach* (advertising, product development, etc.) and the *aggregate approach* (society's consumption patterns).

▶ THE MARKETING APPROACH ◀

We have chosen to work from a single primary source in this discussion in the interest of brevity, although we realize the risk of misconception in doing so. The source is *Consumer Behavior: Contemporary Research in Action,* by Robert J. Holloway, Robert A. Mittelstaedt, and M. Venkatesan (Boston: Houghton Mifflin Company, 1971). Although there are many other fine sources, we have chosen this one because it is current, written by qualified people in the field, an excellent source of other references, and has a practical-action orientation rather than a philosophical–conceptual one. In deference to psychologists and economists, it must be said that the book is neither a psychology book nor an economics book; it is a modern marketing book. But marketing is a major area where psychology and economics abut.

Consumer Behavior is a more advanced book than this text, and thus a higher level of competence is needed to thoroughly comprehend it than to comprehend this book. No matter. It is not our intention that you should "eat and be filled"; it is our intention that you should "get a taste." Accordingly, we first reproduce the table of contents, after which we present several selections from the text which are pertinent to our discussion. If you are really interested in this field, you will find much of the book valuable, even though beyond your complete comprehension. In addition, you will find numerous other references in it that you may wish to investigate.

Influencing Forces of Consumer Behavior: External Forces

CULTURAL FORCES

SOCIAL FORCES

Parts II–A and II–B are probably the most specifically oriented toward psychology and thus evidence an interdisciplinary approach. Accordingly, the following brief statements from *Consumer Behavior* about each of the four headings in Part II–A (perception, learning, personality, and attitudes) and the two principal headings in Part II–B (cultural forces and social forces) are instructive.

SELECTIONS FROM THE INTRODUCTION TO PART II-A

Perception

Perception may be defined as the ". . . complex process by which people select, organize, and interpret sensory stimulation into a meaningful and coherent picture of the world." [3]

Learning

Learning "refers to a more or less permanent change in behavior which occurs as a result of practice." [4]

Personality

In their classic review of behavioral theory and research, Berelson and Steiner did not include a separate section on personality. They explained that "Within psychology now, except for the clinical literature, there is little concern with individual personalities or with personality *per se* as an independent category of study." [7]

---

[3] Bernard Berelson and Gary A. Steiner, *Human Behavior: An Inventory of Scientific Findings* (New York: Harcourt, Brace and World, Inc., 1963), p. 88.

[4] Gregory A. Kimble, *Conditioning and Learning* (New York: Appleton-Century-Crofts, 1961), p. 2. Kimble devotes a chapter to the definition of learning citing 12 definitions, many of which imply different theoretical positions.

[7] Berelson and Steiner, p. 63.

Earlier, Hall and Lindzey claimed that "no substantive definition of personality can be applied with any generality . . . personality is defined by the particular empirical concepts which are a part of the theory of personality employed by the observer." [8]

In spite of this lack of conceptual clarity, the continued popularity of the term in ordinary usage and the need for practical predictors of individual behavior have combined to produce an almost overwhelming array of measurement instruments which purport to measure personality. Because some of these have proven useful in clinical, counseling and personnel management contexts, it is only natural that researchers of buying behavior attempt to relate some of the variables measured by these instruments with certain aspects of buying behavior.

Attitude

Attitude may be defined as a "relatively enduring system of affective, evaluative reactions based upon and reflecting the evaluative concepts or beliefs which have been learned about the characteristics of a social object or class of social objects." [9] Because an attitude has no existence independent of the attempt to measure it, much research effort has gone into the development of attitude scales.

SELECTIONS FROM THE
INTRODUCTION TO PART II-B

Although all readings in this section are concerned with external forces, they have been divided into two broad categories, *cultural forces* and *social forces*. The distinction between the two may be illustrated by an example from Kluckhohn and Mowrer: "If a random third of the parents of Cambridge, Massachusetts, were to die tomorrow and their children were to be socialized by their surviving relatives and friends in Cambridge, it may be safely predicted that what these children would learn would be approximately the same—taking the group as a statistical whole—as if their parents had survived." [2]

---

[8] Calvin S. Hall and Gardner Lindzey, *Theories of Personality* (New York: John Wiley and Sons, Inc., 1957), p. 9.

[9] Marvin E. Shaw and Jack M. Wright, *Scales for the Measurement of Attitudes* (New York: McGraw-Hill Book Co., 1967), p. 10.

[2] Clyde Kluckhohn and O. H. Mowrer, "Culture and Personality: A Conceptual Scheme," *The American Anthropologist*, Vol. 46 (January–March, 1944), p. 15.

In short, the *cultural forces* are those whose existence is not contingent on particular persons or small groups but are, in a sense, supra-individual. In contrast, *social forces* are those which are mediated by socially revelant "others."

Cultural Forces

Because of its all-inclusive nature and pervasive effects, culture, as a concept, is both easy to talk about and difficult to define.[3] Sheth has observed, "The role that culture plays in developing buying motives and habits has been implicitly accepted by researchers and specific research has been lacking." [4]

Social Forces

The readings in social influence begin with two studies of group influence. Conforming to group pressure is a rather natural consequence of our relationship with one another. Groups are of varying size, structure and function and each may have different norms. Everyone is a member of a number of groups and each may have an impact on what we buy.

---

[3] Bernard Berelson and Gary A. Steiner, *Human Behavior: An Inventory of Scientific Findings* (New York: Harcourt, Brace and World, Inc., 1964), pp. 643–646, examines the concept of culture. Their discussion is based, in part, on a 1952 paper by A. L. Kroeber and Clyde Kluckhohn which analyzed, in detail, 164 definitions of the term.

[4] Jagdish N. Sheth, "A Review of Buyer Behavior," *Management Science*, Vol. 13 (August, 1967), p. B–729.

▶ THE AGGREGATE APPROACH ◀

The name most closely associated with psychology and consumer economics at the aggregate level is that of George Katona, retired Professor of Economics and Psychology and Director of the Economic Behavior Program of the Survey Research Center at the University of Michigan. Katona has been instrumental in the periodic publication of the results of the Center's survey of a sample of consumers' attitudes as they might be expected to influence their buying behavior. Since the economy tends to move upward if consumers are buying abundantly and downward (or upward more slowly) if consumers are "frightened" and saving for an anticipated rainy day, the results of this kind of work are of some interest—just how much interest depends on how much you believe that the volume of consumer purchases is affected by the consumers' frame of mind. In any event there is much food for thought in Katona's work; you may ask yourself about the extent to which *your* perception of things influences *your* willingness to spend—and for what.

Most of us probably believe that we are relatively immune to personal euphoria or depression as a factor in our buying plans. After all, most of us say, "I am hardnosed; I look at the facts; I am not swayed by my moods." Yet if you are really hardnosed, you recognize that, from the standpoint of personal action, the facts are what you perceive them to be. It can be no other way. If your income is $10,000 per year and you *really* believe that it is $15,000 per year you will act as though it is $15,000 per year, will you not? To be sure, you will soon be in trouble and your belief will undoubtedly be altered, but you must necessarily act on your "belief" and not on the "facts" as conventionally defined. It might be argued that "beliefs" supported by, or largely in accord with, the "facts" are essential to function satisfactorily in this world. Nevertheless, it is our perception of our situation that dictates action; and the perception of our situation is influenced by a wide variety of things, including the weather.

A second reason that most of us probably attach little importance to perception, attitudes, and expectations as factors in our personal economic behavior is that most of us personally experience fairly narrow ranges of these variables. That is, most persons lean toward optimism or pessimism but do not normally swing from extreme optimism to extreme pessimism, so we do not see the importance of the relatively minor changes in ourselves from time to time, even though those changes might have more influence on us than we realize.

One approach to consumption theory is the **permanent income hypothesis,** which holds, briefly, that you spend for goods, not according to your present income, but according to your expectation of "permanent income." In other words you take a long-range view. Thus, as a student, you spend more heavily than your current income justifies because you anticipate enough income in the future to cover your tracks; conversely, in middle age you spend less heavily than your current income might justify in anticipation of old age. The assumption is that you remain at the level of living you think you can swing in the long run so that you do not need to make disruptive changes along the way. Of course it is also assumed that you will make a shift in your level of consumption if your expectations turn out to have significantly missed the mark. Obviously, frame of mind is a significant factor in all this; the hypothesis hinges on what you expect of the future.

Because of the relatively narrow view that most of us have of mental attitude as an economic factor, one of Katona's recent books is of particular interest since it compares attitudes in several different countries. The book is *Aspirations and Affluence,* by George Katona, Burkhard Strumpel, and Ernest Zahn (New York: McGraw-Hill Book Company, 1971). The opening paragraphs (page 3) provide an immediate appreciation of the variation in pattern from country to country and, necessarily, an appreciation of the importance of attitude on economic life.

> Close to two-thirds of the many Americans who have experienced improvement in their financial situation over the past few years expect it to continue in the future. Only one-third of the Germans, French, and Dutch think that their progress will continue, although they, too, have enjoyed substantial and steady improvement in the past.
>
> About one-half of all Americans both approve of and use installment credit. At the other extreme, only one-fourth of the Germans approve of it, and only one out of ten actually has any installment debt.
>
> About forty percent of American husbands think it is a good idea for wives with school-age children to go out to work. Only one out of ten German household heads approves of mothers working if any children live at home, even if the children themselves are already working. Every second American wife, and only every third Western European wife, between the ages of forty and fifty has a job outside her home.
>
> More than two-thirds of American fathers expect their boys to go to college. Only one-third of German fathers approve of boys staying in school beyond the age of eighteen. In fact, today almost every second American youngster, boy or girl, eighteen years of age is in college, while in Western Europe only every tenth youngster of that age goes to school full time.

The goals of the authors in writing the book provide further clues as to its content (page 4).

> . . . In choosing their subject matter, the methods used, and the nature of the empirical evidence collected, the authors set three tasks for themselves:
>
> 1. To indicate the similarities as well as the differences in the economic behavior of American and Western European people and to contribute to an understanding of economic trends and prospects in these countries by means of behavioral analysis.
>
> 2. To indicate what "affluence" means and how the participation of private households has contributed to its development and growth. Different ways of adaptation to changing conditions may

have altered both the use consumers make of their income and the ways in which they attempt to increase their earning power.

3. To develop and enrich the new discipline of behavioral or psychological economics. Behavioral economists believe that in order to understand the functioning and the prospects of an economy, it is necessary to study people's behavior as influenced by psychological no less than by economic factors. It was thought, and our studies confirmed, that the influence of expectations and aspirations on economic behavior would emerge more clearly in a comparative analysis of trends in different countries than in observations made in one country alone.

This book is essentially nontechnical. An earlier book by Katona, *The Powerful Consumer* (New York: McGraw-Hill Book Company, 1960) is based more directly on his survey research work among U.S. consumers. It, too, is essentially nontechnical and is frequently cited by other authors in the field.

▶ AN OVERVIEW ◀

There is at least one other book worthy of mention as an excellent overview of the field of consumer economics from the standpoint of both the marketing and aggregate approaches (and some others as well): *Consumption Economics: A Multidisciplinary Approach,* by Marguerite Burk (New York: John Wiley & Sons, Inc., 1968). Although the book is moderately technical, the uninitiated will still find it useful as a portal to the field. Many parts of it are instructive in their own right, even if the reader has no previous background in the field. In addition, the book provides abundant references.

chapter
3

SOLVING THE PROBLEM: THE NEED FOR A SYSTEM

The general assumption of this chapter is that a systematic way of doing things is superior to a random, unsystematic way. If a goal is desired, a systematic approach will lead more quickly and efficiently to it. This is true for whatever the goal may be: spiritual contentment, money, new car, education, love, or friendship.

A systematic approach does not stifle you. It provides opportunities for greater, not less, fulfillment in life. The use of a systematic approach in attacking life's problems, whether they are economic, political, philosophical, moral, spiritual, or social, does not imply an impersonal, Orwellian, 1984 world. Quite the contrary. It is the identification of the problem, the ferreting out of alternative solutions, the evaluation of these solutions, the making of a decision, and the implementation of the decision that leads to personal fulfillment. You will never make it without a systematic approach.

▶   **AN EXCURSION**   ◀

▷   **from reality . . .**   ◁

Ah—the morning paper! Let's see what's new today. Front page headlines:

- Border Clashes in the Middle East
- Consumer Prices at All-Time High
- President Presents Record Federal Budget
- Inflation Rate Still Climbing
- State Unemployment Highest Since 1933
- New Record in Auto Accident Deaths
- Local Taxpayers in Revolt
- Bus Drivers on Strike
- Air Pollution in City at Danger Level

This is news? I read this every day. Maybe the editorial page will have something less negative. Here is Jack Panderson's column on "Group Challenges the Rights of the Individual." That should be interesting! Or, what about this: "The Individual's Right to Challenge Group's Decisions"?

What's the weather forecast? Clear and warm—high in the mid 70s. Extended forecast predicts ideal weather for the weekend. This seems to be the only bright spot in the newspaper.

▷   **. . . to fantasyland . . .**   ◁

The coconut palms rustle in the gentle ocean breeze. The beach sand seems almost white in the bright reflection of the sun on the warm blue ocean. I'm secure and content on my South Sea Island with no morning paper to disturb me or relay the message about the mess I left behind.

My simple thatched hut, which I built myself, is all I need for shelter. Food comes easy from the fish in the lagoon, from the fruit and nut trees and vines on the Island.

Lie in the sun all day—if I want. Sleep when I want. Little or no work. No boss—or teacher—or parent—or anyone else to push me around. No taxes to pay—no pollution to contend with—no "keeping up with the Joneses." . . . Dream on!

Though each of us may not entertain a South Sea Island retreat dream, the rush and bustle of today's living drives most of us to consider occasionally a simpler less pressure-packed way of life.

Our South Sea Island dreamer could very well live a simple, uncomplicated life—if he could find his island. But he would probably still be unhappy. The psychological and emotional stress of loneliness would soon become a reality. Maybe the dreamer would be more satisfied if four or five other companions were included. But now the conditions have changed dramatically. The effect of an action on the other people must be considered. Our dreamer will ask himself, "Can I do exactly what I want, when I want, how I want, disregarding the effect on, or the wishes of, my companions?"

▷ . . . **and back to reality** ◁

What evolves is a certain, agreed-upon way of doing things for the benefit of all or for the greater benefit of most. A way of doing things to provide greater efficiency, satisfaction, and contentment is one way of defining a **system.**

Our South Sea Island dreams may be an enjoyable, and perhaps even beneficial, relief of stress from modern-day living. Nevertheless, they must be recognized for what they are—dreams. The 200 million people in the United States or the 3.5 billion people in the world today cannot all move to a South Sea Island. Today's societies involve large numbers of people and deal with very complex, interrelated, social and economic realities. As people live together in closer proximity and the number of people increases, the number of related problems multiplies and the magnitude of the complexities increases. Therefore, systems have evolved to attempt to cut through the complexities and to provide the greatest satisfaction to the greatest number. The necessity for systems is self-evident.

─────────────── **EXAMPLE 3–1** ───────────────

The need in our economy for a transportation system to move people and goods around is apparent. It is ridicu-

lous to question its necessity. We have a variety of transportation subsystems: airline systems; railroad systems; trucking systems; local transportation systems of buses, subways, and taxis. We need transportation for short-distance and long-distance travel. A road network (system) is essential.

The point need not be belabored that transportation is essential to our modern socioeconomic life. The consequences of a breakdown in the transportation system are almost beyond comprehension. Contemplate it for a moment. Certainly, the random functioning of transportation facilities would result in utter chaos. Without some agreed-upon rules or guidelines, planes would fly when and if pilots and crews felt so disposed; buses would have no scheduled routes or departure and arrival times; roads would be built that did not interconnect. The result would be a mess. The mere availability of transportation facilities is not enough. It is when these facilities are made to function together via published schedules, standardized fares, and identified routes that the satisfaction potential from transportation facilities is realized. A system exists.

▶ A SYSTEMATIC APPROACH ◀

What may *not* be so self-evident is the need for a systematic *approach* to the solution of *any* problem. Modern society has evolved so many systems that the awareness of their existence may be lost. Students are involved with one of the largest, most complex systems our society has developed—the educational system. Bearing in mind all the complaints, fair and unfair, about our educational system, imagine, nonetheless, what would happen if education were attempted under a random behavior pattern. Students would attend classes if, or when, they wished. And, of course, so would teachers. There would be no assigned classes, no time schedules, no providing of facilities, no curriculum planned. School buses might run—or they might not. Without some system, which implies a purposeful pursuit of a goal and the planned application of techniques and materials, education would soon grind to the proverbial halt.

It is necessary to recognize that what society has developed as a particular system will probably not be perfect. The present-day educational system is not perfect. This is not a valid argument for denying the necessity for a system's approach, but it is a valid argument for the need to seek improvement of the system. It is possible that society must evolve new systems—ways of achieving goals and satisfaction never before employed. The significant point is that, without a system, undesirable and unacceptable consequences occur. If a system is ill, the antidote is not necessarily arsenic.

A highly developed, modern economy is dependent on efficient systems in almost every area of endeavor.

EXAMPLE 3–2

The following are some of the systems that allow a nation, such as the United States with its 200 million people, to live—producing, consuming, communicating, interrelating, and interacting.

1 • Transportation system.
2 • School system.
3 • Communication system.
4 • Postal system.
5 • Political system.
6 • Tax system.
7 • Legal system.
8 • Welfare system.
9 • Banking system.
10 • Money system.
11 • Economic system.

It may be deduced that a system becomes more and more useful and necessary as certain conditions exist:

1 • The number of people involved becomes larger.
2 • The results of decisions affect larger numbers of people.
3 • The results of decisions affect other systems or areas of concern.
4 • The numbers of decisions to be made increases.
5 • The complexity of decisions increases.

▷ **the individual as a self-contained** ◁
system

Points 3, 4, and 5 from the preceding list relate to a single person as well as to groups of persons. That is, you, *individually*, make large numbers (point 4) of complex decisions (point 5) that interrelate with other areas of concern in your life (point 3). If we look at those decisions that are economic, it is evident that each of us is, among other things, a small economic system.

An economic system entails *production, distribution,* and *consumption.* Most of us *produce;* we work at a job, or at home, or at school providing goods and services; we do things for ourselves and others. We are providing or using resources in production: We work and do things (labor); we decide how best to use our time and talent (management); we own and use tools and machines (capital); and we own and use natural resources (land). We *distribute* our income and wealth. We are all *consumers.* Each of us is really a self-contained microeconomic system; we each use that system to solve our economic problems. Do you use it as well as you can?

Two points are significant: You are a self-contained system which also relates to a larger system—that is, you function within a socioeconomic system that includes many subsystems; second, you are constantly making decisions—either within your self-contained system or within the larger socioeconomic system.

▶ **THE GOAL: SATISFACTION** ◀

The *satisfaction of needs* is the consumer's goal. The system for reaching a more rational consumer decision recognizes the necessity for constant review of desires and needs. In developing a long-range plan, you should assess your personal values, desires, and needs. Why do you desire or want something? Do you need it? Is it consistent with your values?

It is necessary to recognize yet another problem—income. You must assess your desires and needs in relationship to your ability to satisfy them. If you have many needs you cannot satisfy, it becomes necessary to think of ways to increase your ability to satisfy them. This generally means increasing your money income. If you "want lots" but plan little about how to generate the income to provide for these wants, you will probably be very dissatisfied in life. If your ability to satisfy your needs cannot be raised, you must make a reassessment of your desires and a reordering of your needs. If you can neither lower your needs nor raise your ability to satisfy them, you will dwell in Consumers' Hades.

The gap between needs and the ability to satisfy them is the basis for the degree of contentment or discontentment with economic life. Let us call this gap a **satisfaction gap** (Figure 3–1). The wider the gap, the more dissatisfied you will be.

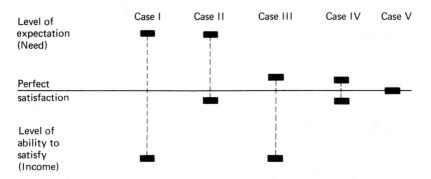

FIGURE 3–1 • An illustration of the satisfaction gap.

▶ Case I

This individual has low ability to satisfy in relationship to his need. The result is great dissatisfaction.

▶ Case II

This individual has the same level of desires and needs as I.

▶ Case III

This individual has the same level of ability to satisfy himself as I; but his needs are much less. He is less dissatisfied than I, and about the same as II. (*Note:* The gaps for II and III are about the same, but the cases are quite different.) II has a much higher ability to satisfy (income) than III, but his desires and needs are much greater. The result is that the gap is the same. This indicates why increases in income too often do not result in greater contentment (or less dissatisfaction). If the level of desires and needs rises faster than the ability to satisfy (income), the gap increases rather than diminishes.

▶ **Case IV**

This individual has a relatively high ability to satisfy (income) in relationship to his desires and needs. Relative to I, he has increased his income and decreased his desires and needs—closing the gap. He is probably as satisfied as is humanly possible. Note that he has not reached perfect satisfaction. Seldom, if ever, does that occur.

▶ **Case V**

Utopia. How realistic is this?

Note that this illustration assumes that you have some control over both ends of the satisfaction gap. Since the level of desire and need is primarily psychological, consumer economics has not paid much attention to it. But, in a sense, desires and needs are half the matter. The ability to *satisfy* needs is the other half. Control over the ability to satisfy needs within limits is well recognized; but our needs are subject to more control than we often realize. Changing expectations (needs) are a major force in world economics. On a more personal level, frequent discontentment at middle age is at least partly a matter of a wide satisfaction gap that shows no signs of diminishing. At younger ages, persons accept the gap in anticipation of a higher income later in life. But income doesn't always rise enough to close the gap, and a crisis results. A major part of a happy life is the adjustment of expectations.[1]

▶ # ACHIEVING THE GOAL: ◀
A MODEL SYSTEM

Assume that you have a particular set of needs, one of which is a textbook for an English course. Your satisfaction gap will be narrowest by satisfying as many of your needs as possible, which, of course, means satisfying your need for the textbook as cheaply as possible so that your income will stretch as far as possible to satisfy your other needs. The general outline of a system for decision might be as follows; its application to the textbook decision follows the general model.

▷ ## the general decision model ◁

▷ **Step I**　The Problem

When a need calls for satisfaction, you first recognize the problem. How serious is it? What is the magnitude of the problem?

▷ **Step II** Alternative Solutions

Search out all possible alternative ways of solving the problem. Seek all possible information regarding each alternative.

▷ **Step III** Economic Implications

Ascertain the real and monetary implications of each alternative. This means recognition of opportunities foregone (real costs) as well as dollar and cents costs (monetary). That is, what do you give up for what you get from each possible solution? What are the *opportunity costs?*

▷ **Step IV** Decision

Make a choice based on the information gathered and analysis of the problem and alternative solutions.

▷ **Step V** Reassessment

Reassess the implications of the choice, attempting to avoid possible oversights or mistakes.

▷ **Step VI** Implementation

Time for action.

▷ application of the decision model ◁

"Should I buy a textbook for my English course?" Use the general model backed up by desires and needs to come to a consumer decision.

▶ INSIGHT INTO DESIRE

I want to succeed in the course; at least I do not want to fail. I don't want to appear "stupid" to my friends or family. I want to learn something about the correct way to compose and punctuate sentences. The course is required for graduation.

▶ **INSIGHT INTO NEED**

My feeling of need for the book is dependent on my desires for it—to succeed, to complete the course, to learn, and to graduate. I have been told by other students that the text is absolutely necessary in order to keep up in the course.

▷ **Step I** The Problem

The problem is rather simple: I have to obtain an English book so that I can do my studying. I view this as a fairly serious matter.

▷ **Step II** Alternative Solutions

1 • Buy a new book.

2 • Buy a used book.

3 • Rent a used book.

4 • Borrow a book from a friend.

5 • Try to study with someone in class—using their book.

6 • Trade a math book I have for an English book.

7 • Try the library and see if they have a copy.

8 • Go without a book and try my luck.

▷ **Step III** Economic Implications

Monetary

1 • A new book costs $9.00.

2 • A used book costs $6.00, but they are often in bad shape.

3 • A good used book can usually be sold for one third off the new price.

4 • Renting a book generally runs $3.00 a semester.

5 • Borrowing would be the cheapest.

Real

1 • Studying with a friend would involve time and planning.

2 • Trading with someone would also cost time and planning.

3 • Library copies involve renewing and possible recall.

4 • Going without a text would cost nothing directly in money terms but a great deal in other terms if I fail the course.

5 • What else could I buy that I want and need with $9.00?

6 • What else could I buy that I want and need with $6.00? If I buy a used one, I give up having a good, complete, clean new copy.

7 • Renting means I wouldn't be able to write in the book. I would also be responsible if I lost it—just as if it were mine.

8 • Borrowing is cheap, but that's just the problem. My friend might prefer selling it. He needs the cash. But, he might lend it to me if I prevail on our friendship, which I am not sure I want to do.

9 • Studying with someone else means that I'd have to give up some independence and study when he wants to study. Also, I wouldn't be able to use the book as a reference whenever I would like. I'd have to spend time planning for and around our get-togethers for study sessions.

10 • Trying to find someone to trade with takes time and pure luck. I know enough about economics to know that barter is generally time-consuming and inefficient.

11 • Going without a text means that I give up the opportunity to study and in all probability means that I give up the opportunity to successfully complete the course.

▷ **Step IV** Decision

Unacceptable Choices

Choices 7 and 8 of the "alternative solutions" are completely unacceptable. I am not going to jeopardize myself before I start by not having a text, and all the copies are signed out of the library.

Poor Choices

Choice 6 is not attractive because it is generally too hard to find someone to trade with and none of my close friends needs any of my books. Choice 5 might be all right if I have class with someone I know well. But that's risky because we might have trouble getting together to study. And this semester I'm going to carry a heavy load and will need all my time for studying.

Fair Choices

Choice 4 would be acceptable if I felt I could lend another book to my friend at another time. However, I think that it's unfair for me to ask to borrow a book and let my friend bear the cost. If I didn't borrow it, he would sell the book and have the cash. Choice 3 isn't too bad. There is a rental shop on campus, and the money cost of renting is about the same as buying and reselling it when I'm through with the course. But if I rent, I lose the option of keeping the book for future reference if it should prove useful; and I would want to jot notes in it. On that basis I prefer not to rent.

Best Choices

Choices 1 and 2 seem the best for my circumstances and needs. If I buy a new book, I can resell it for one third off—or $6.00. I can buy a used one for that price and resell it also, though for something less than $6.00, of course. I need to buy a lot of books this semester, and I am a little short of cash. So I'll look for a good used book; but if I can't find one, I'll buy a new one and plan to resell it at the end of the semester.

▷ **Step V** Reassessment

I dismissed alternatives (choices) 3 through 8 because they were impractical, unfair, or there was no financial advantage. The major gain of buying a used book is the smaller original outlay of cash.

▷ **Step VI** Implementation

I go to the used-book store early so I can get a good, clean, used copy.

A likely reaction to this example? "So what's new? I always buy used books when I can." Buying a used text has become a habit. There would be nothing wrong with this habit unless (for example)

1 • A friend has a book he will not be using, not going to sell, and would be happy to lend you if you had not been too lazy or careless to ask.

2 • You know of a student who had just taken English and was planning to take a course for which you had a "white elephant" text. You could trade and both of you gain.

3 • Renting a text, under different circumstances perhaps, might be much cheaper. You just never thought of it.

The degree of effort put into the decision-making process will vary from individual to individual and from problem to problem. Some decisions become habits.

EXAMPLE 3–3

The effort expended deciding to buy a pack of gum, a pair of socks, an automobile, or a house will, and should, be greatly different. The habitual spearmint-gum chewer will not spend time assessing the "problem" of buying another pack of gum. Similarly, the Salem-cigarette smoker will not go through an analysis of whether or not to buy a pack of cigarettes or what brand. An analysis of the *habit* and its financial, medical, and dental implications would certainly be wise in these cases; however, there is certainly no point in analyzing each *individual* action. But the housewife who spends several minutes analyzing the choice of a $.10 package of radishes and then steps into a dress shop and buys a $60 dress on the spur of the moment has probably made a serious error. Conclusion: There are good habits and there are bad habits.

Although you cannot agonize over every little decision, the total effect of many, poor, minor decisions made over a long period of time may be the root of serious problems. Are the habits you have developed in making small decisions good ones? You should assess them occasionally and keep an eye open for situations that warrant an exception to your habit. If you have an ear for old sayings, it might be well to remember both of the following and strike a middle ground within the contradiction they present.

"Watch the pennies, and the dollars will take care of themselves," or "Don't be penny-wise and dollar-foolish."

In other instances the decision may hinge on noneconomic considerations. A professor may know that time spent gardening during the summer will be at the sacrifice of other professional activities that could make more money than the value of the garden produce. It is conceivable that $200 worth of fruits and vegetables might cost several thousand dollars in foregone opportunities. But a decision to garden is still a good one *if* he realizes what he is giving up and is willing to forego it for the change of pace gardening provides. If he believes he is cleverly beating the high cost of food, he is in trouble!

SUMMARY

1 • Consumption provides satisfaction, the final goal of economic activity.

2 • You are a miniature, self-contained, economic system that is part of a larger socioeconomic system. You engage in consumption (and probably production), the two primary economic activities.

3 • A system—or systematic approach—is a requisite of a satisfying life. Willy-nilly leads nowhere. Rational behavior implies a systematic approach.

4 • A systematic approach to consumer choice is a relatively simple matter.

	VALUES AND PRIORITIES	Attempt to understand yourself by more clearly identifying your personal values and priorities.
	DESIRES	Recognize the desires (wants) you have and attempt to understand the basis for them.
	NEEDS	Identify, analyze, and reorder your needs on a basis consistent with your values and desires.
Step I	PROBLEM	Determine the need that will be satisfied. Define as specifically as possible the problem confronting you. Seek information regarding the problem.
Step II	ALTERNATIVE SOLUTIONS	Dig up all possible ways of solving the problem—all alternative solutions.
Step III	ECONOMIC IMPLICATIONS	Assess the economic implications of each alternative in real and monetary terms. Recognize the opportunity costs involved.

Step IV	DECISION	Make the decision on the basis of the best alternative—the greatest gain for the least loss (cost).
Step V	REASSESSMENT	Ask if the decision is sensible. If not, you may have overlooked something.
Step VI	IMPLEMENTATION	Put the decision to work.

5 • Every consumer choice does not require such thorough analysis. Some choices may be routinized as a habit. But periodically the habit ought to be reevaluated.

study materials

1 • Discuss those problems of modern living which you would like to avoid. How does (or could) your view of these problems affect your consumer choices?

2 • Define a system. Give examples of systems used in our society. What elements make these systems? (To be considered systems, what elements do they have to have?)

3 • Explain how and why an individual could be considered a self-contained economic unit? A self-contained system?

4 • Explain what is meant by the term "satisfaction gap."

5 • List 10 specific ways of narrowing the satisfaction gap.

6 • Why is it unrealistic to attempt to eliminate the satisfaction gap and reach perfect satisfaction?

7 • State the six steps of the "general decision model."

8 • Why is it important to recognize the problem, as stated in Step I of the decision model?

9 • Information about specific goods and services is necessary in reaching good consumer decisions. In what step(s) should specific information be sought and used?

10 • It is obvious that all consumers do not reach the same decision on very similar kinds of concerns. Why is this true?

footnote

[1] Lest you conclude that the message of consumer economics is: "Be happy with what you have—no matter how little," we hasten to explain the obvious. Satisfying all your *many* needs is certainly preferable to satisfying all your *few* needs, is it not? As a more intelligent consumer, your ability to satisfy is enhanced (your income goes further), and you can then let out a little more "psychological rope" and cultivate some additional needs. More formally, a narrow satisfaction gap is not the *most* desired goal; it is a *minimum* goal. A closed gap at a high level of need is preferable to a closed gap at a low level of need.

appendix

COLLECTIVE DECISIONS

We have implicitly assumed that decisions are made by individuals. However, frequently a group must make a decision, whereupon different preferences among individuals within the group must be reconciled. The family is the most notable case in point, but group decisions are common in other instances. The family must decide who shall work in the home, who shall work outside the home, and how much leisure each member shall have. Each member has his individual preferences, but he is frequently not free to exercise them because his action has a direct impact on other members of the family, who act as a constraining influence. In addition, it is frequently necessary for the family to present a united front to the rest of the world to preserve itself for the benefit of all members. The same observations may be made of any group that has a community interest: the family, the commune, the dormitory, the church, the garden club, the nation, the business firm, and so on. Persons in a modern urban setting are probably as much affected by group decisions as by individual decisions in the course of normal living.

Environmental issues are a good example. The condition of the environment is a group "decision" if it is *possible* to alter it. Miserable conditions exist because of a "decision" to refrain from doing anything about it. The group (society in this case) can make the offenders stop polluting or not. It may be that the group in charge of the situation (society) is disinclined to function or, conceivably, even unaware that it is responsible for a given situation. But everything, everywhere, always, is under someone's control, individually or collectively, if it is capable of being altered. You may object to the suggestion that neglect through ignorance or indifference represents a "decision"; the objection may be well taken, but that is not the point. The point is that your well-being is frequently as much or more a product of group action or inaction as of action or inaction by you as an individual.[1]

Although it may seem a strange marriage at first thought, it should not be surprising that there exists such a subject as economic anthropology, and a book so entitled. The following quotation suggests the central importance of group decisions.

> *Choices are not discrete, unrelated. They form a system, they have continuity. Each is related to the others which succeed it, behaviourally—not only in a time-sequence but in an action sequence. They are related also conceptually, in terms of values—that is, in regard to a series of qualities assigned to the relations involved in action.*
>
> *In all this, the fact of sociality is vitally important. The choice, the behaviour, the values of any one person are all conditioned by other people. They, too, are exercising their choices. They compete for a common set of resources. By their very existence they are significant elements in the individual's total appreciation of his own position. Relations with them are then assigned specific qualities—values. This is so in part because the actions of these other persons give sense to the conceptual and symbolic system of the individual. His notions of economic reality are confirmed by seeing the type of choice made by others around him. The less any individual acts in isolation, the more he must be responsive to choices, or the expectations of choices, by others. Economic organization is set in a social framework of relations between persons and between groups, expressed in different conceptual ways and with different emphases, as values, symbols, rules of conduct, patterns of behaviour.*[2]

You now begin to recognize that your place in the group, and the influence you may exercise over it for your individual well-being, is a result of two things: *the position of the group* and *your relative position within the group*. Thus there are now two ways to enhance your position: *Elevate the group* of which you are a part, possibly at the expense of other groups; or *elevate your position within the group,* possibly at the expense of other members in the group. Which course you follow may be a difficult decision and depend on a great many things, particularly your relationship to other members of the group.

Your relationship to other members in the group is crucial to both your own welfare and that of the group. The skillfulness of relating to a group varies widely among individuals. Some people can get along with anybody; others can get along with nobody. But "getting along" is essentially a neutral position. The best position for you as an individual is to lead the group in your direction so that the entire group supports your decisions! If this sounds crass, it is only because you are assuming something improper about influence. It need not be improper at all. As a member of a group, you cannot escape influencing and being influenced, so you might as well determine what constitutes acceptable influence in your mind and then be as influential as possible. Exert leadership (which, incidentally, does not necessarily mean getting elected president). The difference between real leaders and apparent leaders is often considerable. What do you have to work with (resources) to exert influence? The following quotation is an interesting thought starter.

> *By* social power *we shall mean an individual's potentiality for influencing one or more other persons toward acting or changing in a given direction. According to this definition, social power is the ability to exert interpersonal influence. What, then, is the basis of interpersonal influence? Such influence is established by inducing other persons to perceive that acceptance or rejection of a given influence attempt will lead either to satisfying or depriving experiences for them. In other words, interpersonal influence implies the manipulation of valences in another person's psychological environment.*
>
> *In formally structured groups, the basis of such influence is grounded in the established rules of organization. In informal groups, however, the members' differing abilities to influence one another arise out of their continuing interaction. In a newly formed group of relative strangers the prospective member has no rank or status. In such a setting he brings with him merely his individual properties such as his personal characteristics; his knowledge, information, and skills; his material possessions; and his social-emotional capacities. If the prospective member's properties are relevant to the needs of other group members, these properties may become re-*

sources which he can use in his dealings with them. He can satisfy or deprive other members to the degree that his intrapersonal properties are convertible into interpersonal resources.[3]

The *size* of the group may affect your relationship to it. If it is small, you may be inclined to see it as essentially an extension of yourself and act accordingly. If it is large, you may see it as impersonal and beyond your influence and therefore treat it with indifference. If the group is small and closely knit (a family, for instance), you are probably more inclined to prefer to try to elevate your position by elevating the group rather than by trying to elevate yourself within the group. There are at least two major reasons for this preference: In a small group, you get a larger share of the total pie, so you can see that a relatively large portion of your efforts to elevate the group flow to you directly; second, you are more apt to receive direct satisfaction yourself from seeing other members of the *small* group improve their position. Not so for a *large* group. For example, you would probably be willing to get a job and work extra hours so that your family could buy a new stereo. It is a family decision to buy the stereo, but you might nonetheless be willing to bear most of the cost simply because your benefit from it as part of this small group would be very large; moreover, you would experience satisfaction (additional benefit) from seeing other members of the group enjoy it, since you feel a close bond with them. For the very same reasons you would be much less inclined to make the same effort toward the purchase by your dormitory of a stereo for the lounge.

All this leads to the conclusion that small groups are more inclined to hang together and function effectively than large groups. Hardly a big surprise. Large groups may function effectively where the stakes are large—a war that threatens national existence, for example. But this simply leads to the conclusion that it is the size of the issue in terms of its impact on the individual members *relative* to the size of the group that determines the tendency of the group to act effectively. Thus, *other things being equal,* a small group will act more effectively and have a greater tendency to remain intact than a large group.

This leads to a key observation on the decision-making behavior of a member of a group. There are always two questions: *What is the impact of the decision on you as an individual member of the group? What is the impact of the decision on the* continued life *of the group itself?* That is, to pursue the stereo example, you make the decision to favor or disfavor this purchase based on the cost to *you* relative to the benefit to *you* (including the satisfaction you get from the enjoyment of other members of the family) just as you would proceed if you were making the decision

as an individual who was not a member of a group. But, *in addition,* you
consider the impact of the decision on the continued existence of the
group itself, since you perceive that your well-being is directly dependent
on the group's existence in the future. As a consequence, you may support
the decision to purchase the stereo and contribute to it even though you
get direct disutility from it (it's only noise to you). Thus if it is desired
strongly by other members of the group, you go along with it to "keep
peace in the family," knowing that your contribution to group solidarity
is in your interest. It is an investment, if you will, from which you expect
to have a future payoff either in support for your desire for something
unpopular with the other members of the group or because you receive
other psychological satisfactions from membership in this group and do
not wish to strain the bonds that hold it together.

We have now arrived at the crux of the difference between the group
decision and a purely individual decision. In addition to the merit of the
direct "fruit" of the decision,

> The group decision is necessarily the result of group
> members' evaluation of the impact of the decision on the
> life of the group itself.

The individual decision does not entail this additional consideration,
obviously, since no group is involved; the individual decision only looks
at the merit of the action flowing from the decision per se.

A group will necessarily provide for the reconciliation of different
preferences within the group, as agreement must be reached if the group
is to survive. Thus the dynamics within a group are an important matter.
Indeed, one of the most important things a group can do is provide for
a means of arriving both at consensus and at an acceptable level of individual expression (dissent) within the framework of group cohesiveness.
Clearly, this is not an easy task. A mechanism that works and is acceptable
to one group is not acceptable to another. For example, one group may
feel that an authoritarian leadership is in its interest; another group may
provide for democratic decisions.

Curiously, a given individual may belong to several groups run in
quite different ways. That is, although there is surely a strong bias in
favor of democratic institutions in the United States, any one person may,
for example, prefer a democratically run nation but an authoritarian
church. There is not necessarily anything inconsistent about this; it is
only a bit curious. Perhaps you believe that certain *kinds* of decisions
ought to be made one way, and other kinds another way. People are
always jockeying around to get into or out of groups on the basis of the

way group decisions are made. ("I left because I didn't like the way the outfit was run.") People move from business to business, from church to church, from bridge club to bridge club, from political party to political party, from university faculty to university faculty, and even from household to household for largely noneconomic reasons centered on the way in which decisions are made.

Any group has a framework that provides for group decisions and for individual action within that framework. The framework may be elaborate and formal such as might be contained in a national constitution; it may be sketchy and informal such as commonly found in a family. But the framework is there. It has to be if the group is to survive. Groups that fail to survive frequently fail for one of two related reasons: The group did not provide an adequate framework for reconciling individual members' differences; or the majority of members did not consider the survival of the group sufficiently important to them, individually, to cause them to honor the framework. The group collectively, therefore, is unlikely to provide enforcement of the framework in light of widespread indifference. In other words, groups frequently fail because there were no rules, or because the rules were not enforced because nobody cared enough to take the trouble.

▶ SUMMARY ◀

Many decisions are made by groups of which you are a member and your role is that of participant rather than arbiter. The consideration interjected when you are part of a group decision is the value you place on your continued participation in and/or survival of the group itself. You may accept, and actually favor, group decisions you would reject as an individual because you value the solidarity of the group and your participation in it.

footnotes

[1] It must be recognized that your individualism always has "preemptive capability," so to speak. That is, although you are *normally* heavily influenced by groups of which you are a part, you can always jump overboard by becoming a hermit (yes, there are still enough unoccupied corners of the world) or, in the ultimate, by shooting yourself. That is, you can bolt the group. Thus the discussion is relevant to "normal living" and particularly to "normal urban living."

[2] Raymond Firth, "The Social Framework of Economic Organization," in *Economic Anthropology: Readings in Theory and Analysis,* ed. by Edward E.

LeClair, Jr., and Harold K. Schneider (New York: Holt, Rinehart and Winston, Inc., 1968), pp. 66–67.

[3] George Levinger, "The Development of Perceptions and Behavior in Newly Formed Social Power Relationships," in *Studies in Social Power,* ed. by Dorwin Cartwright (Ann Arbor: Research Center for Group Dynamics, Institute for Social Research, University of Michigan, 1959), pp. 83–84.

chapter
4

THE WORLD
OF UTILITY

Economic measurements and ideas are most commonly pre-
sented in terms of money. This is a necessary practice in the
practical, personal world, but it contributes little to under-
standing the basic workings of an economic system and the
place of the individual in it. Indeed, money may be a
hindrance to understanding fundamental economic issues.
As an aid to the investigation of economic bedrock, we will
therefore proceed in terms of utility rather than money.
Since utility is an abstraction, you will probably feel freer
to accept fundamental economic ideas heretofore obscured
by a monetary surface.

▶ MAJOR ASPECTS OF THE WORLD ◀ OF UTILITY

Since all consumers are acquiring satisfaction—they only acquire products because satisfaction comes embodied in them—we need to invent some unit of satisfaction so that we can tell how much satisfaction you are receiving. Let us call a unit of satisfaction a **utile**. This stems from the word **utility** which relates to usefulness. A product is considered "useful" if it has the ability to satisfy its possessor. Since your goal as a consumer is satisfaction, it seems fair enough to say that anything that is capable of satisfying you is useful to you. This definition of "useful" differs only slightly from the meaning given to it in everyday conversation. Ordinarily, a certain physical practicality is expected of anything useful, but since it is the consumer's desire to be satisfied, anything that contributes to that satisfaction would seem to be useful in that broader context.

The world of utility (like Gaul) may be divided into three parts:

1 • Utility from noneconomic sources: love, affection, companionship, self-fulfillment, peace of mind, etc.
2 • Utility from free goods: air, sunshine, water, space, etc.
3 • Utility from economic goods: cars, houses, food, movies, education, etc.

The distinction between the economic world and the noneconomic world was discussed in Chapter 1, where the point was made that the distinction is by no means clear-cut. However, you probably have a fairly good general idea of the broader social, philosophical, and practical considerations that determine the general location of the boundary between the economic and noneconomic worlds as they were discussed in Chapter 1. The broad distinction between utility from economic sources and that from noneconomic sources (categories 1 and 3 above) is therefore probably reasonably clear. What about utility from free goods (category 2)? Free goods have not been previously discussed. The question naturally arises: "Are free goods part of the economic world or the noneconomic world?" The answer? "It depends." Although **free goods** will be discussed in more detail below, they are defined as those goods that are available simply for the taking—you can have all your heart desires—no cost, no price, no sweat, free. Space, sunshine, air, and water (in their natural states) would seem to fall in this category.

The most restrictive definitions of economics would exclude free goods from the economic world. Since economics centers on scarcity and since scarce goods are defined as those goods that must be created by direct or indirect human effort (produced), it seems obvious that, since free goods are *not* scarce, they cannot be part of the economic world. On the other hand, although economic goods must be created by direct or indirect human effort, it will be argued below that production is impossible without using some free goods—space, in particular. Thus if economic goods cannot exist without free goods, must it not be argued that free goods *are* part of the economic world? Obviously, free goods must be considered relevant to serious economic issues whether or not they form an actual part of the economic world.

The point here is that, for the time being, we wish to focus more closely on only part of the entire spectrum of utility—that part consisting of economic and free goods. The economic world is a good deal more concrete than the noneconomic world and, therefore, perhaps a bit easier to understand; so we will begin with it. Developing the relationships within, and characteristics of, the economic world (including free goods) will establish the foundation from which to extend our thinking to the issues relating to utility in the noneconomic world, to which we will return later.

One further word of caution: Utiles and utility are words invented to give substance to the abstract. Satisfaction cannot be measured precisely in specific units (quantified). Nonetheless, we know that some things give more satisfaction than others.

► KEY ELEMENTS ◄
OF THE ECONOMIC WORLD

For purposes of illustration of the principles of economic choice, we define a number of fundamental economic words in terms of utility. These words will be defined in more detail in the rest of the chapter. They are presented here to provide an overview of utility as a common economic denominator.

- *Goods:* anything having utility.
- *Production:* creation of utility.
- *Consumption:* diminution of utility that increases human welfare.
- *Waste:* diminution of utility that does not increase human welfare.
- *Income:* a flow of utility.
- *Wealth:* a stock of utility.

- *Cost:* diminution of utility undergone in the acquisition of a (hopefully) greater utility.
- *Capital:* a stock of utility (wealth) to be used in the creation of wealth (production).
- *Depreciation:* diminution of capital (cost) as it is used in the creation of wealth (production).

In everyday conversation these words are usually defined in terms of money. Their definition in terms of utility shows their true economic nature. Money is only a rough representation of utility. In everyday life we are preoccupied with money because it will buy utility. There is no point in thinking in terms of the representation, money, when we can think in terms of the real thing, utility. Thus, in thinking about utility rather than money, we get to the real economic heart of the matter. Indeed, the tendency of most people to think in financial terms and perhaps even to equate finance with economics is unfortunate, for it often obscures the *real* issues. The use of the word **real** here is deliberate. **Real wealth** comprises the actual products and the utility from them; **money wealth** is the dollar representation of the actual products and utility. **Real income** is the actual products and utility your **money income** will buy.

Let us examine the key economic words listed above in greater detail as they apply to society as a whole. Upon completion of this examination you should have a reasonably good idea of the fundamental working of *any* economic system. At this stage we are concerned only with basic relationships and not with other things that tend to occupy our thoughts in everyday living. For example, we are not at all concerned with the ownership of goods—we are only concerned with whether they exist. We are not concerned with whether the economy is capitalistic, socialistic, communistic, or whatever.

▷ goods: anything having utility ◁

Goods can be subdivided so that all goods fall into any pair of two different sets of categories. Goods are either free or economic *and* tangible or intangible. Any single good will therefore be either free and tangible, free and intangible, economic and tangible, or economic and intangible. Free goods are goods that are available simply for the taking. Their utility came about through no human effort or cost to society—that is, they are free to society as a whole. They are available without anyone having given up anything to get them. Economic goods are all other goods for which someone has given up something. In other words, economic goods are available only at a cost. Free goods are all natural resources, although not all natural resources are necessarily free goods. The virgin forest is a free good, but the forest that is the product of reforestation is an economic good. Water in a lake may be a free good, but water from the faucet in your home or apartment is an economic good.

Tangible goods have physical substance and form. Goods may also be intangible, however. Intangible goods, if also economic, are generally called **services.** A waiter in a restaurant provides you with utility just as a merchant does when you buy a product from him. You get utility added to the product through the service the retailer provides in making it available to you when and where you want it. Table 4–1 shows the major

Table 4–1
TYPES OF GOODS

	Tangible		Intangible	
Free	Timber Minerals Land Water	all in their natural state	Sunshine Space Air	
Economic	*Products* available only at human sacrifice	Food Clothing Automobiles Buildings Highways etc.	*Services* available only at human sacrifice such as	Labor, generally, or the service of Barbers Dentists Entertainers Teachers etc.

categories of goods available and the kinds of goods that fall into each category.

The quantity and quality of free goods available is apparently decreasing as time goes on. In the case of air and water, the pollution problem indicates that *clean* air and water are often not free goods. In the case of timber and land (as used for agricultural purposes) human effort has gone into the resource as currently available. For example, farmland is partially an economic good if it has had fertilizer added to it, rocks removed from it, and trees cut from it. Although the role of free goods seems to be diminishing, man is still unable to accomplish the creation of economic goods without some free goods to start with. This will apparently be true until such time as man can create matter. Even then, he must have space in which to operate, and it seems most unlikely that we will ever be able to create that. The moral is clear: Ultimately man is dependent on that which he did not create himself. The concern for man's environment may be viewed as a belated recognition of that fact.

Labor is probably best viewed as an economic good, since people who provide labor are not free—as any parent well knows. On the other hand, it is clear that society does not view the "production" of labor in the same way as it views the production of an automobile. As in Chapter 1, the personal nature of labor makes it something of a special case. In any event, it seems more appropriate to view it as economic than free if one is forced to a choice.

Although it may be argued that free goods are ultimately of more significance than economic goods, we are more concerned here with economic goods than free goods. The reason is simple enough: Since free goods are given to man, there is no point in concerning ourselves with them except from the point of view of conservation. There are no choices to be made as to which goods to forego and which to have because there is nothing we can do about creating more or fewer free goods; there is nothing to decide regarding their production. In the case of economic goods, we are interested not only in conserving them as in the case of free goods, but in making good decisions as to which ones to create as well. In other words, there are more decisions to be made with respect to economic goods than free goods, hence we are more interested in economic goods than free goods.

▷ production: creation of utility ◁

Production refers to economic goods only. We will simply say that free goods are created by "divine effort" or "nature" and let it go at that. Production refers to utility created through human effort. The basic anatomy of production is simple but revealing. A number of elements must be present for production to occur. These are the **factors of production:**

1 • Land.
2 • Labor.
3 • Management.
4 • Capital.

Land refers to the natural resource base (free good) that is necessary for production to occur. In everyday conversation, land usually means the dry portion of the earth's surface. In basic economics, land is really synonomous with free goods, as defined in Table 4–1. Every kind of production requires land. A minimum of space is also required in every instance. Land is therefore defined, basically, as a free good.

Labor refers to direct human effort that goes into the production process at the time the production is taking place. Labor physically performs the tasks that make the production occur.

Management also refers to direct human effort expended at the time the production is taking place, but, more specifically, management refers to human effort that is concerned with providing coordination and direction to the entire project. Land, labor, and capital must be brought together at a particular time and place and in the right proportions, or production will not occur.

Capital is a stock of utility (wealth) to be used in production. Capital is all the economic goods presently available for use in production (excluding labor). In more common terms, capital is factories, machinery, tools, equipment, highways, and so on. Thus, to return to the basic definition of capital, we are saying that factories, tools, equipment, and the like have utility that has been created (produced) previously and stored up, and that is available for use in current production. Indeed, capital has utility primarily because it is capable of contributing to the creation of greater utility. As an end in itself, most capital would seem to have little utility. The modern student does not need to be told that the use of capital facilitates a much greater quantity of production than would be possible in its absence. It is interesting to note that capital formation will not occur unless we are willing to "back off" from the production of consumer goods to take time out to produce capital. We then later use the capital to produce a greater final quantity of utility in the form of consumer goods than we could have produced initially with our bare hands.[1] Reduction or disappearance of capital as it is used in production is called **depreciation** or **capital consumption.**

In summary, production requires

1 • Land, or free goods.

2 • Labor, or current human physical effort.

3 • Management, or coordination and direction.

4 • Capital, or economic goods previously produced.

The division between some of these categories is obscure in the real world. As noted earlier, land and capital may be intermingled. An acre of farmland as now available is usually part capital and part land, as defined here. The acre was originally a free good, but improvements (fertilizer, drainage, fencing, etc.) are capital. Labor and management also overlap. Most jobs have at least some element of each, although one or the other often predominates. The small businessman usually supplies management and some labor simultaneously; that is, he decides what to do and then does it himself. There may also be overlap between capital and management and/or labor. Educational "improvements" on human beings may qualify as capital. Some education is a form of capital. If education makes human beings more efficient producers, then, since education is an economic good, human beings may have capital embodied in them just as land has capital embodied in it in the form of improvements that enhance its productivity. The production of human capital, that is, a more skillful labor force, has been a major factor in the economic success of the United States. (Note that the concept of human capital through education requires "bending" the definition of capital as tangible.) The fact that we cannot clearly classify a given good or person neatly into one of the categories is of no concern here. The point is that the *elements* of land, labor, management, and capital must be present in one way or another for production to occur.

You may wonder why we are placing so much emphasis on production when our primary focus will eventually be on consumption. To consume you must have income, and production is what generates income. Most people have more discretionary control over the amount of money income they receive than they realize, simply because they have not stopped to consider what it takes to generate that income. Therefore, it might be argued that the first order of business in consumption is an assessment of what it takes to generate income and what you have under your control to do it with. A general view of production then becomes an important starting point. Indeed, the most common denominator of poor people is that they control a very small quantity of the factors of production; or if the quantity is large, the quality is low. That is, they have no productive horsepower. The solution to their problem is somewhat self-evident: Make them capable of greater productivity. It is no accident that education and job training are (or should be) integral parts of most programs to deal with the poverty problem.

▷ **consumption: diminution of utility** ◁
that increases human welfare

Consumption is the motivation for production. As a society we are certainly not interested in production for its own sake. Consumption is the actual "ingestion" of utility by the consumer. It is interesting (and disturbing) to note that since utility is only the *ability* to satisfy, the *actual* satisfaction comes only when the goods having the utility are used, which destroys some of their ability to satisfy further. For example, a new car has utility (*ability* to satisfy) as it sits in your garage, but as it *actually* satisfies you, it is wearing out, which, of course, diminishes its ability to further satisfy you. Thus when a good is consumed, its utility is diminished and someone is better off for it.

> ## ▷ waste: diminution of utility that ◁ does not increase human welfare

Persons are not necessarily more satisfied as utility diminishes. For example, the destruction of property and the failure to preserve free goods (forest fires, floods, etc.) constitute waste. Involuntary unemployment is also a form of waste, since the utility that the persons could have created during their unemployment is lost forever.[2]

> ## ▷ income: a flow of utility ◁

From a practical, personal point of view, income is a flow of goods toward you. Presumably, however, income may also be negative, in which case you are giving up goods you once had. Defining income in terms of utility leads to a startling conclusion. In the *real* economic sense, you do not receive income when you get money but rather when you spend money! It is when you spend money that you get goods that have utility. If there were no goods to spend your money on, your money would provide you no utility at all. So don't count your monetary chickens before they hatch into utility. The seriousness of the error of defining income as *receipt* of money rather than the *spending* of money is probably clear enough once it is pointed out; however, we may then be led to ask how it is that everyone gets along so well operating under this glaring misconception. It is simply that the economy of the United States (and that of many other nations as well) has performed so well that we have never had a problem finding goods to spend our money on, and we therefore do not anticipate a problem in converting money into utility. In such a situation it never occurs to us not to view the receipt of money as income.

In summary, **income** (the flow of utility) as defined and used in economics refers to receiving real goods and services from which satisfaction (utility) is derived. Money, in and of itself, provides no satisfaction; it is what the money will buy which provides the satisfaction. It should be clearly understood that if our economy were producing no goods or services for us to purchase, our money income would be worthless. It is therefore the receipt of real goods or services which provides income in the real economic sense. Real income is derived, then, by spending money income.

It should be quickly pointed out that this in no way implies that economists minimize or disregard the usefulness of money. In a highly specialized, industrialized economy a sound money system is essential. Money becomes the catalyst which makes the system function—hopefully smoothly. Money facilitates the flow of real income or satisfaction (utility). One does not have to be apologetic about concerns for money. Only if the concern stops with money is the consumer in trouble, for ultimately the real concern is for satisfaction that is derived from real goods and services received in exchange for money.

▷ wealth: a stock of utility ◁

Wealth is a stored-up quantity of economic goods. Wealth must consist of tangible economic goods alone because it is not generally possible to store intangible goods. The relationship between money and wealth is analogus to that between money and income. Defining wealth in terms of money presupposes that there will always be tangible economic goods present into which the money may be converted. Since this need not be the case, we want to look at real wealth, just as we looked at real income.

Again, the plea is to think in terms that have real economic meaning. Real wealth implies, in the true economic sense, a stock or collection of tangible, economic goods; real wealth stems from real goods. To the economist, the significance of emphasizing the concept "real" as opposed to "money" is to attempt to focus attention on that which is ultimately important. A simple analysis illustrates the point:

▶ **Analysis 4–1**

You might say: "I know of a man who has $10 million. I say he's wealthy. Now you try to tell me he is not."

First, let it be said that there is much implied in what you say. The economist will agree that the man is "wealthy," in the everyday sense of the word and in all probability in the true economic sense. The $10 million monetary measurement of his worth undoubtedly involves ownership of such real goods as factories, real estate, and equipment, and not a pile of 10 million dollar bills. The factories, real estate, and equipment are certainly wealth (collection of tangible, economic goods). In this case, the real wealth has been measured in money terms. Indeed, even if the man had a pile of 10 million dollar bills, it might be logical to assume him to be "wealthy," in a practical sense. He could very quickly convert this money into tangible, economic goods—and at this point the economist would have to accept his "wealth." But such a conversion is not necessarily possible.

EXAMPLE 4–1

From history, you can read that Germany experienced one of the world's worst depressions and inflations after World War I. Imagine two Germans, each with 10 million marks. The prewar worth of a mark was about $.23. One of the men had his "wealth" in the form of cash monies, and the other owned factories and land worth 10 million marks. All other things being equal, and in the everyday usage of the term "wealth," one would conclude that the two were equally wealthy. But by 1923 the economy of Germany had collapsed. Very few real goods and services were being produced—and much of what was being produced was going as "reparations" for the war to the "allied countries." Practically no goods and services were available to the German citizens—not even food or clothing. Money (marks) had become practically valueless. At the height of the inflation, in 1923, one U.S. penny was worth 40 billion marks. Assume that our two men each held their prewar 10 million marks of "wealth." The one man with his cash money would now be worth 1/4,000 of a penny; the other would still have his factories and land. Whom would you now consider the "wealthier"? It is for this reason that it is dangerous to measure "wealth" in money terms. It is for this reason that the economist emphasizes a stock or collection of tangible, economic goods as being real wealth. In a later chapter, we will discuss the preservation of your wealth in the face of inflation.

We have referred to income and wealth as flows and stocks of utility from *economic* goods only in the definition of these key economic words. The utility from free goods is excluded—perhaps somewhat arbitrarily. The reason for this exclusion is that we are interested in focusing on how much we are *improving* our welfare through economic activity. A nation with abundant natural resources is sometimes said to be wealthier than

a nation with few natural resources. On the other hand, if the quantity
and quality of natural resources available do not result in more productivity than occurs in a nation with few natural resources, the nation with
the greater number of natural resources would seem to be little, if any,
better off than the nation with few natural resources. We conclude that
natural resources are a better indicator of a nation's *potential* wealth than
actual wealth. There is nothing to assure that a nation will necessarily
achieve its potential. Hence our focus is on wealth that results from economic activity (production) rather than on the quantity of natural resources that may or may not be closely related to the level of production
occurring in an economic society.

SUMMARY

1 • Key economic words, ideas, and measurements may be
   presented in terms of utility rather than money,
   thereby getting at economic fundamentals directly.

2 • Utility (the ability to satisfy) comes from noneconomic and economic sources and from free goods
   (available for the taking), which are not strictly economic goods but are most conveniently viewed as part
   of the economic world.

3 • Key economic terms defined in terms of utility are
   Goods: anything having utility.
   Production: creation of utility via the use of *factors
   of production.*
      a. Land, or free goods.
      b. Labor, or current human physical effort.
      c. Management, or coordination and direction.
      d. Capital, or economic goods previously produced.
   Consumption: diminution of utility that increases
   human welfare.
   Waste: diminution of utility that does not increase
   human welfare.
   Income: a flow of utility.
   Wealth: a stock of utility.
   Cost: diminution of utility undergone in the acquisi-
   tion of a (hopefully) greater utility.

> *Capital:* a stock of utility (wealth) to be used in the creation of utility (production).
>
> *Depreciation:* diminution of capital (cost) as it is used in the creation of wealth (production).

study materials

1 • State activities in which you engage in which you do *not* seek utility (if you can).

2 • Why is utility difficult to measure quantitatively?

3 • State the difference between free goods and economic goods.

4 • Income is commonly expressed in monetary terms: "My income for the year was $10,000." Explain income using the concept of income as a flow of utility. How and to what extent is the utility concept of income related to the monetary concept of income?

5 • State or explain the following in monetary terms and in real terms as they relate to utility:
   a. Income.
   b. Wealth.
   c. Cost.
   d. Capital.
   e. Depreciation.

6 • Name the four factors of production and give examples of each.

7 • Explain how education can be considered as capital.

8 • State the relationship in real and monetary terms between production and income.

9 • List personal and societal examples of waste.

10 • Assume this situation (admittedly a strange one): A man buys a piece of pie with the idea of looking at it and saying to himself that he is not going to eat it because he is on a diet. Is this waste? Explain.

11 • Assume that two very similar individuals receive $10,000 annual monetary income. One lives in the United States and one lives in Mexico. Is it likely that the real income of both individuals is identical? If not, why not? (*Note:* The $10,000 is in U.S. dollars.)

12 • Defend one or the other of the following statements:
   a. Talking about utility in consumer economics is nonsense because utility is an abstract concept and not a precise measurable

entity. Therefore, utility has no meaning or significance to a consumer.

  b. Utility is an abstract concept that is impossible to measure directly. It is important for the consumer to understand that what he is seeking is utility and that he should therefore focus and develop a stronger feel for this concept if he hopes to improve his consumption decisions.

footnotes

[1] Eugen von Böhm-Bawerk (1851–1914), an Austrian economist who developed a theory of capital, cited the advantages of "indirect" means of production as opposed to "direct" means of production, using labor and nature only. He referred to the use of capital as "the roundabout process"—a most revealing phrase about the nature of the creation and use of capital.

[2] *Involuntary* unemployment means that those who want work cannot find it—at least at a skill level reasonably near their capability. If you do not get paid unless you work, *voluntary* unemployment—the failure of persons to work more than they do by choice—does *not* represent economic waste, since these people are apparently getting more utility from leisure than they would get from the economic goods that they could buy with the earned money income. This, of course, is not true of the *in*voluntarily unemployed, hence the economic waste.

chapter 5

THE CENTER
OF THE
ECONOMIC UNIVERSE:
COST

The centrality of scarcity and choice in economics implies the centrality of cost, since cost is simply what is foregone to have something else. Since individuals make choices in the economic and noneconomic world and since societies or nations make choices in the economic and noneconomic world, the concept of cost is all-pervasive. Increases in technology are improvements in economic efficiency which reduce cost. Diplomatic skills in interpersonal relationships are at least one noneconomic equivalent of technology which reduces the "cost" of getting what you want. Finally, it will be suggested that businesses operating in a competitive market economy provide the most utility to consumers at the lowest possible cost.

At the beginning of Chapter 4, several key economic words were defined in terms of utility. The remainder of the chapter was devoted to the elaboration of those definitions and the explanation of the economic significance of each —save one: Cost *was not expanded. It was not omitted because it was unimportant. On the contrary, it was omitted there so that additional emphasis could be placed on it in a chapter devoted entirely to cost.*

Recall the definition of cost from Chapter 4:

Cost is the diminution of utility undergone in the acquisition of a (hopefully) greater utility.

Cost is all-pervasive in the economic world. The concept *or* principle *of cost is all-pervasive in the noneconomic world of human experience as well. Thus the concept of cost applies to every fragment of life. The reason is disarmingly clear: If cost is the diminution of utility undergone to acquire a greater utility, then cost simply translates into* that which is given up to get something else. *Since a decision to do something necessarily entails* not *doing something else, whatever is chosen will entail the cost (utility from) that which could have been chosen alternatively but was foregone to have that which* was *chosen.*

The pervasiveness of cost should not be surprising when the intimate relationship between cost and the definition of economics is considered. If economics is defined as dealing with the problem of scarcity, and scarcity is defined as a condition where wants exceed our ability to satisfy them, then it follows that choices must be made as to which things to have and which things to forego. As soon as a choice is made, it is evident that the utility realized from that which was chosen has as its cost the utility in that which was foregone. Thus since the central issue in economics is scarcity, and scarcity requires choice, and choice entails cost, it follows that the core of economics consists of cost; hence the devotion of an entire chapter to it. Although the basic idea of cost is simple, we want to be sure that its various applications are explored thoroughly.

To adequately impress ourselves with our inability to escape cost, we will look at the principle of cost as it relates to the economic and noneconomic world of the individual and to the economic and noneconomic worlds of societies or nations. Finally, as an acknowledgment of the practical world to be investigated later, the money representation of cost will be discussed briefly at the end of the chapter.

. . . On Cost . . .

Reprinted by permission of New York News Inc.

► PERSONAL ECONOMIC COST ◄

What is the real cost of a new car? If you say $3,000 or respond to the question with some other dollar figure, go back to the beginning of the chapter and try again. You are still not convinced. Three thousand dollars is *not* the *real* cost; it is the money representation of the real cost or, simply, the money cost. The *real* cost is what you could have had with the $3,000 but chose to forego to have the car. The cost of the new car is a boat or, in utility terms, the cost of the utility from a car is the utility from a boat at the same dollar price as the car. Obviously, you should choose the boat if it has more utility than the car. You could also have saved the money, in which case your cost might be a college education for your children 15 years from now or a more comfortable retirement.

The cost of the car would be the *largest* amount of utility foregone, which would, of course, be the *most valuable* alternative foregone. If the $3,000 would have bought a car *or* a boat *or* a year in college for the children, the cost of the car would be the utility from the one with the *most* utility. Remember, cost is that which you *could* have had. The cost is obviously not the utility from *both* the boat and the year in college because you could not have had both as an alternative. Only one or the other was available for the $3,000. If you accept as the cost of the car the alternative with the *least* utility, the concept of cost becomes meaningless, because one alternative in every situation is to have nothing—to burn your money, to destroy your resources, to waste your time. Zero utility then is always an alternative, which leads to the conclusion that everything is free because you conclude that you gave up nothing! But we can readily see that virtually nothing is free, so this is a nonsense result. It forces us to the conclusion that cost is not only what could have been had, but specifically, the *most* that could have been had as an alternative. To conclude otherwise is to delude yourself that things are cheaper than they really are. It will also necessarily lead to bad decisions that fail to maximize utility. More on that in Chapter 6.

▶ **PERSONAL NONECONOMIC COST** ◀

Any noneconomic human action (or inaction) illustrates the concept of cost also. The cost of the utility from being where you are now is the *most* utility you could get from being somewhere else. The cost of the utility from a reasonably tranquil relationship with your neighbor is possibly the utility lost from his dog digging up your flowers or his children running across your lawn. The cost of marrying Karen is not marrying Susan. The cost of going to church is the utility lost from sleeping late on Sunday or going fishing. Your decision on each of these issues is dictated by the amounts of utility gained relative to the amounts lost. Choices should be made so as to give the greatest benefit for any given amount of cost; that is, always choose the alternative with the highest utility relative to cost. The decision to endure the trespassing dog in your flowers is a bad one if you get more utility from the flowers that the dog is digging up than you do from a harmonious relationship with your neighbor. Go over there and tell him (in language he can understand) to keep his dog out of your flowers. The utility you would gain would be more than you would lose, so the decision would be a good one.

The concept of noneconomic cost leads along fascinating paths. For an example from the world of politics turn to the Appendix.

▶ SOCIETAL ECONOMIC COST ◀

The issue of cost pervades the life of a society as well as the life of an individual. In this section, the broader issues of cost are investigated as they relate to social priorities and to society's decisions about resource use. Many of these decisions are the direct result of personal decisions made by individual members of society. Others are collective decisions made through elected representatives in units of government. The basic issues are the same regardless of the mechanics of the process of choice. The fundamental issue, as always, is cost. The primary application relates to production.

Cost is of concern to economic society in two very closely related ways: (1) *How many* factors of production should be converted into economic goods? (2) *Into which* economic goods should factors of production be converted? The first question will be referred to as **production level** and the second as **production mix**. Both questions can be answered with the same general principle. The principle is that society should always proceed to maximize its total utility. Its total utility will be maximized *if whatever is chosen* has more utility than *whatever must be foregone* to get that which is chosen.

▷ production level ◁

The utility of the resources that are used up in the production process is lost in order to gain the greater utility in the goods produced. Thus the cost of economic goods is the resources that went into them. All the factors of production, land, labor, management, and capital, had some utility in their original state. Free goods provide some utility as wilderness, aesthetic beauty, and so on. Labor and management would realize the utility of leisure if they were not engaged in production. Capital also probably has some utility, although we earlier concluded that capital's utility consists primarily of its ability to create additional utility. You may conclude that the utility in all the factors of production is very low compared to the utility of the goods into which they may be converted. Perhaps so. Indeed, if the utility in the factors of production is more than the utility of the goods into which they are converted, we would certainly be foolish to engage in production at all, because production would result in a reduction rather than an increase in total utility—we would lose more than we gained from the activity of production.

Starting from zero level of production, it would appear from the vast amount of production undertaken that we do believe that the factors of production have much less utility than the goods produced. However, if we start from the level of production *currently occurring,* it is *not* clear that we believe that additional goods would have more utility than the resources used up. Whenever anyone complains that our production of goods causes polluted air and water, crowded space, and a harried personal existence, he would seem to be saying that *his utility is increased less* from the economic goods than *it is decreased from the destruction of factors of production.* He therefore feels worse off than he would be if production were to be cut back. Assuming that the participants in the discussion really understand the choices involved, the great ecological debate may be viewed, in large part, as an argument over the amount of utility contained in the factors of production as opposed to the amount contained in the economic goods into which they are converted.

The decision to increase or decrease the level of production from its present level depends a great deal on what the current level of production is. If a nation is already producing a great quantity of economic goods, it would be expected to be less interested in expanding production than the nation currently producing at a very low level. This would suggest that if two nations are equal in other respects, we should expect to find the wealthy nation (in terms of economic goods) less anxious to expand production than the poor nation.

When a nation has no economic goods at all and many factors of production, a few economic goods would have great utility because people would be very "hungry" for them. Factors of production would have little utility because they would be so plentiful. Consider the case of labor. (Remember: Labor is a factor of production.) If you had no economic goods at all and spent all your time at leisure, you would be very anxious to go to work. You would greatly increase your total utility by giving up a small amount of utility in leisure in exchange for a great deal of utility in the economic goods you could produce. But there is a limit to this. In general, the more you have of something (say, economic goods or leisure), the less utility you get from *additional* amounts. If you are working more and more and therefore taking less and less leisure, you are less inclined to work still more. The reason is obvious. The more you work, the less leisure you have, and you therefore value leisure more highly relative to the economic goods you are getting by working. There comes a point at which you are unwilling to work more because you are losing more utility in the leisure than you were gaining in the economic goods. The point at which you decide to quit working, then, clearly must be the point at which your utility from leisure just equals your utility from the economic goods into which the leisure may be converted. A lesser amount of work will overprovide you with leisure and under-provide you with economic goods from a utility standpoint. You will work more to trade a lesser amount of utility from leisure for a greater amount of utility from economic goods.

On the other hand, a greater amount of work will overprovide you with economic goods and underprovide you with leisure from a utility standpoint. You will work less to trade a lesser amount of utility from economic goods for a greater amount of utility from leisure. You will always end up with the division of your time between work and leisure so that the utility from another hour of work just equals your utility from another hour of leisure. Therefore, utility is maximized for an individual or society at the level of production where the losses in utility from the use of extra factors of production is just equal to the gains in utility from the extra economic goods into which they can be converted.

▷   production mix   ◁

The answer to the first question (What level of production?) assumed that economic goods are all alike or, put another way, that what we are really producing is one gigantic economic good. This, of course, is not true. A decision must be made not only as to how much to produce but what to produce. In fact, we may need to answer the second question first in real life, because we may not know whether we want to produce until we know what goods we can produce. To return to the labor example, it is entirely possible that you may be willing to forego a given amount of leisure to get a car but not to get a boat. Therefore, if it is possible to get a car for the sacrifice of the amount of leisure in question, your decision is to produce. However, if it is possible to get a boat but not a car for that amount of leisure, your decision is to not produce.

The second question (production mix) is answered the same way that the first question (production level) was answered. Specifically, we need to be sure that *our gains in utility are always at least as great as the losses in utility* undergone to get the gains. The fact that there is any decision to be made as to what to produce implies that factors of produc-tion are capable of producing a variety of different economic goods. If any given batch of factors of production were capable of producing only one single economic good, we would not need to decide what to produce.

ALTERNATIVES

Copyright © 1971 The Chicago Sun Times. Reproduced by
courtesy of Wil-Jo Associates, Inc. and Bill Mauldin.

A bundle of factors of production X could produce economic good B, and we could take it or leave it. Actually, a bundle of factors of production may produce economic goods A or B or C or D, in which case we have to decide which we want—if any. It is apparent that a choice in favor of C is necessarily a rejection of A, B, and D. The utility in economic good C is gained. The utility in A or B or D is foregone, since we could have had any one of them if we had not had C. If, say, A had the next highest amount of utility compared to C, we diminished or lost utility by the amount contained in economic good A in order to gain the utility in economic good C.

▶ SOCIETAL NONECONOMIC COST ◀

Just as an individual has an economic and a noneconomic side, a society has an economic and a noneconomic side. And just as the concept of cost relates to the noneconomic side as well as the economic side of the individual, so the concept of cost relates to the noneconomic as well as the economic side of a society. It may be a bit difficult to find a good real-world example of a purely noneconomic benefit for a purely noneconomic cost, noneconomic benefits for economic costs, or economic costs and benefits that have noneconomic aspects. The most outstanding examples probably cut across the political–economic boundary. The appendix leads to the conclusion that major wars are increasingly less likely to occur on cost–benefit grounds.

▶ OPPORTUNITY COST ◀

Cost is that which is given up to get something else. Cost is therefore sometimes referred to as **opportunity cost** or **alternative cost.** The selection of one opportunity or alternative entails foregoing another; hence the real cost of anything is an *opportunity* or *alternative* foregone. This should be clear enough by now. Only one possible point of confusion should be clarified. Occasionally a writer refers to cost and then at another point refers to opportunity or alternative cost. It is only natural to ask what the difference is between just plain cost and opportunity or alternative cost. There is *no* difference. A simple reference to cost rather than to opportunity or alternative cost is purely a matter of convenience. All cost is either opportunity or alternative cost. The basic definition of cost is such that it *must* be defined as alternative or opportunity cost.

The point of each of the preceding four sections (personal economic cost, personal noneconomic cost, societal economic cost, and societal noneconomic cost) was to show that all cost is opportunity or alternative cost and that it is relevant to the individual in his economic and noneconomic life and to aggregates of individuals (societies) in their collective economic and noneconomic lives. The identification of cost is central to the decision-making process. What you have now is simply one alternative; another alternative is to forego what you have now in order to acquire something else. The cost of what you have now is the next most valuable opportunity foregone; the cost of the next most valuable alternative is what you have now. Obviously, if the utility is greater in what you have now than in the next most valuable alternative, your decision is to retain what you have now and forego the alternative. If the utility of the most valuable alternative is greater than the utility in what you have now, your utility-maximizing decision is to forego what you have now in exchange for the more valuable alternative. Such is the simple relevance of cost to decision making. In fact, decision making might be defined as "cost analysis," to use more flowery terminology.

► ECONOMIC EFFICIENCY ◄

Efficiency is an important economic topic that relates very closely to cost. In fact, the question of efficiency might be viewed as simply another way of looking at cost, although there is an additional dimension. Cost was defined as the diminution of utility undergone in order to acquire a greater utility. The previous discussion explained that choices as to what things to have or to forego were based on a determination of the amounts of utility in the various alternatives. The alternative with the most utility would be chosen, and the alternative *foregone* with the most utility would be the cost of the alternative chosen. But another question remains.

What determines *how much* utility is gotten for the utility foregone? It is one thing to say that alternative *A* has more utility than alternative *C*, so alternative *A* should be chosen and alternative *C* foregone. It is another (but related) matter to say that alternative *A* has twice as much utility as alternative *C*, or half again as much, or three times as much. What determines specifically how *much* better the best alternative is compared to the second best?

Suppose that you have $20. Your alternatives are to have food or a new pair of shoes. The amount of each that $20 will buy is such that the $20 buys more utility by spending it on food than on shoes, so you choose the alternative food and reject the alternative shoes. A year later you again have $20 and, since your preferences have not changed, you again are faced with a food–shoes choice. Again, you see that $20 will buy more utility in food than in shoes, so you choose the alternative food again. But there is a difference between the situation this year and last year. You discover that this year food is not only the more attractive alternative but that it is attractive by a wider margin. In other words, the $20 will buy the same amount of utility in shoes this year as last year, but it will buy *more* utility in food this year than last year. It seems that although food was the best buy last year, it is an even better buy this year. Food has gotten cheaper in real terms. You can get more for the same sacrifice as earlier. Looked at in money terms, the same conclusion results. If you were to buy the same amount of utility from food this year as last, the money cost would be less than $20. Food is cheaper no matter how you look at it. Why?

Apparently there has been an increase in the efficiency of food production. **Efficiency** is defined as *the* amount *of utility gained relative to the* amount *of utility foregone.*[1] If the *amount* of utility from a given expenditure on food *increases* and the same *amount* of utility is foregone from shoes, and your desire for food versus shoes has not changed, something has changed with regard to the efficiency of production. You are able to get more food for the same sacrifice, apparently because someone is willing to let you have food more cheaply. But presumably no one is going to let you have things more cheaply unless he in turn gets them more cheaply (at less sacrifice). You got the food, ultimately, from the producer. The producer will supply you with food at a lower cost only if he in turn can get it at a lower cost. So the question becomes a matter of asking what determines the producer's cost. That, of course, is a matter of determining the cost of production. If production is the creation of utility, it must be that, since the producer will now let you have food more cheaply, the producer is able to create more utility than he once was from the same resources because the loss of utility to the producer equals the amount of resources used up. Thus we come to the conclusion that apparently the cost of food went down because the same utility in resources (cost) will now generate more utility in food than it once did. When the producer's costs went down, the benefit was transmitted through the economic system to the consumer. The producer is realizing a *greater amount* of utility *gained* (food produced) for the *same amount* of utility lost in resources (land, labor, capital, and management); that is, the producer has realized an increase in efficiency.[2] Thus an increase in efficiency is, by definition, a reduction in cost.

What causes an increase in efficiency? In this example, how is it that the food producer can get more utility for the same amount of utility given up? In everyday terms, why is it that a farmer now finds that two blades of grass grow where only one grew before, that the cow now gives more milk, and that the pig gets fat more quickly and on less feed? It takes about the same amount of time and equipment to cultivate an acre that grows little as one that grows much, so, obviously, if that acre produces twice as much as it did before, there is twice as much utility gained for the same utility lost in resources. The cost of production has fallen. What can cause this to happen? There may be several specific causes, but they can probably all be grouped under a single heading, technology.

Technology is defined as *the* skillfullness *with which resources are* *converted into economic goods.* This is a key issue in production. It is possible to have a given *quantity* of land, labor, capital, and management resources and to increase production through increased *quality* of technology. The more skillful we are at using resources, the more we get out of them. In fact, technology has sometimes been called "the fifth factor of production." It is perhaps not really a separate factor of production because it is not "free standing." That is, it does not have a separate identity such as land, capital, or labor. Technology exists only as it is embodied in one of the other factors of production. The laborer who is more highly trained and skilled has more technology built into him and is more productive than the unskilled and untrained laborer. The capital equipment that is well designed, lightweight, runs dependably, performs intricate tasks, and does them rapidly has more technology built into it than equipment that is slow, heavy, and undependable. Technology is the intangible input; it is the implementation of "the better idea." But technology can exist only as it is incorporated into either human or nonhuman resources.

To return to the specific example of agricultural technology and the cost of food, the farmer now uses bigger and better designed machinery, plants and animals bred to produce more abundantly, and chemicals (fertilizers, insect and weed killers) that allow him to be much more productive than he ever could have been earlier. The real cost of most goods in the United States is low, because the United States has realized tremendous technological success. As most people are well aware, technological success also has its cost.

The food example shows that technology in production generates economic efficiency which reduces the real cost of the economic good produced. As the level of technology rises throughout the economy, it translates into generally rising *real* incomes. If income is a flow of utility, obviously, rising technology, which generates more utility from the same resources, will cause the flow of utility to increase in the economy as a whole, allowing each individual to draw off an ever larger amount in return for the resources he supplies. Put plainly, the typical member of economic society ends up with more economic goods for a shorter work week.

The modern student is generally aware of ubiquitous technology: Should we praise it for our high level of economic well-being or damn it for creating environmental problems and diverting attention from other nontechnical problems that need attention? Either position, dogmatically held, is unwarranted. Like everything else, technology is subject to evaluation on the grounds of cost: What are the gains from it and what are the losses (costs), economic and noneconomic? Part IV will explore this issue further.

▶ NONECONOMIC EFFICIENCY ◀

If there is utility from noneconomic alternatives, it follows that the specific *amounts* of gains and losses in utility from these alternatives are subject to the same efficiency analysis that existed in the economic world. In the economic world, it developed that the greater the *amount* of gain relative to loss, the higher the level of efficiency. The amount of gain relative to loss could be increased in the economic world through an increase in technology. There is a counterpart to technology in the noneconomic world.

Consider your neighbor's dog who digs in your flowers. You like both your flowers and your neighbor. You believe, however, that if you do anything to stop the digging, it will scuttle a happy relationship with your neighbor. Your present utility-maximizing decision is to get the dog out of the flowers, since you have decided that you value them more than your neighbor's friendship. Once you have taken action, you will have gained utility from the flowers and lost utility from the friendship. The amount of the gain is going to be greater than the amount of the loss, so you decide to have it out with your neighbor. Having acted, you will have a utility "profit"—the *amount* by which the utility gained exceeded that lost.

But there is another dimension not yet considered. You may have some control over the amount of utility lost for this gain. If you charge over to your neighbor's house and yell at him, he may go out of his way to be nasty, in which case your utility "profit" is very low. The gains barely exceed the cost, because the losses are very great. If you are nice about it, you may get the dog out of the flowers with less damage to your relationship, in which case the cost is reduced, increasing "profit." If you are extremely astute and clever, you may convince him that it is not good for his dog to be in your flowers. He then volunteers to keep the dog out of your flowers with virtually no damage to your friendship, thereby reducing the cost greatly and leaving substantial "profit." Thus the more subtle you are in your approach to him, the more efficient is the solution to the problem. In this case, it seems that diplomatic skillfulness appears to be to noneconomic efficiency what technical skillfulness is to economic efficiency. Both are cost reducing.

> Conclusion: Political skills (broadly defined to include all interpersonal relationships) are at least one example of the noneconomic equivalent of technology.

An interesting development.

▶ PRACTICAL EXAMPLE ◀

After having roamed through the world of cost in a general way, a concrete example may be helpful. It will also allow us to view gains and losses in dollar terms, which is necessary if we are to return eventually to the world of practical decisions.

▶ Analysis 5–1

1 • Assume that the following resources are available:

	Labor	40 machinists.
	Capital	Factory with machinery, equipment, and tools capable of producing machinery.
X Bundle of Factors of Production	Land	The lot the factory is situated on, plus other natural resources.
	Management	Two executives trained in directing machinery production.

2 • An engineering and production analysis has indicated that X bundle of factors of production is capable of producing one of the following quantity of economic goods each month:

Alternative A: 300 power lawn mowers
Alternative B: 200 power garden tillers
Alternative C: 500 hand lawn mowers
Alternative D: 50 boat trailers

3 • Pick an alternative! If you pick alternative C of 500 hand lawn mowers, the real cost is alternative A or B or D. Stating it in real terms, you would be giving up 300 power lawn mowers *or* 200 power garden tillers *or* 50 boat trailers. The opportunity cost is the most desirable alternative foregone.

4 • Assume that you had available information regarding the utility of each of these products:

ALTERNATIVE	UTILITY/ UNIT	TOTAL UTILITY/ ALTERNATIVE (UNITS × UTILITY/UNIT)
A	4	1,200
B	8	1,600
C	1	500
D	15	750

It now becomes apparent that alternative *B* would provide the greatest total satisfaction and is therefore the best economic choice. It must be remembered that, although alternative *B* is the best choice, alternative *A* or *C* or *D* is foregone. The opportunity cost of 1,600 units of utility gained from garden tillers is 1,200 units of utility foregone in lawn mowers. The correct choice provides a "profit" of 400 units of utility.

5 • Let us consider how the choice might have been made in a practical way. As has been mentioned a number of times before, we are trying to grasp an abstraction—the abstract measurement of utility or satisfaction. In step *D* the utility per unit was provided. A valid question, but one impossible to answer, would be: "How was this utility measured?" In a practical way utility cannot be measured directly. Relating to this problem, the practical question of what to produce with the given bundle of resources is ultimately to be answered by the managers. As businessmen, their primary concern is to make the most profit possible for their business. Business profit is computed by subtracting money costs from money revenue. In this case the money costs would be the same for each alternative, and thus the managers' decision would be based on money revenue. Assume that the managers, with the assistance of sales personnel and cost accountants, determined that the products could be sold for the following prices, resulting in total revenues indicated:

ALTERNATIVE	PRICE	TOTAL REVENUE
A	$ 80	$24,000
B	160	32,000
C	20	10,000
D	300	15,000

With these prices, alternative *B* is the best choice in a business sense. Price has become the practical and perfect measurement of utility, which we could not measure directly. A word of caution: It must not be assumed that price is always a perfect, direct measurement of the utility of a product. If this were true, consumer decision making would be a very simple matter. Nonetheless, since consumers are trying to get as much utility as possible, *they can be expected to be willing to pay in proportion to the amount of utility in each product.* Thus if consumers are willing and able to pay $80 for 4 units of utility in a lawn mower, they could be expected to be willing to pay twice as much ($160) for 8 units of utility in a garden tractor. Consumer desires therefore translate into revenue to the firm. Consumers' willingness to pay dollar prices is the way the consumers tell the business which alternative to select.

Notice that alternative *B* provides $8,000 ($32,000 minus $24,-000) more revenue and therefore $8,000 more profit than the next best alternative. (The dollar *cost* of each alternative is the same.) This is a happy state of affairs indeed. The consumers wanted alternative *B*, and this is just what businessmen, who are trying to make profits, gave them! Notice also that it is necessary for businesses to try to maximize profits in order to give the consumers what they want. If businesses are not interested in profits, they will not necessarily select alternative *B*. This is the essence of the working of "the invisible hand," which guides resources to the use that consumers desire. The term "invisible hand" appears in *The Wealth of Nations* (1776), by Adam Smith, who is generally recognized as the founder of economics, particularly of market economics.

SUMMARY

1 • The cost of any alternative chosen is the most utility foregone in order to get that which was chosen.

2 • Cost is applicable to the economic and noneconomic world.

3 • Cost is applicable to individuals as such and to groups of individuals in aggregate.

4 • Cost as defined here is synonymous with alternative cost or opportunity cost.

5 • Choices should be made so that the gains in utility are always greater than the losses in utility from alternatives foregone.

6 • Efficiency is the *amount* of utility gained *relative* to the *amount* foregone.

7 • Technology increases economic efficiency, that is, increases the gains for any given loss.

8 • Political skills increase noneconomic efficiency, that is, increase the gains for any given loss. There may be other noneconomic equivalents of technology.

9 • If competition exists, businesses, by selecting the production alternative yielding the highest profit (a money representation of utility for the owners of businesses), will inadvertently give the consumers the alternative that gives them the most utility.

study materials

1 • Define and explain the concept of cost.

2 • Define personal economic cost.

3 • List three examples of personal economic cost, using real and monetary examples.

4 • Define personal noneconomic cost.

5 • List three examples of personal noneconomic cost.

6 • Define societal economic cost.

7 • List three examples of societal economic cost.

8 • How do polluted air and water, crowded space, and harried personal existence relate to production? What is the basic question or concern implied in this relationship?

9 • Define societal noneconomic cost.

10 • List three examples of societal noneconomic cost.

11 • Define the concept of compromise. Give an example of how compromise might relate to consumption. (*See* Appendix.)

12 • State the relationship between technology and efficiency. Give both economic and noneconomic examples to illustrate the relationship.

13 • List examples of how consumers might improve their "consumption efficiency."

14 • In Analysis 5–1, it became apparent that alternative *B* was the best choice. What part of this example would be the most difficult to state or determine exactly?

15 • Under what conditions would it be reasonably valid to consider price as an "indicator" of utility in a good or service? What conditions affect price which make it incorrect to assume that price provides a valid and direct measurement of utility?

footnotes

1 It would be somewhat more adequate to say that the cost of food *relative* to shoes has fallen, which would leave open the possibility that rather than food having fallen in cost, food has not changed but shoes have risen in cost. It greatly simplifies the example at no sacrifice to the basic point to "lock in" shoes and assume that all changes take place with regard to food.

2 The unstated assumption here is that competition prevails in all markets. This is not always so, in which case the example is not really false but somewhat less adequate. If there is not competition, consumers get only part rather than all of the benefits of increased efficiency in production.

appendix

MORE ON NONECONOMIC COST

▶   PERSONAL   ◀

Politics is sometimes defined as the art of compromise. As such, it is based on the noneconomic application of the principle of cost. Suppose that you are an elected representative of your constituency. You receive utility from your position in office, from the feeling that you are doing a good job, and from the esteem in which you are held. You want to stay in office, which means pleasing the voters most of the time. (You may be able to go your own way to a moderate degree, but in general your actions have to be in accord with the wishes of the voters.) This means getting your voters what they want. But this may be contrary to the wishes of other representatives' constituencies, who want something different. Since your adversary in the legislature also wants to get reelected, circumstances boil down to each of you trying to get what you want, and this entails preventing your adversary from getting what he wants—if I win, you lose, and if you win, I lose. Each side is equally determined. The result is a stalemate.

For example, if the new state office building and the new university branch are both built in Podunk, they will not be built in Last Chance, and vice versa. But both Podunk and Last Chance want both installations. Neither will get either one, unless one side gives in to produce a majority vote for one location or the other. However, if the Podunk legislator gives in and supports Last Chance, the Podunk voters will turn him out in the next election, and he well knows it. Ditto for the Last Chance voters and their legislator. Each legislator refuses to support the other, perhaps on the grounds that it is less painful to go without the installations if no one else gets them either; at least no legislator gets branded a traitor for an unrewarded sellout. Thus if one party wins totally and the other party loses totally, one party has gotten "something for nothing" and the other party has gotten "nothing for something"! But each party knows that the other party is just as determined as he is and therefore realizes that the "whole hog" strategy is out of the question, for to win is to have your cake and eat someone else's, so to speak. The opposition can be expected to be very vigorous in preventing your "free lunch" from coming out of his pocket. Each side contributes to the stalemate because the stalemate represents "nothing for nothing" for each side, which is certainly superior to the "nothing for something" that one side will realize if the other side wins. The situation would seem to suggest that the political process is incapable of ever accomplishing anything. Which way out? [1]

Compromise can make both sides better off by allowing each side to give up that part of his package which he values least for a part of the other side's package which he values more than that which he has to give up to get it. The utility gained exceeds the utility lost for each side. Both get a good "buy" through the compromise. The strategy simply requires the abandonment of the "whole hog" strategy—a strategy that each side quickly saw as impracticable. There are probably aspects of the position of each side which are valued more highly than other aspects by the respective parties. If the two sides do not each value the various parts of their positions identically, they have opened up the opportunity to trade that part of the package which they value little for a part of the opposition's package which they value more. Each side makes a decision to enter into a compromise according to the cost principle: What can I get and what do I have to give up to get it? If each party sees that, by being less hard-nosed, he can get something that he values more than that which he had to give up to get it, he is simply concluding that the cost of the "acquisition" should be borne and the compromise entered into, because the trade will increase his total utility. If each side finds itself in this position, the compromise can be expected to take place. The haggling over the terms of the compromise is the noneconomic counterpart to bargaining over price in the economic world. Acceptable terms are hammered out in either case.

The Podunk–Last Chance example contains an obvious compromise. Give the office building to one and the university branch to the other. If this was your immediate reaction to this situation, you are apparently convinced, whether you realize it or not, that cost is extremely relevant indeed. The two legislators agree to support one another on the basis of compromise. The cost to each legislator of the support of the other legislator is the abandonment of any hope whatsoever of attaining both installations. Since each legislator recognized that the probability of getting both was very low anyway, each legislator sees the acquisition of one of the installations through compromise as very attractively priced—he gave up relatively little to get it. Since the benefits from a compromise so greatly exceed the cost to each legislator, the compromise is eagerly sought by both. (Which city gets which installation would be hammered out in the terms of the compromise according to the relative preferences of each city for each installation. For our purposes it is adequate to note only that the gains to each city are substantial no matter which installation each gets, since each is losing only the very slim likelihood of getting both.)

Most people stand ready to compromise both because complete selfishness gets nowhere and because compromise so greatly increases utility at such a reasonable cost. For precisely these reasons, compromise tends to constitute a common denominator of interpersonal relationships. In fact, a compromise is probably the closest approximation to the free lunch that one can find. But in this case the lunch is not free; it is only very reasonably priced. Since the benefits typically greatly exceed the costs to all parties, compromises are sometimes referred to as "everybody wins" situations. The description may be apt, but it does not refute the cost principle. Winning in this context is not defined as something for nothing, only as getting more than is given up. If the gains exceed the losses by a wide margin (as in many compromises), the win is decisive. A situation where all parties can score decisive wins tends to be eagerly sought, hence the interest in compromise.[2]

▶ SOCIETAL ◀

Although wars have an economic cost and perhaps, at least in early history, an economic benefit as the winner took over the resources previously controlled by the conquered, the noneconomic dimensions of war are also substantial. Isolating the noneconomic costs and benefits from war leads to the conclusion that the costs tend to exceed the benefits, which leads to the conclusion that wars are to be avoided if possible. Hardly a surprising conclusion. The noneconomic costs consist of loss of life, which has noneconomic (as well as economic) utility, physical pain and suffering by the direct participants, emotional pain and suffering by the participants and their friends and relatives, a possible brutalizing effect on society which makes life in general less desirable, and so on.

You may be hard pressed to find noneconomic benefits from war, but they are there. In a "popular" war there is a feeling of righteousness and national purpose generated which unifies the nation and spurs it to great accomplishment and minimizes internal problems. The focus is on the common enemy. Fight it, not each other. There is a feeling of national satisfaction from fighting "the war to end all wars" or "to make the world safe for democracy." In an "unpopular" war, such as the Viet Nam war, the benefits were particularly small, which is precisely why the war was unpopular. In fact, the degree of "popularity" of a war would seem to boil down to the relationship of benefits to cost. In the case of Viet Nam, the United States came to have a difficult time finding any package of benefits, economic and noneconomic, sufficient to offset the costs, economic and noneconomic.

As a slight digression, it is interesting to note how a changing relationship between costs and benefits from war may be affecting international relations. Although the speculative premise on which the following arguments are based may be false, it provides opportunity for interesting cost-related contemplation. The premise is that *the probability of war is diminishing and the reason is that the costs relative to the benefits are increasing rapidly for virtually all nations.* The post-World War II period has seen numerous abrasions and conflicts—Berlin, Russia–United States, China–United States, China–Russia, Cuba, Middle East, Northern Ireland, India–Pakistan, Pakistan–Bangladesh, Viet Nam, and so on. Some of these conflicts did erupt into wars and very costly wars. Yet the wars were generally unpopular and localized. Twenty-five years ago, it was generally feared that local squabbles would drag the major powers into World War III. Yet today, local fracases tend to remain local fracases. The mood and tone in the United States seems to be less preoccupied with the prospect of a conflict of the international scale of World War I or World War II. Why? Perhaps it is because war is not as good a "buy" as it once was.

Consider early history. What were the costs and benefits from war? Wars were relatively cheap; economic systems were rudimentary; little capital existed; most labor was manual labor; technical know-how was very limited; and wars were easy (cheap) to stage. Round up some horses, chariots, men, spears, clubs and what have you, and go get 'em. If you win, you take over their lands, force their people to work for you, and take life easy. Little cost; relatively good payoff.

But the presence of substantial capital and technology changes all that. Wars are more expensive. It requires more resources to stage a modern war. Furthermore, the technology of war now causes wars to be more broadly disruptive. An all-out war does not destroy key installations; it wipes out whole cities, which substantially reduces the value of whatever is left for the winner to claim. Furthermore, the enslavement of a people doing manual labor is a good deal easier than enslavement of people who are primarily the manipulators of capital. Manual laborers can be forced to produce by standing over them with a club. Manipulators of capital need only to surreptitiously fold, staple, and mutilate to sabotage a modern economy. The manpower required to coerce the labor force of a modern economy to function at anywhere near the level at which it would function voluntarily would undoubtedly constitute a major portion of the entire labor force itself, which creates a monumental drain on the captor for "supervision." The economic aspects of modern warfare for economic payoff seem to work out to paying the price that one might expect to pay for the acquisition of a modern economy and getting in return (1) ashes, (2) a modern economy that requires an exorbitant quantity of resources by the captor to keep it running, or (3) sufficiently lenient rewards to those conquered to keep them from sabotaging the system, so that nothing is left for the captor.

As for the noneconomic costs and benefits, they seem to be primarily ideological and political. The crux of the noneconomic aspect of the issue seems to be education. Educational levels throughout the world are rising—at different rates at different places in the world, but nonetheless rising. As people are better educated they tend to be somewhat more objective in their outlook, which means that they are less uptight about ideology. They adopt a live-and-let-live attitude. They are less inclined to blindly follow political leaders who, in order to divert attention from their own inadequacies, convince their people that their neighbors are about to do them in, so "let's get them before they get us." This substantially reduces the benefits to those who actually make the war–peace decisions. The nation is less inclined to go to war on ideological grounds because it gets less utility from its ideological position than it once did. It also means that war loses its unifying potential within a nation as the citizenry is more able to accurately identify costs and benefits from war. Wars are therefore more apt to be unpopular.

Combining the economic and noneconomic costs and benefits from war, the previous arguments suggest that, since the trend internationally is toward more capital, technology, and education, the benefits to the typical nation from war are becoming less and less relative to the cost, and the typical individual is increasingly able to recognize that fact. End result? Diminishing likelihood of World War III deliberately initiated. It is interesting to note that concern about major war has tended to shift from the deliberately initiated war to the war initiated by an irresponsible leader pushing the panic button. Irresponsibility in this context might be defined as the incurring of cost without regard to benefit. Clearly no rational person incurs cost without considering the benefit.

You may now ask why it is that nations go on preparing for wars that we have nearly concluded they will not fight. You probably have a notion of possible answers—some legitimate when the broader complexities are considered. We will simply put our tongues in our cheeks and say, "That is a good question, isn't it? Speaking of costs without regard to benefit. . . ."

The *specific* arguments above leading to the conclusion that major wars are less and less likely on cost–benefit grounds are full of innumerable holes. The *general* substance of the arguments and the conclusions may or may not be correct. That is beside the point. The point is that total (economic and noneconomic) costs and benefits are an ever present and powerful force in the course of human events.

More specifically, societal costs and benefits are present in virtually every major historical event. The benefit of the cultural revolution in the People's Republic of China was to be ideological indoctrination that would produce a national unity resulting in sundry benefits to society; but as the cost in disruption of economic and social activity was apparently greater than anticipated, the program was toned down. In Hitler's Germany, the benefit from the purge of the Jews was perhaps some national determination and political stability, but the cost in terms of scientific and cultural leadership foregone was enormous. The list of examples is endless.

footnotes

[1] This example assumes a contest between approximate equals. If one side is strong enough to browbeat the other side into submission, it would appear that we have the noneconomic equavalent of robbery—the taking of something without a voluntarily accepted reward (pay) in return. In a civilized society, we assume that interpersonal relationships are on a *voluntary* basis.

[2] The Podunk–Last Chance illustration and related discussion might be considered as a brief introduction to some of the ideas behind game theory. Game theory is a procedure for developing winning strategies under conditions found in such diverse activities as business, poker, war, and politics. It deals particularly with the determination of the most desirable strategy when all the parties to the contest (game) know all the circumstances faced by the other "players" and when those circumstances include the virtual impossibility of any player scoring a complete win at the total expense of the other players.

chapter
6

ECONOMIC SYSTEMS: COMMON FEATURES

production, consumption, income, wealth

In Chapter 3 we discussed various systems and their role in the efficient solution of problems. For purposes of this chapter, we note that you, yourself, are a small economic system, which in turn is part of a larger economic system— or simply, the economy—which your nation has established to provide for its economic needs. The national economy is in turn part of the world economy. In many respects the three economies (personal, national, international) are identical. That is, because they all seek to generate utility, they therefore all engage in production and consumption. In addition, in all of them, factors of production must be employed for production to occur.

In this chapter we will proceed under the tacit assumption that we are looking at a national economy—a convenience based on our suspicion that you will find this view the most comfortable. But for purposes of a look at the basic elements of an economic system, we could consider you personally a "nation" undertaking production and consumption, creating income and wealth through the employment of factors of production, and engaging in "foreign trade" with other "nations."

We hasten to add that in Chapter 7 we will consider some ways in which economies are not identical, most notably with regard to (1) the way the utility produced is divided up among individuals in the economy, and (2) the way decisions are made as to what to produce and how to go about it. When examining these questions, we will not be able to assume that your personal economy and the national economy are identical, since the crux of the issue lies in your personal relationship to the economic world of which you are a part and in what determines its impact on you.

In this chapter we will also look more closely at the two basic sides of any economic system: production and consumption. Although the three major categories of consumer goods (durables, nondurables, and services) are physically different, the differences are overshadowed by their similarities. They all have utility and all require factors of production in their creation. We will then examine the flows of utility (income) and the stocks of utility (wealth) in the economic system.

▶ LIFE CYCLES ◀

A fact that we must begin to acknowledge more overtly is the presence of *time*. As one measure of human experience, it frequently gets little attention in its own right. However, when we discuss investment, the concept of time will be central. Let us begin to acknowledge time by looking at the **life cycles** of some different kinds of economic goods. Since the economic system generates utility as time elapses, it should come as no surprise that economic goods have a life cycle much as other entities in this finite world have life cycles.

▷ in general ◁

Imagine some good called economic good X. Its life cycle is depicted in Figure 6–1. At some point in time the factors of production are combined

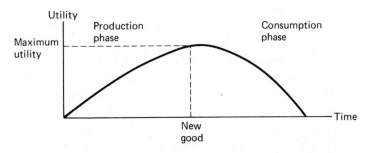

FIGURE 6–1 • The life cycle of economic good X.

which will eventually emerge as good X. *As long as utility is increasing, production is occurring.* The good is not fully produced until the factors of production that are put into it have the most utility they will ever have. When the maximum level of utility is reached, we have a new good. The utility of the good has not reached a maximum until it is actually in the hands of the consumer. Certainly a new car has more utility in your possession than it does as it comes off the assembly line, or even as it stands in a dealer's showroom. This means that relocating a good in time or space may add to its utility. It also means that what is sometimes called marketing or distribution is simply a particular form of production. As the good is consumed, its utility diminishes. If ownership of the good changes during the consumption phase, this obviously constitutes trade in used goods. The good's utility will finally diminish to zero when it is completely "worn out."

There is no predictable relationship between the length of the production phase and the length of the consumption phase. The length of each phase is determined by the nature of production and the way that the good is consumed. These two elements are determined by entirely separate circumstances.

▷ **nondurables** ◁

Most food products, for example, have a production phase that is very long relative to the consumption phase. It takes more than a year to produce beefsteak only 15 minutes to consume it. A life cycle of a steak would take the general form of Figure 6–2.

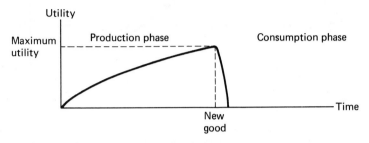

FIGURE 6–2 • The life cycle of the nondurable economic good "Steak."

▷ **durables** ◁

On the other hand, some goods are rapidly produced and slowly consumed. Such a good (an automobile, for example) is represented by Figure 6–3. It takes a relatively short time to produce an automobile but

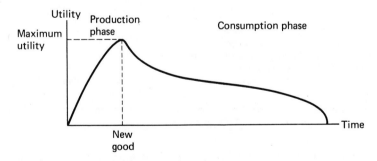

FIGURE 6–3 • The life cycle of the durable economic good "Automobile."

years to consume it. Figure 6–4 considers the life cycle of the automobile in greater detail.

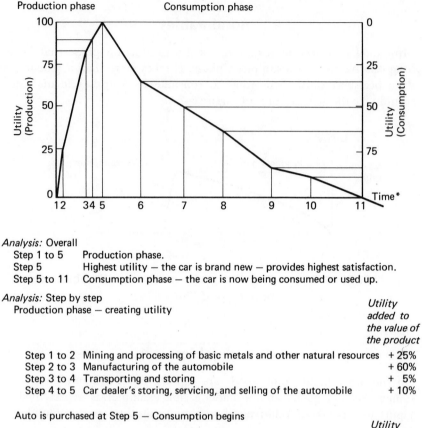

Analysis: Overall
Step 1 to 5	Production phase.
Step 5	Highest utility — the car is brand new — provides highest satisfaction.
Step 5 to 11	Consumption phase — the car is now being consumed or used up.

Analysis: Step by step
Production phase — creating utility

Utility added to the value of the product

Step 1 to 2	Mining and processing of basic metals and other natural resources	+ 25%
Step 2 to 3	Manufacturing of the automobile	+ 60%
Step 3 to 4	Transporting and storing	+ 5%
Step 4 to 5	Car dealer's storing, servicing, and selling of the automobile	+ 10%

Auto is purchased at Step 5 — Consumption begins

Utility diminished

Step 5 to 6	Car is brand new; however, much of the utility is used up the first year — satisfaction of owning a brand new car, etc.	− 35%
Step 6 to 7	Car is still quite new	− 15%
Step 7 to 8	Good used-car phase	− 12%
Step 8 to 10	Fairly good second-car phase	− 26%
Step 10 to 11	Teen-age hot-rod	− 12%
Step 11	Junking stage	approaching	0

* The time represented by Steps 1 to 11 may, of course, be anywhere from 5 to 20 years, depending on the particular car and the circumstances.

FIGURE 6–4 • The life cycle of an automobile in detail.

▷ services ◁

Durable goods are necessarily tangible. Nondurable goods may be either tangible or intangible. Those goods which are intangible and have no durability whatsoever are generally referred to as "services." The life cycle (Figure 6–5) of a service is unique, since no time can elapse if it has

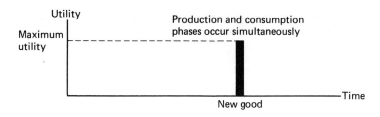

FIGURE 6–5 • The life cycle of services.

no durability at all. It must be consumed as it is produced—there can be no lapse between production and consumption. The barber who cuts your hair and the salesman who sells you insurance produce their "goods" at the precise moment that you consume them.

Although Figures 6–1 through 6–5 serve to illustrate some of the basic differences in the nature of different goods, different kinds of production, and different kinds of consumption, the term *durability,* of course, refers to consumption characteristics only. That is, goods that are consumed over a relatively long period of time are **durables;** goods that are consumed relatively quickly are **nondurables;** goods that are consumed more or less instantaneously are **services.** In the case of services, production at the time of consumption is necessarily implied. The distinction between durables and nondurables is necessarily a gray one, since all goods fall somewhere on a "durability continuum" and any division between durables and nondurables is necessarily somewhat arbitrary. In general, durables are items of hardware (appliances, automobiles, recreational vehicles, etc.) or furniture. That is, even though your shirt or dress may last 10 years, economists would still call it nondurable. Figure 6–6 is a simple durability continuum. Economists would probably draw the line between durables and nondurables at about 3 or 4 on the scale. The issue is not terribly important for our purposes.

In any event, it is clear that production and consumption take place only as time elapses, albeit a very small amount of time in the case of services. Production and consumption are therefore **flow concepts.** Production creates a flow of utility over time. Consumption can occur only

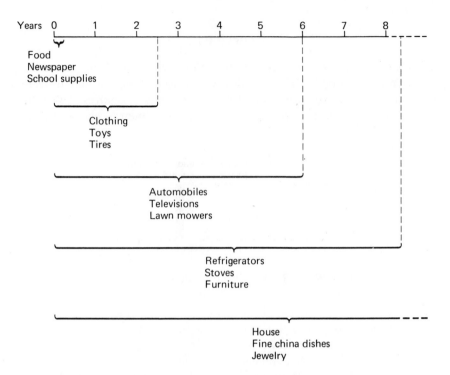

FIGURE 6–6 • Consumption phase time line: Durability continuum.

as time elapses. Similarly, income is a flow, because if time stopped, no income could flow to you. On the other hand, wealth is a **stock concept,** because if time stood still, wealth would still exist, even though production, consumption, and income would not. To use the analogy of a horse race, if the winning of the race is income, the race cannot be won unless time elapses; but if the horses and track are wealth, if time stopped in the middle of the race, everything would still be in place. Everything is there if time stops, but time must elapse for anything to be accomplished.

► A RUDIMENTARY ECONOMIC SYSTEM ◄

An economic system consisting of production, consumption, income, and wealth may be thought of as a plumbing system through which utility flows. Additions and subtractions are continuously being made to a "tank" (stock) of wealth as economic goods go through their life cycles:

Production continuously creates income, part of which (durables, non-durables, and capital goods) are additions to the stock of wealth, and *consumption* (including capital consumption or depreciation) continuously draws down the stock of wealth. Figure 6–7 represents such a system.

Throughout this "plumbing system" it is really utility that is being created, that flows, that is stored, and that is destroyed in consumption.

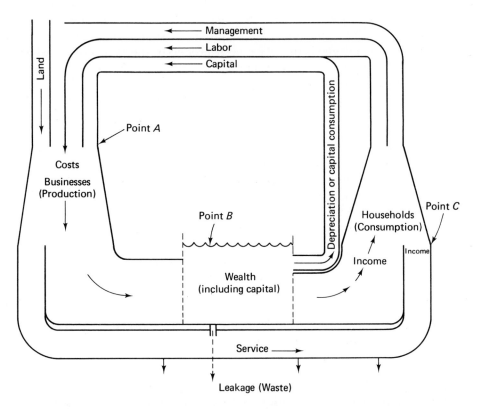

Analysis:

1. Note that the flow begins to widen at Point *A*. The four basic resources are combined in production to create utility. The widening process indicates production in a pictorial way. The whole (produced goods) is greater than the sum of its parts (each resource considered separately).

2. Point *B* indicates the "tank" of wealth. At any point in time a given stock of goods (wealth) is available in the economy.

3. Note that the flow begins to narrow at Point *C*. The flow (income) is diminished as consumption occurs.

4. Note that services are produced and consumed immediately and do not become a part of wealth.

FIGURE 6–7 • Basic economic system.

Businesses create utility through production. Utility then flows directly to households as services or flows into the wealth tank as durable and nondurable goods—which then flow either to households as consumer goods or back to businesses as capital. As households reduce utility through consumption, the only utility that is left in households is the utility of the householder himself (his time and skills), part of which he puts back into production as labor and management. Also flowing into the productive process is land (free good). Businesses incur costs (use up factors of production) in order to produce. As households receive the actual economic goods that have been produced, they get income, which they divest by using up (consuming) the utility in the economic goods they got from businesses.

Waste is represented by whatever leakages may be present in the system. Utility that escapes provides no one with satisfaction and is therefore waste.

The relationship among production, income, wealth, and consumption is simple. The level of wealth will rise if the faucet of production generating income adds more to the tank of wealth than the drains of depreciation, consumption, and waste draw off. Obviously, then, the only way for an economy to build a capital stock, and therefore to enable higher future production, is for current production to exceed the sum of current consumption, depreciation, and waste. Furthermore, the only way for an economic society to increase its consumption in the long run is to increase its production. If the society increases consumption without increasing production, it will deplete its tank of wealth (capital stock) and thereby reduce its ability to maintain even the present level of production. When its capital stock runs out, it will have to start over from scratch and will of course be confined to a very low level of consumption.

> **Thus the only way for an economic society as a whole to increase consumption and maintain a level of increased consumption in the long run is for it to increase production.**

Lest you think this is an obvious conclusion, we can only say that a great many people act as though they don't know it.

SUMMARY

1 • **Economic goods go through "life cycles" as utility is added to a good during production and as it then diminishes during consumption.**

2 • Consumer goods are typically divided into durable goods, nondurable goods, and services (having no durability at all).

3 • *Any* economic system (economy) generates income through production, which constitutes additions to wealth from which consumption is undertaken.

4 • Income, production, and consumption are flow concepts in that time must elapse for them to occur.

5 • Wealth is a stock concept since it would exist even if time stood still.

6 • An economy may be likened to a plumbing system in which utility flows into the wealth tank as production occurs and flows out of the wealth tank as consumption occurs. The level of wealth, then, depends on the rate of consumption compared to the rate of production.

7 • In the short run, if consumption exceeds production, wealth will diminish.

8 • In the long run, it is impossible for consumption to exceed production since the stock of wealth will eventually be exhausted.

study materials

1 • Explain how and why an individual can be considered an "economy."

2 • What is the "life cycle" of a good?

3 • Explain the relationship between time and production and consumption.

4 • What is the relationship between time and durables and nondurables? To which phase of economic activity do *durable* and *nondurable* relate?

5 • What is the unique characteristic of services as related to time, production, and consumption? Explain.

6 • Approximate the length of the consumption phase of an automobile, a steak, and a haircut.

7 • Is there a relationship between the consumption phase of goods and their prices? Their values? (Clues: Are plastic salt and pepper

shakers priced higher than a tenderloin steak? Is an emergency appendectomy valued less than an automobile?) Why are price and value frequently different?

8 • Income has been defined in the chapter as a *flow of utility*. Economic income is derived from goods, services, and resources. Prepare a list of your income in real and monetary terms for the past 24 hours.

9 • Wealth has been defined in the chapter as a *stock of utility*. Prepare a list of your wealth in real and monetary terms at the present time.

10 • Now compare your present wealth with the income computed in question 8. Which is larger? Must wealth always be larger than income—or vice versa? What significance did time have in arriving at your income? At your wealth?

11 • List four problems or conditions that may modify the income distribution patterns away from productivity as the sole criterion for income distribution.

12 • Why is waste within the production phase of concern to the consumer?

13 • Using Figure 7–2, indicate what is occurring at each point of the diagram and indicate its significance to the consumer.

chapter 7

ECONOMIC SYSTEMS: UNIQUE FEATURES

decision,
control,
money,
income distribution

In this chapter we will move from the consideration of production, consumption, income, and wealth, which are part of any economy, to the consideration of some features of an economy that vary from case to case, such as provision for economic decisions, economic control, and money and income distribution.

Some economies allow a great many decisions by individuals and provide for economic control by individuals. Others place a much lower priority on the individual as such. Although all modern economies use money, it is not an absolute requirement for economic activity. Primitive economies can do without it, though its absence will greatly curtail the level *of production, consumption, income, and wealth realized. Finally, the manner in which the fruits of production (income) is distributed varies greatly from economy to economy.*

Our discussion will proceed primarily from the standpoint of competitive market capitalism, which is the foundation stone of the U.S. economy. Lest the skeptics among you point out that big government, big business, big labor, big agriculture, and a plethora of economic regulations have rendered competitive market economics obsolete, we can only say that many of the difficulties and stresses and strains that attend economic regulation and departures from competition are due to market forces that keep coming to the surface for air regardless of attempts to suppress them. It is imperative that you understand at least a little about them. It is chiefly the adequacy of decision and control mechanisms and monetary and income distribution systems that cause the levels of production, consumption, income, and wealth to vary from economy to economy— particularly after accounting for differences in technology, population, and natural resources.

▶   **ECONOMIC DECISION**   ◀

Our primary focus in Parts I, II, and III is on you as an individual householder; how you make decisions and the consequences of those decisions to you and your family or immediate associates is our first concern. Householders are the focal point of economic interest. Householders are consumers. Production is undertaken only in order that households may consume—individually, or collectively in the case of government services. In fact, it may be said that businesses are simply organizations or devices that householders collectively (society) create to convert factors of production into economic goods so that you will be more satisfied. Needless to say, the way you go about *deciding* which goods to have and how many factors of production to supply and to which businesses are very important questions. The household is your home base from which you make decisions about your life as a producer as well.

Most of our investigation will deal with your decisions and how they affect you directly as an individual rather than their effect on you as a part of the group that controls government and business. However, the principles laid down for good decision making when the decisions affect you directly are in large measure the same principles that relate to good decision making when you are part of a group.

The activities of production, distribution, consumption, and decision making are necessarily performed in some "agreed-upon pattern." Some societies stress decision making on an individual basis—others on a group basis. Some societies have "decisions" forced upon them by a "command" system. The command system is manifest where the "government" is all-powerful. Tribal societies where the chief would have the last word on all activities is an example of a simple command economy or system. Ancient monarchies are another example. Present-day, all-powerful dictatorial governments are yet another example.

Societies may pursue economic activities, and the decision-making process, based on tradition or custom. Modes of production, distribution, and consumption evolved over long periods of time, perhaps hundreds of years. Economic activity changed very slowly and was carried on in a "traditional" manner because "that's the way it has always been done— it's the custom." Apparently no one really made decisions; the decisions were preordained by tradition. Feudalism and some tribal systems are examples of a "custom" economy.

Some societies stress group decision making, minimizing the individual. Certain religious colonies in the United States, South Sea Island groups, modern day communes, as well as some modern industrialized nations stress the group approach. The decisions relating to production, distribution, and consumption are made by the group, with the group's interest of foremost concern.

Yet other societies stress the individual approach to economic decision making. Production, distribution, and consumption decisions are pursued on the basis of satisfying individual wants and desires. The individual's wants and desires all meet in a common arena called a *market*. Market capitalism is an example of such an individualized pattern.

The point to be stressed and remembered is that regardless of the "agreed-upon pattern," the *decision mechanism* of an economic system is the result of that pattern. All societies employ an economic system containing a decision mechanism; some are very simple, some very complex; some are based on command, others on tradition or market; decisions may be group-based, others individually oriented. What is important is that a pattern develops; provision for decision exists.

► ECONOMIC CONTROL ◄

When we begin to talk about economic decisions, we are talking about economic control. He who decides, controls. Thus the essence of the last few paragraphs about economic decision making may be repeated in terms of economic control. All economies are much less alike than when we simply talk about the occurrence of production and consumption and the existence of income and wealth. Competitive market economies are quite directly under household control. The U.S. economy as a modified market economy, or mixed economy, has a major share of control resting directly in the hands of units of governments and large corporations. Since individual householders exercise control over U.S. governments and corporations by ballot (one person, one vote, in the case of government; one share of stock, one vote, in the case of corporations), household control is indirect. In a centrally planned economy where participatory democracy is absent (such as the U.S.S.R.), household control is either absent, or, if you wish, present only to the extent that decision makers are constrained by what the householders will stand for. In other words, household control is very indirect indeed, and can be exercised assuredly only through open rebellion. Thus there are all shades of gray when it comes to economic control.[1]

We are now in a position to modify the simple economic system of Figure 6–7 to show economic control where that control rests with householders. It is people in the act of making decisions and exercising control that are the "pump" that makes the utility flow in the system. Everything is under the jurisdiction of someone. Even though land is a free good, someone exercises authority over it. Someone, somewhere, decides; someone, somewhere, controls.

Figure 7–1 is modified from Figure 6–7 to show control over the basic economic system. There are two modifications: (1) The end of the land and capital pipes are connected into the households; (2) wealth is moved into the households. We are not necessarily ignoring government and its control of economic affairs. We are simply saying that the government is made up of householders who, indirectly through elected representatives, exert control over government and its economic actions. The same is true for businesses. Although businesses, like governments, take economic action, they are controlled by households. The household control of the business is direct if the business is a proprietorship or partnership, as are most doctors, lawyers, small retailers, and farmers. Household control of business is indirect or on a group basis if the business is a corporation. In that case, the householders are stockholders in the corporation and elect representatives (board of directors) to run the corporation for them, much as they elect representatives to run their government.

▶ **MONEY** ◀

A step back to real-world practicality is the reintroduction of money now that the fundamentals have been laid out. From Figure 7–1 it is evident that householders are, in *real* terms, trading factors of production that they control for economic goods from which they get more utility than they did from the factors of production that they exchanged for the goods. If they do not get more utility from the goods than from the factors, engaging in production will reduce their level of utility. If they are rational, they will not continue to offer factors of production to businesses.

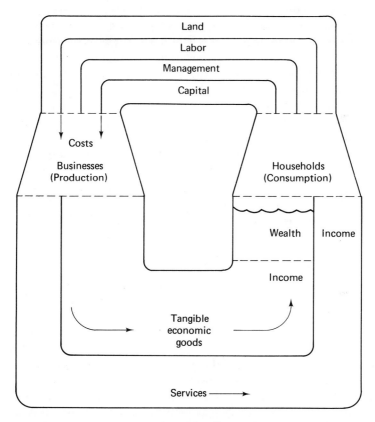

FIGURE 7–1 • Control by households in a basic economic system.

As a practical matter we know that an outright exchange of factors of production for goods does not occur. This is barter. Actually, the householder trades factors of production for money and then later trades money for a variety of goods. Thus, finally, factors of production have been exchanged for goods, but involving extra steps converting factors of production to money and money to economic goods. Money, then, is purely a matter of convenience.

Money, like other modern wonders, was invented because there was a need for it. Barter was cumbersome. To trade a factor of production directly for an economic good would require you to (1) consume only those particular goods made by the factors that you, yourself, supplied, (2) find someone else who supplied factors to a different line of production and trade goods with him, or (3) supply your factors to a wide variety of production activities. None of the three alternatives is satisfactory. In the first case, you do not want a single good; you want a variety of goods. In the second case, you get a variety of goods but only after a time-consuming search for someone else who has the good you want *and* who wants the good you offer in exchange. The third case results in your getting a variety of goods; however, the *total* amount of goods that you can have will probably be fairly low because the factors of production you supply are not equally well suited to the production of all kinds of goods. Specialization in production allows higher total production than would be possible in the absence of specialization. As an extreme example, the Iowa corn farmer who decides to satisfy his hunger for seafood by offering the resources he controls to the production of seafood will likely find his hunger unabated. His resources are completely unsuited to that use. Better to stick with corn and trade it with a fisherman.

All these problems can be alleviated if we can get everyone to agree to trade *every* good and factor of production for one *single* commodity, money. Then everyone can produce his specialty for which his factors of production are well suited. You can take your goods to market, a common arena in which all who wish to buy or sell that good have learned to go, and sell for money to all who wish to buy. You can then take your money and go to several other markets to buy that variety of goods you want. All the problems of barter are thereby averted. The factors of production may be used where they are the most productive. The suppliers of the factors of production get the variety of economic goods that they want, and they are able to do it with a minimum of inconvenience.

It matters not the least that the single good, money, which we agree to exchange for all other goods may be only paper with ink on it and has almost no utility in itself. All that is necessary is that everyone agrees to the scheme—which they are likely to do as long as they can exchange money for real goods anytime they want. In any event, money and monetary systems are simply inventions that have been developed to serve a purpose. As long as everyone finds his money readily acceptable for a wide variety of goods, the monetary system can be expected to serve its purpose well. We will discuss money at several subsequent points in more detail. For now it will be convenient to think in money terms as we consider income distribution.

▶ INCOME DISTRIBUTION ◀

All economies embrace certain criteria according to which income is distributed to individual members of society. The generation of income by society as a whole through production is one thing; a decision as to who gets how large a piece of the total pie is another.

▷ on a personal basis ◁

Criteria for income distribution differ widely from economy to economy. "From each according to his ability; to each according to his needs" is a statement about income distribution—or at least the second half is. "Need" is apparently the determining factor. Such a criterion may or may not be good philosophy; it is certainly difficult economics, however, since the "need" of every individual person must be determined. Any volunteers? On the other hand, even the United States, which professes quite a different basis for income distribution, acknowledges the significance of "need." Public assistance programs give money income to people who "need" it. This is certainly a much more restricted concept of need than one on which an entire income distribution system might be based. Nonetheless it is evidence that, in reality, income distribution mechanisms acknowledge several criteria.

In competitive market capitalism, the foundation of the U.S. economy, the income distribution system is based on the contribution you make to the economy. To paraphrase: "From each according to his inclination (and ability); to each according to his contribution." The bigger the contribution you make to the creation of the pie, the bigger the piece you may claim for yourself. The operation of the market generates this end result. If you recognize that the size of your contribution is measured by the *value* the market places on your contribution, the essence of this income distribution mechanism is self-evident. It also illustrates the importance of economic *control* over resources and the *consumer orientation* of a market economy.

───────────────── **EXAMPLE 7–1** ─────────────────

1 • **Consumers' preference for widgets rises.**
2 • **Consumers are willing to pay a higher price for widgets.**

3 • Businesses acquire resources for widget production more aggressively because it is now more profitable to produce widgets.

4 • Businesses pay resources used in widget production higher prices to attract them to widget production.

5 • Thus since the market values widgets more highly, the resources that can be converted to widgets are valued more highly by the market.

6 • As the controller of widget-producing resources, your money income rises allowing you to buy (claim) a larger share of the total economic pie.

7 • Conclusion: Consumer demand is transmitted through the market to businesses (consumer orientation), who in turn transform that demand into higher money incomes for those persons who supply (control) resources.

Notice that it is *control* of valuable resources that generates income for an individual member of society. This is why a minimum understanding of the income distribution mechanism is necessary for personal economic success. *What do you control, or can you get under your control, that can be converted into a high-value end product?*

Notice however that this mechanism has a certain social sterility about it. It does not pass judgment as to whether your resources are converted into "desirable" products. "If people are buying it, it is desirable," says the market.

EXAMPLE 7–2

People are buying drugs like crazy and killing themselves consuming them. If you control the drug supply, you get a high income for producing this valuable product.

In addition, notice that "work" as typically defined is not necessarily required: It is *control* of something valuable that counts, which, of course, may be skills offered in "work." "Work" is not necessarily involved, however; the idle rich may also be productive.

EXAMPLE 7–3

Great Grandfather Bullgravy was too lazy to carry his own weight in the westward-moving pioneer party, so they threw him out of the wagon and he lived his life on a worthless patch of brush. As his only heir (and a delinquent one at that), you have inherited this worthless piece of property. On it, however, a well is discovered which produces the only source of Eternal Twinkle Water, which will cause people to live forever. Consumers are climbing over one another to buy your product and bidding the price to astronomical levels in the process. You become the world's richest person. Why? Because you are also the world's most productive person, obviously.[2]

▷ on a resource basis ◁

With this general understanding of the income distribution mechanism, we return to our circular flow diagram in Figure 7–2, modified from Figure 7–1 to depict the division of income according to productivity— this time not among individuals but among the four factors of production (or resources). The same principle applies: Each factor receives a share of the income according to its contribution to the total production endeavor. This is readily convertible to a personal basis because persons control the factors of production.

▶ IN REAL TERMS

Income distribution begins at point A in Figure 7–2. Each resource receives the same proportion of the total income as the proportion of its contribution to the value of total production (value input). Assume that 200 units of goods and 50 units of services are produced and are available for distribution at point A. Table 7–1 shows the distribution. Of course, if the amount of value input of the resource is different, the amount of goods and services claimed by each resource is different.

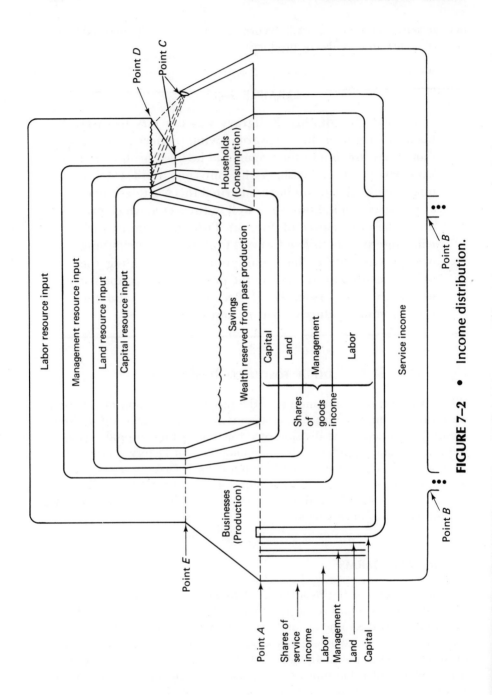

FIGURE 7-2 • Income distribution.

Table 7–1

DIVISION OF PRODUCTION
AMONG RESOURCES

RESOURCE	VALUE INPUT (%)	GOODS TO RESOURCE	SERVICES TO RESOURCE
Labor	70	140	35
Management	20	40	10
Capital	5	10	2.5
Land	5	10	2.5
Totals	100	200	50.0

▶ **IN MONEY TERMS**

Assume for simplicity's sake that the money value (price) of each unit of good is $10 and each unit of service is $20. The total money value of the production is derived in Table 7–2, and the distribution of that money

Table 7–2

CONVERSION OF PRODUCTION
TO MONEY VALUE

	UNITS	PRICE/UNIT	MONEY VALUE (TOTAL)
Goods	200	$10	$2,000
Services	50	20	1,000
Total money value			$3,000

value among the various resources is shown in Table 7–3. In the next step, the money is exchanged by the householder for consumer goods, as shown in Table 7–4.

We have now come full circle back to Table 7–1—from real to money to real. *Income distribution in monetary terms is the same as income distribution in real terms.* As concluded earlier, money is merely

Table 7–3

DIVISION OF MONEY VALUE
AMONG RESOURCES

RESOURCE	VALUE INPUT (%)	MONEY VALUE (GOODS)	MONEY VALUE (SERVICES)	MONEY VALUE (TOTAL)
Labor	70	$1,400	$ 700	$2,100
Management	20	400	200	600
Capital	5	100	50	150
Land	5	100	50	150
Total money value		$2,000	$1,000	$3,000

Table 7–4

CONVERSION OF MONEY INCOME
TO GOODS AND SERVICES

RESOURCES	MONEY INCOME (GOODS)	UNITS OF GOODS ($10/UNIT)	MONEY INCOME (SERVICES)	UNITS OF SERVICES ($20/UNIT)
Labor	$1,400	140	$ 700	35
Management	400	40	200	10
Capital	100	10	50	2.5
Land	100	10	50	2.5
Totals	$2,000	200	$1,000	50.0

an economic tool invented by man for his convenience. A good monetary system facilitates the economic activities of production and distribution. It does not change the economic realities. The real satisfaction (utility) to the consumer is in the real goods and services—money merely represents them. Money allows specialization and division of labor to occur. A highly developed industrialized economy is dependent on a sound monetary system. However, this should not obscure the real roots of your concern—obtaining the real goods and services and the satisfaction from them.

▶ MODIFICATIONS TO THE INCOME ◀ DISTRIBUTION MECHANISM

The pattern up to this point assumes that goods and services will be distributed to resources based on the value-input proportion. A number of problems prompt modifications to this simple pattern in the real world.

1 • The value-input proportion is very difficult to ascertain exactly. In a very simple production system the proportion may be fairly easily assessed. When production occurs on a very large scale using complex techniques and a variety of mixes of resources, the contribution of each resource is more difficult to ascertain. Many of the labor–management battles that occur today in collective bargaining are based on a disagreement of the value-input of each resource. Each resource owner feels that he has evidence to support a higher value-input proportion and therefore has a claim on a larger part of the goods and services produced. In the appendix you will find an example taken from banana production which illustrates something about *how* the proportion of value contributed by each resource might be determined.

2 • In the real world the resources are paid a money income, which they convert to real income. Using money creates some problems because (1) the value of money changes over time as prices *in general* change (inflation and deflation), and (2) the relative value (price) of individual products also changes over time. Power production has changed dramatically in the United States during the last two or three decades. The switch has been from coal to petroleum. The real value of coal went down at the same time that the general price level went up (inflation) for several years. These two occurrences have made it difficult to determine the value input of coal miners and coal mine owners.

3 • The assumption that income *should* be based on the value input of the resources may be challenged. Some people feel it necessary to modify or change the pattern to encompass considerations other than value input. Their line of reasoning might go something like this. Just because someone owns a great deal of land, there is no justification for a claim to a large income—or a claim to a large bundle of goods and services. Assume that you own land that produces $1 million money income per year. Though the value input of the land has been fairly valued at $1 million, the question arises as to the equity of your claim for an equal amount of goods and

services. A progressive income tax might tax away $400,000 of your income. The money may be used to pay for schools and roads that other resource owners use also. Other resource owners have realized increased real income at your expense. To the extent that this redistribution of income occurs, the productivity (value-input) pattern of distribution is modified. No one can specify precisely the extent to which redistribution should occur. Quite obviously, it is a question of values and judgment. Equally obviously, substantial modifications are effected in the United States through the tax system and public assistance programs.

4 • Another fact of life in real-world income distribution is the *market power* of the resource owners. Regardless of the value input of a resource, the return to the resource can be changed to the extent that the resource owner can force a claim for a higher proportion based on market power. Assume that labor has a value input of 70 percent. Through powerful unions (market power) the workers could force a claim of 90 percent. If the other resource owners were less powerful in the market, they would have to accept this claim. However, if the workers were in a weak market position and the other resource owners were in a strong position, the workers might receive only 50 percent. Market power has had a profound effect on income distribution patterns in the United States.

The extent to which distribution is modified from the basic value-input pattern varies from time to time and situation to situation. The prevailing philosophy in the United States seems to be a value-input income distribution mechanism with substantial modifications that reflect social judgments.

► LEAKAGE AND RESIDUE ◄

No system operates with perfect efficiency—economic systems included. There are always losses along the way and residues at the end. Waste is a critical matter when resources are scarce. Remember our definition of waste: the diminution of utility that does not increase human welfare. For example, goods may be produced but never consumed. Food stuffs may spoil before they are eaten. Metal goods may rust before they are used. Some goods may be declared illegal by the government and thus cannot be sold after they have been produced. If waste were to occur at Points *B* in Figure 7–2, for example, the goods and services available for consumption would be decreased.

Waste may occur in the service sector also. The person who goes to the barber or beautician and comes out with a hair style you wouldn't believe has gotten "negative utility." The service was wasted. Surgery that fails and the entertainer who doesn't entertain are service wastes. Of course, waste may occur at any point in the system. Points *B* are only isolated illustrations.

Another waste problem is the disposal of consumption residue— economic ashes and gases. This, of course, is part of the pollution problem. Consumption is generally considered the culminating activity on the economic merry-go-round. But some part of the leftovers from consumption may be recycled for reuse in the production phase. Our awareness of recycling has generally focused on natural resources. The automobile is produced from resources. When it arrives at the junkyard, the metal becomes available for a second trip around. Our long-range welfare requires us to learn to reuse our natural resources.

Labor, management, and capital are recycled also. The worker learns in the act of production to be more efficient. This know-how is recycled —used over and over. The manager learns new techniques as to more efficient combinations of resources. These new techniques and know-how are recycled.

The more we learn about recycling our resources, the more we can produce and the greater will be our welfare. Obviously, the environmental movement is arguing for, and seeking means of, increased feasibility of recycling. The alternative is to let the "exhaust" of the economic system blow off into the "atmosphere." As the economic system gets bigger, this becomes a less satisfactory policy. Hence Point *C* shows the economic residues being blown back into the system as a resource at Point *D*.

SUMMARY

1 • **Every economy contains provision for economic decisions (who shall make them), economic control (who shall exercise it), and income distribution (who shall get what). Clearly these three elements of an economy are closely related.**

2 • **These provisions vary widely from economy to economy. Some economies emphasize individual decision and control; others emphasize group decision and control. Some economies distribute income according to need; others distribute it according to the contribution made to the total economic endeavor. Still others distribute it on the basis of custom or the social standing of the individual or on other grounds.**

3 • The United States seems to favor primary reliance on income distribution according to productivity, with substantial modifications to equalize income among individuals, to compensate for market power, and to accomplish various social purposes.

4 • All modern economies use money—a common good used to express the values and rates of exchange of all other goods. Money is a convenience designed to eliminate the debilitating inconveniences of barter, the direct exchange of goods for goods or resources for goods.

5 • Householders ultimately realize the exchange of resources for goods, but the immediate exchanges are resources for money and then money for goods.

6 • Income distribution in money terms results in the same distribution pattern as income distributed directly in real terms.

7 • Recycling is a means of reducing economic waste by feeding the residue of economic processes (including consumption) back into the economic system as a resource.

study materials

1 • Four types of economic systems were identified in the chapter—command, traditional, communist, and capitalist. Identify the basic "agreed-upon pattern" of each. Try to assess each in terms of strengths and weaknesses or problems. Give examples of each.

2 • Defend the view of the market as the "common arena" in which individuals' wants and desires meet. What takes place in the arena?

3 • How can it be concluded that ultimate control rests with households? Relate or explain household control over government and business. Some economists argue that household control over big business is more fiction than fact. How do their arguments run? What rebuttal can you offer?

4 • Analyze the assertion that "the individual's potential control over his economic life is much greater than the actual control generally exercised."

5 • Does the apparent dismissal of the significance of money as "merely an economic convenience" minimize its importance? In other words, to what extent must we be interested in money if we hope to understand economics?

6 • Under a barter system, what three alternatives do you have in using your resources to satisfy your economic needs. What are the problems with each alternative?

7 • Explain how money facilitates specialization.

8 • Explain why "work" as typically defined is not necessarily required to be productive or to command income.

9 • What is a windfall gain? Give three examples.

10 • Using the resources land, labor, capital, and management, make up your own example to illustrate value input and production of goods and services attributable to each resource. Assume a price for the goods and services. Divide the money value among the resources. Show that the distribution in monetary terms is the same as the distribution in real terms.

11 • Why is it valid to consider noneconomic income within the context of economics (granting that it is very difficult to measure directly)?

footnotes

[1] There is a significant part of the economics profession in the United States that maintains that household control of the U.S. economy is more fiction than fact. They argue that governments and large corporations, particularly, go their own merry way without regard to the wishes of householders. Even if they are right, our little diagrams showing household control are still reasonably adequate from an instructional point of view, since householders have a good deal more control than they are frequently inclined to exercise. Perhaps our main purpose in this book is to bring you sufficient understanding and motivation to exercise the control you possess over your economic life. Clearly the potential is much greater than the actual for most people. Consumer movements, though still relatively weak and frustratingly ineffective in many cases, have shown more muscle than most people probably would have thought 10 years ago.

[2] This is an example of a **windfall gain,** which is income received simply by being in the right place at the right time. Of course **windfall losses** may also occur by being in the wrong place at the wrong time through no fault of your own. Windfall gains and losses take many subtle forms, not the least of which is who your parents happen to be. Not everyone starts from ground zero.

appendix

MORE ON PRODUCTION
AND INCOME DISTRIBUTION

▶ CREATION OF THE PHYSICAL ◀
PRODUCT

Return to Figure 7–2. If the income flow is viewed in real terms, we are simply looking at the physical products produced by the resources. At point E the diagram begins to widen to depict increasing utility from production. Production is the mixing of resources in a meaningful way; the result (output) is greater than the sum of its parts (resources). Consider three qualities of mixers and possible reasons for the differences as given in Figure 7A–1.

Assume in each case that the resources available are identical. Independently and individually the resources have the capacity to provide satisfaction—assume 100 units of satisfaction (utiles). The production resulting is not the same in each. Why? The resources are coupled with a different mixer—a different means of production. If we use national economies as an example, the difference might be due to different levels of technology or different political or social conditions. Some economies are not as productive as others because of lower technological development. Others are less efficient because the political or social climate is not conducive to efficient production. Unstable governments or social unrest can contribute to economic inefficiency.

In Figure 7A–1, illustration I, the utility available within the resources independent of one another totals 100 utiles. The mixing of the resources produced 50 more units of satisfaction. This "creation" or increase in available satisfaction is called production.

Mixer II starts with the same resources as I but ends with a total of 200 units of satisfaction—adding 100 utiles in the production-mixing

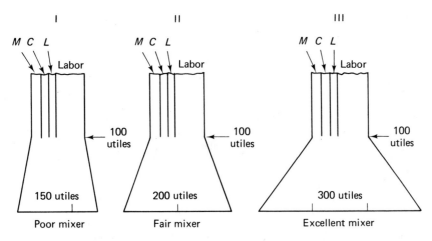

FIGURE 7A–1 • Three qualities of production "mixers": Identical resources.

process. Mixer II, with the same resources available, outproduces Mixer I by doubling the utiles. Mixer II is more efficient.

Mixer III ends with 300 utiles and is the easy winner in the contest.

The real significance of the efficiency of production becomes apparent when the issue of distribution is considered. The welfare of a society, and ultimately the individual consumer, is dependent on the amount of goods and services which are available. To be available, the goods and services must be produced. How much is produced is dependent on the quantity of resources available and the efficiency of the production side of the economy.

In Figure 7A–1 the available resources for each different illustration are the same. Suppose, however, that the mixer has the same efficiency but starts with different resources. Each mixer has the capability (level of efficiency) to double the units of satisfaction by combining the resources, but resources available are not the same. Figure 7A–2 illustrates the results.

The efficiency in the use of resources is the same in each illustration. In each, the results of production have doubled the utiles. Assume that the three illustrations represent different countries. "All other things being equal"—meaning that each country has the same number of people, political and social stability, means of transport, and so on—the consumers in the country represented by illustration III have three times the goods and services available as the consumers represented by illustration I. The difference is in the resources available to each country.

It has been illustrated that differences in available goods and services

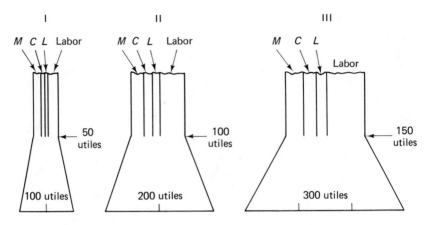

FIGURE 7A–2 • Three levels of resources: Identical effi-
ciencies.

for consumers occur either through differences in the means of production
(mixer) or in the quantity and quality of resources or both. Consumers
living in a country that has few resources and that has a poor production
system will have few goods and services available. A country with few
resources can overcome some of its handicaps by improving the means
of production via technology, political and social stability, and work
attitudes.

► DISTRIBUTION OF THE PHYSICAL ◄
PRODUCT

To this point our major concern has been with the combination of
resources in the production phase. It should be obvious that the consumer's welfare is directly dependent on the quantity of goods and
services produced. The production aspect is certainly a proper concern
of the consumer. However, an important question, and one perhaps more
difficult for an economy to answer, is how to distribute the fruits of production among individuals. As discussed in Chapter 7, the distribution of
the physical product of an economy that uses money is necessarily the
same as the distribution of the value product (physical product with
money prices attached to it); he who gets the money gets the goods. Since
we need to equate different goods and resources, we will proceed in
money terms, in which case the physical product becomes the value
product.

► DISTRIBUTION OF THE VALUE ◄
PRODUCT

A competitive market economy distributes income according to productivity. But, more specifically, income is distributed according to the contribution of each unit of resource to the *last* (or marginal)[1] unit of production. The illustration of this mechanism requires consideration of the law of diminishing marginal productivity:

> **The more of a particular resource you have, the less productivity you get from each *additional* unit of that resource as it is combined with a given quantity of other resource(s).[2]**

Thus, as it turns out, it is the marginal productivity of the *last unit* of resource employed that governs the payment (income distributed) to *all* units of that resource employed.

Notice that this is not really an economic law as such. It is a physical or engineering law that has substantial economic implications, one of which relates to income distribution.

Let us examine both the operation of the law of diminishing marginal productivity and its connection to income distribution by considering an example taken from banana production. For the sake of simplicity, assume that there are only two factors of production—land and capital—and that there is a given quantity of land available and used by the banana-producing business but that the business can hire any quantity of capital it wishes. Suppose that the capital employed is in the form of a "tiller–irrigator," rented for as many hours as the business wishes. The principles unfolded here can be extended to a situation in which there are more than two factors of production and in which all of them may be employed in any quantity (in this example, land is "fixed"); however, since the analysis of such an example requires rather sophisticated mathematics, we will settle for a simple example that illustrates the principle of income distribution very well in spite of its simplicity. Table 7A–1 contains the data we need. A column-by-column explanation follows.

- *Column 1 (Units of Land)*: We agreed that land would be held constant. We represent it with a given number of "native trees." Remember that land is defined as a free good—natural resources; thus a given quantity of native trees is a quantity of land. A unit is a tree: 100 units, 100 trees.

Table 7A–1

BANANA PRODUCTION: TOTALS

(1) LAND ($10/UNIT)	(2) CAPITAL ($100/UNIT)	(3) TOTAL PRODUCTION	(4) TOTAL COST OF LAND	(5) TOTAL COST OF CAPITAL	(6) TOTAL COST	(7) TOTAL INCOME ($20/UNIT)	(8) TOTAL PROFIT
100	0	70	$1,000	$ 0	$1,000	$1,400	$400
100	1	80	1,000	100	1,100	1,600	500
100	2	88	1,000	200	1,200	1,760	560
100	3	94	1,000	300	1,300	1,880	580*
100	4	98	1,000	400	1,400	1,960	560
100	5	100	1,000	500	1,500	2,000	500
100	6	100	1,000	600	1,600	2,000	400

* The profit-maximizing level of production is 94 units of bananas, which requires 3 units of capital (to the nearest whole unit of capital).

- *Column 2 (Units of Capital)*: Define a unit of capital as a certain amount of use of the tiller–irrigator. Conceptualize it any way you like. It is only important that 2 units is twice as much use as 1; 4 units is twice as much as 2, and so on.

- *Column 3 (Total Production)*: Assume that each native tree either grows and produces fruit or it doesn't. With no capital applied, 60 trees make it. As capital is applied, production rises, of course. But how fast? The first unit of capital "saves" 10 trees as it is used "on them." Fine. But do you expect that the second unit of capital will save another 10 trees. If yes, then the third also? And the fourth? Fifth? Sixth? You are getting into trouble if you answer "yes" all along the way, since the obvious maximum productivity is to save all 100 trees; sooner or later, therefore, additional capital accomplishes nothing. The world being what it is, the *first* units of capital are, in general, the most productive. (This is not always true if the first quantities of capital are very, very small, but we will ignore this extreme case.) Column 3 is constructed accordingly. Each unit of capital *adds* less to productivity than the previous one. This is the law of diminishing marginal productivity. When there is no capital, production is limited because of its absence; when capital becomes very abundant, production is limited because of an absence of land, so to speak. In other words, there is inadequate land to accommodate more than so much capital. The point is obvious: Production requires resources in proper combination; a *relative* deficiency of any one resource inhibits production.[3] Colume 3 is constructed to show diminishing marginal productivity, since each *additional* unit of capital makes a smaller *addition* to total production.

How does the banana producer decide how many units of capital to use? If we assume that he is seeking profits, he will *add* units of capital as long as they *add* to profits, and each unit of capital will *add* to profits as long as it *adds more* to his income than it *adds* to his costs. So we make some price assumptions. Land is $10 per unit (tree). As a free good, land is available to society as a whole without cost; but someone controls the land and may well be in a position to assess this business at cost. If banana production is profitable, banana producers will bid against one another for the supply of land and drive the price up. Capital is $100 per unit, and the bananas from one tree will bring $20.

- *Column 4 (Total Cost of Land)*: Units of land multiplied by the $10 price per unit of land.

- *Column 5 (Total Cost of Capital)*: Units of capital multiplied by the $100 price per unit of capital.

- *Column 6 (Total Cost)*: Cost of land plus cost of capital.

- *Column 7 (Total Income)*: Units of production (trees of bananas) multiplied by the $20 price per unit of bananas.

- *Column 8 (Total Profit)*: Income minus cost.

Obviously, this banana producer will produce 94 units of bananas if he wants to get the most possible profit and he is unable to use fractional units of capital. The 94 units of bananas requires 3 units of capital. (We will see later that between 3 and 4 units of capital would probably be somewhat more profitable.)

But what does this say about income distribution? We can get at that by presenting the profit-maximizing conclusion in another form in Table 7A–2. It is a table of *marginals*.

- *Columns 1, 2, 3:* Same as Table 7A–1.

- *Column 4 (Change in Capital)*: From the *changes* in column 2.

- *Column 5 (Change in Production)*: From the *changes* in column 3.

- *Column 6 (Change in Cost)*: *Change* in capital multiplied by the $100 price per unit of capital. (Since land does not change, it does not enter into the marginal picture.)

- *Column 7 (Change in Income)*: *Change* in production multiplied by the $20 price per unit of production.

- *Column 8 (Change in Profit)*: *Change* in income minus *change* in cost. The level of production and capital use is the same as in Table 7A–1. Indeed, Table 7A–2 could be produced simply by adding all the changes within the columns in Table 7A–1. Of course, the profit-seeking banana producer keeps *adding* capital as long as it *adds* to profit. As more capital is added, starting from zero, profits go up at an ever slower rate (the changes get smaller), but as long as they are positive, all is well. Only after the changes become negative, does the producer quit adding capital.

We are now able to nail the income distribution mechanism down solidly. Remember:

1 • As long as another unit of resource *adds* more to income than it *adds* to cost for the business, it will be hired by the business.

2 • The cost of the unit of resource to the business is its price.

Table 7A-2
BANANA PRODUCTION: MARGINALS

(1) LAND ($10/UNIT)	(2) CAPITAL ($100/UNIT)	(3) TOTAL PRODUCTION	(4) CHANGE IN CAPITAL	(5) CHANGE IN PRODUCTION	(6) CHANGE IN COST	(7) CHANGE IN INCOME (INCOME: $20/UNIT)	(8) CHANGE IN PROFIT
100	0	70	—	—	—	—	—
100	1	80	1	10	$100	$200	+$100
100	2	88	1	8	100	160	+ 60
100	3	94	1	6	100	120	+ 20
					100 =	100	0 *
100	4	98	1	4	100	80	− 20
100	5	100	1	2	100	40	− 60
100	6	100	1	0	100	0	− 100

* The profit-maximizing level of production is 94 units of bananas, which requires 3 units of capital (to the nearest whole unit of capital). If fractional units of capital could be used, it would be profitable to use between 3 and 4 units of capital (say 3½ units) and produce between 94 and 98 units of bananas (say 96 units).

3 • The price paid for the unit of resource is income distributed to the holder of that unit of resource.

The business keeps adding resources until the income generated by the last unit of resource has fallen to the price of that unit of resource. And, of course, as more units of resource are added, each unit adds less to income because each unit is less productive, owing to the operation of the law of diminishing productivity. Additional resources are hired until the cost and income additions from the last unit are the same. Thus income is distributed to the controller of each resource according to the productivity of the last unit employed; or more formally, each resource is paid the *value of its marginal product,* which is the ability of the last unit employed to generate value (income).

To reemphasize, notice that, since the price of the resource applies to *all* units of resource hired but the decision to hire more units is based on the cost–income relationship of the *last* (marginal) unit hired, *all* units of resource hired will have income distributed to them according to the productivity of the *last* unit hired. That is, as stated previously, income is distributed according to marginal conditions. If it were to be otherwise, many conditions impossible to maintain in the real world would have to prevail. Foremost would be the necessity for the business to pay a different price for each and every unit of resource it employed. Normally, conditions in markets do not allow such a situation. One price prevails to all buyers buying under like conditions (terms of payment, delivery, quantity, etc.). Thus the decision to buy another unit of resource is based on the price of all units relative to the productivity of the last unit only.

▶   **USING THE MODEL**   ◀

You may verify the income distribution mechanism by making some simple assumptions and then envisioning the occurrence of certain events. The reworking of the data in Table 7A–2 under these changed conditions demonstrates a formal conclusion consistent with your intuitive expectations. Assuming that we can guess your intuitive reaction, consider the following examples. These assumptions are required for the examples that follow.

1 • You control a certain quantity of capital to sell to a banana producer to generate income for yourself.

2 • The banana producers to whom you sell the capital want as much profit as possible.

EXAMPLE 7A–1

The quantity of capital available in the economy of which you and this banana producer are a part rises, but the quantity you have remains the same.

1 • *Intuitive Result:* An increase in the supply of anything, including resources (capital in this case), tends to lower the price. Your capital commands a lower payment, so you get less income from the quantity of capital you control.

2 • *Formal Verification from Table 7A–2:* Column 6 falls, so banana producers use more capital at a lower price. But since *you* have the same quantity of capital as before, *your* income drops in proportion to the drop in the price of capital. (Before you conclude that the road to prosperity lies in restricting the quantity of resources available in an economy, remember that as the price of capital falls and more is used, banana production rises in response to the increased quantity of resources employed. As banana production rises, the price of bananas tends to fall, causing you to be able to buy more bananas for the money income you receive—a rediscovery of production as the generator of income. To state it another way, remember that this example looks at money income only; *real* income is what the money income will buy, and that depends on production.)

EXAMPLE 7A–2

Return to the original conditions of Table 7A–2 and suppose that banana producers become more efficient users of capital; that is, they get more bananas from each unit of capital (there has been an increase in technology).

1 • *Intuitive Result:* A unit of capital will now generate more profit for the banana producer under present prices, so banana producers try to hire more capital;

but since the supply of capital is limited, they tend to bid the price up, thereby increasing the money incomes of capital suppliers.

2 • *Formal Verification from Table 7A–2:* Marginal productivity, and therefore total productivity, rises (columns 3 and 5). This raises columns 7 and 8. Maximum-profit capital usage is higher than before, but if the quantity of capital does not change, the banana producers cannot hire more capital; they can only bid the price up as they try to hire more capital (column 6 rises). The price of capital rises until it is high enough to equal the new, higher, column 7 at the old level of capital usage. Thus the increased productivity of capital has been bid into the price of capital, and the suppliers (controllers) of capital are the recipients of the benefits of the increased productivity of their resource.

EXAMPLE 7A–3

Again return to the original conditions of Table 7A–2 and suppose that the demand for bananas rises.

1 • *Intuitive Result:* Banana prices will tend to rise, making banana production more profitable. Banana producers will try to hire more capital to cash in on the bonanza. This will bid up the price of capital, thereby increasing capital suppliers' income.

2 • *Formal Verification from Table 7A–2:* Columns 7 and 8 rise, and the remainder of the example is the same as Example 7A–2. The suppliers of the capital are the final recipients of the "benefits" from the increased demand for the product.

Perhaps you will wish to envision other changes and follow them through the example under different kinds of assumptions to examine their income distributions implications. Indeed, by elaborating on assumptions and tracing fully the consequences of events, we could go on to illustrate many things touched briefly or not at all: the fallacy of composition; price discrimination; noncompetitive forms of market organization; long run versus short run; static versus dynamic analysis; and general equilibrium analysis—to mention a few. But we are not about to describe the economic universe. The message for our purpose is clear: The road to personal prosperity is to gain control over a large quantity of resources capable of conversion into end products eagerly sought by consumers, particularly under conditions such that everybody and his brother cannot also easily become a supplier of similar resources. Hardly a big surprise. It is always comforting to see that formal analysis substantially supports the expectations of common sense. Such is not necessarily always the case.

footnotes

1 The concept of "margin," explained more fully in Chapter 10, simply deals with *changes*. Thus words such as "additional," "more," "less," "first," "last," "next," and so on are marginal in their orientation. The margin is very interesting because it relates to "where do we go from here," which is what economic life is all about.

2 There is a very interesting symmetry between consumption and production as opposite sides of the economic coin. Note the similarity between the law of diminishing marginal productivity given here and the law of diminishing marginal utility given in Chapter 10. Some of the business–household symmetry may be expanded in table form:

	BUSINESS	HOUSEHOLD
Major activity	Production	Consumption
Goal	Profit	Utility
Source of goal	Resources	Goods
Noneconomic law governing rate of conversion of source of goal	Law of diminishing marginal productivity	Law of diminishing marginal utility

3 It has been suggested [Campbell R. McConnell, *Economics*, 5th ed. (New York: McGraw-Hill Book Company, 1972), p. 442] that if the law of diminishing marginal productivity did not operate, the world could be fed from a flowerpot. Why not? Keep adding labor, water, fertilizer, capital, and so on (variable inputs) without limit to this fixed input, and production flows forth without limit.

chapter
8

YOUR INDIVIDUAL
ECONOMIC WORLD

We now turn from the economic world of which you are a part to your own economic world. We will examine more closely what you control that may be converted into utility. Clearly each of us is "richer" than is commonly believed. We will develop a broader concept of income which more nearly captures the full extent of your economic horsepower. Good decisions cannot be made looking at only part of the picture. And money income, as conventionally defined, is a very small part of the picture for most of us. In other words, we are now going to lay out in its entirety the economic base from which you operate personally.

▶ TRANSITION ◀

As we begin to examine your world as an individual more closely, it is helpful to review briefly some major relationships and conclusions about the world of which you are a part, since you are a miniature world of your own in many respects. Much of what we concluded about the world in general is also true of you as an individual. Ideas about cost are the outstanding case in point.

What were the relevant highlights of the earlier chapters? We might cite such things as utility (the ability to satisfy) as the common denominator of human acquisitiveness. We want things that satisfy us. Utility stems from both economic and noneconomic sources. The classification of the sources of utility as to their nature, economic or noneconomic, is not always easy; but then, it is not really necessary either. Presumably we try to get as much satisfaction as possible, that is, to maximize utility. Since it is not possible to have unlimited utility because of our limited ability to generate utility, we have to make choices as to which sources of utility to acquire and which to forego. The most utility foregone is the cost of the utility that was chosen. Every choice exercised requires that an alternative choice be foregone. Skillfulness, both economic and noneconomic, decreases the cost of the alternative chosen—that is, increases efficiency.

The preceding paragraph serves not only as review but makes another point as well. The paragraph may be read with respect to either a single individual or with respect to a group of individuals collectively. It would be true for a nation as well as for an individual. But *everything* that is true for an individual is not necessarily true for a nation, and vice versa. To conclude that what is true for an individual is also *necessarily* true for a group of individuals is to fall victim of the **fallacy of composition.**

Statements such as "Any one of us may enter this phone booth, therefore we may all enter this phone booth," or "As a corn farmer, I can grow more corn without causing the price of corn to fall; therefore, all corn farmers can grow more corn without causing the price of corn to fall" are examples of the fallacy of composition. The first part of each statement, which applies to the individual, would seem to be true; the last part of the statement, referring to the group of individuals, is obviously false (a fallacy). The purpose in citing these fallacies is to recognize that the material that follows relates specifically to you and your world. The larger world is considered primarily because you must operate in it. You cannot make good decisions from your own point of view unless you understand the opportunities and their consequences. This entails knowledge of conditions around you. But do not conclude from this that what is good for you is necessarily good for everyone. That may or may not be the case. These larger issues are generally outside the scope of the immediate discussion to follow; however, much of the analysis applied here can be used to evaluate issues of public policy, which will be discussed in Part IV.

We fall victim to the fallacy of composition because we are all tempted to view ourselves as the center of the universe. The typical person operates with the attitude: "Of course I know what the world looks like. I've been there. I can stand up on my tippy-toes and see plainly that it is flat. I also know that the sun rises in the East and sets in the West." But we all know better. The world is not flat, and the sun does not rise and set at all. These are merely appearances. Yet it is interesting to note that for the living of one's personal life, these erroneous conclusions are harmless, indeed it might be argued, necessary. So it is with economics. The entire economic system may be a different-looking entity when viewed from the outside than when viewed from a personal position on the inside. The same is true for any other system as well—political, social, and so on. You must bear in mind that what you conclude is good for you may or may not be good for the nation or any other *group* of individuals of which you may or may not be a part.

For example, the simple likes and dislikes of different persons are different, so there is no reason to presume that what constitutes a good decision for you necessarily constitutes a good decision for someone else. In a larger dimension, the fact that different component parts of a system are intimately related has profound significance for the behavior of the system as a whole. Interrelationships between individuals as they constitute an economic system can cause one individual to be able to accomplish what all together cannot accomplish. For example, it may be good for you to save a high proportion of your money income. If everyone tries to do this, however, sales of economic goods and services fall drastically as people quit buying as they save more. Businesses lay off employees, and money incomes drop. Hard times beset everyone. The amount saved actually decreases because money saving is done out of money income—but money income dried up when people quit buying to save. Thus a single individual can save all he wants to with no ill effects; but, when everyone tries to increase savings, no one is able to accomplish it, because one person's saving deprives another of money income and therefore destroys his ability to save. Such is the nature of the fallacy of composition. But our focus will be primarily on the individual and not on the group. Generalizing your experience may therefore be useful at times when analyzing broader issues, but may also constitute a hindrance to your ability to see the whole picture. Forewarned is forearmed. Don't read more into a situation than is there.

▶ ECONOMIC CONTROL ◀

In Chapter 7, which explored the nature of the economic system of which you are a part, we saw that the link between you and the rest of the world was *control*. Personal decision begins with an assessment of what you control. Someone controls, actually or potentially, every fragment of utility in existence. In more formal language, someone possesses claims against all utility. After all, if utility is desirable, any that is floating around loose will be grabbed by someone. To get utility for yourself, you must entice it away from someone, which requires giving him utility in return—that is, incurring cost.

Utility may be controlled by individuals as such, or it may be controlled by groups of individuals. Your personal belongings represent utility controlled by you as an individual. Schools, highways, parks, and so on represent utility controlled indirectly by individuals through units of government. Individuals also group together to form businesses (corporations), which represent utility. Each owner shares in it. Again, the control is indirect but accrues, eventually, to individuals.

Control is distinct from ownership. They are not synonymous and to assume that they are is to blind yourself to many opportunities on the one hand or to delude yourself on the other hand. Ownership is legal; control is operational. Ownership in itself does not guarantee utility—unless, of course, the simple fact of ownership provides utility. The behavior of misers might be explained in this way. Society also considers the miser's behavior to be abnormal, however. Most people do not derive substantial utility simply from ownership. They derive most utility from possession and use (control).

The father of the teen-age son may own a car, but does he control it? In many cases it would seem that control rests with the teen-ager. The father may possess the *capability* for control by virtue of ownership but refrains from exercising his prerogative because the cost in terms of family relationships and personal stress is too great. Father gets more utility from his weak-kneed position than from exercising his capability for control and having the fur fly.

Some of the most successful business ventures are built on control rather than ownership. Franchising, leasing, renting, borrowing money, and so on are all means of extending control without necessarily extending ownership. In fact, it might be argued that astute businessmen *always* look for control of resources and economic goods. They consider ownership only if it facilitates control. Things under your control are, by definition, subject to your decision-making power. Things you own may or may not be subject to your decision-making power. Certainly, in most cases ownership facilitates control. But ownership is secondary; control is primary. Ownership facilitates control because the law will support your claim to control, but in the real world this may prove to be a technicality. Invoking the law to support your claims to control may also be expensive in terms of both economic and noneconomic costs. Legal proceedings, if it comes to that, are expensive in several ways. "Possession is nine tenths of ownership" is a saying of considerable merit.

Control is seldom unqualified. Indeed, if the previous paragraph seems to disparage ownership, it must be acknowledged that the owner of resources or goods is invariably recognized as *capable* of some measure of control. It is doubtful that control is ever completely in the hands of any single individual, or group of individuals for that matter—regardless of ownership.

For example, who controls the telephone in your home? Who owns it? The telephone company probably owns it and therefore controls it to some degree. They can take it out and replace it if they want to. They can prevent you, legally, from damaging it. You control it with regard to location in your home, the amount of use it gets, and, most importantly, how it is used (who you call). Who has the most control? Rather obviously it is not the owner. Control is absolute by neither the owner nor the nonowner, but it seems clear that the majority of the control is with the nonowner in this instance. Even ownership of your own phone would not give you complete control, since your fellow citizens have decreed that you may not make obscene phone calls. Of course, you can do it anyway, but in that case you might have the phone taken from you. Thus, if you exercise *full* control in the short run, you may lose *all* control in the long run. It seems that control is never quite complete regardless of ownership.

Your ability to acquire utility appears to relate directly to control of economic goods and resources. The issue is not what you own but what you control. Personal choice is based on the answer to the question "What do I control?" Whatever you control is under your decision-making power. Since gains in utility come only at the expense of utility foregone or lost, it is self-evident that your basic choice is either to keep what you have now or to exchange it for other utility. In any event the foundation of your position and action is that which you control. You cannot either use or exchange what you do not control. Intelligent decision making therefore requires a careful assessment of just what you do control and to what extent. Then you can decide what to do with it.

► COMPREHENSIVE INCOME ◄

Identification of your sphere of control is through the use of a concept we will call **comprehensive income.** *Comprehensive income* is similar to *income* as defined in Chapter 4 but somewhat broader in scope and more fundamental in nature.

Recall from Chapter 4 that income was defined as a flow of utility. As defined there, income really included only that utility which *actually* flowed from economic goods. Comprehensive income is different in two respects: (1) It includes utility from both economic and noneconomic sources, and (2) it is the amount of utility that *could* flow from everything you now control. In other words, comprehensive income is basically *potential* utility from everything you presently control. Stated in still another way, income as defined in Chapter 4 was *actual* and *economic;* comprehensive income is present *potential* and *economic* and *noneconomic* combined. It is that into which the resources you control may be converted. Comprehensive income therefore represents the most utility you can gain with what you now have at your disposal. If you make perfect utility-maximizing decisions with regard to the deployment of what you control, the utility you realize will be an amount equal to your comprehensive income. If the utility you actually realize from what you control falls short of comprehensive income, you have made some bad decisions. Thus comprehensive income serves (1) as a focal point in identifying fully what you control at any point in time and (2) as a standard against which to measure your performance as a decision maker.

For purposes of exposition it will be useful to break comprehensive income into component parts. Since income, basically, is a flow of utility, the various income segments or categories relate to the major sources of utility realized by you. We will cite (somewhat arbitrarily) four major sources of income.

▷ regular income ◁

Regular income is the most utility from economic goods that could be purchased wtih money income. It is utility from the economic goods that are obtained through markets—that is, produced by someone else.

▷ self-sufficiency income ◁

Self-sufficiency income is utility from economic goods that are produced by you for your own consumption. They are the goods that could have been purchased in markets but instead were produced by you for yourself. Self-sufficiency income would include such things as housework, home repairs, lawn mowing, snow shoveling, pest extermination, and so on. The value of these activities can be readily calculated by determining what they would have cost had they been purchased.

▷   resource income   ◁

Resource income is utility from resources that could have been converted into economic goods but instead were consumed directly as resources. Utility from leisure would seem to be the main source of resource income. Time consumed as leisure could have been spent in gainful employment, in which case money (regular) income would have been earned and utility from economic goods would have been realized, or the time could have been spent in do-it-yourself projects that would result in economic goods produced, in which case you would have realized self-sufficiency income. If you spend your time and skill in playing a game you are using up your resources and gaining utility, but you are producing nothing that has or could have concrete market value.

▷   noneconomic income   ◁

Noneconomic income is utility derived from activities, conditions, and personal characteristics that could not be converted directly into economic goods under any circumstances. This would be the utility derived from friendships, inner reflection, maintenance of good health, and so on.

The sum of *regular income, self-sufficiency income, resource income,* and *noneconomic income* constitutes *comprehensive income.* Since we will eventually end up in the practical world of personal decisions, we will need some concrete measure of comprehensive income. The monetary equivalent of comprehensive income can be determined by relying on the opportunity cost principle, which identifies what is given up in order to have something else. At this stage the money values assigned to utility from various sources will be the values that the market assigns to it, which may or may not be the same as the value that you assign to it. The key to your personal decision making will be how *you* value the utility relative to the way the *market* values it. But that will come later. For the time being, we will simply try to identify what the dollar value of your comprehensive income is according to the market, which represents a consensus of value by all buyers and sellers of economic goods.

▶   THE MONEY MEASURE   ◀
OF COMPREHENSIVE INCOME

For this example, assume that a husband and wife team is making decisions and realizing comprehensive income as a unit. Assume also that only the husband has a job in the conventional sense. Women who complain that their contribution to household welfare is unrecognized by conventional income measures will be delighted to see that the value they create is specifically accounted for in comprehensive income.

The money measure of *regular income* is self-evident. Since regular income is defined as the utility that money income will buy, the money measure of money income is simply the amount of the money income itself. This would be primarily wages and salaries for most persons, plus perhaps the interest from some savings and investments and small amounts of miscellaneous cash receipts. Obviously the money that you are paid for offering resources in the production of economic goods represents the consensus of the market of what these resources are worth. Let us suppose that for our hypothetical family money regular income is $12,000 per year. There is nothing sacred about a year as the length of time over which we accumulate income before expressing it as a specific amount. A year however is a convenient and conventional time period, so we will use it. We could just as well use a month, in which case money regular income would be $1,000.

The money measure of *self-sufficiency income* is revealed by determining what it would cost in money to acquire the economic goods you produce for yourself by yourself. Let's suppose that it would cost $15,000 to buy your housework done, your lawn mowed, your pests exterminated, and to do the work on your car that you did yourself. If it would cost $15,000, apparently the consensus of the market is that resources that would produce this much self-sufficiency income are worth $15,000 per year. For many families this is a conservative estimate, but the figure will do for purposes of illustration. The $15,000 was ascertained by looking at the money cost of this much utility. The market price is the market price regardless of whether you are a buyer or a seller. If this utility would have cost $15,000, then it follows that $15,000 could have been received if the services had been performed for someone else rather than for yourself. Thus $15,000 was foregone in order to have this much self-sufficiency income. $15,000 is therefore the money measure of the opportunity cost of the self-sufficiency income, and it was the opportunity cost principle that allowed a monetary expression of the value of these services, even though there was no actual monetary transaction involved.

The money measure of *resource income* can be determined by looking at the money income foregone by consuming resources directly. This again relies on the opportunity cost principle. Assume that husband and wife are each consuming 4 hours per day as leisure and that each could earn $5 per hour if they offered these resources in outside employment. Four hours per day times 2 persons equals 8 hours per day for the couple. Eight hours per day times $5 per hour equals $40 per day. $40 per day

times 365 days per year equals $14,600 per year—say, $14,000 for convenience. This is the money value that the market places on the resources that this couple is consuming directly as resources.

The money measure of *noneconomic income* is probably impossible
to determine directly. It is assumed in computing the value of regular
income, self-sufficiency income, and resource income that this husband
and wife are withholding sufficient resources to provide a minimum
level of rest, nutrition, health, and so on. Of course, it might be argued
that by physically and mentally abusing themselves they could push their
income even higher. Perhaps; but we will assume that a *minimum* level
of personal maintenance has a very high priority and that the typical
individual strips from the top of his resource block enough resources to
provide these minimum levels.

You may feel that these minimum levels of personal maintenance
have very high priority and are therefore very valuable. Undoubtedly a
minimum amount of sleep and nourishment has very high utility. You
therefore view the resources used in producing these minimums as very
valuable to you. Yes, of course. But remember that at this point we are
measuring comprehensive income according to the value the *market*
places on these resources, which relates to their ability to produce economic goods. The market places a very low value on resources that consist of a half-starved worker asleep on his feet. Thus it might be said
that the resources used to "produce" minimum levels of personal maintenance are very low quality resources, so the opportunity cost of minimum rest and nutrition is very low. Since the value to you is very high
and it comes at a very low opportunity cost, you therefore automatically
elect to have minimum personal maintenance. We will concern ourselves
with utility above and beyond these bare minimums for the moment.
We will simply recognize that there is such a thing as noneconomic
income but that our money measure of comprehensive income does not
include it. We will discuss the issues relating to noneconomic income in
more detail shortly.

The comprehensive income of this family is therefore the total of
the regular income, self-sufficiency income, and resource income. Noneconomic income is listed without a specific dollar value just to keep its
presence before us.

Regular income	$12,000
Self-sufficiency income	15,000
Resource income	14,000
Noneconomic income	?
Comprehensive income	$41,000

Since all money income is disposed of in one way or another, this amount of comprehensive income might be viewed as a family's money income of $41,000—of which it spends $14,000 for leisure time, $15,000 for household and personal maintenance, and $12,000 for economic goods produced by parties other than themselves. It should come as no surprise, then, that income as typically defined, earned in a paltry 40 to 50 hours per week for the typical worker, constitutes a small part of the total utility block realized.

The implications of the magnitude of comprehensive income as compared to regular income are monumental. You exercise control over substantially more than your earned money income. This suggests that your decision as to whether to take a second job, to spend more time in social activities, or to change occupations or life styles is more important than a decision about what kind of car to buy. It is unfortunate that consumer economics has focused so heavily on the way in which money income is spent and tended to ignore the larger issues, where the stakes are far greater. Looking at only the tip of the iceberg (what money income will buy) and dismissing the allocation of other resources controlled can hardly result in utility-maximizing decisions for you. One of the most fundamental decisions you must make is to decide how much of the resource block you control should be converted into money income and how much should be "spent" in other ways. You have a great deal of discretion as to how much money income you earn. You can vary the length of your workweek; you can choose to work in a metropolitan area as opposed to a rural area; you can specifically prepare to enter occupations that generate high or low money incomes. If all that was important hinged on money incomes, it would seem that everyone should always move to where money incomes are the highest. Of course, this tendency does prevail if "other things being equal" conditions are met. But other things are not equal. The relatively high money income of urban employment comes at the price of polluted air and congested traffic, a distinct source of disutility. Many, if not most, people make some money income concessions to enjoy other things that they value. It is generally recognized that there is substitutability among different economic goods, but it is generally less well recognized that there is also substitutability between economic goods as a group and other sources of utility. Thus consumer decisions must begin with comprehensive income as the base of reference in order to capture the tradeoffs that exist between regular income (which buys economic goods) and utility from self-sufficiency income, resource income, and noneconomic income. Deciding what kind of car to buy without first deciding whether you are willing to sacrifice, for example, the social life necessary to earn the income to buy *any* car is to stumble over a boulder while looking for a speck.

Comprehensive income can explain a good deal about personal welfare and behavior that cannot be explained in terms of regular income alone. Comments such as "How do they live so well on what they make?" or "I don't see why he is always broke—he makes good money" obviously miss the fact of their own explanation. The tendency is to equate human welfare with money income. People who live well on modest money incomes may have high self-sufficiency incomes. A low money income can be supplemented tremendously by such things as repairing your own car, appliances, and plumbing and by doing your own painting, refinishing of furniture, or even remodeling and construction of furniture and homes. Some people have become moderately wealthy in money terms by creating what is, in the first instance, self-sufficiency income and then selling their production. Earning self-sufficiency income is obviously a form of self-employment. Your real income of course will also be high if you do not sell the fruits of your self-sufficiency but choose instead to enjoy them yourself. Other persons may possess very little in the way of economic goods either through the earning of regular income or self-sufficiency income but are satisfied and happy because of the utility they receive through resource and noneconomic income. There are many choices available. The total level of utility you realize is, as always, dependent on the total quantity and quality of resources controlled by you.

The use of comprehensive income causes many fundamental economic ideas, particularly about cost, to be cast in a clearer light. For example, as you relax in the evening, you observe that you could earn $5 per hour by working instead of watching TV. The opportunity cost principle says that the cost of the utility in leisure is $5 worth of utility in economic goods. You are $5 per hour worse off for having taken the leisure. You are therefore "paying" $5 per hour for the leisure and are apparently "paying" it willingly. Yet somehow you find it hard to accept the fact that you are willing to pay $5 per hour to watch TV; but, on the other hand, you are not about to jump up and go to work to collect the $5 either. Which way out of the puzzle? The hang-up is in viewing the $5 cost as coming out of your $12,000 money regular income. You are "paying" the $5 out of $41,000 of comprehensive income. If your money income were $41,000 instead of $12,000 you probably would be willing to actually pay $5 to watch TV for an hour.

The only way good decisions can be made in regard to the living of your life is to consider it in its totality and proceed from there. It does not make sense to proceed only in terms of a small segment of what is at your disposal. Everyone knows that the quantity of earned money income available to purchase economic goods can be influenced by such things as the amount of housework foregone, the extent of involvement in community affairs, and the amount of leisure taken; yet, frequently, little attempt is made to systematically analyze how individuals make these major decisions. We will try to remedy this. The concept of comprehensive income and its approximation in money terms through reliance on the opportunity cost principle will be our point of departure.

► MORE ON NONECONOMIC ◄
INCOME

Although comprehensive income is a concrete measure of utility for an individual or family, it remains first and foremost a concept designed to act as a framework for analytical thinking about consumer decisions. As a framework for analytical thinking the inclusion of noneconomic income is essential. Every economic action has its noneconomic dimension and it must be considered to arrive at satisfying decisions.

It is impossible to put a dollar value on noneconomic income for two reasons: (1) The market cannot measure it, since it flows from a resource incapable of direct conversion to economic goods, and (2) to some extent noneconomic income is generated simultaneously with other forms of income, the value of which has already been included in another category. We will refer to (1) as the measurement problem and to (2) as the double-counting problem. They are interrelated.

▷ the measurement problem ◁

With regard to the measurement problem, we see that the establishment of a dollar value via the opportunity cost route requires determining the dollar value of goods that the resource could produce. But noneconomic income, by definition, is income from resources possessing no capability for conversion to economic goods. So how can the market value them? It cannot and therefore we cannot.

For example, consider the utility received from a friendship. Cultivation of friendships is perhaps essentially a leisure-time activity. However, the value of the leisure has been counted as resource income, so it cannot be counted again as it produces a friendship. Some people may possess skills that generate more utility from friendships in a given amount of time than others do. The ability to make friends certainly differs among individuals. The market can value the amount of time put into cultivation of friendships, and we included it as resource income. But, beyond this, we have no way of valuing your personableness, which is a form of resource that finds one person acquiring much utility from friendships in a given amount of time and another person acquiring little utility from friendships in the same amount of time—even though the second person has no other utility to compensate for his lower utility from friendship. In other words there are different degrees of skillfulness in the use of leisure, and the market cannot measure them.

▷ the double-counting problem ◁

With regard to the double-counting problem, there is potential overlap between noneconomic income and resource income. The activities that generate noneconomic income are often essentially leisure-time activities. Clearly the utility from a friendship cultivated, for example, must not be included in both categories. Similarly, there may be overlap between self-sufficiency income and resource income. Working on a car may have value to you beyond the market value of the work you do. You may enjoy the activity and receive utility beyond the value of the economic goods you create. If so, assigning a dollar value in the amount of the economic goods created will understate the amount of utility from the activity. Extending the argument, employment for money income may also, in a sense, be viewed as partially a "leisure-time" activity. Despite most persons' professed desire to escape the world of work, there is considerable evidence that employment for money income has some utility *per se*. The person who can afford to retire early but later goes back to work, the vacationer who looks forward to going back to work, and the person who gets antsy sitting around on sick pay or unemployment compensation would all seem to get utility from their work, as evidenced by their preference and behavior. If you get utility from the *fact* of your employment, then your money income received will understate the utility generated by your employment. You perhaps get noneconomic income from the personal satisfaction of a job well done and from the social contacts that work may involve.

The existence of utility from the very fact of an activity (as opposed to the end result of the activity) in general, and work in particular, is well recognized by sociologists and psychologists, although they may not refer to the noneconomic rewards of work as utility. Even economists make this acknowledgment. John Maynard Keynes, who was probably the most influential economist of the twentieth century, observed: "When involuntary unemployment exists, the marginal disutility of labour is *necessarily* [emphasis supplied] less than the utility of marginal [additional] product. Indeed it may be much less." [1] This would seem to suggest that Keynes thought that, frequently, work as an end in itself had utility. It is interesting to note also that neither Keynes nor anyone else to our knowledge has attempted to put a money value on it.

In summary, it seems that we must value the resources you control by looking at the value of the end products they could produce that could pass through markets. The market is the "device" that establishes value. But resources produce not only an end product that has value, they produce value to the resource controller in the *course* of their use as well as in the end product created. A productive activity may have utility purely as an activity, as opposed to the utility from the end result of the activity. Since there is no way that the utility from the activity itself can be marketed, there is no way that we can establish a reliable dollar value on it. It seems that noneconomic income, rather than being a category of income in its own right, is really diffused throughout regular income, self-sufficiency income, and resource income. It is, in a sense, an extra dividend.

What an impasse! Utility from noneconomic sources is substantial and must be considered, but there is no way to get our hands on it. In Part II we will develop a procedure whereby we can isolate the money cost of whatever noneconomic utility is associated with any decision, without specifying its value ahead of time. This will make the noneconomic utility visible and allow you to decide whether you believe the cost of it is warranted. The effect is to reduce decisions on noneconomic utility to an acceptance–rejection basis. It's either worth it or it isn't. This is a somewhat weaker stance than placing a specific value on the noneconomic utility beforehand. This approach, though not a first choice, is better than ignoring the noneconomic utility and will prove to be remarkably useful. The money measure of comprehensive income therefore represents the utility from resources available for use over and above the *minimum* levels of rest, personal health, social relationships, and so on. Since the typical consumer wishes to maintain certain minimums at practically any cost, we will assume that he satisfies these minimums and consciously allocates resources beyond those minimums. Our approach to the evaluation of the cost of noneconomic utility to be developed later will allow you to evaluate these minimums as well, however —in case you are concerned that you have set your minimum too high.

SUMMARY

1 • What is true for you as an individual may or may not be true for an entire group of which you are a member. It is therefore hazardous to extend conclusions about your personal life to social affairs.

2 • Economic control links you, an individual, to the economic world. Ownership is significant primarily because it facilitates control.

3 • Comprehensive income is the amount of utility that could be generated from the resources you control as an individual.

4 • Comprehensive income is made up of four income categories:

    a • Regular income—the utility from the economic goods that could be purchased with money income received.

    b • Self-sufficiency income—the utility from economic goods produced for your own consumption.

    c • Resource income—the utility from the resources that could have been converted to economic goods but were consumed directly without first being converted to economic goods.

    d • Noneconomic income—the utility from resources above and beyond their ability to produce economic goods.

5 • The money measure of comprehensive income (excluding noneconomic income) is the market value of the goods that the resources controlled are capable of producing. This determination utilizes the opportunity cost principle.

6 • A money measure of noneconomic income cannot be established, since there cannot be a market for these sources of utility. The utility tends to stem from the fact of the use of the resources, as opposed to the end products resulting from their use. Thus a resource tends to generate noneconomic income at the same time that it generates other forms of income that can be measured in monetary terms.

study materials

1 • Define and give two examples of the fallacy of composition.

2 • What are the essential differences between ownership and control? Of what significance is this to the consumer?

3 • List at least five things that people typically control (through renting, leasing, borrowing, etc.) that they do not own. Decide whether or not these are wise consumer decisions in general, and why.

4 • List as many things as possible that are available for consumption through control without ownership that are *not* typically or commonly rented, borrowed, or leased.

5 • Explain how the consumer can improve his consumption by concentrating on control rather than ownership. Under what conditions or in what cases is this wise? Unwise?

6 • Name the four types of income that make up comprehensive income.

7 • Differentiate money income from comprehensive income. Why does comprehensive income provide a more accurate indication of the consumer's economic status than money income?

8 • List several ways a consumer might increase or decrease each of the following: regular income, self-sufficiency income, resource income, noneconomic income.

9 • Assume that the following represents a valid measurement of each income type for two different individuals. Explain the possible reasons for the differences and the significance of each. Note that each has the same regular income.

	CONSUMER A	CONSUMER B
Regular income	$10,000	$10,000
Self-sufficiency income	15,000	8,000
Resource income	10,000	5,000
Noneconomic income	+	−
Comprehensive income	$35,000 (+)	$23,000 (−)

footnote

[1] John Maynard Keynes, *The General Theory of Employment, Interest and Money* (New York: Harcourt Brace Jovanovich, Inc., n.d.), p. 128.

appendix

A SOCIOLOGIST ON RESOURCE AND SELF-SUFFICIENCY INCOME

The following quote is offered as evidence of the recognition of economic contributions through other than traditional economic channels—that is, via transactions. The author has not used the terms *resource income* or *self-sufficiency income,* which we have coined, but it is clear that that is what he is talking about when he concludes that the value of a housewife's time is not determined by whether she actually works outside the home. The quote is from *The Modern Family,* by Robert F. Winch [3rd ed. (New York: Holt, Rinehart and Winston, Inc., 1971), pp. 86–88].

THE ECONOMIC CONTRIBUTION OF THE MODERN HOUSEWIFE

If we think of utility in the economic sense as the capacity of a good or a service to satisfy a human want, then we may speak of the economic activities carried on within a household as "consumer production," which Kyrk asserts is largely represented by "the utilities provided by the unpaid activities of the family members for the family members." [25] Having noted that much economic activity has moved outside the home, we are entitled to inquire what is left. Ogburn and Nimkoff offer the answer: "cooking and preparing meals, housecleaning and decorating, some laundering, a little sewing and marketing." [26]

---

[25] Hazel Kyrk, *The Family in the American Economy* (Chicago: University of Chicago Press, 1953), p. 47.

[26] *Op. cit.,* p. 129.

By now the reader may have gained the impression that in the old days the housewife had an economic function, that the "working" wife has an economic role, but that the contemporary housewife has no economic significance. Such an observation is not justified. In the early American farm family there was a division of labor both in production and in consumption. In the modern urban family a new division of labor has arisen. The husband and father now has the major role of producer. He produces, however, not directly for the consumption of the family members but for the market. The wife and mother, on the other hand, now assumes charge of consumption. Through the activity of shopping she adds to the commodities purchased what the economists call "place utility" and "time utility." In other words, she sees that goods are available in the home when needed. Her day-to-day shopping, therefore, brings home food for the family table, supplies for household maintenance, and clothing for family members.

Besides shopping, other productive activities of the housewife include the exacting job of child care, the final processing and serving of foods, and the maintenance of clothing and home furnishings. To summarize, then, the bulk of the economic contribution of the modern housewife is in housekeeping, marketing, and child care. It is not possible to make a very accurate estimate of the monetary value of the contribution of the average housewife. Yet her contribution can be appreciated when one tries to hire a competent worker to manage a home.

chapter
9

INTRODUCTION TO PRACTICAL PERSONAL DECISIONS

If you are going to make good decisions, you have to know two things: what you want; what you can get. Your "wants" for various goods are reflected in the utility each of those various goods provide. Your "can get" is determined by your income—in the conventional sense, money income, or your ability to command goods. This, of course, is the central issue in personal economics: How can you get the most for what you have at your disposal? The two sides of the problem, utility and income, can be brought together by assuming that you are rational, in which case what you are willing to pay for a good and what you must pay for a good to acquire it are powerful insights into your preferences and basis for action. The "best buy" is the good for which you are willing to pay the most relative *to what you must pay to get it.*

Obviously, decisions can be made and action taken only in the present—not the past or future. We will look closely at **marginalism,** *which deals with* changes, *since decision implies change. In addition, the total of your experience and situation is necessarily the result of all changes ever made, and changes can be made only in the present. Therefore, the concept of the* margin *is extremely relevant, widely used in economic analysis, and, in fact, rather thoroughly accepted in an intuitive way by everyone. We will look at matters a little more deliberately.*

▶   **CHOICE BETWEEN GOODS**   ◀

The framework within which you make your decision is built on cost—that is, opportunity cost or alternative cost. Recall that cost was defined in terms of utility as "the diminution of utility undergone in the acquisition of a greater utility." In the circular flow diagrams of Chapters 6 and 7, cost for an entire economic system consists of the loss of the utility in the factors of production that was borne in order to get greater utility in the form of economic goods. Similarly, as a single individual or consumer, you lose the utility from the factors of production you control in order to get money income, which you intend to spend on economic goods that have more utility than the factors of production you supplied.

But a second important question exists. Not only do you have to decide how many of your factors of production to supply in return for the money income that you intend to convert into economic goods as a *group* but you also must decide specifically *which* economic goods to spend your money income on. In making that decision, you encounter cost again. This time you find that whichever good you choose to buy will automatically entail giving up another good, which you *do not* buy *but could have* bought. Thus you lose the utility of that good which you did not buy to have that good which you did buy. This means that the "real cost" of any good bought is the utility foregone in the next best alternative.

For example, suppose that a hypothetical consumer has $3,000 to spend as a result of having supplied factors of production and that he must decide which goods to spend it on. For the sake of simplicity, assume

Table 9–1
UTILITY FROM FOUR DIFFERENT GOODS

ECONOMIC GOOD	(1) PRICE	(2) UTILES/UNIT	(2)/(1) = (3) UTILES/DOLLAR SPENT
Car	$3,000	4,500	$1\frac{1}{2}$
Boat	3,000	3,600	$1\frac{1}{5}$
Trip to Europe	3,000	3,000	1
Remodel house	3,000	6,000	2

that the $3,000 will be spent in a lump sum on a single item. Table 9–1 lists four possible goods and the utiles (amount of utility) from each. Which should he buy? Obviously, he should remodel the house. Since he is really buying utility, he gets the most for his money from that particular economic good(s). This is formalized common sense, to be sure. But what is the real cost? What utility did he give up? He gave up the car *or* the boat *or* the trip to Europe. He did not give up all three, because he couldn't have had all three. He had $3,000, so he could only have had one of the three. He therefore gave up either 4,500 utiles (car) *or* 3,600 utiles (boat) *or* 3,000 utiles (trip to Europe). Did he lose 3,000 or 3,600 utiles? Not really. He lost more than that. He lost 4,500 utiles that he could have had in a car. Thus our consumer made a "profit" of 1,500 utiles by making a good decision rather than by choosing the best alternative.

} **Pursuing the alternative cost reasoning will always lead to a good decision, that is, one that maximizes utility.** }

Note that it is immaterial just how we arrived at the absolute number of utiles for any given item. What is important is the *relationship* in the number of utiles between items. To start with the trip to Europe for example, we may assign it any number of utiles that strikes our fancy as long as the boat has one fifth more, the car one half more and remodeling the house twice as many. We would still find that the best buy was the remodeling job. This reveals the purpose of inventing utiles, even though we cannot use them in real life. Utiles allow us to specify relationships concretely so that we may organize our thinking about things that have a relationship to one another but no relationship to an absolute standard. *You cannot state how much you like something except in relationship to something else which you like more or less.*

You should go through the same kind of reasoning when deciding whether to supply factors of production. Your time may be consumed directly as leisure or may be offered in production as labor. The money income from labor will buy utility in the form of economic goods; leisure itself has utility. Utility gained through leisure, therefore, comes at the expense of utility lost from economic goods, and vice versa. Thus the opportunity cost of leisure is the most utility you could have bought in the form of economic goods with the money income you would have earned if you had worked instead.

Cost is therefore relevant to you in two ways: (1) You must decide how much utility to give up by supplying factors of production in return for economic goods as a group, and (2) you must decide how much utility you are willing to forego in one set of economic goods in order to gain another set of economic goods. In other words, you must decide *how much* in economic goods to have and then *which* economic goods to have.

► ## THE RELATIONSHIP BETWEEN UTILITY AND MONEY ◄

Utility and money are both common denominators for economic goods in terms of which various dissimilar economic goods can be compared to one another. Various economic goods can be compared on the common ground of the utility contained in each. A relationship may also be established on the basis of money. This relationship is what we call **price,** or more specifically, **money price.**

While money and utility are both common denominators for economic goods, each has an advantage the other does not. Utility looks at the ability of the economic good to satisfy, but because utility has no concreteness, it is useless in the real world for expressing the terms on which goods may be exchanged for one another. Utility is an abstraction, invented to represent that which we are really interested in—the ability of the economic good to satisfy. On the other hand, prices (in money) are concrete and useful in the real world for expressing the terms of exchange of goods for one another, but they miss the main point: the amount of satisfaction contained in the various economic goods. We need to bring both the concreteness of money and the fundamental importance of utility together if we are to make good decisions. *If you know the relationship between economic goods in terms of money only (their prices), you know what you can get but not what you want. If you know the relationship only in terms of utility, you know what you want but not what you can get.* To get the most possible utility you need to know *both* what you want and what you can get. This would imply the necessity of establishing a link between money and utility in the mind of the consumer.

We can establish the link between utility and money only by making an assumption. It is a crucial assumption.

{   **Assumption: The consumer is rational.**   {

By this, we mean that you will behave in such a way as to get the most utility possible, considering what you know about the choices available and considering the amount of money income you have with which to buy utility. Knowledgeableness and money income level may be termed *constraints*. They establish a limit on the amount of utility you may get. If your knowledge of the choices is not perfect (complete), you may not have made the best possible choice because you did not know about it. Obviously, the higher your money income, the higher the level of utility you can get. Rational behavior under constraints may be defined in an ordinary way as "making the best of it under the circumstances."

▶   WILLINGNESS TO PAY   ◀

How does the assumption of rational consumer behavior connect money and utility? You know you are buying satisfaction even if you have not formulated your knowledge as carefully as on the preceding pages. You have money to spend on economic goods that bring you satisfaction. You will therefore be *willing* to pay different amounts of money (prices) according to the different amounts of utility contained in the various economic goods. If economic good *A* has twice as much utility as economic good *B*, you would be *willing* to pay twice as much for *A* as for *B*. If you pay twice as much for *A* as for *B*, the price of utility from *A* is equal to the price of utility from *B*, and you are indifferent as to whether you spend your money for one of *A* or two of *B*. Either choice gets the same amount of utility for your money. However, if the price of *A* is *less* than twice the price of *B*, you will pick *A* because you get twice as much utility as from *B* but need pay less than twice as much; you thus get more for your money from *A* than from *B*. Conversely, if the price of *A* is *more* than twice the price of *B*, you will get more for your money by taking two *B*'s instead of one *A*. We may then state clearly how the assumption that the rational consumer, who always buys so as to get the most for his money, connects utility and money into one system that is both practical and fundamentally meaningful.

{ The schedule of prices that a rational consumer is *willing* to pay for various economic goods automatically reveals the amount of utility contained in each economic good for this particular buyer. }

To illustrate the point, let us restate the economic goods from Table 9–1 in Table 9–2. We restate the utiles per dollar on a constant level so

Table 9–2
MAXIMUM PRICE WILLINGLY PAID

ECONOMIC GOOD	(1) UTILES/DOLLAR	(2) UTILES/UNIT	(2)/(1) = (3) MAXIMUM PRICE WILLINGLY PAID
Car	2	4,500	$2,250
Boat	2	3,600	1,800
Trip to Europe	2	3,000	1,500
Remodel house	2	6,000	3,000

that the price column will show how much the buyer can pay to get the same utiles per dollar on each good. Since, from Table 9–1, the consumer found the remodeling of the house to be the best buy, let us start from there and find what prices it takes to get 2 utiles per dollar from each good. These are the maximum prices you would be *willing* to pay. At the prices listed above, you get the same amount of utility per dollar spent from any of the goods listed. In summary, we may determine the utility from a series of economic goods by asking the rational consumer, "What would you be *willing* to pay for each good?" *The* relationship *between prices he is* willing *to pay is necessarily the same as the* relationship *between the amounts of utility in each of the goods.*

▶ WILLINGNESS TO PAY ◀ VERSUS MARKET PRICES

Table 9–2 viewed alone has limited value. The word "willing" has always been emphasized. The reason is that there is absolutely nothing to assure that you will be *able* to buy at as low a price as you are *willing* to pay or that you will *need* to pay as high a price as you are willing to pay. If we want to know what you will *actually buy*, we have to look at Table

9–1 as well, where those prices are the prices at which you are *able* to buy. Table 9–3 combines Tables 9–1 and 9–2.

Table 9–3

COMPARISON OF WILLINGNESS TO PAY AND MARKET PRICE

ECONOMIC GOOD	(1) UTILES/ UNIT	(2) PRICE BUYER IS WILLING TO PAY	(3) PRICE BUYER IS ABLE TO BUY FOR	(1)/(2) = (4) UTILES/ DOLLAR (WILLING TO PAY)	(1)/(3) = (5) UTILES/ DOLLAR (ABLE TO BUY FOR)
Car	4,500	$2,250	$3,000	2	$1\frac{1}{2}$
Boat	3,600	1,800	3,000	2	$1\frac{1}{5}$
Trip to Europe	3,000	1,500	3,000	2	1
Remodel house	6,000	3,000	3,000	2	2

On the basis of Table 9–1 we concluded that you would remodel the house because you got more utiles per dollar there than elsewhere. By comparing columns 4 and 5 of Table 9–3, the conclusion from Table 9–1 is borne out. You are willing to buy a car at a price that would give you 2 utiles per dollar. However, you are able to buy it at a price that gives you only $1\frac{1}{2}$ utiles per dollar. You therefore reject the car. You reject everything else also, if it gives you less utility per dollar than you are willing to accept for the money. Only the remodeling gives you as much utility as you are willing to pay for, so you choose to remodel the house and reject the other choices.

There is another even simpler way to determine what the consumer will actually buy. It is to compare columns 2 and 3. You obviously will not buy anything that has a price higher than you are willing to pay. Immediately it can be seen that only the remodeling is acceptable.

Note that there are three ways that Table 9–3 will indicate what you will buy: (1) You can look at column 5 alone, where you will take the economic good that gives the most utiles per dollar that you are able to buy; (2) you can compare columns 4 and 5, where you will buy what gives you the most utiles per dollar relative to what you are willing to pay; and (3) you can look at columns 2 and 3, which compare what you are willing to pay with what you are able to buy for. You will not buy anything that can be had only at a price higher than you are willing to pay. Any of the three approaches leads to the same conclusion—you will remodel the house.

Which approach is best? Clearly the third one, because it deals with money only and is therefore the only practical way of making decisions in the real world. Why did we drag utility into it at all? Because we had to in order to determine what you would be willing to pay—that is, to get column 2. This is the result of the assumption that you are rational and would be willing to pay according to the amount of utility you get from each economic good.

We need to make one more adjustment to Table 9–3 before making a general conclusive statement. Column 2 is determined partly by the level of your money income. Earlier we noted that what you could buy was subject to constraints such as knowledge and the level of money income you had. We assume that the knowledge constraint is not binding by virtue of the fact that you are willing to buy the four economic goods. If you know about the economic goods and the prices at which they are available, you obviously are not hampered by your ignorance. But suppose that your money income is substantially higher. This may make you willing to pay more for all the goods. We will assume that the higher money income does not alter your tastes—that is, that the higher money income does not change column 1. We will also assume that column 3 is unchanged—that is, that the price is the same to rich and poor alike. Column 5 is unchanged also, then, because it is column 1 divided by column 3, neither of which changed.

For the sake of simplicity, assume that your money income is enough higher so that you would be willing to pay twice as much for each economic good. The results are in Table 9–4. Column 2 is of course doubled

Table 9–4

COMPARISON OF WILLINGNESS TO PAY AND MARKET PRICE HIGH MONEY INCOME

ECONOMIC GOOD	(1) UTILES	(2) PRICE BUYER IS WILLING TO PAY	(3) PRICE BUYER IS ABLE TO BUY FOR	(4) UTILES/ DOLLAR (WILLING TO PAY)	(5) UTILES/ DOLLAR (ABLE TO BUY FOR)
Car	4,500	$4,500	$3,000	1	$1\frac{1}{2}$
Boat	3,600	3,600	3,000	1	$1\frac{1}{5}$
Trip to Europe	3,000	3,000	3,000	1	1
Remodel house	6,000	6,000	3,000	1	2

and column 4 is cut in half, because column 4 is column 1 (unchanged) divided by column 2 (doubled).

Now which is the best buy for the rich consumer? No! The answer is not the trip to Europe where he is *able and willing* to buy 1 utile per dollar. The best buy is always where he gets the most satisfaction from what he is able to buy *relative* to what he is willing to pay. After all, he may be able to buy for less than he would have been willing to pay. The fourth unit for a *total* of 300 utiles. The entire picture appears in Table 9–5 shows the differences between Tables 9–3 and 9–4 with respect to

Table 9–5

COMPARISON OF DECISIONS OF POOR AND RICH CONSUMERS

ECONOMIC GOOD	(1) COLUMN 2 MINUS COLUMN 3 FROM TABLE 9–3	(2) COLUMN 2 MINUS COLUMN 3 FROM TABLE 9–4
Car	−$ 750	+$1,500
Boat	− 1,200	+ 600
Trip to Europe	− 1,500	00000
Remodel house	00000	+ 3,000

the final decision made in terms of money. Table 9–5 is really a summary of the information contained in Tables 9–3 and 9–4.

From Table 9–5 it can be quickly seen that whether your income is low, as in Table 9–3, or high, as in Table 9–4, you get the most utility from $3,000 spent by remodeling the house. In Table 9–3, that is the only choice you can afford; in Table 9–4, where your income is higher, you can afford (are willing to pay for) any of the goods, but there is still one choice that is better than the others. The price of any choice is $3,000, so you should take the one where the surplus of what you would have been willing to pay over what you had to pay is the greatest and that is in remodeling the house (Table 9–5, column 2).

If you are wealthy, you now have another decision to make, however. The remodeling job only cost you $3,000; you still have another $3,000 to spend. After you remodel the house, the best buy is the car, which you then buy. When you have the car, you find the income constraint now binds, even though you are wealthy. When you were poor, you had to settle for the remodeling job because at that point your income ran out.

You therefore got a total of 6,000 utiles from your income. When you are wealthy, you got both the remodeling and the car for a total utility from your income of 6,000 + 4,500 utiles or 10,500 utiles. The higher your income, the more total utility—hardly a surprising result. The most important result, however, is that a wealthy and the poor consumer both get the maximum possible utility from their respective incomes. And they each accomplished it in exactly the same way. They always bought that item next which gave the most utility relative to its price—that is, the most utility per dollar spent. They kept spending in this way until their income was all spent. *The following rule for utility maximization may therefore be offered:*

> **A consumer gets the most utility possible by always purchasing that item next which gives him the most utility per dollar spent.**

This will assure that you have gotten the most possible utility from your money income.

▶ MARGINALISM ◀

Notice that we always talk about which good you should buy *next*—in the present. The past is water over the dam, and the future isn't here yet. We can do nothing about either one—except insofar as present action may influence the future. The present is where the action is. It is only in the present (not the past or future) where decisions can be made and action taken.

This means that the focus is always on what happens *next*, on what should be done *now*, on what good should be bought *next*, and so on. The fact that what is done now may influence the future is beside the point. Consider the future all you like; consider anything else also that you think is appropriate. But when you come to making a choice and taking action, you are limited to the present. To attempt otherwise is, at best, to cry over spilled milk (living in the past) or to be a worrywart (living in the future). At worst, you may make a psychiatric case of yourself. In terms of the goods in Tables 9–1 through 9–5, the utilities assigned to each good by the consumer are probably influenced by the past. Perhaps you assign a low utility to a trip to Europe because you have just been there. Perhaps you assign a high utility to remodeling the house because nothing has been done to it in 20 years. Perhaps you assign a somewhat higher utility to the car because, although your present car is performing satisfactorily, you expect it to roll over dead shortly and you wish to avoid a crisis by trading now. *Thus although past experience and future expectations are relevant, their influence must always be translated into a "present equivalent."* It is only in the present that anything can be done, so it is the present utility in which we are interested. Only *now* will you decide to buy or not to buy good X; therefore, you need to know its utility now.

When we talk about making *decisions,* we are necessarily talking about what happens in the *present,* and when we talk about what happens in the *present,* we are necessarily talking about *changes.*

Your decision to buy good X rather than good Y will *change* the total amount of good X you have ever bought, which will *change* the total amount of utility you have ever realized, which will *change* the total amount of money income you have ever spent.

The *total* of anything is necessarily the result of all the *changes* that have *ever* been made to the total. Thus if you are interested in having the largest possible total of anything (say utility), you can assure yourself of that result by always making sure that the changes in the total utility are as large as possible. Changes can be made only in the present. Thus you can concern yourself only with *changes* made in the present, and the *total* will take care of itself. A desire to have the highest possible total utility will automatically be fulfilled if you see to it that you always make the largest possible additions to total utility.

Analysis that deals with changes is called **marginal analysis.**[1] Margin refers to the edge. Changes occur at the edge. The margin on a sheet of paper is the space around the edge. The marginal business is the one at the edge of economic viability. The marginal student is the one at the edge of academic viability. Indeed, life is lived at the margin of time. Everything that we do is necessarily at the margin and changes the total of our experience. The marginal utility from an economic good is the *change* it makes in total utility. The marginal expenditure is the *change* its purchase makes in total expenditure. Although it is repetitious, it will serve to show how succinct the simple rule for utility maximization is if we restate some of the information in Tables 9–3, 9–4, and 9–5 in terms of the new terminology.

We determine how much additional utility you get per dollar spent $(MU/\$)$ by expressing the marginal utility of each economic good relative to the price at which it is available (Table 9–6).

We may simply substitute the prices you would be willing to pay from column 2, Table 9–3, for marginal utility in the previous series of inequalities (Table 9–7). The remodeling still comes out the best buy, as it did previously. The preceding has been generalized in terms of *willingness* to pay and *ability* to pay. Everything is in money terms, so it has become a practical operating mechanism for decision making. You

Table 9-6

MARGINAL UTILITY RELATIVE
TO MARGINAL EXPENDITURE

CAR	BOAT	TRIP TO EUROPE	REMODEL HOUSE
$\dfrac{4,500}{\$3,000} = 1.5$	$\dfrac{3,600}{\$3,000} = 1.2$	$\dfrac{3,000}{\$3,000} = 1.0$	$\dfrac{6,000}{\$3,000} = 2.0$

Arranging in order from highest to lowest yields

REMODEL HOUSE	CAR	BOAT	TRIP TO EUROPE
$\dfrac{6,000}{\$3,000} = 2.0 >$	$\dfrac{4,500}{\$3,000} = 1.5 >$	$\dfrac{3,600}{\$3,000} = 1.2 >$	$\dfrac{3,000}{\$3,000} = 1.0$

Table 9-7

WILLINGNESS TO PAY RELATIVE
TO MARKET PRICE

REMODEL HOUSE	CAR	BOAT	TRIP TO EUROPE
$\dfrac{\$3,000}{\$3,000} = 1.0 >$	$\dfrac{\$2,250}{\$3,000} = .75 >$	$\dfrac{\$1,800}{\$3,000} = .60 >$	$\dfrac{\$1,500}{\$3,000} = .50$

For the high-income consumer from Table 9–4 the inequalities become

$\dfrac{\$6,000}{\$3,000} = 2.0 >$	$\dfrac{\$4,500}{\$3,000} = 1.5 >$	$\dfrac{\$3,600}{\$3,000} = 1.2 >$	$\dfrac{\$3,000}{\$3,000} = 1.0$

make decisions by comparing what you are willing to pay with what you must pay to have the good. This comparison is called the **benefit–cost ratio.**

Table 9–6 expresses the benefit in real (utility) terms and the cost in money terms for the low income consumer. Table 9–7 expresses the benefit in money terms as revealed by willingness to pay, and again the cost is in money terms for both the low- and high-income consumer. Notice that, in all three cases, the decision as to the best buy came out

the same and that it was determined at the margin (what to do *next*) by looking at the benefit–cost ratio—specifically the *marginal* benefit–marginal cost ratio. Table 9–8 contains a summary of these results.

Table 9–8

COMPARISON OF VARIOUS BENEFIT–COST RATIOS

	REMODEL HOUSE	CAR	BOAT	TRIP TO EUROPE
Low-income consumer				
real benefit / money cost	2.0 >	1.5 >	1.2 >	1.0
money benefit / money cost	1.0 >	.75 >	.60 >	.50
High-income consumer				
money benefit / money cost	2.0 >	1.5 >	1.2 >	1.0

The relationship between the goods is identical in each case. The choice between goods is the same measured in money and real terms because we assume that the rational consumer's willingness to pay is a perfect reflection of utility received. The high- and low-income consumers make the same choice because we assumed that money income level did not affect his basic likes or dislikes or the prices he would be charged. It is evident that the size of the benefit–cost ratio for any given product is of no consequence in making a choice among products. It is the *relationship* of the benefit–cost ratios between products that dictates choice.

You may object to the assumption that the level of money income has no effect on tastes and preferences or prices charged to the consumer. No problem. It is not a necessary assumption as far as individual choice is concerned. The assumption was introduced here to illustrate the importance of the *relationship* of the benefit–cost ratio *between* products for a given consumer and the unimportance of such things as the level of money income, the level of money prices, or the level of utility received —each viewed in their own right. You look at the prices that *you* are willing to pay for various goods relative to the prices *you* must pay to get them, and you make your choice on that basis. If you believe that poor people tend to be charged higher prices (or vice versa) or that wealthy people have different tastes because of their station, well and good. That is a broader issue.

Having determined how you choose between goods, it is now necessary to investigate the choice as between goods compared to additional units of a good previously purchased. This will involve the **law of diminishing marginal utility.** It is basically a simple law, and our decision will again draw on a comparison of willingness to pay with market price —that is, on the benefit–cost ratio.

▶ DIMINISHING MARGINAL UTILITY ◀

When the two-year-old daughter of one of the authors discovered salt shakers, she promptly engaged in some self-instruction in basic economics. She was fascinated with the mechanics of the use of this marvelous device. She also found that her hot dog tasted better with a little salt on it. Since her discovery yielded utility from two sources—the use of the salt shaker and the enhanced flavor of the food—she quickly expended a considerable amount of the resources she controlled in salting her food. Since a shake or two yielded tremendous utility at a very minimal cost, she wisely increased her resource allocation to this activity. It was a good "buy." But, to her disappointment, she discovered that additional quantities of the "product" yielded considerably less additional utility than did previous units, and, upon discovering that she could not eat her hot dog with six shakes of salt, she reduced her resource allocation to this activity. It seems that she had discovered the *law of diminishing marginal utility.*

This law, which is fundamental in explaining consumer behavior and preference for a variety of goods as opposed to only larger quantities of a given set of goods, may be stated simply as:

> The more of a good you have, the less utility you get from each *additional* unit.

To pursue the lesson of the salt shaker, the law of diminishing marginal utility was set forth especially forcefully in this instance, because the marginal utility from this particular activity happens not only to diminish, but to diminish very rapidly. In other situations, marginal utility may diminish much less rapidly, but in every instance it will eventually diminish. There would seem to be no good for which marginal utility does not diminish when the quantity possessed becomes large. In other words there is nothing that you don't eventually get tired of. Of course, as you get more of a good and its marginal utility diminishes, your willingness to pay declines, which makes additional units of the good less attractive and causes you to purchase a different good eventually. For example, consider the real cost of the use of the salt shaker. The cost would seem to be only a short period of time that could have been expended differently. Assume that the cost of a unit of this good (1 shake) is 5 seconds.

Let's suppose that the first shake yields 100 utiles, the second shake 90 utiles, the third shake 70 utiles, the fourth shake 40 utiles, the fifth shake 10 utiles, and the sixth shake −20 utiles. The *total* utility from, say, *4* units would be 100 utiles from the first unit, *plus* 90 utiles from the second unit, *plus* 70 utiles from the third unit, *plus* 40 utiles from the fourth unit for a *total* of 300 utiles. The entire picture appears in Table 9–9.

Table 9–9

MARGINAL UTILITY AND TOTAL UTILITY FROM A GIVEN GOOD

UNIT	MARGINAL UTILITY	TOTAL UTILITY
1	100	100
2	90	190
3	70	260
4	40	300
5	10	310
6	−20	290

Expressing the marginal utility from each unit relative to its real cost gives the following:

- *First unit:* 100 utiles/5 sec = 20 utiles/sec
- *Second unit:* 90 utiles/5 sec = 18 utiles/sec
- *Third unit:* 70 utiles/5 sec = 16 utiles/sec
- *Fourth unit:* 40 utiles/5 sec = 8 utiles/sec
- *Fifth unit:* 10 utiles/5 sec = 2 utiles/sec
- *Sixth unit:* −20 utiles/5 sec = −4 utiles/sec

This example is entirely in real terms. It relates the actual utility received to the actual sacrifice necessary to get it. It shows that if diminishing marginal utility exists (as it must), then the fewer the units possessed, the more valuable each unit is. Notice that this little illustra-

. . . On diminishing marginal utility . . .
© 1971 United Feature Syndicate, Inc.

tion does not tell us how many units should be "bought." It is clear,
however, that 6 units should *not* be bought, for even if the units were free,
there would be no point in taking another unit when it makes you worse
off. Obviously if utility diminishes, eventually it will become negative—
you get saturated and are worse off for having more units. Taking the
sixth unit would seem to be a form of gluttony in which you gorge yourself even though you are worse off for it. But as for units 1 through 5, there
is no way to know how many you should take *until* you know what the
alternatives for the spending of your 5 seconds are. If the 2-year-old
could get 80 utiles from a 5-second tiff with her 1-year-old sister, she
should spend the first 5 seconds available salting her food and collect 100
utiles, spend the second 5 seconds salting her food and collect an additional 90 utiles, and spend the third 5 seconds with her sister and get 80
utiles—10 more than the 70 utiles from a third unit of salt. The opportunity cost principle scores again! It told us whether to take another unit
of the same product or to switch·to another. The acquisition of 80 utiles

from the argument with her sister exceeded the cost of 70 utiles foregone from a third unit of salt.

It should now be clear that the decision as to whether to acquire another unit of the *same* product is no different from the earlier decision as to *which* product to acquire next. Obviously, another unit of something you already have is an alternative, and it is evaluated in the same way as any other alternative. It is, as always, the margin that is relevant. The units of a good already possessed relate to the margin only indirectly in that they are a factor in determining the utility you will get from the next unit, which is the immediate question.

Marginal utility may diminish very rapidly or very slowly as more units of a good are acquired, depending on the nature of the good and your attitude toward it. In the salt example, marginal utility diminished quite rapidly. You soon have had enough. In other cases marginal utility may diminish very slowly. If we define a 5-mile joy ride in an automobile as a unit of economic goods, it would seem that the marginal utility of that good diminishes very slowly as more of the good is obtained. The evidence is that, for most people, after having had one, they are willing to have another at the same cost quite quickly—and another—and another.

SUMMARY

1 • The choice between different economic goods relies on the opportunity cost principle just as did the choice between economic goods as a group and other outlets for resources such as self-sufficiency income, resource income, or noneconomic income.

2 • Investigation of the relationship between goods in terms of the amount of *utility* they each supply gives you insight into what you *want*.

3 • Investigation of the relationship between goods in terms of their *money prices* gives you insight into what you *can get*.

4 • Your wants are converted into concrete terms by expressing *willingness* to pay. The rational consumer is willing to pay in proportion to the utility he receives.

5 • You can make a decision on which good to choose by comparing your willingness to pay with the price

at which the good is offered you (market price). You will get the most utility from your money income by purchasing that good where your willingness to pay is greatest relative to market price.

6 • The most possible utility from any quantity of money income can be gotten by following the procedure in (5) above until money income is exhausted.

7 • The margin is the edge. The margin deals with changes.

8 • Only the margin is relevant in decision making. Nothing else is subject to influence or control.

9 • Decisions are necessarily marginal in nature because life itself is lived at the margin with respect to the flow of time. Action can be taken only in the present.

10 • In a more concrete sense, decisions as to which alternatives to choose and which to forego are marginal with respect to specific products, since total utility is necessarily the sum of the utilities of each alternative chosen up to the present. Always choosing the next alternative that makes the largest possible addition to utility necessarily results in the most possible utility.

11 • Utility is maximized by choosing those alternatives for which the utility received—as evidenced by willingness to pay—is greatest relative to the payment required to get the alternative.

12 • A given decision may be produced through analysis in real terms or money terms.

13 • The law of diminishing marginal utility says that as more of a good is acquired, less utility is provided by each additional unit.

14 • Willingness to pay for additional units therefore declines as more of a good is obtained. As willingness to pay declines, a switch is eventually made to a different good. The law of diminishing marginal utility thus constitutes an explanation of the observed tendency for the typical consumer to prefer variety.

study materials

1 • Defend or criticize the idea that "to be as well off as possible, you should keep spending money income on items that provide the most satisfaction per dollar spent until your money runs out."

2 • What are the strengths and/or weaknesses of measuring goods in terms of utility?

3 • What is meant by the assumption that the consumer is "rational"? Why is this perhaps a hazardous assumption? Why is it also a necessary and, undoubtedly, usually substantially correct assumption?

4 • Why does the recognition of utility become significant in determining your willingness to pay?

5 • Which is the most relevant—willingness to pay or ability to pay—in determining which alternative good to choose, assuming that you are a rational consumer?

6 • State the utility-maximizing rule that applies to wealthy consumers; to poor consumers.

7 • Why should the consumer concentrate on the present, or what to do next?

8 • Explain what is meant by marginal analysis.

9 • What is the marginal utility and marginal expenditure per item in the following?

ITEMS	TOTAL UTILITY	MARGINAL UTILITY	TOTAL EXPENDITURE	MARGINAL EXPENDITURE
1	100	———	$200	———
2	150	———	280	———
3	190	———	350	———
4	220	———	410	———

10 • Explain what is meant by the benefit–cost ratio. How is it computed?

11 • Explain why it is the *relationship* of the benefit–cost ratios between products and not the *size* of a ratio for a given product that dictates choice.

12 • Explain the law of diminishing marginal utility and its significance to the consumer. Give examples.

13 • Is it possible for marginal utility to be negative? If so, under what conditions may this occur? Try to think of examples where and when people may push consumption to the point where negative utility is experienced at the margin. Is this rational consumer behavior?

footnote

[1] For some purposes, the changes must be infinitely small to qualify as *marginal*. However, for our use, we may consider changes that are larger.

appendix

CONSUMER EQUILIBRIUM

Equilibrium is a condition of stability. It is a position from which there is no tendency to move. You are in equilibrium with regard to the combination of products you buy if you are taking a combination such that

$$\frac{\text{marginal utility from good } A}{\text{price of good } A} = \frac{\text{marginal utility from good } B}{\text{price of good } B} - - -$$

$$- - - - - - - - - - - = \frac{\text{marginal utility from good } N}{\text{price of good } N}$$

where N is the number of different goods bought. Since willingness to pay is a revelation of marginal utility for the rational consumer, the equilibrium condition may be restated as

$$\frac{\text{willingness to pay for good } A}{\text{price of good } A} = \frac{\text{willingness to pay for good } B}{\text{price of good } B} - - -$$

$$- - - - - - - - - - - = \frac{\text{willingness to pay for good } N}{\text{price of good } N}.$$

The recognition that you try to get as much utility as you can from your expenditure and the operation of the law of diminishing marginal utility indicate that the above condition must prevail if you are to be satisfied with the combination of goods you have.

Assume a two-good world. If $MU_A/P_A > MU_B/P_B$, you are getting more per dollar spent on good A than you are getting per dollar spent on good B, so you spend less on good B and more on good A. As you do, $MU_A/P_A > MU_B/P_B$ tends to become $MU_A/P_A = MU_B/P_B$, since as you get more of good A and less of good B, the MU_A drops and MU_B rises. This is because the law of diminishing marginal utility says that MU depends on how much of the good you already have. When $MU_A/P_A = MU_B/P_B$, you get the same utility from an additional expenditure on each. You are therefore satisfied with the combination of goods and tend to stay with it. The prices, of course, may also be expressed in real terms; that is, the actual loss in resources or alternative goods entailed in the acquisition of the utility gained may be substituted for the money representation of the loss. This condition establishes the *combination* of goods bought; the *level* (or total amount) of goods bought in this combination is determined by your level of income. That is, keep buying in this combination until your money runs out.

II

CONSUMPTION, INVESTMENT, INSURANCE DECISIONS

In Part II, we will apply the understanding and procedure developed in Part I to the making of specific personal economic decisions. Those decisions can be categorized according to (1) whether they relate to the present only or whether they involve a relationship between the present and the future, and (2) whether they entail a high degree of certainty or a high degree of uncertainty in the level of benefits and costs to be realized from the selection of a given alternative. The types of decisions may therefore be loosely categorized as relating to *present certainty, future certainty, future unavoidable uncertainty,* or *future avoidable uncertainty.* Future avoidable uncertainty entails converting uncertainty to the equivalent of certainty. A preview of each of the four categories may be helpful.

1 • Decisions relating to *present certainty* are commonly referred to as *consumption decisions.* They are the simplest decisions because there are few unknowns lurking around. Decisions as to whether to go to a movie rather than to a concert or whether to buy a steak rather than a pork chop or even whether or not to buy a new car are relatively simple. You know precisely what you are getting and precisely what you must give up to get it. Little estimation is required.

2 • Decisions relating to *future certainty* might be called *safe investments.* The essence of investment is relationship between the present and the future. Usually the cost is borne in the present and the benefit received in the future; a reversal of this relationship (benefit in the present–cost in the future) though atypical, does not alter the fundamental nature of the problem. For working purposes, we might accept government-insured savings accounts, United States government securities, and perhaps very high-grade corporation bonds held to maturity as safe invest-

ments. The return, or benefit, is quite certain since you know precisely what you will get and when. You also know what you must pay now to get this future benefit.

3 • Decisions relating to *future unavoidable uncertainty* might be called *risky investments*. Perhaps common stocks could serve as an example. There is a great deal of uncertainty about the size of the benefit. Furthermore, you must bear this uncertainty if you are going to play the game. There is no way you can own these investments without accepting the risks that go with them. To be sure, there are myriad methods and volumes written about strategies, simple and complex, to minimize this risk, but there is no way to escape it completely. You must bear, ultimately, whatever uncertainty is there.

4 • Decisions relating to *future avoidable uncertainty* are basically *insurance questions*. Under some conditions, uncertainty may be transferred onto other shoulders. It is uncertain whether your house will burn down, but you can escape the uncertainty by insuring against fire, in which case you know your costs and what you can expect as a benefit.

A word of clarification. The preceding four paragraphs are a sketch of what is to follow in Part II. As such they are woefully incomplete; elaboration will follow. It must be recognized at the outset, however, that the world is gray, not black and white. For example, it is clearly unwarranted to stamp any investment as "safe" or "risky." All investments are risky. There are only various degrees of risk. Further, it is unclear where the division between the present and the future lies. In the strictest possible sense, neither "the present" nor "certainty" exists. Everything is uncertain to some degree; you may not like the concert as well as you thought you would, for example. Everything happens in the future to some degree; the present is instantaneous, so nothing can happen except in the future. In reality, then, there is only the "near future" and the "distant future." In the strictest sense, it appears that there is no such thing as a consumption decision. Everything is really an investment. Perhaps so. Your purchase of a movie ticket, though commonly viewed as a consumption expenditure, is really an investment. You pay *now* for *future* utility in an undetermined amount because you are not sure how well you will like the movie. However, since you are *quite* certain how well you will like the movie and will receive the benefit in the very *near* future, we agree to view the decision in the light of *present certainty* for working purposes.

Also, you may have blown your mental whistle at the very suggestion of *future certainty*. The future is inherently uncertain— almost by definition. There can be no absolute certainty about the future. Will the sun come up tomorrow morning? "It always has" does not persuasively support your claim to certainty that it will tomorrow. For working purposes, however, such a response is probably sufficient evidence of certainty, particularly when considered against the reasons for it having done so in the past. Thus the return from any investment is uncertain to some degree. All investments are risky. Doing anything is risky. Doing nothing is risky. Nothing is certain. (Death and taxes? Science is making progress on at least one of these!) If uncertainty characterizes the world, paragraph (4) does not make sense since it talks about avoiding uncertainty. Avoiding uncertainty is a matter of avoiding sufficiently much of the uncertainty, so that, for working purposes, we may say that it has been avoided because it is *sufficiently* avoided to be unimportant.

Hopefully, the lesson is clear: Pigeonholing a decision according to its home category is pointless; there is a point in recognizing that *when* (present versus future) benefits and costs will be realized and to *what extent* the expected benefits and costs are likely to be realized (certainty versus uncertainty) is important. Therefore, every decision has two important dimensions—the present–future dimension and the certainty–uncertainty dimension. As the distance in time between realization of the benefit and the cost *lengthens,* new considerations must be taken into account. As the extent to which a given cost or benefit becomes *less* certain, new considerations must be taken into account. For these reasons, consumption decisions, made under conditions of present certainty, tend to be somewhat simpler than investment and insurance decisions. The basic issue in investment and insurance choices, however, remains the same as in other choices. The relevant decision criteria is benefit relative to cost. But new dimensions enter into the determination of benefit and cost.

Comparison between the present and the future relies on the concept of *interest,* particularly *compound interest.* Interest rates are the economic link between the present and the future. Decision making under conditions of uncertainty relies on *probability.* Probability allows conversion of uncertainty to a "certainty equivalent" —the next best thing to certainty itself. *Interest* and *probability* as they relate to personal economic decisions will be developed in detail later.

chapter
10

CONSUMPTION DECISIONS: SERVICES, NONDURABLES, RESOURCES

This chapter will focus on decisions made under conditions of approximate present certainty, that is, consumption decisions. We will look at a decision about services, nondurables, and direct resource consumption. The decisions about services and nondurables will serve as vehicles for investigation of the concept of substitutability as it relates to consumer choice. We will also discover that the decision-making process itself is subject to economic analysis.

Perhaps a word of qualification or friendly advice is in order before proceeding. You may conclude from the examples in Part I and those to follow here that we believe that every action must be carefully analyzed. Not so. The analysis of every action leads to worrying about whether to lead off with your right foot or left foot when getting up from your chair. Indeed, the shortcut to misery and ultimate disutility is to analyze your every action. The purpose of the discussion is not to lead to the analysis of every action but to provide the wherewithal by which all action may be analyzed from time to time. Certainly it is appropriate to ask yourself occasionally whether you are doing the kinds of things that you really want to do. You should be sufficiently cognizant of the conscious and unconscious choices you are making to recognize habits and patterns in your behavior that are contrary to your preferences. To determine whether your actions are in accord with your goals, you need to know how to make good decisions.

▶ IDENTIFICATION OF ALTERNATIVES ◀

Every practical choice has two major aspects: (1) identification of the alternatives, and (2) selection of the best alternative. Maximization of utility from the resources you control requires that you score on both counts. It is obvious that you must choose the best alternative from among those available. It should be equally obvious that you cannot maximize utility from your resources if you overlook some of the alternatives. You cannot select what was not under consideration, and one of the alternatives you overlooked might have proved to be the best one had you considered it.

It might be said that the identification of the alternatives requires imagination and reflection and that the selection of the best alternative requires technical competence. Sorting out the best alternative from among a group of alternatives is largely a mechanical procedure, but identifying what the alternatives are calls for cleverness and imagination. Since the material that follows will tend to focus on the selection of the single best alternative and the identification of costs and benefits, it is worthwhile to stop here for a moment and reinforce the material in Chapters 2 and 3 in a more specific way.

It was suggested in Chapter 2 that the range of alternatives open to you may be somewhat greater than you first thought. For example, we will shortly determine how a consumer chooses between a concert and a movie. Although we will assume for the purpose of simplification that he considers these to be the only alternatives, there certainly must have been more than two alternatives.

What, then, was the process by which the consumer came to choose between a movie and a concert? Chapter 2 suggests that consumer choice grows from a desire that manifests itself in a need that culminates in specific wants. Desires are, to some degree, subject to cultivation or extermination. By looking at your desires carefully, you may see different alternatives than you first thought existed.

We will assume momentarily that the want of a movie or concert grew from a desire for entertainment—whatever that means. Can you be more specific? Do you specifically desire exposure to the performing arts? If so, there may be other forms you have not yet considered, such as the theatre. Is your desire for entertainment socially founded? If so, other

There is *always* a choice! (But some may be uninteresting.)

social activities might be feasible alternatives. A card game with your friends can be cheaper than the movie or concert (or more expensive, depending on who your friends are and what the card game is). Is your desire for entertainment founded on simple need for a change in routine? If so, a walk alone in the woods might be an alternative. Is your desire for entertainment essentially an escape from dissatisfaction with your lot? If so, participation in social service activity or religious experience may be a feasible alternative. Clearly, the feasible alternatives depend on something quite basic within yourself. Explore yourself. Separate what you *really* want from what you *assume* that you want. Then use your imagination to come up with feasible alternatives. The high level of well-being of many persons seems often to be built more on imaginatively and aggressively ferreting out substitute sources of utility than it is on selecting from a dog-eared list of standard alternatives. Knowing yourself is the starting point.

▶ DECISIONS UNDER PRESENT ◀ CERTAINTY: SERVICES

The general decision-making framework laid down in Part I sets the stage for rapid disposal of personal choice about consumer services once the alternatives have been identified. Suppose that you have a felt need for entertainment and have concluded that either a movie or a concert will satisfy your need at an acceptable cost considering nonentertainment alternatives for your money. The issue, then, is to determine which is the better buy—a movie or a concert. Suppose that the movie costs $2.00 and the concert costs $5.00. The fact that the movie costs less than the concert does not mean that you necessarily choose it, of course. Choice is dictated by the benefit *relative* to the cost. The ticket price is only half the issue. Assuming that you are rational, the benefit (utility received) will be reflected in your *willingness* to pay to go to the movie or to go to the concert. Suppose that if only the movie were available, you would pay $4.00 rather than go without; if only the concert were available, you would pay $6.00 rather than go without.

The benefit–cost ratio from the movie is $4.00/$2.00 = 2 and for the concert is $6.00/$5.00 = 1.20. Since a dollar spent on the movie yields $2 worth of utility but a dollar spent on the concert yields only $1.20 worth, the movie is clearly the better buy and is therefore chosen.

It seems almost certain that a rational consumer would arrive at a decision in this general manner, but it seems unlikely that this much formality would be followed or is even necessary in this instance. It was not necessary to determine precisely that the benefit–cost ratios were

2.00 and 1.20; it was necessary only to determine that the benefit–cost ratio was higher for the movie than for the concert. The consumer simply evaluated his preferences *relative* to the costs and concluded that, considering the cost, he preferred the movie to the concert. It is good to actually specify what you might be willing to pay occasionally. It helps identify actions taken from force of habit or out of ignorance as opposed to actions taken because they get what you really want.

This example was simple because the costs and benefits were quite easily identified and somewhat similar for each alternative. The economic cost was simply the ticket price in each case. Additional costs, both economic and noneconomic, were minor and very similar for each alternative. The benefits were also easily identified. They consisted largely of the utility from the performance itself. That's about all there was to it. More complex decisions are difficult, not because the decision-making process is different but because it is more difficult to accurately assess the costs and benefits. After these have been identified, the actual decision is always a simple matter.

As a sidelight, it is evident that many alternatives can be eliminated because your willingness to pay is *less* than the required payment. Only if your willingness to pay is greater than the required payment does an alternative become viable. For example, if the cost is $2.00 and you would be willing to pay only $1.50, the benefit–cost ratio would be $1.50/$2.00 = .75. You gain $.75 for every dollar lost. You are better off making no expenditure at all; therefore, this alternative is not seriously considered as a possible choice. It might be said that whether or not the benefit–cost ratio is greater than 1 will determine whether or not an alternative has a *possibility* of being selected. If the benefit–cost ratio is less than 1, all alternatives are rejected; your present state is preferable to all others. From among those alternatives that have benefit–cost ratios greater than 1, you select the alternative where the benefit–cost ratio is the *most* above 1.

► DECISIONS UNDER PRESENT ◄ CERTAINTY: NONDURABLES

Consumer nondurables are those alternatives which possess physical substance but have no important lasting qualities. Obviously, we are again dealing in approximations, since everything having physical substance would seem to have *some* lasting quality. Perhaps food and clothing are the most prominent broad categories of consumer nondurables. The durability of these goods is sufficiently low so that we assume that their utility flows forth almost instantly. Services, which were just discussed, might, in a sense, be viewed as simply the least durable of the nondurables. Having no physical substance whatever, they are obviously incapable of any lasting quality whatever. Thus the analysis of a choice among consumer nondurables is essentially a repeat of the analysis of a choice among services. The benefits and costs are usually quite evident.

Suppose that your need for food has led you to the grocery store. You have decided to buy meat, and it will be either steak or pork chops. As you peer into the meat counter, you see that steak is $1.72 per pound and pork chops $1.18 per pound. In the dusk of your consciousness you note that you have an absolute preference for steak but perhaps not sufficiently so to warrant the extra cost. As your hand reluctantly moves to the pork chops, you are concluding that the benefit–cost ratio is higher for the pork chops priced at $1.18 than for the steak priced at $1.72. You might, for example, be willing to go as high as $2.00 for the steak and $1.50 for the pork chops. If so, the benefit–cost ratio would have been $2.00/$1.72 = 1.16 for the steak and $1.50/$1.18 = 1.27 for the pork chops. Since these benefit–cost ratios were fairly close together, your decision was not particularly clear-cut. You pondered a moment. On the other hand, you did not spend a great deal of time on the matter because there was not enough involved to warrant spending a lot of time. *Herein lies an inadvertently discovered lesson.*

The decision making process itself is subject to economic analysis. No decision should absorb more resources than the good decision is worth. In the steak–pork chops example, a good decision as opposed to a bad one is not worth very much because the total amount of resources that will go into either steak or pork chops is small. Since it is nearly a toss-up between them anyway, it is evident that the value of the right decision is not much greater than the value of the wrong decision; so obviously you cannot afford to spend much time deciding between them. Make up your mind and get on with it.

The point can be illustrated by observing that perhaps $5.00 will be spent on meat here. Steak will give $1.16 benefit per dollar spent and pork chops $1.27 per dollar spent. $1.27 − $1.16 = $.09. The right decision rather than the wrong one seems to be worth about $.09 per dollar spent. $.09 × 5 = $.45. Clearly, giving up more than $.45 worth of time and effort from your comprehensive income to make a decision is unwarranted. How much less than that is warranted depends on your value of the alternative uses for the resources expended on the decision. On the other hand, suppose that a new Ford comes up with the same benefit–cost ratio as the steak, 1.16, and a new Chevrolet the same benefit–cost ratio as the pork chops, 1.27. Even though you find the Chevrolet to be a better buy than the Ford by the same "amount" than the pork chops were a better buy than the steak, you can afford to expend more resources making the auto decision because the total resource block at stake represented by the expenditure is larger. If the expenditure on the car will come to about $4,000, the value of a good decision relative to a bad one is about $.09 × 4,000 = $360.00. It is obvious that you can afford to spend more time and effort buying a car than buying 3-days' supply of meat.

Before you scoff at the conclusion as obvious, ask yourself how many people you know who make decisions about new cars out of habit yet look at every head of lettuce in the bin before selecting one. You, of course, are smart enough to be careful to put more into the major decisions than the minor ones, but are you sure that you are putting enough into the major ones relative to the minor ones—or perhaps too much? It is an interesting question. Some people, of course, get utility from the simple fact of shopping (making decisions). If that is the case, the amount of resources going into the effort can be justifiably increased.[1]

▶ SUBSTITUTABILITY AND CONSUMER ◀ CHOICE

Insight into the economic fundamentals of substitutability is provided by looking at the benefit–cost ratios for the concert versus the movie and the steak versus the pork chops. Economic choice is influenced heavily by the extent to which various goods substitute for one another as sources of utility. The issue of substitutability in economic analysis is encountered frequently and at various levels of sophistication. Our encounter is, shall we say, a lower-level encounter, but significant nonetheless. Is the steak a substitute for the pork chop? Is the steak a substitute for the concert? Most people would probably answer "yes" to the first question and "no" to the second. But is it not true that steaks and concerts are both sources of utility? Having more steaks necessarily entails having fewer concerts and vice versa, since our resources are limited. Are they not then substitutes? Of course they are. It is sometimes said that everything is a substitute for everything else to some degree.

Again, the world is not black and white but gray. The question is not whether any two goods are substitutes but to what extent they are substitutes. The ability of any two goods to substitute for one another in consumption at any point in time is necessarily given by comparing their benefit–cost ratios. Since you are pulled toward that good with the highest benefit–cost ratio, it is necessarily true that the farther apart the benefit–cost ratios of the two goods, the more decisively you are pulled to the good with the higher benefit–cost ratio. The good with the low benefit–cost ratio is a poor substitute. Conversely if the benefit–cost ratios are close together, the goods are excellent substitutes, so a choice is less clear-cut. If the benefit–cost ratios for two goods are equal, they are perfect substitutes, since you are completely indifferent as to which you choose. (*Note:* Substitutability is defined more narrowly in everyday conversation.)

Notice that the closer that goods substitute for one another, the more difficult it is to make the right decision. However, the wrong decision hurts you less when they are close substitutes. This is a fortuitous circumstance since it tends to cause more important decisions to be easier to make, *assuming* that benefits and costs have been accurately assessed. But, as stated earlier, that is usually the toughest part of the matter and will occupy most of our attention in later chapters. For the moment, notice that apparently steak and pork chops (benefit–cost ratios of 1.16 and 1.27) were fairly close substitutes for one another *at the moment* that that choice was made. If you want to assume for purposes of illustration that this consumer lived in a four-good world and that the steak–pork chop decision was being made *at the same moment* as the concert–movie decision, the order of preference would be movie, pork chop, concert, steak (2.00, 1.27, 1.20, 1.16); he would spend his money on them in that order until his income ran out. Since he was making his choice *at a particular moment* in time, his willingness to pay takes everything into account that affects the amount of utility received from each of these alternatives, including how recently he has had steak or pork chops, or has been to a movie or concert. This is the practical essence of the conclusion in Part I that only the margin was relevant to decision making. The here-and-now automatically takes the past into consideration when it comes to utility from various goods.

As further insight into the working and significance of substitutability as it relates to consumer decisions through investigation of benefit–cost ratios, ask yourself what you would be willing to pay for a single $1.00 food item if you were told that it was the *only* food item you could have. In other words, view all food as a single good. How would the benefit–cost ratio compare to the benefit–cost ratios for steak or pork chops? Undoubtedly the benefit–cost ratio would be much higher than the benefit–cost ratio for steak or pork chops. The reason is that there are no close substitutes for all food as such, so you would be willing to pay a good deal for it; there are, however, excellent substitutes for any *single* food item, so your willingness to pay is reduced in accord with the greater substitutability possible for each food item taken singly.

Conclusion: The extent to which substitutes are available affects *willingness to pay*, which affects consumer choice. Thus the extent to which substitutes are available affects consumer choice. Hardly surprising. Why such care in arriving at that conclusion? *Be sure that you have selected from among all the possible alternatives.* "Substitute" and "alternative" are virtually synonymous. This illustration shows that lack of substitutes tends to increase your willingness to pay. Thus if you fail to consider attractive alternatives, you will tend to be willing to pay more than you otherwise would for less desirable alternatives. An inflated willingness to pay for less desirable alternatives will lead you to accept alternatives that you would not accept if you had considered all the substitutes (alternatives), one of which would prove to be the most desirable.

In summary, the discourse on substitutability verifies an elementary point: *Since you cannot choose what you did not consider, don't overlook anything, or you will necessarily accept less than the best.* Ascertaining that the best alternative is among those considered requires considering all of them.

▶ DECISIONS UNDER PRESENT CERTAINTY: RESOURCE CONSUMPTION ◀

Perhaps the most important decision you make in the deployment of the resources at your control is their division between direct consumption as resources or consumption in the form of economic goods—particularly economic goods produced by other people (as opposed to self-sufficiency goods). To work or not to work—that is the question. Resources provide utility directly. When resources are consumed directly, they provide utility in recreational activity, social and family life, personal enrichment, and so on. Most direct resource consumption would probably fall under the heading of leisure-time activity. Resources may also be consumed indirectly by first converting them to economic goods and consuming them. This conversion may involve market transactions in which you first offer your resources for sale for money and then use the money to buy back economic goods; it may involve *no* market transactions if you use the resources to generate self-sufficiency income (economic goods produced by yourself for yourself).

We can make dollar approximations of the value of resources consumed directly by relying on the opportunity cost principle and the concept of comprehensive income. The money value of the economic goods you create and can create from your resources is the money measure of comprehensive income. In the example in Part I, this was $41,000 for a husband and wife where the husband only was employed in the conventional sense and earned $12,000 from that employment.

The decision to consume resources directly or indirectly must proceed from the base of comprehensive income rather than regular income.

All the alternatives considered must always be in the same "arena." For example, the choice between the concert and movie and between the steak and pork chop did not proceed from the base of comprehensive income; it proceeded from the base of regular income. Both alternatives were within the "arena" of regular income. But the direct versus indirect consumption of resources considers trading utility from economic goods for utility from resources directly, so the "arena" has to be expanded to include both the sources of utility. The "arena," then, is necessarily defined as the sphere bounded by the extent of substitutability. In the steak–pork chops and movie–concert choices, the extent of substitutability —that is, all the alternatives—were within the regular income arena. In the direct versus indirect resource consumption example, some of the alternatives lie inside and some outside the regular income arena, so the arena has to be expanded to include all the alternatives. The concept of comprehensive income does the job. To fail to get all the alternatives into the same arena is to try to compare something with nothing, or perhaps more accurately, to compare a known quantity with an unknown quantity, or possibly, to simply eliminate feasible alternatives. Such an attempt obviously cannot lead to any valid conclusion.

Previously when we were working entirely within the regular income category, it was concluded that the way to maximize utility from that portion of the resource block represented by regular income was to allocate it to various economic goods so that the good purchased was always the one with the highest benefit–cost ratio. You would keep spending in this manner until your income (that portion of your total resources represented by regular income) ran out. The procedure for allocating *all* resources controlled is exactly analogous: Keep picking that alternative next that yields the highest benefit relative to the cost until all resources are expended. As you pick off alternatives, some will lie within the regular income category, some within the self-sufficiency income category, and some within the resource income category. The resource you are allocating is basically the skills and talents you possess per unit time. Since your skills and talents are what they are at any point in time, your allocative decisions consist primarily of an allocation of time. ("Time is money," it is said.)

Let us pursue the example from Part I of the husband and wife with $12,000 regular income from a single wage earner, $15,000 in self-sufficiency income between them, and $14,000 in resource income for a total of $41,000 comprehensive income, plus an unspecified amount of noneconomic income. In money terms, the allocative process may be viewed as beginning with the husband and wife having $41,000 and the time necessary for a minimum of eating, sleeping, and personal maintenance but nothing else—no economic goods, no leisure. They then spend the $41,000 to buy (from themselves, so to speak) whatever they want that the $41,000 worth of resources they control can provide.

How might this couple proceed from a zero level of utility from economic goods and resource income? The first hours should go to the activities with the highest priority (utility). Surely minimums of food, clothing, and shelter would take top claim. The benefit (utility) relative to cost (an hour spent) is highest here. Next, perhaps, small amounts of self-sufficiency income in the form of housekeeping services, for example, might be desired. Then probably some leisure would be desired in the form of various recreational diversions. Education, tastier food, more elaborate clothing and shelter, more and a wider variety of leisure-time activities, and so on would absorb all resources. Certainly none would be unused. If the primary resource is time, it is impossible to refrain from "using" it. It is simply a matter of how effectively it is used.

When all resources are allocated in this manner, this couple has accepted that particular mix of regular income, self-sufficiency income, and resource income (and specific goods in each category) which represents the greatest utility possible from this resource block controlled.

Although this discussion shows the procedure involved in arriving at an optimum resource allocation, it is not yet really practical because it proceeds in terms of a "zero start" assumption. The allocation proceeded under the assumption that you make decisions starting with nothing—a clear slate. But you must proceed from where you are now. Is your current resource allocation the best one, or can you improve your position by reallocating? The test is really quite simple.

> If a change can be made where the benefit is valued more than the loss necessary to get it, an increase in utility can be realized by making the change (reallocation).

This is pure marginal analysis. It looks at changes from where you are now.

We can now approach our example in a more practical way. This couple has $12,000 regular income, $15,000 self-sufficiency income, and $14,000 resource income, for a total comprehensive income of $41,000. The realistic approach would be for this couple to ask themselves, "If we had $41,000 per year with which to buy everything we have, is this the way we would allocate it?" The division between categories is a revelation of what they are saying about their preferences. Since the $41,000 represents, in a sense, maximum potential regular income, it is realistic to view the $12,000–$15,000–$14,000 as reflecting this couple's values. They have made what they are doing somewhat more visible so that they might inspect it more closely. When they see these relationships, they may or may not like what they see, depending on whether they have actually been doing what they presumed they were doing or intended to do. They may conclude, for example, that they are overallocating to self-sufficiency and resource income and underallocating to economic goods. Corrective action? The wife takes a full- or part-time job, or the husband takes a second job. This might allow them to continue to realize two-thirds of the self-sufficiency income but to increase by one-half their regular income. Thus a $5,000 loss in self-sufficiency income (a reduction from $15,000 to $10,000) resulted in a $6,000 gain ($12,000 to $18,000) in regular income, for an increase in comprehensive income of $1,000. An increase in utility represented by a money value of $1,000 resulted from the reallocation.

The usefulness of comprehensive income as a reference point and analytical framework now becomes evident. Since comprehensive income is the maximum potential regular income, it is clear that the relationship between the categories is a reflection of the decision-maker's values of economic goods relative to other sources of utility. For example, this couple is saying that they receive 25 percent *more* utility from their self-sufficiency activity than they do from the economic goods purchased outright: $15,000/$12,000 = 1.25. If they do not really feel this way about it, they are not allocating properly. They should expand or contract either category so that they bring the dollar figures into line with what they believe to be their true feelings.

Comprehensive income can also help evaluate alternatives by serving as a reference point. Suppose that you are considering other ways of providing your current level of utility. Does an alternative constitute an improvement—that is, is it cheaper? Suppose that this couple is considering hiring household help so that the wife can accept outside employment. Suppose that she can earn $7,000 and that the household help will cost $5,000. The $2,000 difference represents a net gain. In other words, by reallocating their resources, they can boost their comprehensive income from $41,000 to $43,000. The fact that this can be accomplished suggests that, relative to the resources controlled by an "average" person on which market prices are based, this wife has resources that are more valuable producing goods other than household services. In formal language, she has a *comparative advantage* in nonhousehold employment. She is a stronger competitor in the nonhousehold labor market than she is in the household labor market relative to other persons in these markets. But before you conclude that the $2,000 improvement in comprehensive income from this resource allocation indicates that the wife should go to work, we must consider something else that we quietly put on the back burner some time ago. That is the matter of noneconomic income. So far, the decision has hinged only on the fairly concrete economic aspects of the problem.

Tackling the noneconomic aspects of this problem requires more wrestling with what has developed to this point. What is the *real* issue? What has *really* happened? How can we *really* comprehend the consequences? Perhaps we can't, but we can certainly come close by looking at a couple of angles. The first angle has been covered. The family increased the monetary value of its resources by $2,000 by redeploying them. They increased the total utility by $2,000 by getting the wife into a situation where she was a stronger relative competitor. The second angle is to look at the $2,000 in relative terms. Is $2,000 much or little? That depends on the size of the "base," which in this case was $41,000. This couple increased the utility from their resources by $2,000/$41,000 = .0487—say, 5 percent. We suspect that the 5 percent looks less robust than the $2,000 to the reader. Perhaps it is because you are used to comparing the $2,000 to regular money income which, unfortunately, leads to an invalid conclusion. Now that we see something of the magnitude of the economic changes, we are in a position to investigate the noneconomic aspects and reach a final decision.

The wife needs to ask herself, "Other things being equal, would I rather take outside employment or stay and work at home?" This will give her some idea of her assessment of the noneconomic utility in one alternative relative to the other. She can then compare her reaction to that question with the 5 percent gain in utility from economic sources connected with outside employment and come to a reasonably enlightened, if not quantifiable, decision. The woman who has never worked outside the home and has been tied down with children for 15 years might react, "Let me out of this madhouse." She seems to be saying that the noneconomic utility from outside employment would substantially exceed the noneconomic utility from "inside" employment. For her, the $2,000 gain in comprehensive income is an understatement of the total utility gains from taking the job. She earns $2,000 with a bonus of an undetermined amount of noneconomic utility thrown in besides. Easy decision. A second woman has worked for 20 years, married late, enjoys homemaking but has not really had a chance to do it until now. Her reaction: "Get out there in that rat race again for a lousy 2,000 bucks a year on top of $41,000 a year now? You gotta be kidding!" Easy decision. The noneconomic losses of outside employment would exceed the economic gain for a reduction in total utility from economic and noneconomic sources.

You can go on with whatever modifications and applications you like. The example of the working wife is a good one to pursue further. Household services constitute a major source of utility; noneconomic utility from outside employment as compared to household employment varies widely among individuals; husbands' inclinations to perform household services vary widely; the earning ability of husband and wife and husband relative to wife affect the decision; women's liberation says that it's time we thought about women in the home—to name a few of the factors making the household service aspect of self-sufficiency income an interesting one to explore. The procedure is of course capable of generalization to any decision with regard to any possible reallocation of personal resources. The issue, as always, is whether the benefit is greater than the benefit from the next best alternative. The benefit in the next best alternative is, of course, the cost of the alternative chosen. Thus changes (reallocations) must always be made so that the benefit exceeds the cost. If such a change cannot be made, you are realizing maximum possible utility from the resources you control.

▶ REVIEW OF THE DECISION-MAKING ◀ MECHANISM

By now it may seem that more than one decision mechanism has been employed. This review is presented to reinforce the conclusion that it is always a comparison of benefits and costs that dictates a choice. Even though the manner or form in which the comparison is presented or used may vary, it is always basically the same. It might be helpful to review the decision model in Chapter 2, plugging what follows into it. This is an expansion of steps III and IV of that model.

First, examine the case for the possible conclusion that two methods of choice were employed in the present chapter. The decision between the pork chops and the steak was reached by comparing willingness to pay (which was a reflection of benefit) with the required payment (which was the money cost). This comparison was the benefit–cost ratio. The utility-maximizing choice was the selection of the alternative with the highest benefit–cost ratio. It was 1.27 for the pork chops and 1.16 for the steak, so the pork chops were selected. In the example of the wife who could earn comprehensive income as self-sufficiency income in the home or as regular income in outside employment, the utility-maximizing decision consisted of changing resource allocation if the gains associated with the change exceeded the losses from the change. A gain–loss ratio was established.

Reworking these two examples in tandem should illustrate that they are actually identical methods. Only the form in which the method appears is different. Gain–loss ratios and benefit–cost ratios are really two ways of arriving at the same conclusion.

STEAK VERSUS PORK CHOPS	HOUSEWORK VERSUS OUTSIDE EMPLOYMENT

Decision Rule
  Pick the alternative with the highest benefit–cost ratio.

Decision Rule
  Pick the alternative where the gains exceed the losses—i.e., pick the numerator of the gain–loss ratio when it is greater than 1.

Benefit–Cost Ratio

$$\frac{\text{willingness to pay}}{\text{required payment}}$$

Gain–Loss Ratio

$$\frac{\text{value of alternative chosen}}{\text{value of the most valuable}}$$
alternative foregone

Data from this example

$$\text{Steak} = \frac{\$2.00}{\$1.72} = 1.16$$

Data from this example

$$\frac{\text{Housework}}{\text{Outside employment}} = \frac{\$5,000}{\$7,000}$$
$$= .79 < 1$$

$$\frac{\text{Pork chops}}{} = \frac{\$1.50}{\$1.18} = 1.27$$

$$\frac{\text{Outside employment}}{\text{Housework}} = \frac{\$7,000}{\$5,000}$$
$$= 1.40 > 1$$

Decision
  Choose pork chops.

Decision
  Choose outside employment.

But the *real* cost of the steak is not $1.72. It is actually the loss of utility from the pork chops; similarly, the *real* cost of the pork chop is not $1.18 but the loss of utility from the steak. Looking at the benefit–cost ratios for each, we can see that a gain of $1.16 in utility from a dollar spent on steak required a loss of $1.27 in utility from that same dollar if it had been spent on pork chops, and vice versa. With the aid of the benefit–cost ratios for the two goods, we can now establish gain–loss ratios for the steak–pork chop example.

$$\frac{\text{pork chops}}{\text{steak}} = \frac{\$1.27}{\$1.16} = 1.09 > 1$$

or

$$\frac{\text{steak}}{\text{pork chops}} = \frac{\$1.16}{\$1.27} = .91 < 1$$

The decision? Choose the pork chops, of course.

It becomes apparent that comparison of benefit–cost ratios leads to the same end as does the examination of a gain–loss ratio. In fact, the ratio of two benefit–cost ratios is a gain–loss ratio. In the steak–pork chop example, the block of resources being allocated was represented by a block of money (dollars); in the housework–outside employment example, the block of resources being allocated was represented by a block of time (hours). In each of these cases, and in all others, there is a comparison of utility received with utility foregone, which is the crux of the decision mechanism. It may be more convenient to express this comparison in one way in one situation and another way in another situation. When the choice is between goods that have money prices, the benefit–cost ratios seem to be a little more useful directly; when the choice is with regard to possible redeployment of a resource block controlled between alternatives that do not have specific money market prices determined by an outside condition (the market or government edict or whatever), direct reliance on a gain–loss ratio seems to be the most useful. In any event, the issue is not significant since all roads lead to Rome.

SUMMARY

1 • Economic choices tend to relate to categories of conditions of *present certainty, future certainty, future unavoidable uncertainty,* or *future avoidable uncertainty.* These categories might be labeled *consumption decisions, safe investment decisions, risky investment decisions,* and *insurance decisions,* respectively.

2 • Practical choice consists of two basic parts: (1) identification of alternatives, and (2) selection of the best alternative. They are equally important.

3 • Identification of the alternatives requires reflection on what you *really* want and the ways in which it may be provided.

4 • Selection of the best (utility-maximizing) alternative requires selecting the alternative where the ratio of willingness to pay relative to the required payment (benefit–cost ratio) is highest, or selecting the alternative where the gains relative to the losses (gain–loss ratio) is highest.

5 • The ratio of two benefit–cost ratios is a gain–loss ratio.

6 • No matter how the machinery is designed or how the gains and losses are measured, a decision always

> hinges on the utility gained relative to the utility
> forgone.

study materials

1 • Define and explain decisions that are categorized as *present certainty*.

2 • Why shouldn't every decision be subjected to very close scrutiny?

3 • What are the two basic parts of every practical consumer choice?

4 • Why is each part considered of equal importance?

5 • Why should the consumer who is trying to improve consumption stress the recognition of more and more alternatives?

6 • What is meant by the statement "Services are simply the least durable of the nondurables"?

7 • How can economic analysis be used to analyze the decision-making process itself?

8 • Using benefit–cost ratios, how can the substitutability of goods be determined?

9 • What is the relationship between substitutes and alternatives?

10 • How can resource consumption be analyzed as a decision made under present certainty?

footnote

[1] Professor C. Northcote Parkinson is the author of *Parkinson's Law* (Boston: Houghton Mifflin Company, 1957), which is a humorous yet serious explanation of seemingly peculiar personal, corporate, and governmental behavior. With his tongue only partly in his cheek, Professor Parkinson observes that a decision-making body will purchase vast systems of equipment and otherwise make big decisions with very little deliberation but will agonize interminably over the purchase of a coffee maker. He argues that the coffee maker is of a magnitude that every member of the decision-making body can understand, so he takes an interest in it. The deliberative process therefore grinds on and on. Complicated decisions, however, are beyond the grasp of most individuals, so they gloss over the issues, hoping that their ignorance will not surface in the process. Individual consumers seem bent on supporting his theory when they fail to get the facts and fail to weigh the issues relating to important decisions where the stakes are great but nit-pick over minor matters.

chapter
11

CONSUMPTION
DECISIONS:
DURABLES

transportation:
a model analysis

Every consumer has a need for transportation. Just as it is absolutely essential for you to have certain minimums of shelter (housing) and nutrition (food), it is absolutely essential for you to be able to move from one place to another (transportation). This chapter will examine some of the alternative forms and means of transportation. The framework will be as it always is—where can you get the most utility for the least cost? This will lead to utility maximization.

This analysis will consist of (1) investigating the ways in which utility flows from sources of transportation, and (2) tallying the costs of various forms of transportation. Point (1) above will lead to determination of the alternatives available, and point (2) will lead to selection of the best alternative. The emphasis in this chapter (which will center on the automobile) will be on costs. We will see that costs fall into one of two categories, fixed costs *or* variable costs. *The division of costs between fixed and variable is a condition encountered when you are dealing with durables, as opposed to nondurables or services. The significance of this is that the utility-maximizing alternative is different as the durable good is used in different amounts. In other words, the best buy depends on a relationship between the proportion of costs that are fixed or variable and on the amount of use the good will get. Our focus in this chapter will be on the durable good, automobile, and the identification of benefits and costs associated with its ownership and use. We are following the decision model of Chapter 2 but elaborating some of the steps in great detail for instructional purposes.*

▶ IDENTIFICATION OF THE ◀ ALTERNATIVES

Although we will finally focus on automobile ownership, let's back up for a moment to the issue of transportation in general. What is the nature of the utility from transportation and its alternative sources? This is a much more complex question than it first appears, and answering it carefully is absolutely essential if we are to be spared the necessity of concluding later that most automobile owners are stupid. Although it seems unlikely that such a sweeping condemnation should be made, it is nonetheless possible that many decisions on car ownership would be made differently if consumers organized their thoughts more carefully. Perhaps many car owners are not stupid—just careless in their decisions.

Although transportation is primarily concerned with getting from one place to another, much utility from transportation stems from sources other than the transport itself. It is necessary to consider negative as well as positive utility. For example, the net utility of a ride in a cab is the positive utility of getting from one place to another minus the negative utility (disutility) of dealing with a cantakerous cabbie or, possibly, plus the additional utility of a cabbie who is a stimulating conversationalist. It is the nontransport (noneconomic) utility from transportation that often tips the scale as to what is finally chosen. Table 11–1 lists alternative methods of transportation, their sources and nature of utility, and their sources of costs. It is offered as an example that you may be able to extend.

The possibility of negative utility creates a point of possible confusion that must be clarified. Recall that costs were defined as the loss of utility undergone to get a greater utility. Should not any negative utility, then, simply be listed as a cost? To be sure, you could proceed in this way and be correct. The positive utility of the cab ride for which you would be willing to pay $5.00 costs $3.00 for the fare and $1.00 worth of disutility from the disagreeable cabbie (you would be willing to pay $1.00 to avoid him). Your total costs are $3.00 + $1.00 = $4.00 against $5.00 utility from the ride. "Profit" = $5.00 − $4.00 = $1.00. On the other hand, suppose that we view the utility as $5.00 positive utility less $1.00 negative utility. Net utility = $5.00 − $1.00 = $4.00. Cost = $3.00. "Profit" = $4.00 − $3.00 = $1.00. Same conclusion.

Calling this item a negative utility rather than a cost simplifies the analysis. It will be easier to proceed if we agree to label as costs only those things to which dollar values can be unambiguously attached— that is, for which specific money prices are available. Costs then will consist of economic costs only. This will leave all those utilities (positive and negative), for which dollar values are less readily available, in one group under the benefit heading. This procedure therefore expresses all noneconomic benefit and costs as "net noneconomic benefits" as a single entry under "noneconomic benefits." Thus consideration of the noneconomic utility from an alternative will cause the utility from economic sources only to understate the attractiveness of the alternative if the noneconomic utility from the alternative is greater than the noneconomic disutility (cost); the utility from economic sources only overstates the attractiveness of the alternative if the noneconomic utility from an alternative is less than the noneconomic disutility (cost).

Let us examine some of the major alternative forms of transportation, listing the major sources of benefits and costs and listing under costs only those items to which a specific dollar value can be attached by virtue of our ability to compute them on the basis of market prices or opportunity cost. Under the benefit column will be listed all major sources of utility gained plus any source of utility lost that could not appear under the cost column because we could not attach a dollar value to it (Table 11–1).

Notice that, according to the previously agreed-on rule, everything that appears in the cost column can be specifically identified in dollar terms. Some things under the utility column are more difficult to evaluate. For example, there is no market price for the utility of making a favorable impression on the neighbors. Thus the utility column contains

Table 11–1

ALTERNATIVE METHODS OF TRANSPORTATION

ALTERNATIVE FORMS OF TRANSPOR-TATION	UTILITY (POSITIVE OR NEGATIVE)	COSTS
Walking	1 • Very limited mobility	1 • Negligible cost in time
	2 • Exercise	2 • Some clothing costs: weather
	3 • ?	3 • Shoe wear
	4 • ?	4 • ?
Bicycle	1 • Limited mobility	1 • Bicycle and upkeep
	2 • Exercise	2 • Some special clothing
	3 • Worry about theft	3 • ?
	4 • ?	4 • ?
Motorcycle	1 • Good mobility	1 • Motorcycle and upkeep
	2 • Exhilaration	2 • Special clothing and equipment
	3 • Dangerous	3 • ?
	4 • ?	4 • ?
Keep old car	1 • Excellent mobility	1 • Remaining value of car
	2 • Comfort	2 • Cost of operation
	3 • Feeling of "command"	3 • Cost of storage and parking
	4 • Feeling of "attachment"	4 • ?
	5 • Knowing what to expect	5 • ?
	6 • ?	6 • ?
Buy used car	1 • Excellent mobility	1 • Cost of car
	2 • Comfort	2 • Cost of operation
	3 • Feeling of "command"	3 • Cost of storage and parking
	4 • ?	4 • ?
Buy new car	1 • Excellent mobility	1 • Same as used car or old car but generally higher
	2 • Comfort	
	3 • Feeling of "command"	2 • ?
	4 • "Personalized" aspect of new car ownership	3 • ?
	5 • The "talk of the town"	
	6 • Safer?	
	7 • ?	

Table 11–1 (continued)

ALTERNATIVE FORMS OF TRANSPOR- TATION	UTILITY (POSITIVE OR NEGATIVE)	COSTS
Lease new car	1 • Excellent mobility 2 • Comfort 3 • Feeling of "command" 4 • No capital outlay 5 • Less responsibility? 6 • ?	1 • Rental payments 2 • ? 3 • ?
Public transport	1 • Fair mobility, depending on location 2 • Limited to schedules 3 • No responsibility 4 • ?	1 • Tickets 2 • ? 3 • ?

some things for which prices can be computed and some things for which they cannot. For example, a new car provides miles of transportation. It is *relatively* easy to compute this cost since we know all the necessary prices of the inputs (the car itself, gas, oil, tires, insurance, taxes, etc.) and we know how much output (miles) we can get for the inputs. Thus we can determine the cost of utility from the *transport* (economic) services per se for any given car. If we conclude that 10,000 miles per year will be driven and that they will cost $1,500 from a Cadillac, but only $1,000 from a Ford, we have inadvertently concluded that all the nontransport utility from the Cadillac over and above the nontransport utility from the Ford costs $1,500 − $1,000 = $500. You then ask whether the extra comfort and prestige of the Cadillac over and above the Ford was worth $500. You base your decision to buy on the answer. In general, this is a useful procedure because it allows you to make a yes–no decision on a residual figure (the $500 cost of the package of noneconomic benefits and costs), which was derived from fairly "hard" information on the cost of mileage (the economic benefits).

If you do not adopt this procedure, you must state beforehand whether you are willing to pay $147, $528, $1,025, or what for the extra comfort and prestige. That may be hard to do. But chances are that you can look at the $500 and see fairly clearly whether you think the package of "net noneconomic benefits" is worth a $500 sacrifice in other economic goods. If so, you have avoided a lot of troublesome input to the problem.

Shortly we will reach a conclusion as to which form of transportation represents the best buy. This would suggest that there is one, and only one, correct decision, which applies universally. Not true! If it were, we would observe that since wealthy people tend to select more costly forms of transportation than poor people, wealthy people as a group tend to make poorer personal economic decisions. After all, is not the best buy the best buy regardless of your level of money income? Not at all. Remember that both the wealthy and poor consumer are desirous of getting the maximum utility their money will buy. The presence of noneconomic utility can cause the wealthy consumer to make quite a different decision than a poor consumer on the same good. Recalling the law of diminishing returns and the role of the income constraint, we can verify that a cheap form of transportation for a poor person and an expensive form of transportation for the wealthy person may represent good decisions by each.

The key lies in the noneconomic utility associated with transportation. Assume that the cost of operating any given car is the same per mile whether owned by a wealthy or a poor person. This means (to go back to our earlier example) that either person driving 10,000 miles per year will find his dollar cost to be $1,500 in a Cadillac or $1,000 in a Ford. In each case the cost of the noneconomic utility is $1,500 − $1,000 = $500. Assume also that the noneconomic utility represented by this $500 is the same for the wealthy and poor consumer alike. Suppose that this noneconomic utility is represented by 1,200 utiles. Suppose also that the poor consumer is getting 4 utiles per additional $1.00 spent (a utile therefore costs $.25), which is the maximum price he is willing to pay, and that the wealthy consumer is getting only 2 utiles per additional $1.00 spent (a utile therefore costs $.50), which is the maximum price he is willing to pay.[1] The following table shows the route to a different decision by the two consumers, even though each would have gotten the same utility from either car and it was available to each at the same money cost.

	WEALTHY CONSUMER	POOR CONSUMER
1 • Utiles per additional $1.00 spent	2 utiles	4 utiles
2 • Willing to pay for additional utile	$.50	$.25
3 • Noneconomic utility	1,200 utiles	1,200 utiles
4 • Price at which these 1,200 utiles can be bought	$500	$500
5 • Price willingly paid for the 1,200 utiles [(2) × (3)]	$600	$300
6 • Decision	Buy Cadillac	Buy Ford

The decision between the Ford and the Cadillac for each consumer was reached by comparing what the noneconomic utility from the Cadillac would cost and what it could be purchased for. The ratios of $600/$500 = 1.20 for the wealthy consumer and $300/$500 = .60 for the poor consumer are benefit–cost ratios with respect to the noneconomic utility from the Cadillac. Recall from the previous chapter that a benefit–cost ratio of less than 1 indicated clearly that the alternative being considered would *not* be chosen because the required payment was higher than the willingness to pay. Whether the wealthy consumer actually buys the Cadillac depends on whether there are other alternatives for the $500 with higher benefit–cost ratios.

Following good decision-making procedures therefore produces the resultant differences in living style often observed at different money income levels.[2]

► SELECTION OF THE BEST ◄
ALTERNATIVE

The following analysis sets forth in more detail the actual accounting of costs that can be measured. For simplicity at the outset, we will assume that the only choices to be considered from Table 11–1 are whether to keep the old car, buy a used car, or buy a new car. We are not saying that leasing or walking are out of the question; we are just saying that, given the utility schedule of this individual, he can eliminate all but these three possibilities because they are so obviously inferior. He is required to use a car in his job and leasing in his area is not available. Some additional assumptions will make the problem relatively simple. Assume that (1) if the decision is to buy, there will be no financing—cash deal, (2) if he buys a car, it will be a car of about the same size, model, and price as the one he has now, and (3) the market reflects perfectly the conditions of the cars. In other words, if he puts $100 of tires on his old car and then trades immediately, the dealer will give him $100 more for his old car. This eliminates any problem of timing the purchase advantageously.

In accord with previous suggestions, we will compute the cost of the product per unit of utility for those utilities that can be identified in fairly concrete terms (mileage in this case) and then ask ourselves whether the noneconomic utility from a car providing more expensive mileage is worth the difference.

The discussion, as always, focuses on cost. There are two major categories of costs: (1) fixed costs, and (2) variable costs. *Fixed costs are those costs that are the same no matter how much the good is used or not used.* *Variable costs are costs that rise or fall as the good is used more or less.*

In the case of an automobile, fixed costs are such things as the license; probably insurance, the cost of which is usually largely independent of mileage driven; interest foregone on the money tied up in the car; and the largest fixed cost item, depreciation. Depreciation is the decline in the car's value from one year to the next. This may be very substantial, particularly for a new car. Although the mileage driven can be expected to have some influence on the amount of depreciation realized, it seems that the age of the car is the most important determinant of its value; hence depreciation is most appropriately visualized as a fixed cost. Variable costs include such things as gasoline, oil, tires, and maintenance.

The division of costs between fixed and variable costs has far-reaching significance for our problem. To illustrate the basic issue, imagine that you owned a car and all the costs were fixed costs and that they were $1,000 per year. If you drove that car only 1 mile that year, your costs would have been $1,000 per mile ($1,000/1 = $1,000 per mile); if you drove 100 miles, your cost would have been $10 per mile ($1,000/100 = $10 per mile); if you drove 10,000 miles, your costs would have been 10 cents per mile ($1,000/10,000 = 10 cents per mile); if you had driven 100,000 miles, your costs would have been 1 cent per mile ($1,000/100,000 = 1 cent per mile). Cost per mile drops as the number of miles driven rises because the lump sum of $1,000 is spread over more miles.

Now imagine the opposite extreme: all costs are variable costs. If you do not drive the car at all, you have no costs. If you drive 1 mile, you have, say, 10 cents in costs, which is the cost per mile. Assuming that costs *per mile* do not rise as you drive more miles, your cost per mile is 10 cents no matter how many miles you drive.

In reality, costs are partly variable and partly fixed. Thus total costs per mile = fixed costs per mile + variable costs per mile. Since variable costs per mile are constant as more miles are driven, but fixed costs per mile drop as more miles are driven, total costs per mile will also drop as more miles are driven. How much they drop as more miles are driven depends on what proportion of the costs are fixed and what proportion are variable. The higher the proportion of fixed costs, the more rapidly cost per mile will drop as more miles are driven. This introduces an interesting complexity if a comparison is made between two cars that have different proportions of fixed and variable costs. It means that the comparison is valid only for some specified number of miles. A conclusion as to which is the better buy if you drive 10,000 miles a year may not be the same as your conclusion if you drive 25,000 miles per year. The distressing result is that you may not know how many miles you want to drive until you know what they will cost, but you cannot determine what they will cost until you know how many miles you will drive. The practical solution is to estimate the cost per mile for, say, 5,000, 10,000, 15,000,

20,000, and 25,000 miles for each car if you think that the two cars have importantly different proportions of fixed and variable costs.

Table 11–2A

TOTAL VARIABLE AND FIXED COSTS FOR 1 YEAR FOR THREE AUTOMOBILES (10,000 MILES DRIVEN; ALL COSTS CONSTANT EXCEPT DEPRECIATION AND INTEREST FOREGONE)

	1969 MODEL	1973 MODEL	1975 MODEL
Variable costs			
Gas and oil	$ 400	$ 400	$ 400
Maintenance, tires, etc.	150	150	150
Total variable costs	$ 550	$ 550	$ 550
Fixed costs			
Insurance	$ 300	$ 300	$ 300
License	50	50	50
Depreciation	160	600	1,000
Interest foregone at 8%	51	176	320
Total fixed costs	$ 561	$1,126	$1,670
Total costs (fixed and variable)	$1,111	$1,676	$2,220

Assume that the comparison shown in Table 11–2A represents your estimate of the costs for your car—a 1969 model, a 1973 model you are considering as a replacement, and a 1975 new car also considered as a replacement. Assume that each car cost $4,000 new and that each would be driven 10,000 miles per year. Assume also, for the moment, that all costs except depreciation and interest foregone are the same on each car. This will focus attention on these two major items of fixed cost. Other costs will be varied later to add more realism.

Interest foregone must be listed as a cost, even though the purchase is not being financed and no interest will actually be *paid*. Recall that cost is that which is lost or sacrificed to gain something else. We assume that if you did not own the car, you would have had that money available to earn interest; therefore, that interest you did not receive because you owned the car is a cost in every sense of the word. The fact that you might have bought a boat if you had not bought the car and would therefore not have collected the interest anyway does not alter the argument. In that case, the interest foregone would have been part of the cost of owning the boat. Cost is identified by asking: "How much worse off am I for owning the car than I *could* have been if I had not owned the car?" The best you could have done would have been to collect interest on the money you tied up in auto ownership.

The derivation of the figures for depreciation and interest foregone is presented in Table 11–3. Column 3 of Table 11–3 is a reasonably close approximation of the annual depreciation you can expect to realize on an "average" automobile. In general, depreciation is substantially greater in the early years of a car's life. This apparently reflects the strong preference of the average consumer for a new rather than an old car. The

Table 11–3

SCHEDULE OF DEPRECIATION AND INTEREST FOREGONE ON A $4,000 AUTOMOBILE

(1) MODEL YEAR	(2) AGE OF CAR	(3) ANNUAL DEPRECIATION AS A % OF INITIAL COST	(4) ANNUAL DEPRECIATION ON A $4,000 CAR [(3) × $4,000]	(5) VALUE OF CAR AT BEGINNING OF YEAR ($4,000 MINUS PREVIOUS DEPRECIATION)	(6) INTEREST FOREGONE AT 8% [8% × (5)]
1975	1	25	$1,000	$4,000	$ 320
1974	2	20	800	3,000	240
1973	3	15	600	2,200	176
1972	4	10	400	1,600	128
1971	5	8	320	1,200	96
1970	6	6	240	880	70
1969	7	4	160	640	51
1968	8	2	80	480	38
1967	9	2	80	400	32
1966	10	2	80	320	26
1965	11	2	80	240	19
1964	12	2	80	160	13
1963	13	2	80	80	6
1962	14	0	0	0	0
		100	$4,000		$1,215

exact percentages can be substituted for any particular car by consulting the *Official Used Car Guide,* which gives wholesale values of various makes and models in various parts of the country. It is published by the National Automobile Dealers Association and is reasonably accessible to anyone interested; automobile dealers, automobile financers, and many libraries can be expected to have it. If the *Guide* says that the wholesale value of a car at the end of its third year of life is $2,000 and at the end of its fourth year of life is $1,200, the fourth year's depreciation is $800. If the car's new value is $5,000, the percent of new value represented by the fourth year's depreciation is $800/$5,000 × 100 = 16 percent. By completing these computations for each year, you can get a reasonably good idea of depreciation patterns for various cars.

The other fixed cost that varies with the age of the car is interest foregone. Assuming an interest rate of 8 percent, the interest foregone is 8 percent times the value of the car that year. If you are tempted to take 8 percent of the initial cost of the car every year for interest foregone ($320 every year in this example), you are still unconvinced as to the nature and role of depreciation. You are not committing $4,000 to this use every year. Only the first year did you have $4,000 tied up. By the second year your car was worth $1,000 less, so you forewent the interest on only $3,000. What happened to the $1,000? Did it simply disappear? Certainly not! It appeared as part of your costs in the first year. To take an interest charge of the full $4,000 and to take depreciation as well would be to count some costs twice. Cars are costly enough without doing that! This is the essence of a durable good. You do not really spend for it when you purchase it; you spend for it each year according to the amount of it you use up.

It is a simple matter to convert all the values in Table 11–2A to a cost per mile basis by dividing all the figures by 10,000 miles, the assumed number of miles driven per year. Per mile costs are given in Table 11–2B.

If we assume that variable costs per mile remain at 5.5 cents per mile when 25,000 miles are driven, they are $1,375 for the 25,000 miles. Fixed costs by definition remain as they were when only 10,000 miles were driven. Total costs for 25,000 miles per year are therefore

$1,375 + $561 = $1,936 for the 1969 model
$1,375 + $1,126 = $2,501 for the 1973 model
$1,375 + $1,670 = $3,045 for the 1975 model

Dividing each of these figures by 25,000 miles gives per mile costs of

7.74 cents for the 1969 model
10.00 cents for the 1973 model
12.18 cents for the 1975 model

Figure 11–1 shows costs per mile for the three cars for any mileage driven.

Table 11–2B

PER MILE VARIABLE AND FIXED COSTS IN CENTS FOR 1 YEAR FOR THREE AUTOMOBILES (10,000 MILES DRIVEN; ALL COSTS CONSTANT EXCEPT DEPRECIATION AND INTEREST FOREGONE)

	1969 MODEL	1973 MODEL	1975 MODEL
Variable costs			
Gas and oil	4.00	4.00	4.00
Maintenance, tires, etc.	1.50	1.50	1.50
Total variable costs	5.50	5.50	5.50
Fixed costs			
Insurance	3.00	3.00	3.00
License	.50	.50	.50
Depreciation	1.60	6.00	10.00
Interest foregone at 8%	.51	1.76	3.20
Total fixed costs	5.61	11.26	16.70
Total costs (fixed and variable)	11.11	16.76	22.20

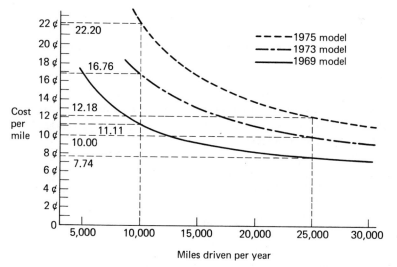

FIGURE 11–1   •   Cost curves for three automobiles. (All costs constant except depreciation and interest foregone.)

Some characteristics of the curves should be considered. They all slope downward to the right, indicating that costs per mile drop as the number of miles driven increases. This is due to the spreading of the fixed costs over more miles. Second, the 1969 model gives the most economical mileage and the 1975 model the least economical mileage, regardless of the number of miles driven. This is shown by the fact that the curves never cross—the lowest curve is always the lowest and the highest curve always highest. Third, although the 1969 model always gives the most economical mileage, its advantage diminishes as the number of miles driven rises. This is shown by the fact that the vertical distance between the curves lessens as the miles driven increases. At 10,000 miles the cost difference between the 1969 and 1973 models is

16.76 cents per mile − 11.11 cents per mile = 5.65 cents per mile

At 25,000 miles the difference is

10.00 cents per mile − 7.74 cents per mile = 2.26 cents per mile

Fourth, it follows, then, that 5.65 cents is the cost per mile of the noneconomic utility if you drive 10,000 miles per year, and 2.26 cents per mile if you drive 25,000 miles per year. The distance between the curves is always the cost per mile of the noneconomic utility over and above the cost of the utility of the next cheapest transportation. If you drive 25,000 miles per year, you can ask yourself whether you are willing to pay 2.26 cents per mile for noneconomic utility. If your answer is no, you should keep the 1969 model. Obviously, these comparisons can be made for any models considered for any mileage driven. Fifth, you can always convert from a cost per mile basis to a total cost basis by multiplying the cost per mile for any given mileage by that mileage. For example, the cost per mile for the 1969 model if driven 25,000 miles is 7.74 cents per mile. 25,000 × 7.74 cents = $1,936 total cost.

For some purposes it may be more meaningful to view things on a total cost basis. It is entirely possible that it may be more meaningful to view the cost of the noneconomic utility in terms of costs per year rather than cost per mile. If so, multiply 2.26 cents, the difference in cost per mile of the noneconomic utility between the 1969 and 1973 models, by 25,000 miles. 25,000 × 2.26 cents = $565, which is this year's cost of noneconomic utility from the 1973 model over and above the cost of the 1969 model. Similarly, 10,000 miles × 5.65 cents per mile cost of the noneconomic utility = $565 annual cost. The annual cost of noneconomic utility is the same no matter how many miles are driven because the only costs that are different among the different models are fixed costs, which do not change as mileage changes.

The next major step toward realism is to recognize that the maintenance expenditure on an older car can be expected to be higher than on the new car. In fact, the cost of mileage for different-aged cars often boils down to the relationship between depreciation and interest foregone on new cars compared to maintenance expenditure on old cars. At some point, added maintenance costs can be expected to more than cancel out the depreciation and interest economies of an older car. Assume that maintenance costs are 3.50 cents per mile higher for the 1969 car than for the 1973 car and 1.50 cents per mile higher for the 1973 car than for the 1975 car. This would make maintenance costs 1.30 cents per mile for the 1975 car, 2.80 cents per mile for the 1973 car and 6.30 cents per mile

Table 11–4A

TOTAL VARIABLE AND FIXED COSTS FOR 1 YEAR FOR THREE AUTOMOBILES (10,000 MILES DRIVEN; DEPRECIATION, INTEREST FOREGONE, AND MAINTENANCE VARY WITH AGE OF CAR)

	1969 MODEL	1973 MODEL	1975 MODEL
Variable costs			
Gas and oil	$ 270	$ 270	$ 270
Maintenance, tires, etc.	630	280	130
Total variable costs	$ 900	$ 550	$ 400
Fixed costs			
Insurance	$ 300	$ 300	$ 300
License	50	50	50
Depreciation	160	600	1,000
Interest foregone at 8%	51	176	320
Total fixed costs	$ 561	$1,126	$1,670
Total costs (fixed and variable)	$1,461	$1,676	$2,070

for the 1969 car. Tables 11–4A and 11–4B are the same as Tables 11–2A and 11–2B except for this change in maintenance costs.

Table 11–4B

PER MILE VARIABLE AND FIXED COSTS IN CENTS FOR 1 YEAR FOR THREE AUTOMOBILES (10,000 MILES DRIVEN; DEPRECIATION, INTEREST FOREGONE, AND MAINTENANCE VARY WITH AGE OF CAR)

	1969 MODEL	1973 MODEL	1975 MODEL
Variable costs			
Gas and oil	2.70	2.70	2,70
Maintenance, tires, etc.	6.30	2.80	1.30
Total variable costs	9.00	5.50	4.00
Fixed costs			
Insurance	3.00	3.00	3.00
License	.50	.50	.50
Depreciation	1.60	6.00	10.00
Interest foregone at 8%	.51	1.76	3.20
Total fixed costs	5.61	11.26	16.70
Total costs (fixed and variable)	14.61	16.76	20.70

If we again assume variable costs per mile are the same for each car, no matter how many miles driven, we get the following for 25,000 miles:

25,000 miles × 9.00 cents per mile = $2,250 variable costs
    + $561 fixed costs = $2,811 total costs for the 1969 model

25,000 miles × 5.50 cents per mile = $1,375 variable costs
    + $1,126 fixed costs = $2,501 total costs for the 1973 model

25,000 miles × 4.00 cents per mile = $1,000 variable costs
    + $1,670 fixed costs = $2,670 total costs for the 1975 model

On a per mile basis the costs would be

$2,811/25,000 miles = 11.24 cents for the 1969 model
$2,501/25,000 miles = 10.00 cents for the 1973 model
$2,670/25,000 miles = 10.68 cents for the 1975 model

The data from Table 11–4B plus the same data for other mileages driven is given in Figure 11–2. Figure 11–2 is the counterpart to Figure

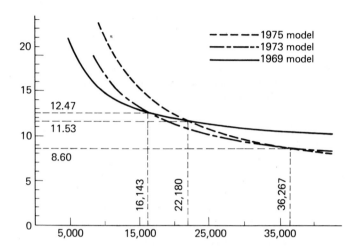

FIGURE 11–2 • Cost curves for three automobiles. (Depreciation, interest foregone, and maintenance vary with age of car.)

11–1, where it was assumed that maintenance costs were the same on all cars. When maintenance costs vary with the age of the car, the most economical car is determined by the mileage driven.

The graph shows clearly a number of things. At low mileages the cost relationships between cars depicted in Figure 11–1 is preserved. However, things change dramatically when more miles are driven. At mileages over 16,143 the 1973 model becomes more economical than the 1969 model; at 22,180 miles the 1975 model becomes more economical than the 1969 model but less economical than the 1973 model; at more than 36,267 miles per year the 1975 model becomes more economical than even the 1973 model.[3]

Again, why does all this work out this way? The result hinges on the substitutability of variable operating costs (maintenance) for fixed capital costs (depreciation and interest). At low mileages the fixed costs are very high per mile because there are few miles over which to spread them. Thus any car that has low fixed costs is more economical than a car with high fixed costs. It does not matter that maintenance may be high because maintenance relates to miles driven.

As before, the cost of noneconomic utility can be readily determined by multiplying the cost per mile by the mileage to get the difference in the cost of this utility. Obviously, if you drive more than 36,267 miles per year any noneconomic utility from the new car is free because the new car is the best buy of the three on transportation grounds alone. Similarly, any noneconomic utility from a 1973 model not contained in a 1969 model is free if you drive more than 16,143 miles per year. The possibility should not be overlooked, however, that for some people an old car has more noneconomic utility than a new car. People who like to talk about how many miles they have on their cars seem to fall into this category. This, too, can be taken into account from the graphs. At 25,000 miles the cost of the 1969 model is 1.24 cents per mile higher than for the 1973 model (11.24 cents − 10.00 cents = 1.24 cents). 25,000 miles × 1.24 cents = $310.00. Are you willing to pay $310.00 per year or 1.24 cents per mile if you drive 25,000 miles to be able to say that "Old Bertha has 200,000 miles on her and is still going strong." If so, keep Bertha; if not, trade.

You now have before you the framework that will lead to a good decision. If you have not already done so, rework the previous problem comparing three (or more) cars you might consider owning. This is a good time to come to a concrete decision as to just how economical that economy car really is for *you* and how much the Belchfire 8 you have had your eye on would *really* set you back.

The foregoing examples assumed that the car would not be financed. How is the procedure altered if the car is financed? Very simply. Instead of entering interest *foregone* as a cost, enter interest *paid* as a cost. Do not fall victim to a possible temptation to enter interest paid in *addition* to interest foregone. Remember that cost refers to what is lost or sacrificed to get something else. Your car is worth, say, $3,000. If the going rate of interest is 8 percent, the cost of the $3,000 is 8% × $3,000 = $240. If you *have* the $3,000 and buy the car with it, you are $240 worse off than if you did not own the car. If you do *not* have the $3,000 but borrow it and actually pay the $240 in interest, you are again $240 worse off than if you did not have the car. You do not add $240 of interest foregone because you do not forego it unless you have the $3,000 in the first place!

If the car is only partly financed, you add the interest actually paid on the money borrowed to the interest foregone on that part of the car you own—your equity.

Interest foregone must be considered for durables because you have more money tied up than is actually providing utility at any one point in time. The depreciation schedule reveals the rationale for this argument. Since a year's depreciation represents the amount of the good actually used up that year, a durable might be viewed as several year's worth of nondurables hooked together. In order to get any one year's worth of "nondurable" you have to take several together in a lump, which means, in the car example, that the first year's value of the "nondurable" was $1,000 (first year depreciation), but $4,000 had to be spent to get it. You could not buy $1,000 worth as you could an actual nondurable. Since you have to wait to collect the rest of the benefit, you should charge as a cost of the future benefit to be secured the interest that could have been earned while you were waiting.

SUMMARY

1 • Money income is subject to diminishing marginal utility because economic goods as a group are subject to diminishing marginal utility with respect to noneconomic sources of utility.

2 • The diminishing marginal utility of money income will frequently lead a wealthy consumer to purchase what a poor consumer will not purchase because the wealthy consumer is willing to spend more of his less valuable dollars for the noneconomic utility of luxury goods.

3 • A decision between different durable goods is influenced by the proportion of fixed and variable costs and the amount of use the good will get.

4 • A durable good with *low fixed costs* and *high variable costs* will tend to be the best buy on purely economic grounds if the good will be used *little*.

5 • A durable good with *high fixed costs* and *low variable costs* will tend to be the best buy on purely economic grounds if the good will be used *much*.

---

study materials

1 • List the alternative transportation choices that are reasonable for you. Assess each in terms of utility and costs.

2 • Explain what nontransport utility is in an automobile.

3 • Why would a "good" decision on an automobile for a relatively poor consumer not necessarily be a "good" decision for a wealthy consumer?

4 • List the desirable features and characteristics of an automobile for you.

5 • What parts of a used automobile should you check very carefully before deciding to buy?

6 • Which automobile costs are generally considered to be fixed? Which variable?

7 • Summarize the analysis used in the chapter in considering the 1969, 1973, and 1975 model automobiles.

8 • Which model was considered the best choice and under which circumstances?

9 • Why would adding interest paid to interest forgone be an error?

10 • State a best-buy-rule-of-thumb for durable goods with fixed and variable costs being high and low, respectively, and vice versa, with regard to the amount of use the durable good will get.

footnotes

[1] This suggests that money income itself is subject to diminishing marginal utility, although some economists object to this particular statement on other technical grounds. If any particular economic good is subject to diminishing marginal utility as compared to other economic goods, it would seem to follow that economic goods in general are subject to diminishing marginal utility as compared to noneconomic sources of utility. Since money is a representation of economic goods, it follows that money income is subject to diminishing marginal utility. There is no reason to suppose that the law of diminishing marginal utility ceases to function at the bounds of conventional economies. Although the law has profound economic implications, it is not basically an economic law. It is basically a human law which applies to human experience. Since human experience certainly transcends the bounds of conventional economics, it is reasonable to suppose that the law of diminishing marginal utility does also.

[2] This is obviously an issue apart from whether money income should be redistributed more evenly or whether we should try to cultivate in the wealthy a greater utility from philanthropic uses of their money. This analysis does not address itself to the ethics of income distribution or of shaping the utility function of certain classes of people.

[3] The appendix shows *precisely* how the 16,143, 22,180, and 36,267 figures were derived mathematically.

appendix

"BREAKEVEN" MILEAGES FOR THREE AUTOMOBILE MODELS

It was determined from the graph that the cost per mile was the lowest for the 1969 model if fewer than 16,143 miles were driven, but lowest for the 1973 model if between 16,143 and 22,180 miles were driven, and lowest for the 1975 model if more than 36,267 miles were driven. Although the graph is a useful device for showing relationships, it is important that it be drawn very precisely if it is to yield exact answers. If you want to get directly at the mileages at which any two cars cost equally to operate on a per mile basis, the following procedure is the most efficient. The question is: At what mileage is the cost per mile of (say) the 1969 model equal to the cost per mile of the 1973 model? Or at what mileage is the following true?

(1)   cost per mile of 1969 model = cost per mile of 1973 model

but the cost per mile is made up of fixed costs per mile and variable costs per mile, so

(2)   cost per mile = fixed costs per mile + variable costs per mile

Thus (1) becomes

(3)   fixed costs per mile$_{1969}$ + variable costs per mile$_{1969}$
        = fixed costs per mile$_{1973}$ + variable costs per mile$_{1973}$

or

(4) $$FCPM_{1969} + VCPM_{1969} = FCPM_{1973} + VCPM_{1973}$$

but

(5) $$FCPM = \frac{\text{fixed costs}}{\text{miles}}$$

and $VCPM$ is the same no matter how many miles are driven, so (4) becomes

(6) $$\frac{\text{fixed costs}}{\text{miles}}_{1969} + VCPM_{1969} = \frac{\text{fixed costs}}{\text{miles}}_{1973} + VCPM_{1973}$$

There is a single unique mileage figure that satisfies this equation. Substituting the values from this problem into this equation gives

(7) $$\frac{\$561}{\text{miles}} + \$.0900 = \frac{\$1,126}{\text{miles}} + \$.0550$$

The algebra of the solution follows:

(8) $$\frac{\$561}{\text{miles}} + \frac{\$.0900 \text{ miles}}{\text{miles}} = \frac{\$1,126}{\text{miles}} + \frac{\$.0550 \text{ miles}}{\text{miles}}$$

$$\$561 + \$.0900 \text{ miles} = \$1,126 + \$.0550 \text{ miles}$$
$$\$.0900 \text{ miles} = \$565 + \$.0550 \text{ miles}$$
$$\$.0350 \text{ miles} = \$565$$

$$\text{miles} = \frac{\$565}{\$.0350}$$

$$= 16,143$$

You can now go back to either half of equation (7), substitute 16,143 miles, and solve for the cost per mile, which is the same for the 1969 and 1973 models at 16,143 miles per year.

$$\frac{\$561}{16,143} + \$.0900 = \$.0347 + \$.0900 = \$.1247 \text{ or } 12.47 \text{ cents per mile}$$

As a check, using the other side of the equation,

$$\frac{\$1,126}{16,143} + \$.0550 = \$.0697 + \$.0550 = \$.1247 \text{ or } 12.47 \text{ cents per mile}$$

The mileages at which the costs of the 1969 and 1975 models are equal and at which the 1973 and 1975 models are equal are as follows:

	MILEAGE	COST PER MILE '(CENTS)
1969 model = 1973 model	16,143	12.47
1969 model = 1975 model	22,180	11.53
1973 model = 1975 model	36,267	8.60

chapter 12

INVESTMENT DECISIONS: PRESENT VERSUS FUTURE

Our analysis of personal economics to this point has been somewhat oversimplified—or perhaps more accurately— has been correct as far as it has gone. The criticism of the analysis would be that it has inadvertently assumed that there was no tomorrow. When income was spent and costs incurred, it was assumed that both the cost and the benefit happened at the same point in time—now. We assumed that all money income would be spent for goods and services today. But we know that in the real world persons frequently defer consumption to a later date. Perhaps a much later date. For the average person it is seldom that costs and benefits are precisely matched at any point in time. We will now consider decisions where costs occur at one time and benefits at another.

▶ A PERSONAL LIFE CYCLE ◀

If we arbitrarily divide time up into years and look at *real* costs and benefits, we can see that the average person probably goes through three major economic phases in his lifetime: (1) *formative years,* in which you receive direct, personal, real benefits that substantially exceed personal real costs, (2) the *productive years,* in which you incur real costs that exceed direct real benefits, and (3) the *degenerative years* (or what are normally called "the retirement years"), in which direct, personal benefits again exceed direct real costs. The categories might be relabeled simply *youth, middle age,* and *old age.*

The formative years typically end with the completion of continuous formal education. Until that time, you normally receive more in benefits than you incur in personal costs in the form of personal resources given up. Normally parents make up most of the difference. Society as a whole makes up some of the difference by supplying education to you at less than your immediate personal share of its full cost.

The productive years constitute a repayment for the windfall you received during the formative years. They also constitute anticipation of the degenerative years, during which you know that you will wish to receive benefits in excess of their immediate real cost to you. This excess of benefits will now come either from costs incurred by you in the past during the productive years, or from other individuals—perhaps your grown children—or from society as a whole in the form of public assistance of some sort.

The typical pattern can be explained in terms of resource control. The problem is that during your formative and degenerative years, you do not control very much in the way of resources. The resources you do control are capable of conversion into very little, so your comprehensive income is very low. Utility received will have to come from your wealth or someone else's income or wealth. In fact, the formative years might be viewed as a period of acquisition of resources, since you become knowledgeable and skilled and otherwise learn the ropes of living in a modern society. All the while someone else supports you—the next best thing to a free lunch. But the day of reckoning cometh. Sometime, someone will expect you to pay it back in one way or another. How fortunate it is that costs and benefits do not need to be equated for every person at every point in time! Life would be nearly impossible. Clearly the whole issue of the mechanics and decisions that relate to the divorcing in time of costs and benefits is a major one.

The matter of costs at one time and benefits at another need not be considered only within the broad dimension of your lifetime. In a narrower and more specific way, the present-versus-future issue gets right down to a decision as to whether to pay cash or buy on credit. Buying on credit and paying interest is essentially a decision to have something now rather than in the future. The price of your impatience is, of course, interest paid. A decision to send a child to school today entails a less luxurious retirement tomorrow. The examples are myriad.

As somewhat of an aside, it is interesting to note that there is more than one approach to the reconciliation of the problem created by personal benefits that are different from personal costs at any one point in time, but that all the approaches are the same in the most fundamental sense. For example, a purely *individualistic approach* to this issue would require that each person work this out by himself over his lifetime. In money terms, he would borrow during his formative years. During his productive years he would pay back his previous borrowing and save for his degenerative years, during which he would spend his savings (all the while hoping that he comes out about even—he doesn't want to come out short; on the other hand, he doesn't want to come out long either, thereby providing his heirs with a free lunch that he might as well have eaten himself). A purely *collectivist approach* says, "I'll pay your costs during your formative years if you'll provide my benefits during my degenerative years." This approach relies on the relationship between individuals in a society, whereas the individualistic approach does not. In the individualistic approach the emphasis is on *private saving;* in the collectivist approach the emphasis is on *public saving.* The common denominator is obviously *saving.*

▶ SAVING AND INVESTMENT ◀

Although our professed concern is with personal investment, the matter of saving is central since personal investment decisions are usually a matter of deciding on the particular form that savings will take. Similarly, a decision not to invest at all is the working equivalent of a decision not to save. In money terms, saving without investing might be viewed as simply hoarding a pile of cash in your mattress; however, this pile of cash might also be viewed as a particular form of investment. You have simply chosen to invest in dollars per se as opposed to some other form of value. The point is that once saving is done, there is necessarily some disposal of those funds (in money terms) or resources (in real terms). If so, it does not really make sense to view saving and investment as separate at all. It may be helpful, however, to view saving as the essentially negative act of nonconsumption and investment as the essentially positive act of commitment of those resources to some use, pending their consumption in the future. Linking saving and investment together, then, simply says that if the first act (saving) is performed, the second act (investment) is necessarily performed even if only by default. Thus, from a personal point of view, saving and investment are virtually synonymous. If one is done, the other is done.[1]

Having agreed that saving and investment are nearly synonymous, the following paragraphs may be read substituting "investment" for "saving." The discussion proceeds in terms of saving to focus somewhat more on the negative aspect of the activity. Shortly we will switch over to the positive investment side. Let us define **saving** (and **investment**) formally as *costs incurred, the benefits from which will be received at a later date*. Clearly the concept of saving captures the divorcing in time of costs and benefits. The concept of saving from a personal point of view as costs now versus benefits later is intact whether the saving is in the form of public or private saving and whether in the form of money or real saving.

Private money saving is money *you* set aside *now* to be spent *later*.

Private real saving is the factors of production you supplied *now* (utility lost), the fruits from which *you* will consume *later* (utility gained). It is the factors of production supplied that generated the money income from which money saving was done. As always, the link between the real and money measure is intact.

Public money saving is the money *society* sets aside *now* on behalf of its members to be spent *later* on their behalf or given back to them for their own spending. Some of this is done on behalf of specific individuals in society, and some of it is done without regard to individual identification. The social security system is an example of public saving done for specific individuals. Each member has his own account and his specific account is credited with contributions on his behalf. General assistance funds would be an example of public saving done without regard to specific individuals. There is simply a kitty into which the public contributes and from which the public draws. Obviously, the individual members who pay in and those who draw out are frequently not the same people.

Public real saving is the factors of production *society* supplied *now* (utility lost), the fruits from which it will consume *later* (utility gained). The money payments generated by supplying the factors of production is the money income from which taxes are paid into society's collective "saving account." [2] Again, the real-money link is identifiable.

It is clear that in each case the central issue in saving is present versus future. This is not to suggest that it is immaterial whether saving is public or private. There are important differences, but they are less basic than the fundamental nature of saving under scrutiny here. One of the important differences is the rather complete discretion you personally have over your own private saving—it is largely voluntary. Public saving requires that you must go along with the preferences of the majority for saving to a substantial extent—it is largely involuntary.

A second issue is somewhat more philosophical in nature. When saving is totally private, you must work out your own plan completely. Whether it succeeds or fails, it is totally your own doing, and you reap whatever results it produces. Public saving allows "undersaving" by some persons and compensating "oversaving" by others. The total program for all participants must "come out even" in the end but need not "come out even" for each and every individual in the program. In other words, public saving programs can have income redistribution among individuals built into them. This, in fact, is the major purpose of general public assistance funds cited above as an example of public saving.

Whether saving should be compulsory or voluntary and whether real income should be redistributed or not are important issues that reach into all corners of human experience and preference. Since our focus is on personal choice and since the explanation is easier to grasp when applied to personal money saving, we will proceed in those terms. However, since most societies—and certainly American society—provides for a combination of private and public saving together, it is necessary to consider the package of private and public saving together when making personal saving decisions.

If present versus future is the core of personal saving and investment, we need to explore the relationship of time to economics a bit more carefully than we have to this point.

▶ THE ECONOMICS OF TIME ◀

When we assumed in previous chapters that costs and benefits occurred in the same time period, we were necessarily making a somewhat arbitrary assumption. We arbitrarily selected some length of time and declared it to be a time period, and that anything that happened in that length of time happened in the same time period. But a time period can, of course, be of any length. Is a time period a length of time of 1 minute, 1 hour, 1 day, 1 month, 1 year, 10 years, or what? We need a period of time that is long enough so that it is workable and sensible from a practical point of view for you to be able to receive the benefit in the same time period as the costs were incurred but also short enough so that you will not object greatly if you receive the costs at the beginning of the time period and do not receive the benefits until the end of the time period. In other words, the time period must be short enough so that you are indifferent as to *when within* the time period you incur the costs and *when within* the time period you receive the benefit—you consider all points *in* the time period to be the present from a practical point of view. A number of different lengths of time period would seemingly satisfy these criteria, although, for working purposes, we will define our time period as 1 year.

▷   time preference   ◁

The general preference of the average person to have something now rather than later is called **time preference.** Bear in mind that the preference for things presently rather than later is based upon the very important qualification "other things being equal." This means that, after paying now, you can have a given car this year or next year; that, after paying now for food, you can have it this year or next year; that, after paying now for an education, you can have it this year, wait until next year, wait for 5 years, or whatever. If there are no costs involved other than the direct cost of the item itself, you cannot possibly be worse off

. . . On time preference . . .

Reprinted by permission of Newspaper Enterprise Association.

by having it now than by waiting. If you take it now, you enjoy the possibility of having some utility from it between now and the subsequent date, which is the alternative given to you to receive the good. Furthermore, the dollar cost of the good could have been earning interest for you if you had not paid for the good until you were going to use it.

▷ risk ◁

There is a second element that is involved that tends to cause people to elect to have things now rather than later after having paid for them. That is the element of **risk.** If you pay for the car now and agree to receive it next year, there is the possibility that between now and next year it may become impossible for you to receive the car for any number of reasons. The party you paid and who agreed to deliver the car may have skipped the country. It is possible that the manufacturer of the car may not be able to supply the car in the future. Presumably you know whether or not he can in the present. It is possible that between now and the future you may change your mind about what you would want. A realization of any of these eventualities constitutes a loss to you, the buyer. It means that you would have overpaid for the car. These and other similar kinds of possible losses are risks. These risks must be accounted for in some way. It seems clear that the greater the risk or probability that the car will be unavailable or that you would not want it in the future, the less you would be willing to pay presently for it. Considerations regarding *time preference* and *risk* are the two main factors that complicate your determination of the benefits to be received in total or in part in future time periods. Some way or another risk and time preference must be taken into account.

▶ INTEREST ◀

Interest rates are the economic mechanism that ties the present and the future together. Although an elaboration of the workings of the interest rate will follow, you are probably aware that at a given interest rate on a given amount of principal, more interest is collected as the time period lengthens. When you pay (or forego) interest, this is essentially the cost of choosing to have things now rather than waiting. As you receive or are paid interest, you are collecting your reward for foregoing things now and waiting until the future to have them. In a very real sense, then, the interest rate is the "price" of time. At a high interest rate, time is high priced in every sense. At a higher interest rate you will pay (or forego) more dollars interest for having something now rather than having it later. Thus you have found it is more expensive to have things now rather than to wait—that is, time is more valuable than it is at a lower interest rate.

Interest is the compensation for *time preference* and *risk*. If you have a very strong preference for things now rather than waiting until a future date, presumably you would be willing to pay more interest in order to have things now rather than waiting until a future time. If you believe the risks associated with deferring consumption until the future are very high, you would much prefer to have your goods now, and you would therefore demand a very high interest payment to induce you to wait. You demand the high interest rates as compensation for the risk, which you view as very substantial, and for your strong preference to have things now rather than in the future.

▷ simple interest ◁

The importance of the interest rate becomes particularly apparent in those examples where a major cost is borne presently but the utility or a major part of it is not received until the future. This is because the dollar amount of interest is dependent upon the length of the time period involved. Consider the following example, which shows the amount of interest paid for 1 year at 5 percent under simple interest.

(1) $\$1,000 \times 5\% \times 1 \text{ year} = \$50$

However, if that same $1,000 is held at interest for 3 years, the interest paid becomes

(2) $\$1,000 \times 5\% \times 3 \text{ years} = \$150$

The example shows clearly the importance of the length of time involved in the interest cost. But the interest cost is also affected by the interest rate as well as by the length of time. Suppose that the interest rate were 6 rather than 5 percent. The following would then be true:

(3) $\$1,000 \times 6\% \times 1 \text{ year} = \$60$

and

(4) $\$1,000 \times 6\% \times 3 \text{ years} = \$180$

Notice that the interest cost will also be affected by the amount of money that is involved. The initial amount is the **principal.**

(5) $2,000 \times 6\% \times 1 \text{ year} = \$120$

and

(6) $2,000 \times 6\% \times 3 \text{ years} = \$360$

From these simple examples, it can be readily seen that three things affect the amount of interest generated: (1) the principal, (2) the interest rate, and (3) the length of time. From this observation stems the basic general statement of the formula for interest.

$$\text{interest} = \text{principal} \times \text{rate} \times \text{time}$$

Each part must be present to determine the amount of the interest. It is evident from applying simple interest to a modest amount of principal for only a few years that the importance of interest to a consumer over his lifetime would be substantial.

▷   compound interest   ◁

▶   FUTURE VALUE OF A LUMP SUM PAYMENT

But this example still understates the importance of interest. The above example was based on *simple interest;* a more realistic example would be based on *compound interest.* **Compound interest** is interest on interest. Normally, the interest collected at the end of the first time period is added to the principal at that point. For the second time period, the principal becomes the principal at the beginning of the first time period plus the interest collected during the first time period. If we restate Equations 3 and 4 in terms of compound interest, they become

(7) $1,000 \times 6\% \times 1 \text{ year} = \$60$

This is the same as Equation 3 for the first year, but for the second year the principal is higher by $60 interest from the first year, so the interest for the second year is

(8) $(\$1,000 + \$60) \times 6\% \times 1 \text{ year} = \$63.60$

This is added to the second year's principal to get the third year's principal. Thus

(9) $(\$1,060 + \$63.60) \times 6\% \times 1 \text{ year} = \$67.42$

interest the third year. Total interest for the 3 years is $60 + $63.60 + $67.42 = $191.02. This is higher than the interest for 3 years under simple interest by $11.02. The $11.02 is due to compounding and is the interest on interest previously collected. Figure 12–1 illustrates all the aspects of this relationship.

But there is an easier way of getting at all this. Equations 7, 8, and 9 amount to $1,000 × 1.06 × 1.06 × 1.06 = $1,000 × $(1.06)^3$ = $1,191.20. This is the amount of our original principal plus the interest compounded for 3 years. This formula may be generalized in the following way to give us the amount of interest that will accrue to the initial principal at any interest rate specified for any number of years specified.

$$\text{principal} \times (1 + \text{interest rate})^n = \text{final amount}$$

which consists of initial principal and interest compounded for n years

(10) $$P \times (1 + r)^n = S$$

where P = principal
 r = interest rate
 n = number of years
 S = final sum

The effects from compounding are nothing short of spectacular. As time elapses, each year's principal mounts owing to the accumulation of interest. Initial principal will double about every 15 years at 5 percent per year and about every 7 years at 10 percent per year. This doubled amount will, of course, double *again* after the same number of years again elapse. Thus you are doubling ever and ever larger amounts. The net result is that 6 percent of a single sum will be about 1.8 times its original amount after 10 years and 339 times its original amount after 100 years. (The first 50 years are the hardest!) You now begin to see the possibilities for someone who makes a career of frugality.

Table 12–1 allows you to easily determine the amount to which $1 will grow after a specified number of years at a specified interest rate. To determine the amount to which any other number of dollars will grow, you simply multiply the value in the table by the number of dollars you have in mind. You can quickly verify that the table will produce the expected $1,191.02 from $1,000 compounded annually at 6 percent for 3 years.

A few things in particular are worth noticing in Table 12–1. Doubling the interest rate more than doubles the amount of interest collected over a period of years. The interest on $1 at 4 percent for 20 years is

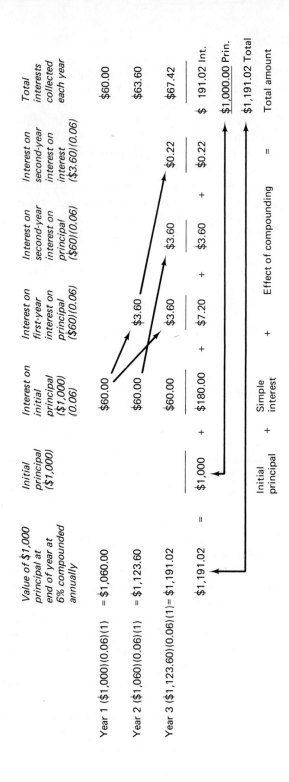

FIGURE 12–1 • Mechanics of compound interest.

Table 12–1

FUTURE VALUE OF $1 PRESENTLY HELD
AT SPECIFIED RATES OF COMPOUND INTEREST

YEARS TO PAY-MENT DATE	2%	4%	5%	6%	8%	10%	15%	20%
0	$1.000	$ 1.000	$ 1.000	$ 1.000	$ 1.000	$ 1.000	$ 1.000	$ 1.000
1	1.020	1.040	1.050	1.060	1.080	1.100	1.150	1.200
2	1.040	1.082	1.103	1.124	1.166	1.210	1.322	1.440
3	1.061	1.125	1.158	1.191	1.260	1.331	1.521	1.728
4	1.082	1.170	1.216	1.262	1.360	1.464	1.749	2.074
5	1.104	1.217	1.275	1.338	1.469	1.611	2.011	2.488
10	1.219	1.480	1.629	1.791	2.159	2.594	4.046	6.192
15	1.346	1.801	2.079	2.397	3.172	4.177	8.137	15.407
20	1.486	2.191	2.653	3.207	4.661	6.727	16.367	38.338
30	1.811	3.243	4.322	5.743	10.063	17.449	66.212	237.376
40	2.208	4.801	7.040	10.286	21.725	45.259	267.864	1,469.772
50	2.692	7.107	11.467	18.420	46.902	117.391	1,083.657	9,100.438
60	3.281	10.520	18.679	32.988	101.257	304.482	4,383.999	56,347.511

$1.19 and the interest on $1 at 8 percent for 20 years is $3.66. This phenomenon is due to the effects of compounding; and, the longer the time involved, the greater is the difference.

Let us return to our earlier conclusion that $1,000 compounded at 6 percent for 3 years would grow to $1,191.02 and see how it fits our concept of cost and utility. Recall that the purpose of this chapter is to analyze situations in which the cost is borne at a different time from that in which the utility is received. Are we not in fact concluding that the present cost of $1,191.02 worth of utility in 3 years is $1,000 if the interest rate is 6 percent? Certainly. To receive $1,191.02 in 3 years, you must give up $1,000 now. In real terms, of course, it means that to receive $1,191.02 worth of utility in 3 years, you must sacrifice or bear the cost of $1,000 of utility today. If you have a high preference for current as opposed to future income or utility, you will necessarily demand a higher interest rate in order to defer the receipt of utility.

▶ **FUTURE VALUE OF A STREAM OF PAYMENTS**

The preceding example assumes that $1 will be committed *now* and left to grow at compound interest for a specified number of time periods (years). It is frequently useful, however, to know the future value of an amount made up of a series (stream) of annual payments. In other words, a contribution to the principal is made *each* year; so the final sum consists of the series of additions to the principal, plus the compound interest on each addition to the principal from the time it was made until the future date specified.

The distinction between the future value of a lump sum and the future value of a stream of payments will become clear if we use a savings account as an example. The future value of the lump sum would be the amount in your account after a specified number of years if you made a deposit now and *no additional* deposits. The future value of the stream of payments would be the amount in your account after a specified number of years if you made *annual* deposits of the same amount each year.

The future value of a stream of payments can be determined by using some common sense and the mechanics of the determination of the future value of a lump sum. Assume an interest rate of 2 percent. If you commit $1 now, what is it worth now? Obviously $1. A year later you again commit $1. What is the whole pot worth now? Obviously, the $1 committed just now, plus the $1 committed the first year, plus the interest on it, or

$$\$1 + \$1 + (\$1 \times .02) = \$1 + \$1 + \$.02 = \$2.02$$

At the beginning of the third year another $1 is committed so the total amount is now the $1 just committed, plus last year's $1, which has earned interest for 1 year, plus the first year's $1, which has earned compound interest for 2 years. It is evident that the future value of a stream of payments can be computed by adding together the series of lump sums represented by the various years' payments. By using Table 12–1, you can quickly see that the value of this stream at the beginning of the third year will be

$1 + $1.02 (the value of a lump sum after 1 year from Table 12–1)
 + $1.04 (the value of a lump sum after 2 years from Table 12–1) = $3.06

This value could have been read directly from Table 12–2, which, it is now evident, is basically Table 12–1 but with the successive years' lump sums already summed for you.

Table 12–3 is a summary of the relationship between Table 12–1 and Table 12–2, using a 6 percent interest rate.

If the amount of the annual payment is different from $1, the figure from Table 12–2 is multiplied by the actual payment, as in the use of Table 12–1. For example, if you are making a $50 annual payment at 6 percent compound annual interest, the amount at the beginning of the fourth year will be $50 × 4.37 = $218.50.

Table 12-2

FUTURE VALUE OF A $1 ANNUAL PAYMENT FOR SPECIFIED NUMBERS OF YEARS AT VARIOUS COMPOUND INTEREST RATES

BEGIN-NING OF YEAR	2%	4%	5%	6%	8%	10%	15%	20%
1	$ 1.00	$ 1.00	$ 1.00	$ 1.00	$ 1.00	$ 1.00	$ 1.00	$ 1.00
2	2.02	2.04	2.05	2.06	2.08	2.10	2.15	2.20
3	3.06	3.12	3.15	3.18	3.25	3.31	3.47	3.64
4	4.12	4.25	4.31	4.37	4.51	4.64	4.99	5.37
5	5.20	5.42	5.53	5.64	5.87	6.11	6.74	7.44
10	10.95	12.01	12.58	13.18	14.49	15.94	20.30	25.96
15	17.29	20.02	21.58	23.28	27.15	31.77	47.58	72.04
20	24.30	29.78	33.07	36.79	45.76	57.27	102.44	186.69
30	40.57	56.08	66.44	79.06	113.28	164.49	434.75	1,181.88
40	60.40	95.03	120.80	154.76	259.06	442.59	1,779.09	7,343.86
50	84.58	152.67	209.35	290.34	573.77	1,163.91	7,217.72	45,497.19
60	114.05	237.99	353.58	533.13	1,253.21	3,034.82	29,219.99	281,732.56

Imaginative use of Tables 12–1 and 12–2 allows you to compute future values under a wide variety of conditions. For example, suppose that you want to know the future value of $200 in 15 years, assuming that it will earn 6 percent the first 10 years and 8 percent the remaining 5 years. At the end of 10 years it will be worth $200 × 1.791 (from Table 12–1) = $358.20. Switching to the 8 percent column in Table 12–1, you see that the factor for 5 years is 1.469. Since you have $358.20 when that 5-year period begins, $358.20 × 1.469 = $526.20, which is the value of $200 at the end of 15 years at 6 percent for the first 10 years and 8 percent for the last 5 years.

Future value that combines lump sum payments and a stream of payments can also be determined. Suppose that you are going to commit $1,000 at interest for 5 years and then add $100 per year to it for 10 years after that 5 years is up. If the rate of interest is 5 percent, what will all this be worth at the end of 15 years? The initial $1,000 will be worth $2,079.00 × ($1,000 × 2.079 from Table 12–1 = $2,079). To this must be added the future value of the ten $100 annual payments. From Table 12–2 we see that their value will be $100 × 12.58 = $1,258.00. Adding this to the final value of the lump sum gives $1,258.00 + $2,079.00 = $3,337.00. It can be easily seen that $2,000 of this represents payments [$1,000 +

Table 12–3

RELATIONSHIP BETWEEN TABLE 12–1
AND TABLE 12–2

VALUE OF $1 ANNUAL PAY- MENT AT BEGINNING OF	TABLE 12–1 VALUES					TABLE 12–2 VALUES
	VALUE OF $1 HELD FOR:					
	0 YEARS	1 YEARS	2 YEARS	3 YEARS	4 YEARS	
Year 1	$1.000				=	$1.00
Year 2	$1.000 + $1.060				=	$2.06
Year 3	$1.000 + $1.060 + $1.124				=	$3.18
Year 4	$1.000 + $1.060 + $1.124 + $1.191			=		$4.37
Year 5	$1.000 + $1.060 + $1.124 + $1.191 + 1.262				=	$5.64

(10 × $100) = $2,000] and that $1,337.00 represents interest ($3,337.00 − $2,000.00 = $1,337.00).

It is not difficult to see that the future value of almost any package involving lump sums and streams of payments and/or different interest rates over different parts of the total time span can be computed easily from the two tables. The key is to recognize that the tables simply tell you how fast your "pot" *grows* under various conditions. You identify the amount that is going to grow (principal) and select the table value according to the length of time of the growth (years), the speed of the growth (interest rate), and whether it is a lump sum or stream that is growing (Table 12–1 or Table 12–2). Any package of conditions can be broken into its component parts and the future values of the parts combined to produce the future value of the package. Needless to say, some care is warranted in identifying correctly the four key elements of each part of the problem: (1) lump sum or stream, (2) principal, (3) interest rate, and (4) time.

Interest tables that contain more refinement than Tables 12–1 and 12–2 both in interest rates and number of years are readily available in published form.

SUMMARY

1 • The incurring of costs and the receipt of benefits frequently occur at different points in time.

2 • The decision that relates costs in one time period to

the benefits in another is essentially the issue of *saving*, which, from a personal point of view, is the virtual equivalent of *investment*.

3 • The economic linkage between various points in time is the *interest rate*. It is therefore no coincidence that decisions about saving and investing are concerned with interest rates.

4 • In general, there is a *time preference* for the present as opposed to the future. This is a force that causes interest rates to be positive (the borrower *pays* interest and the lender *receives* interest). In addition, other things equal, the future represents more *risk* than the present; a reward is demanded for exposure to it. This, too, is a force arguing for positive interest rates.

5 • The general formula for determining the amount of simple interest is principal × rate × time.

6 • Compound interest is interest on interest. Periodically, the previously accrued interest is added to the principal and interest is charged on the new amount. This is called compounding.

7 • Through the use of precomputed tables, it is a relatively simple matter to determine the future value of any amount of principal under compound interest, whether it is in the form of a lump sum left to grow or whether it is an amount to which periodic additions are made.

study materials

1 • With regard to a personal life cycle, explain what is meant by the formative years; the productive years; the retirement years.

2 • Differentiate between the individualistic approach and the collectivist approach to economics.

3 • What is the difference between saving and investment? How are they similar?

4 • Define and explain private money saving, private real saving, public money saving, and public real saving.

5 • Why was the time period of 1 year, rather than 1 minute or 10 years, picked for the time period to be considered in this chapter?

6 • What is the general *time preference* of the average person?

7 • How does the element of *risk* relate to time preference?

8 • Set up a simple example and compute the simple interest.

9 • Using Figure 13–1 as your example, compute and explain the compound interest on $1,500 at 6 percent for 2 years.

10 • What would be the future value of a $100 annual payment for 30 years at 6 percent? At 8 percent?

footnotes

1 Given our conclusion that personal saving = personal investment, it is interesting to note that, for an economy as a whole, saving = investment is also true. The second proposition is *not* true, because the first is true. Personal saving = personal investment, because the same persons are doing each for the same reason. For the economy as a whole, households do most of the saving for their own reasons and businesses do most of the investing for their own, but different, reasons.

2 It is not to be construed that *all* tax payments represent public saving from a personal point of view. Some tax payments go for public consumption.

chapter
13

INVESTMENT DECISIONS: FUNDAMENTAL APPLICATION

the safe investment: the savings account

Having computed the future value of an amount, we can turn the analysis around by specifying what the future value is to be and then computing the present value (the present amount that must be set aside to produce that future amount at a specified interest rate). This is an extremely useful procedure, since investing entails estimating what the payoff (future value) will be and then deciding what you are willing to pay (present value) for that payoff. The simple savings account provides an excellent instructional vehicle: Interest rates act as the connector between present and future.

▶ PRESENT VALUE ◀

The concept of **present value** is a simple one if you are firmly grounded in the concept of future value. Since the interest rate is the economic connection between points in time, it is clear that a known amount of value in the present will be worth some specific larger amount at a given point in the future. The amount by which the future value is greater than the present value depends on the interest rate. Similarly, some known amount of value to be received in the future is worth some specific smaller amount now. The amount by which the present value is smaller than the future value depends on the interest rate.

Working from the future value example in Chapter 12, we can see that at 6 percent interest compounded annually, you are indifferent as

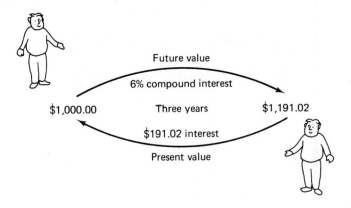

Future value

6% compound interest

$1,000.00   Three years $1,191.02

$191.02 interest

Present value

FIGURE 13–1 • Present value–future value: $1,000.00 as the present value.

to whether you receive $1,000.00 now or $1,191.02 in 3 years. In either case you end up with $1,191.02 in 3 years. Thus the present value of $1,191.02 to be received in 3 years at 6 percent compounded annually is $1,000.00.

> **The present value of a future sum is the amount it takes now to generate that future sum at some specific future time at some specific compound interest rate.**

If the future value is to be $1,000.00—again under the 6 percent, 3-year condition—the *present* value is the amount it takes now to grow to

$1,000.00 in 3 years at 6 percent. That amount is $839.60. Checking from Table 12–2 in Chapter 12, we see that the value of $839.60 in 3 years at 6 percent is $839.60 × 1.191 = $1,000.00.

It is instructive to note that the difference between $839.60 and $1,000.00 is $160.40 but that the difference between $1,000.00 and $1,191.02 is $191.02. Do not be led to the naïve conclusion that one figure should be larger than $1,000.00 by the same amount that the other is smaller than $1,000.00. Remember that the amount of interest generated depends on the principal as well as the interest rate and the time. Figure 13–2 is the

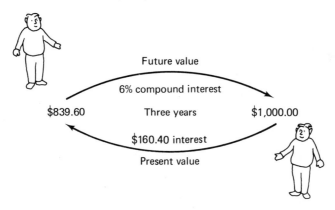

FIGURE 13–2 • Present value–future value: $1,000.00 as the future value.

same as Figure 13–1 except that $1,000.00 is used as the future value rather than as the present value. Note that the amount of interest is different from that in Figure 13–1 solely because the amount of principal (present value) is different.

It will be useful to avail ourselves of precomputed figures that can be used to convert future value to present value, just as we used precomputed figures in Tables 12–1 and 12–2 to convert present value to future value.

Table 13–1 is the *present value* of $1.00 (a lump sum) to be held at various interest rates for various lengths of time. The present value of $1,191.02 to be received in 3 years at 6 percent is $1,191.02 × .8396 = $1,000.00; the present value of $1,000.00 to be received in 3 years at 6 percent is $1,000.00 × .8396 = $839.60. It should come as no surprise at this point to discover that the entry in Table 12–1 is the reciprocal of the comparable entry in Table 13–1. That is, for 3 years at 6 percent, .8396 =

1/1.191 and 1.191 = 1/.8396. If, indeed, future value and present value are merely opposite sides of the same problem, such a relationship would seem inevitable.

Table 13–1

PRESENT VALUE OF A SINGLE $1 PAYMENT TO BE COLLECTED AT A FUTURE TIME AT SPECIFIED RATES OF COMPOUND INTEREST

YEARS TO PAYMENT DATE	2%	4%	5%	6%	8%	10%	15%	20%
1	$.9804	$.9615	$.9524	$.9434	$.9259	$.9091	$.8696	$.8333
2	.9612	.9246	.9070	.8900	.8573	.8264	.7561	.6944
3	.9423	.8890	.8638	.8396	.7938	.7513	.6575	.5787
4	.9238	.8548	.8227	.7921	.7350	.6830	.5718	.4823
5	.9057	.8219	.7835	.7473	.6806	.6209	.4972	.4019
10	.8203	.6756	.6139	.5584	.4632	.3855	.2472	.1615
15	.7430	.5553	.4810	.4173	.3152	.2394	.1229	.0649
20	.6730	.4564	.3769	.3118	.2145	.1486	.0611	.0261
30	.5521	.3083	.2314	.1741	.0994	.0573	.0151	.0042
40	.4529	.2083	.1420	.0972	.0460	.0221	.0037	.0007
50	.3715	.1407	.0872	.0543	.0213	.0085	.0009	.0001
60	.3048	.0951	.0535	.0303	.0099	.0033	.0002	.0000
80	.2051	.0434	.0202	.0095	.0021	.0005	.0000	.0000
100	.1380	.0198	.0076	.0029	.0005	.0001	.0000	.0000

Table 13–2 is the present value of a *series* of annual payments. Table 13–1 shows that the present value of a stream of annual payments is the sum of the present values of each of the individual payments to be received. Recall that this is precisely the relationship between the future value of a stream of annual payments and the sequence of lump sums making up the stream of payments. This relationship was displayed in Table 12–3, which is analogous to Table 13–3.

The analytical tool kit is complete. We can now analyze a variety of situations in which the passing of time is a consideration. Consider three examples as a summary of the mechanics of present value.

Table 13–2

PRESENT VALUE OF A $1 ANNUAL PAYMENT FOR SPECIFIED NUMBER OF YEARS AT SPECIFIED RATES OF COMPOUND INTEREST

NUMBER OF YEARS	2%	4%	5%	6%	8%	10%	15%	20%
1	$ .98	$ .96	$ .95	$ .94	$ .93	$ .91	$ .87	$ .83
2	1.94	1.89	1.86	1.83	1.78	1.74	1.63	1.53
3	2.88	2.78	2.72	2.67	2.58	2.49	2.28	2.11
4	3.81	3.63	3.55	3.47	3.31	3.17	2.85	2.59
5	4.71	4.45	4.33	4.21	3.99	3.79	3.35	2.99
10	8.98	8.11	7.72	7.36	6.71	6.14	5.02	4.19
15	12.85	11.12	10.38	9.71	8.56	7.61	5.85	4.68
20	16.35	13.59	12.46	11.47	9.82	8.51	6.26	4.87
30	22.40	17.29	15.37	13.75	11.26	9.43	6.57	4.98
40	27.36	19.79	17.16	15.05	11.92	9.78	6.64	5.00
50	31.42	21.48	18.26	15.76	12.23	9.91	6.66	5.00
60	34.76	22.62	18.93	16.16	12.38	9.97	6.67	5.00
80	39.74	23.92	19.60	16.51	12.47	10.00	6.67	5.00
100	43.10	24.50	19.85	16.62	12.49	10.00	6.67	5.00
Forever	50.00	25.00	20.00	16.67	12.50	10.00	6.67	5.00

Table 13–3

RELATIONSHIP BETWEEN TABLES 13–1 AND 13–2

PRESENT VALUE OF A $1 ANNUAL PAYMENT TO BE RECEIVED FOR	TABLE 13-1 VALUES					TABLE 13–2 VALUES
	PRESENT VALUE OF $1 TO BE RECEIVED IN:					
	1 YEAR	2 YEARS	3 YEARS	4 YEARS	5 YEARS	
1 Year	$.9804				=	$ .98
2 Years	$.9804 + $.9612				=	$1.94
3 Years	$.9804 + $.9612 + $.9423				=	$2.88
4 Years	$.9804 + $.9612 + $.9423 + $.9238				=	$3.81
5 Years	$.9804 + $.9612 + $.9423 + $.9238 + $.9057				=	$4.71

EXAMPLE 13–1

Present Value of a Lump Sum Payment

You believe that an investment will pay $2,000.00 at the *end* of 10 years. What is its present value at 8 percent? From Table 13–1, the factor for 10 years at 8 percent, is .4632. $2,000.00 × .4632 = $926.40.

EXAMPLE 13–2

Present Value of a Stream of Payments

You believe that an investment will pay $80.00 *per year* for 10 years. If the interest rate is 8 percent, what is the present value of this stream of payments? From Table 13–2, the factor for 10 years at 8 percent is 6.71. $80.00 × 6.71 = $536.80. This means that $536.80 earning 8 percent compounded annually will "throw off" $80.00 per year for 10 years with nothing left at the end of the 10 years.

EXAMPLE 13–3

Present Value of a Lump Sum Payment Plus a Stream of Payments

Combining Examples 13–1 and 13–2, you believe that an investment will pay $80.00 per year for 10 years *and* $2,000.00 at the end of 10 years. What is the present value of this package? It is the present value of its component parts, namely $926.40 + $536.80 = $1,463.20.

▶ PRESENT VALUE IN DECISION MAKING ◀

Although the mechanics of time discounting (present value–future value) have been developed, the significance of the procedure as it relates to personal choice remains to be explored. Rather obviously, the significance is with respect to a choice between consumption and saving (investment). In Chapter 12 it was concluded that personal saving and personal investment were virtually synonymous, except that, perhaps, saving carried the negative connotation of nonconsumption, whereas investment carried with it a more positive expectation of future income, interest earned, future consumption, and so on. In Chapter 12, saving was defined as *costs incurred, the benefit from which will be received at a later date.*

Turning to the positive aspect of investment, let us define **investment** as the *purchase of future income.* A moment's reflection reveals that this definition is essentially synonymous with the definition of saving. The purchase of future income, like the purchase of anything else, entails a cost. The benefit from the investment will be received later. Thus the common denominator of saving and investment is costs borne at one point in time and the benefits received at another point in time.

If it seems peculiar to refer to the "purchase of income," recall that real income is defined as the flow of utility, which is represented by actual goods and services, not money. In that sense, expenditure for food, clothing, entertainment, and so on is the purchase of *present* income. When the consumption expenditure is deferred to engage in personal investment, it necessarily follows that investment represents the purchase of *future* income. Consumption and investment are therefore different only to the extent that consumption expenditure represents the present and investment expenditure represents the future. The choice is not whether to consume or not to consume; the choice is whether to consume now or later. It must be recognized that "later" may mean "much later," even to the extent of subsequent generations if your goal is to leave a wad for your children who may in turn elect to either blow it or add to it and pass it on to yet another generation.

In purely money terms, investment is also the purchase of future income, since dollars are committed in the present to get back dollars in the future. How many dollars you get back for your purchase depends on how good a buyer you are—that is, how skillful an investor you are. There are obviously good buys and bad buys in future income (investment) just as there are good buys and bad buys in present income (consumption).

All decisions between consumption and investment or among various investment alternatives hinge on present value. The reason is self-evident: *All decisions are made in the present; therefore, all costs and benefits must be expressed in their present equivalent.* This observation ties to the arguments set forth in Chapter 9 about the relevance of the present in decision making. Once present value is computed, it is a simple matter to employ the choice mechanism developed in Chapter 9. Consider the following examples, which combine the concept of present value with the decision-making criteria laid down earlier.

EXAMPLE 13–4

Present Value of a Lump Sum and Personal Choice

Should you buy a $2,000.00 car now or a $3,000.00 car in 5 years? You believe that you could swing one or the other but not both. The two cars are not comparable because one is available now; the other is available only after 5 years. The present value of the $2,000.00 with which you would buy the $2,000.00 car now is, of course, $2,000.00. If you can get 6 percent interest, the present value of the $3,000.00 with which you will buy the alternative car after 5 years is $3,000.00 × .7473 = $2,241.90, drawing on the information in Table 13–1. You can now use the comparison of willingness to pay and required payment for the two cars to arrive at a decision. Suppose that the following is representative of the situation:

	WILLING-NESS TO PAY NOW	REQUIRED PAYMENT NOW	BENEFIT–COST RATIO
$2,000.00 car now	$2,800.00	$2,000.00	$\dfrac{\$2,800.00}{\$2,000.00} = 1.40$
$3,000.00 car in 5 years	$2,500.00	$2,241.90	$\dfrac{\$2,500.00}{\$2,241.90} = 1.12$

The decision is to have the $2,000.00 car now at the opportunity cost of the more expensive car at a later date. Notice that willingness to pay captures your time preference. If you have a high time preference for the present, your willingness to pay for the deferred good will tend to be low, which will lead you to decide in favor of current consumption and against investment (saving).

EXAMPLE 13–5

Present Value of a Stream of Payments and Personal Choice

You believe that you will need $2,000 per year for each of the next 4 years if you are to see your offspring through college. Your investments are earning 6 percent. How much do you need to earmark for this? The present value of a stream of four $2,000.00 annual payments spread over the next 4 years is $6,940.00. $2,000.00 × 3.47 = $6,940.00. As in Example 13–1, you can express this cost against your willingness to pay for 4 years of education and compare that with what you would be willing to pay for the most attractive alternative use of the $6,940.00; you can then decide on that basis whether to buy this particular form of future consumption—that is, whether to invest for this purpose.

The examples are endless. Hopefully the point is clear that, since decisions are made in the present, costs and benefits must *both* be expressed in their present equivalent for *all* alternatives considered. Thus the basics of personal choice about investment or saving are the same as the basics of personal choice about consumption per se, except that the preliminary step of conversion to present value must be completed. Your willingness to pay for a future benefit accounts for your time preference.

▶ PERSONAL INVESTMENT ◀

Having investigated the use of present value in the choice between consumption and investment, we now focus on the subject of investment proper in more detail. That is, let us suppose that it is clear that you do wish to forego some present consumption in favor of saving. A decision as to the form that your savings (investment) should take is an important one. Some of the more popular forms come to mind readily. Among the many options are a variety of saving programs offered through banks (e.g., savings accounts), ownership of financial securities (stocks and bonds), ownership of apartment buildings, and ownership of farmland. Other more exotic and/or less understood forms of investment are available through the ownership of foreign money, ownership of rare postage stamps or coins, ownership of agricultural commodities or livestock, or ownership of liquor—to name only a few of the opportunities. All these investment vehicles will provide you with future income as you sell them, or as you sell the services from them to other people (as in the case of apartment buildings), or as you are paid for the capital you supplied to other parties (as in the case of stocks and bonds). In every case, the payoff involves a financial transaction with another party.

In addition, there are investment opportunities where the payoff is "internal" to you. The investment pays off, not in terms of money, but in terms of actual goods and services—"in kind" is the phrase. Home ownership is probably the best example. If you have $25,000 sunk in a house, you would certainly be foolish to forego the interest on the $25,000 if you were getting nothing in return. Of course you are getting something in return—housing services—which have a specific market value. The return to a homeowner's investment in his house is its rental value, which he collects himself so to speak. Education is also somewhat of this nature (although it does involve a financial payment), as you receive a higher money income because of your education. Some investments pay off partly in money and partly in kind. A home may be owned with an eye to selling it later at a profit. Antiques may be both used and held for appreciation in value. The variety of form within the common framework of costs now and benefits later is bounded only by your imagination's inability to discover still other things that may be worth more tomorrow than they are today—for whatever reason.

The categorization of investments will be according to the amount of *risk* that is involved in their ownership. Risk is inherent in investments because investments relate to the future and the future is an uncertain place. The risk consists of uncertainty as to what the future value of the investment will be—that is, what the payoff will be. The present value on which investment decisions are based is necessarily the present value of the *estimated* future value of that investment. Risk is defined by the degree of certainty that can be attached to the best estimate of future value. The degree of risk varies widely, since the best estimate of the future value of a savings account may be perfectly reliable but the best estimate of the future value of a share of stock in Moon Mining, Inc., may be very tenuous. The more tentative the best estimate is of the future value of the investment, the riskier the investment.

Investment analysis consists of two major steps: (1) identification of costs and benefits, and (2) determination of their present value. The identification of costs and benefits is a mixture of art and science that involves estimation and prediction based on a sagacious interpretation of the facts. The major task in investment analysis is the identification of future value accurately—or as accurately as possible. The second step— the determination of present value—is purely mechanical. It is because of the difficulty of estimating future value that everyone has certain investment alternatives that he dismisses immediately. Considerable knowledge about the affairs of the world is required to estimate future value with acceptable accuracy. Successful investing beyond the relative shelter of a savings account, therefore, requires some honest work and some knowledge of the real world as it relates to your investment vehicle.

The individual investor's behavior very frequently betrays lack of understanding of broad fundamentals. The volumes of material that have been written—and sold—on investing staggers the imagination. It ranges in quality from excellent to pure witchcraft. Individual investors walk right into impending doom that was evident to any who really looked. With only a few of the basics under your belt, you should be able to at least sort out some of the sensible ideas and advice from that which is little more than superstition; you should also be able to identify what some of the most attractive and least attractive investment alternatives are for you, given your circumstances. Many persons, not knowing the dangers, fare disastrously; others, knowing that dangers exist but not understanding them, refrain from participating in a fruitful and satisfying activity. There is a middle ground to be traversed by the person who is prudent and reasonably well-informed about a few of the basics.

At the risk of oversimplification, let us look at an insured savings account as an example of a safe (very low risk) investment and, in Chapter 14, a share of common stock as a risky investment. Finally we will look at home ownership and higher education as examples of intermediate-risk situations, since many of you are probably involved with or interested in higher education and/or home ownership.

▶ THE SAVINGS ACCOUNT ◀

Application of the procedures for formal identification of costs, benefits, and the present value of each to an investment in the form of a savings account may seem trivial and pointless since the issues are so simple and clear cut. Actually, it is the simplicity of the example that is so valuable as an instructional device. The example will serve as (1) a review of the mechanics of present value, (2) assurance that the present value approach is valid, and (3) a foundation for more complex examples.

Assume that a bank pays 4 percent compounded annually, which is sufficient to induce you to save. That is, the future value must be greater than the present value by 4 percent *per year* (i.e., compounded) to induce you to defer consumption. The savings account example is simple because the interest rate is specified and you do not really need to estimate future value. If you are willing to save for 4 percent, the specified bank rate on savings either is sufficient or it isn't, and that's that—the future value will be what it will be under a specified rate of return. The problem is over before it begins.

Other types of investments do not return a guaranteed interest rate. You have to estimate the future return, specify the minimum interest rate you will accept, and then compute present value on the basis of the interest rate you specify. If the present value you compute is more than the price at which the investment is available to you, you may be interested in purchasing it, depending on the attractiveness of the other alternatives. If the present value is less than the price at which the investment is available, you conclude that the investment is overpriced. The purchase of an investment for less than the present value will, of course, provide a rate of return higher than the interest rate upon which the computed present value is based. In other words, you will get a rate of return higher than the minimum you would be willing to accept. Similarly, the purchase of the investment at a price higher than the computed present value will give you a return less than the minimum you would accept.

For example, if you pay $100.00 to get $104.00 a year from now, the interest rate is obviously 4 percent. ($104.00 − $100.00)/$100.00 × 100 = $4.00/$100.00 × 100 = 4 percent. If you pay less than $100.00, say $98.00, to get $104.00 a year later, the rate of return is ($104.00 − $98.00)/$98.00 × 100 = $6.00/$98.00 × 100 = 6.12 percent. The rate of return is the gain relative to the cost. When computing present value based on estimated future value, you simply specify the minimum rate of return you will accept, and present value is computed on that basis. That present value is then your willingness to pay, which you compare with the required payment (market price) for the investment in order to make a decision as to which investment to buy. If computed present value is below the market price, you reject the investment as necessarily a bad buy. Among those investments that have a present value above market price, you take the one where the present value is above the market price by the widest margin, since your willingness to pay is above the required payment by the greatest amount for this investment. A choice on this basis assumes that the amount of risk (degree of certainty that your estimate of future value is correct) is the same for all the alternatives considered.

To illustrate the principle of present value as it relates to investment analysis, let us suppose that a bank were to "sell" savings accounts in a manner analogous to the way in which other investments are frequently sold. The bank, then, would not specify the interest rate paid; instead, you would "estimate" the future value of your savings account, which would probably be what the bank says it will pay you when you draw out your savings. The bank would also specify the present amount for which it is willing to "sell" you this future value; that is, the bank would tell you how much you had to put into your account in order to collect the promised amount. The bank would also tell you how much time would have to elapse between your "purchase" and the payoff. Suppose that the bank says, "We will sell you $5.00 *per year* for 10 years *and* $100.00 at the *end* of 10 years, all for $100.00 cost to you *now*." What is your decision? That depends on the minimum interest rate you will accept. Suppose that you have decided that you would be interested in this deal only if it would earn at least 6 percent. You therefore compute the present value based on 6 percent and see how it compares with the $100.00 for which the package is offered. Drawing on the factors in present-value Tables 13–1 and 13–2, we see that the present value of the deal at 6 percent is $92.64.

From Table 13–1:	$100.00 × .5584 = $55.84
From Table 13–2:	5.00 × 7.36 = $36.80
Present value of package at 6%:	$92.64

You reject the bank's offer. The bank would have to price its offer at $92.64 to give you a 6 percent return compounded annually.

Now suppose that you would, under other circumstances, be willing to save for a 4 percent return. The present value of the bank's offer to sell for $100.00 is then $108.11.

From Table 13–1:	$100.00 × .6756 = $ 67.56
From Table 13–2:	5.00 × 8.11 = $ 40.55
Present value of package at 4%:	$108.11

Your willingness to pay for this package to yield 4 percent is $108.11 against a required payment of $100.00. The bank's payoff would constitute a 4 percent return on $108.11. If $100.00 is the lowest price at which any bank will sell you the "$5 and $100" package at about the same convenience to you, it would appear that you should buy it. If you pay $100.00 for the deal, it will yield more than the 4 percent minimum acceptable to you.

It is clear that the bank's offer is priced to yield more than 4 percent but less than 6 percent. As you may now suspect, if indeed it was not evident at the outset, the offer is priced to yield 5 percent.

From Table 13–1:	$100.00 × .6139 = $61.39
From Table 13–2:	5.00 × 7.72 = $38.60
Present value of package at 5%:	$99.99

(The value is $99.99 rather than $100.00 because the factors in the tables were rounded off.) A moment's reflection reveals that the package offered by the bank is exactly what the bank does provide with a conventional 5 percent savings account. If you put $100.00 in your account, the bank pays you $5.00 per year plus your original $100.00 at the end of the series of years.

One final comment may clarify a possible point of confusion about the 5 percent savings account and present value. Perhaps you are inclined to protest that $5.00 per year and $100.00 at the end of 10 years is less than a 5 percent savings account actually provides. Your protest is based on the assertion that in the second year the bank will pay $5.00 plus 5 percent of the $5.00 interest earned the first year, or $5.00 + ($5.00 × .05) = $5.00 + $.25 = $5.25 for the second year. We have ignored the effects of compounding, you say. Not so! If you want to pursue this argument, you also have to argue that your cost in the second year is not $100.00 but $105.00. This is the essence of compounding. Periodically accrued interest is added to the principal, which raises the cost of the package earning the higher interest. The bank's offer here was to give you $5.00 per year and $100.00 after 10 years for the *original $100.00 only.* What you do with the interest you receive is another issue. You can take it and spend it for consumption, put it in another bank to earn interest there, and so on. Now, as a practical matter, you may wish to reinvest the accrued interest in the same account, in which case the bank says, in effect, "O.K., we'll extend a comparable offer to you for subsequent 'purchases' (the accrued interest) in amounts of less than $100.00 for periods of less than 10 years." You can then leave the fruits of compounding in your account, and both the cost to you and the benefits will rise—but still at a rate of 5 percent per year in benefits *based on the current year's cost* as the years elapse. Notice that the actual *payments* that this bank will make to you over the 10-year period under its first offer will be $150.00, consisting of ten $5.00 annual payments plus $100.00 at the end of the 10 years. As you receive the $50.00 over the 10 years, you could perhaps deposit this in another bank that extends a comparable offer. All you would accomplish would be to split the total benefit between two banks—one paying you the simple interest and the second paying you the interest due to compounding. Under this bank's second offer to accept deposits in the form of interest earned on previous deposits with it, the total payment by it to you would be simply the future value of $100.00 left at 5 percent compounded annually for 10 years. From Table 12–1, that amount would be $100.00 × 1.629 = $162.90. Obviously, $162.90 − $150.00 = $12.90 is the additional interest due to the effect of compounding. Your bank might therefore restate its intentions in this manner, "For $100.00 cost to you now, we will give you either (1) $150.00 in the form of ten $5.00 annual payments and $100.00 after 10 years or (2) $162.90, *all* payable at the *end* of 10 years." Having established that the present value of option (1) at 5 percent is $100.00, we should be able to verify that the present value of option (2) at 5 percent is also $100.00. Option (2) is a lump sum to be received at the end of 10 years; thus from Table 13–1, $162.90 × .6139 = $100.00. Option (2) is merely a special case of option (1) in which you decide to "spend" your earned interest in a particular way, namely to invest it in a program in which you are already participating.

The rationale for compounding may now be clearer than it was earlier. The basis for it is the relevance of time to economic affairs. For certain fairly short time periods, any point in the time period is considered equal to any other from the standpoint of time preference. The course of economic events is broken up into a series of such "short" time units. Each unit is a separate ball game. Under option (1) the bank says, "For $100.00 we will pay you $5.00 per time period for as long as you want to leave the $100.00 with us. What you do with the $5.00 is your business. It's yours at the end of the time period." Under option (2) the bank says, "Now if you want to bring that $5.00 in under the same conditions as the original $100.00, we'll take it." The point is that after that $5.00 is paid to you at the end of the time period, it is the same as any other $5.00 received in any other way, and it is subject to the same treatment as $5.00 acquired elsewhere.

▶ EVALUATION OF THE SAVINGS ◀ ACCOUNT

A short discussion of the advantages and disadvantages of a savings account as a specific investment vehicle is in order, since we will be looking at other investment opportunities in the next chapter.

The list of advantages of the savings account is extensive. It is convenient; you may manipulate your account from your own home by mail if you wish. The maximum inconvenience consists of going to the bank where you have an account to do your business. You need no particular expertise; you need know virtually nothing of the complicated world around you to be a "successful" investor. There are virtually no additional costs of managing your investment; you make your investment, and there are no additional decisions or duties required. Your investment decision is reversible on short notice; if you want to discontinue the investment, you can withdraw your money at any time.[1] The risk of loss of your initial investment is very low; in addition to the stability of most banks, most savings accounts are insured by an agency closely related to the federal government. If your bank goes under, the agency will pay your loss. The rate of return is certain; although your bank will probably change the rate it pays periodically, at any moment you know exactly what you are getting.

The list of disadvantages is short and pungent. The rate of return is low. It should come as no surprise that the rate of return would be low for such an extensive list of advantages and virtually no other disadvantages. Other investments carry higher rates of return as compensation for fewer advantages and more disadvantages. If other less convenient and riskier investments carried the same rate of return as the savings account, no one would buy them.

Because the savings account is simple, the advantages extensive, the disadvantages absent, and the rate of return about as low as might be expected from any personal investment, it will serve as a useful foundation from which to compare other types of investment.

SUMMARY

1 • The present value of a future amount is the amount it takes now to produce the future amount at the specified interest rate.

2 • Since an investment is the purchase of future income, present value is the basis for determining the worth of an investment.

3 • The present value of an investment is willingness to pay for it.

4 • The best buy in a relatively low-risk investment is where willingness to pay is highest relative to the cost at which the investment is available.

5 • Investment decisions consist of two major steps: (1) identification of costs and benefits, and (2) determination of their present value.

6 • Although not typically viewed in this way, a savings account is a purchase of a future amount. The present value of a savings account works out to be the amount you must put in the account to generate the future amount.

7 • Savings accounts have several advantages and virtually no disadvantages, which leads to the expectation that the rate of return will be low—which it is.

---

study materials

1 • Relating present value and future value, which will be greater and why?

2 • Why are differences between the future value and the present value not the same in Figures 14–1 and 14–2?

3 • Compute the present value at 5 percent of a lump sum payment for an investment paying $3,000 at the end of 20 years.

4 • What is the present value of an investment that will pay $1,000 per year for 10 years if the interest rate is 8 percent?

5 • Why is present value significant in considering investment decisions?

6 • What two major steps must be considered in making investment decisions?

7 • Name the advantages of a savings account over other types of investment.

8 • Why is the interest return on a savings account relatively low?

9 • How does the concept of present value relate to consumer decisions? Which types of consumer decisions in particular?

10 • Why are savings accounts considered "safe" investments?

footnote

[1] Under law, most savings accounts may be withdrawn only after giving the bank advance notice if the bank wishes to require it. The advance notice is usually 30 days. Banks seldom require that this rule be observed, however. The advance notice provision is the reason that money in a savings account is called a *time deposit*.

chapter
14

INVESTMENT DECISIONS: UNAVOIDABLE RISK

high-risk investments: common stock intermediate-risk investments: housing, education

We proceed from the sheltered world of savings accounts to the more boisterous world of stocks, apartment buildings, education, and so on. Basic principles of present versus future values are the basis of investment analysis here also, but increased uncertainty of future values creates uncertainty about present value and therefore what you are willing to pay. Through the use of probability, we will be able to account for uncertainty and incorporate it into the analysis.

▶ THE COMMON STOCK ◀

The savings account was offered as an example of a low-risk investment that could be bought on the basis of present value that was virtually certain to be accurate—because the estimated future amount was virtually certain to be accurate. The introduction of riskiness causes the present value to be less certain and the decision to be more difficult. The present value is uncertain because the future value is uncertain. To become acquainted with the common stock and to isolate the impact of risk on an investment decision, we will begin by assuming conveniently (but erroneously) that the estimated future value of the common stock is certain. We will then see what new elements are added to the analysis by the introduction of uncertainty later.

What is a **common stock?** Briefly, it is the representation of a piece of ownership in a corporation. The corporation is one form of business organization. Another is the proprietorship. As a proprietorship, the individual simply starts doing business as himself. No red tape. Most small businesses are organized as proprietorships because it is simple. Small retail outlets, farms, small service establishments (e.g., barbers) are most commonly organized as proprietorships. Many professions are characterized by the proprietorship (e.g., doctors, lawyers, dentists, and accountants) or the partnership, which is a close legal cousin to the proprietorship. There is a trend, however, for the professions to operate as corporations.

Most typically it is the larger businesses that organize as corporations. The primary reason is that it is impossible for one person (the proprietor) to raise the capital required for many kinds of business on his own. It would be ridiculous, for example, to suggest that a proprietor could establish a successful firm in the automobile industry, even if there were additional demand for the product. The corporation is a legal device designed to facilitate the raising of large amounts of capital from several persons. The corporation is owned by these suppliers of capital who contribute capital by buying shares of common stock issued by the corporation. The share of stock serves as evidence of the capital supplied and is the stockholder's claim to ownership in the corporation. The stockholders (owners) elect a board of directors to manage the corporation on their behalf. The stock market, then, is simply a market where these shares of ownership are bought and sold.[1]

The question becomes: "What determines the future value and hence the present value of a share of stock?" As a representation of capital supplied, your share of stock represents a claim to the income that capital earns. The corporation is an income generator; it is a block of capital

resources having the capacity to earn income. To illustrate basic relationships, let us assume for the moment that the world is a perfect place—
that everyone sees the same, and true, picture; that expectations are always realized. There is no ignorance and no secrets, in other words. This
is another way of stating the certainty assumption, since under these conditions the future is perfectly predictable. We can predict perfectly the
income that this corporation will generate and each stockholder's share
of it. The present value of the stock is, of course, the present value of that
income.

It must be recognized that this income may be received in either of
two ways: as *dividends* or as *appreciation* in stock value. **Dividends** are
payments by the corporation to its owners (stockholders). **Appreciation**
in the stock is an increase in its value, that is, in the price of the share
of stock. The following examples will illustrate the point.

EXAMPLE 14–1

The XYZ Corporation

(1) Capital supplied by stockholders	$1,000,000
(2) Number of stockholders (each owning 1 share of stock)	10,000
(3) Capital supplied by each stockholder [(1) ÷ (2)]	$ 100
(4) Income generated by the $1,000,000 capital in 1 year (profit after all costs except a return to the $1,000,000)	$ 100,000
(5) Income accruing to each stockholder [(4) ÷ (2)]	$ 10
(6) Rate of return on stockholder capital [(4) ÷ (1) or (5) ÷ (3)]	10%

**As the corporation goes, so goes the stockholder in the
long run. After the $100,000 has been earned, one of two
things happens: Either the $100,000 is retained in the cor-
poration as retained earnings, which causes appreciation
in stock value, or it is paid out to stockholders in dividends. If the earnings are retained in the corporation, the
total amount of capital will now be**

$$\$1,000,000 + \$100,000 = \$1,100,000$$

and each share of stock is worth

$$\$1,100,000/10,000 = \$110$$

or, if the $100,000 is paid out to the stockholders in dividends, each share of stock is worth $100 and the stockholder has $10 cash from the dividend payment. Either way he gains $10 or a 10 percent return on his investment. Thus the present value of the share of stock is the present value of $110 to be received 1 year hence. The present value of the stock is therefore the sum of the present value of the expected future value of the stock plus the present value of the dividend payments expected.

EXAMPLE 14–2

Let us now estimate that a corporation will pay $2.00 per share per year in dividends over the next 5 years and that the price of the stock will be $150 in 5 years based on the outlook for this corporation's earnings; you can compute the present value of the stock. Suppose that you will take a minimum of 8 percent return on this investment. Discounting the $2.00 annual dividend payment and the $150 lump sum for 5 years at 8 percent gives a present value of

Table 13–2   Table 13–1
($2.00 × 3.99) + ($150 × .6806)
                                = $7.98 + $102.09 = $110.07.

This would be the maximum price you would be willing to pay if you demanded an 8 percent return and were certain that your income expectations were perfect. You then look at the market price of the stock and make a decision as to purchase.

▶ THE INTRODUCTION OF ◀
UNCERTAINTY

The assumption that the world is a perfect place and that future value is perfectly predictable must now be formally abandoned and a means of grappling with the specific problem of modest amounts of uncertainty developed. The tool of **probability** will be used.

Probability is fairly simple in the elementary application to be considered here. Most people understand the basic idea of probability, which is simply *likelihood*. About 50 percent of all births are girls, therefore it can be concluded that the probability of the next birth being a girl is about .5. If 10 percent of students flunk a course, the probability of a given student, picked at random, flunking it is .1. If something *always* happens, the probability of it happening is 1.00. If something *cannot* happen, the probability of it happening is 0. Therefore, probability values range from 0, denoting impossibility, to 1.00, denoting certainty. The probabilities of some things happening are **objective probabilities.** Previous experience or air-tight logic are able to predict exactly what the outcome will be. The probability of a birth being a boy or a girl, the probability of a die coming down a 4, and the probability of drawing the ace of spades from a deck of cards fall in this category. Other probabilities are **subjective probabilities.** These are probabilities assigned to events on the basis of "feel" for the likelihood of their occurrence. Improving the best estimate of present value requires the use of subjective probabilities.

As an example, assume that you have estimated that the present value of a share of stock is $50. Assign it a probability that you feel represents the strength of your conviction. If you are *certain* that it is worth $50, assign it a probability of 1.00. (The problem ends here in this case.) But suppose that you also believe that there are about 3 chances in 10 it may be worth $55 and 2 chances in 10 that it may be worth $45. You believe that there is a slight chance (1 in 10) that things could go really well and that the stock could turn out to have been worth $60. Summarizing these feelings, you get the following:

PRESENT VALUE	PROBABILITY
$60	$\frac{1}{10}$ = .1
55	$\frac{3}{10}$ = .3
50	$\frac{4}{10}$ = .4
45	$\frac{2}{10}$ = .2
	$\frac{10}{10}$ = 1.0

Three things in this summarization are significant: (1) The price with the highest probability is your "best" estimate; (2) the sum of the probabilities must equal 1.00; and (3) the relationship between the probabilities shows how you assess the likelihood of any present value being justified as compared to another present value. Since .4 is twice as much as .2, you believe that a present value of $50 is twice as likely to prove warranted as a present value of $45.

The use of this information to improve upon the "best" estimate of $50 is simple. Multiply each price by its probability and sum.

─────────────────────────── **EXAMPLE 14–3** ───────────────────────────

PRESENT VALUE	PROBABILITY	PRESENT VALUE X PROBABILITY
$60	.1	$ 6.00
55	.3	16.50
50	.4	20.00
45	.2	9.00
	1.0	$51.50

You now believe, after taking into consideration other possible present values, that $51.50 is the present value that subsequent events are most likely to support. This result means that if this same decision were made repeatedly, $51.50 would turn out to be the average present value. Hence your expectation is that this stock will more likely prove to be worth $51.50 than $50.00. Considering the range of possibilities arising from uncertainty will therefore lead to better decisions than simply assuming that the most likely outcome is certain.

Lest you be unduly impressed by the mechanics of accounting for uncertainty, the monumental simplicity of the spirit of the procedure should be laid bare. All that is really happening is that you are saying, "I think $50 is the most likely present value, but if that turns out to be wrong, I think it is more likely too low than too high— by $1.50 to be specific. This is evidenced by the fact that the sum of the probabilities attached to present values over $50 is greater than the sum of the present values under $50." It is not likely that you will actually specify these subjective probabilities. More likely you will simply assess them broadly in your mind and adjust your "best" estimate upward or downward, slightly or substantially, depending on where you think you are most likely to be wrong in your estimates of present value. Perhaps the most common

application of what is really this approach is the consumer who decides to have some construction work done. He adds up all the expected costs and then adds 10 percent, because "these projects always come to more than you expect them to." He assigned a very low probability to lower cost estimates and relatively high probabilities to higher cost estimates.

The rule for investing must now be modified to account for *high-risk* conditions: Best adjusted present value is willingness to pay for an investment *provided there is essentially no possibility of a loss sufficiently severe to curtail your future investment program*. If the possibility of a crippling loss exists, the investment should be excluded from consideration. The above statement must be implemented with common sense. Certainly any loss will curtail *something*. It is a matter of degree. What is a high-risk situation for one person may not be for another, depending on how much of your total capital you are committing to the venture. There is always a possibility, of course, of crippling losses. That's life. But you don't have to deliberately and knowingly expose yourself to them. It's one thing to get hit by a truck sitting in your living room because it jumped the curb and came through the wall, but it's another thing to step in front of one on the street because you failed to look.

The *degree* of risk is easy to assess using the probability framework. Risk may be evident in either of two similar ways: (1) *the greater the* **range** *of present values having probabilities above 0,* or (2) *the* **higher** *the probabilities assigned to present values* **different** *from the best adjusted estimate, the greater the risk.*

The savings account with a certain present value has a probability of 1.00 assigned to a single present value, which is why it was defined as

EXAMPLE 14–4

PRESENT VALUE	PROBABILITY	PRESENT VALUE × PROBABILITY
$75	.1	$ 7.50
60	.1	6.00
55	.2	11.00
50	.4	20.00
45	.1	4.50
25	.1	2.50
	1.0	$51.50

minimum possible risk according to either of the criteria just cited. Looking at Example 14–4, which involves common stock, we see that according to criterion (1), a wider *range* of present values would increase the risk even though the best adjusted estimate of future value remained the same. According to criterion (2), which raises the probabilities of values other than the best unadjusted estimate, risk also rises.

EXAMPLE 14–5

PRESENT VALUE	PROBABILITY	PRESENT VALUE × PROBABILITY
$60	.2	$12.00
55	.3	16.50
50	.1	5.00
45	.4	18.00
	1.0	$51.50

Notice that, in the face of a change, according to criterion (1) or (2) the end result is basically the same; the probability of a present value occurring that is different from the best adjusted estimate has risen. Risk might be viewed, therefore, as tied to *the probability of an outcome different from best adjusted expectations.* In Examples 14–3, 14–4, and 14–5, the best-adjusted estimate was $51.50, which, in each case, means that, in the long run, your best strategy would be to buy on the basis of $51.50, since that is what the present value would average out to be in the long run. But this is relevant only if you could survive an unfavorable outcome in the short run, and the probability of an unfavorable short-run outcome is higher in the presence of risk. In fact, risk might be defined in just such terms.

The previous discussion is the basis for many of the rules of thumb and clichés afloat in the investment world.

1 • "Don't risk what you can't afford to lose."

2 • "Don't enter risky investment situations on a scale beyond what you could do three times in a row in the face of unfavorable outcomes." (The laws of chance are not apt to knock you down three times running.)

3 • "Develop a plan to limit your losses." (Decide how much you are willing to lose before you bail out and *then do it.*)

4 • "At least a modest savings account or other form of ready cash comes ahead of other forms of investment."

The possibility of gain is the possibility of loss. . . .

Reprinted by permission of New York News, Inc.

5 • "Preservation of capital, as well as the search for gains, must be an investment goal."

Perhaps there are others that you can add. Like all rules of thumb, they do not deserve to be accepted universally and uncritically, yet it is interesting to note that they are all plausible products of the analysis of risk as it relates to investment.

The advantages and disadvantages of common stock ownership are almost self-evident after considering the advantages and disadvantages of a savings account and discussing the matter of risk. In complete contrast to the savings account, the list of disadvantages is extensive, and the sole advantage is the prospect of a higher rate of return on average. But it is only a prospect, since for long periods of time, common stock owners may fare much worse than the owners of savings accounts; at *any* time the owners of *some* common stocks will fare worse than the owners of savings accounts. It's a cruel world.

► EVALUATION OF THE COMMON ◄
STOCK

The most difficult part of the evaluation of common stock is the estimation of future value. If it is assumed that there is an air-tight link between corporate earnings and future value, you would need to know something about economics and accounting as well as many specific things about the particular corporation whose stock you were considering buying. For example, you would want to know what products it plans to sell and how it plans to produce them, as well as an indication of the general ability of the corporation's management.

But there is not an airtight link between the corporation's earnings and stock prices. Stock prices in the final analysis are set primarily by supply and demand for the stocks. That is, the immediate determinant of stock prices is the number of buyers relative to the number of sellers. Thus it might be said that stock prices are the immediate result of what other people are *doing* with regard to their stocks. Then you conclude that they may be doing what they are doing because they have analyzed the situation. If so, stock prices are based on what *other* people *think* the corporation's earnings will be. Your decision is then based, not on your analysis of corporate earnings directly, but on your analysis of your fellow investors' analyses of corporate earnings.

Now of course there is also the possibility that people are doing what they are doing, not because of their analysis of the situation at all, but on the basis of mob psychology or herd instinct. If so, you need to be a psychologist to ply the investment waters. Certainly all these factors and more operate in different combinations at different times. But sooner or later, and in the long run, it all relates to earnings since it is those future earnings that are being purchased. Fortunes have been made investing according to the "bigger idiot theory." "I know I'm an idiot for paying this much, but an even bigger idiot will surely come along and buy it from me at a profit." There is nothing wrong with this approach if you are aware of some of the unfavorable possibilities. In fact, if you can afford the risk and are a bit careful to limit your losses, there is much very right with such an approach. A profit for you is a profit for you. Who cares if it is "fundamentally warranted"?

On the other hand, the woods are full of the wreckage of babes who knew not where they trod and who held an empty bag when reality struck. Regardless of the final investment strategy you adopt, you should understand the underpinnings. Any investment decision about a common stock, like any other investment decision, must begin with the fundamentals as a point of departure; the fundamentals are *future* earnings and value and their *present* value. Where you go from there is a matter of strategies so numerous as to nearly inundate the imagination. A few of the more comprehensive and perhaps reliable sources of specific investment plans and approaches are included in the references and appendixes at the end of this book.

▶ HOUSING ◀

The examples of the savings account and the common stock both required the calculation of present value of future income. It was assumed that there were no appreciable costs beyond the initial purchase cost. Some investments, however, entail *future costs* as well as future revenue or benefit. Housing is a case in point. The present value of future costs must also be considered. The housing example also serves to illustrate an investment in which there are some uncertainties but of lesser magnitude than in the case of the common stock. Consider the following.

Mrs. Murphy down the street has lived in one side of the duplex she has owned for 30 years. She is getting old and would like a smaller place with less responsibility—perhaps an apartment. She wonders if you wouldn't like to buy her duplex. You own your own home and are content living in it, but you consider the possibility of buying the duplex and renting it out. What can you afford to pay? Determine the present value of all future costs and income. The difference is the present value of the net income or profit and is the maximum you can afford to pay. You decide you need a rate of return of 6 percent on your capital to attract you to this kind of investment. Everything is therefore discounted to the present at 6 percent.

The income you will receive from this investment is in two forms: (1) the series of annual rental payments, *and* (2) what you believe it might be sold for after some specified number of years. Based on what you believe you will be able to rent it for over the next several years, you conclude that you can collect $300 per month rent. But because you recognize that it cannot be rented continuously, you want to pare down your estimate slightly: $300 per month is $3,600 per year; so let's assume for working purposes that you will collect $3,500 per year in rent. How long will you be able to do this? It's hard to say of course, but we must make an estimate of some kind. After looking the duplex over, you believe that it will last another 30 years, at which time it will be valueless and have to be torn down. Thus your income will consist solely of the stream of annual payments with no payment at the end of 30 years.

Subtract the costs. They will tend to fall into one of five categories: depreciation, interest, taxes, insurance, and maintenance.

▶ DEPRECIATION

You have already accounted for the depreciation in your conclusion that the property would be valueless after 30 years. That is, by implication you have concluded that 30 years depreciation will just exhaust the present value—whatever that turns out to be.

▶ INTEREST

Interest has also been accounted for. By specifying a rate of return of 6 percent, you have set the stage so that the present value computed will provide you 6 percent interest which you "pay" yourself. If you are going to borrow the money to buy this property, it would seem likely that you would specify a discount rate somewhat higher than you are paying for the borrowed capital. If you don't, you will gain nothing economically from this endeavor. At any rate the interest cost, whatever it is, is covered when you pick the interest rate on which to base present value. Stated another way, the present value of future income discounted to the present at 6 percent is a present value such that the estimated future income provides a return of 6 percent on that present value which is the amount of capital (principal) committed to the enterprise.

▶ TAXES AND INSURANCE

Taxes, insurance, and maintenance have not yet been accounted for and must be subtracted from the income of $3,500 per year. Assume the taxes to be $800 per year. You may easily determine what they actually are by consulting the appropriate county or city official. Assume that insurance comes to $300 per year. This cost may be determined by consulting insurance agencies.

▶ MAINTENANCE

Estimating maintenance is a little more difficult. Since you have decided that the duplex will be valueless in 30 years, you have necessarily decided against maintaining the property at its current level indefinitely. On the other hand, the property cannot be allowed to deteriorate too rapidly, or it will be difficult or impossible to continue to collect $3,500 per year rent. A second factor that *may* affect maintenance cost is *how* you plan to provide the maintenance. Whether you decide to do the maintenance work yourself or whether you plan to hire it out to be done may or may not affect the cost you wish to assign to this maintenance. If you are going to hire all the maintenance, then, of course, you must include the full cash cost of the maintenance. If you are going to do the work yourself, you still may wish to include the full cash cost of the maintenance as it would have been if you had had it done. The reason rests on the opportunity cost foundation. What are you giving up in order to do the maintenance yourself? You may consider that you are giving up nothing—that this is part of your recreation and a more agreeable form of recreation than it would be possible to have via any other means. Your satisfaction may consist of merely operating this little venture. That is, the maintenance is the cost of noneconomic utility received. If the maintenance cost and the benefit in the form of noneconomic utility equal one another, you charge nothing for your labor. But to ignore the labor in maintenance seems extreme and implies that your next best alternative—another form of leisure—has a value of zero to you. This hardly seems realistic. At the other extreme, if you view this strictly as a business enterprise in every respect, you are likely to say to yourself, "If I am going to paint the place, I expect to earn painter's wages doing so—or at least earn as much as I could earn in my next best alternative business use of these hours." When you fix the front steps, you are contributing a resource, labor, to this enterprise. The labor has an alternative cost—its most productive alternative use—and you would normally expect a return on it over and above the 6 percent return you intend to get for the capital you supply. If you take the latter approach (which is probably more realistic than assuming an alternative cost of zero for your time), you will enter maintenance costs at about the same figure, regardless of whether you hire the work done or do it yourself. If you do it yourself, your duplex is paying you for your labor just as it is paying you for the use of your capital in the 6 percent return. A resource has an alternative cost regardless of whether or not an actual money transaction takes place in its employment.

For working purposes, suppose that you estimate that the maintenance will come to $500 per year. Maintenance, taxes, and insurance then total to $500 + $800 + $300 = $1,600. "Profit" is $3,500 income less $1,600 costs, or $1,900. $1,900 per year at 6 percent for 30 years has a present value from Table 13–2 of

$$13.75 \times \$1,900 = \$26,125.00$$

Alternatively, the present value of the gross income is

$$13.75 \times \$3,500 = \$48,125.00$$

and the present value of the costs is

$$13.75 \times \$1,600 = \$22,000.00$$

The difference, as previously concluded, is

$$\$48,125.00 - \$22,000.00 = \$26,125.00$$

Now suppose you believe that the duplex "can probably be unloaded for $10,000" at the end of 30 years. This seems a bit conjectural since it is hard to predict what may happen in 30 years. Furthermore, what you believe you can sell it for in 30 years probably depends a good deal on what it turns out to be worth now. This is all beside the point, however, since we want to illustrate that *distant returns are not worth very much in the present*. From Table 13–1, $10,000 at 6 percent in 30 years is now worth .1741 × $10,000 = $1,740.00—a rather measly sum when added to the value of $26,125.00 generated by rental value alone. Under the assumption of a resale value of $10,000 (as opposed to $0 resale value), the present value rises from $26,125.00 to $27,866.00, an increase of less than 7 percent. When we consider the roughness of the income and cost estimates, this amount is not highly significant.

Another approach that obviates the necessity of making any estimate of resale value in the future is to assume that you will own the building forever and that it will generate the estimated income forever. This is not as wild as it might first seem. Under this assumption the duplex is worth

$$16.67 \times \$1,900 = \$31,673.00$$

(Appendix A investigates an alternative method of arriving at this figure.) You now have two extreme values. The value is $26,125.00 if the duplex is worth nothing after 30 years and $31,673.00 if its value is unchanged after 30 years (a necessary outgrowth of the assumption that it will generate the same income forever under current conditions). This is a range of $31,673.00 − $26,125.00 = $5,548.00. But this can be narrowed somewhat through a couple of common sense observations. First, you know that maintenance costs will be higher to preserve the property in its present state than to let it deteriorate. This will tend to reduce the upper end of the range to say $30,000 or so, for example. But, second, chances are that the property will have some positive value after 30 years if it is worth $25,000 to $35,000 now. This will tend to raise the lower end of your range to say $27,000 or so. This means that a reasonable price is probably somewhere in the $27,000 to $30,000 neighborhood, a range of only about $3,000 or so. Furthermore, notice from Table 13–2 that as the interest rate rises, this range would drop even more. (Verify by reworking the problem at 10 percent.) Chances are that an investment of this sort would be undertaken for an anticipated return above 6 percent to compensate for some of the uncertainties uncovered here, although, of course, this would depend on the general level of interest rates and your inclination toward risk. Discounting at a slightly higher interest rate for moderately risky situations is a good way to account for that risk, since it will cause you to buy only if the expected return is fairly high—and this will leave some cushion under you for the outcomes that are slightly less favorable than the expected outcome.

In summary, what starts out to look like a problem that will yield a wide variety of answers, depending on how one makes difficult assumptions, turns out to be a problem in which the most difficult assumptions do not really make very much difference. Although most persons would like a nice specific answer to the question, "What is it worth?" we have concluded only that it is worth, perhaps, $27,000 to $30,000, which is still a rather wide range when it comes to actually making an offer to buy.

► MARKET VALUE VERSUS ◄
PRESENT VALUE

At this point it would be a good idea to find out what other similar properties are selling for in the area. This might be done by getting actual information on sales recently made. In addition, a professional appraiser can be expected to be knowledgeable about recent sales of various kinds of properties. Chances are that recent sales—that is, current market conditions—will point to some particular value within the range you have selected and thereby tend to give it credence over and above other values within the range.

But a word of caution is in order also. The question might be raised as to the necessity of computing the present value of future income if one is simply going to wind up paying whatever value the market dictates anyway. Paying the current market price for any investment seems to imply that the market is always correct, that is, that all buyers and sellers in the market are making good decisions from your point of view. This is not necessarily so. Markets occasionally get out of line. The buyers and sellers may be rational and intelligent, but they may nonetheless have failed to do their homework and to bear in mind the basis for value— the ability of an investment to generate income. Investment history is replete with examples of markets that have undergone major corrections because everyone assumed that everyone else knew what he was doing. These corrections can be dramatic, and, afterward, those who got burned look back and say, "Anyone with any sense should have seen it coming." Why wait until afterward to make your evaluation? Much better to be a jump ahead of the pack and do your solid analysis beforehand. It is also possible for market value to understate conditions, in which case you are in a position to identify the exceptionally good buy. If your computation of present value is confirmed by present market prices, all is probably reasonably well. On the other hand, if current market values are substantially different from your estimate of present value, one or both of two general possibilities would seem to exist. Either (1) your estimates of costs and returns are unrealistic, or (2) the market is unrealistic. This should give cause to rethink your estimates and to ask why the market disagrees with you and whether or not you believe a market correction will occur in the foreseeable future. You may then act on your reevaluation.

A final problem on evaluating future costs and returns must be recognized. We glibly assumed that we could state with reasonable accuracy the costs and returns for a long period of time. We entered net income at $1,900 per year for 30 years in calculating present value. What if taxes rise by, say, 25 percent after a few years? Will this not cause us to have understated costs and overstated profits, and hence overstated present value? Not necessarily. Assuming a reasonable amount of competition in the housing market, one would expect costs and rental value to tend to move together. Tenants reimburse landlords for taxes and other costs paid on their behalf when tenants pay rent. Tenants are frequently notified: ". . . owing to rising costs, rents will be $10 per month higher." If *all* landlords are faced with rising costs, a tendency exists for these costs to be passed on to the tenants. This, of course, tends to preserve the landlord's net income in the face of across-the-board cost increases and thereby tends to preserve the legitimacy of the assumption that net income in the future will be *somewhere near* present levels in spite of cost changes.

The owner-occupied dwelling is subject to the same kind of analysis. Just because no rental *payment* is made to you does not mean that you receive no benefit. The benefit is the rental value—that is, what it *could* be rented for. Conceptually, you are renting the house to yourself. Rental value can be determined, of course, by looking at similar properties that are rented. In the case of more expensive homes it may be hard to find examples of rental property. In this case a rental value can usually be established by seeing how costs compare to rental value on other lower-priced properties and projecting that relationship onto the higher-priced property. This procedure has some weaknesses and should be accepted only as a rough guide to value.

▶ EVALUATION OF HOUSING ◀

Whether investment in housing is in an owner-occupied home or in a rental property, the basic issues are the same. It is the comparison of the present value of all future costs and future income that dictates an investment decision. The amount of risk is certainly greater than a savings account but typically less than a common stock. As an intermediate case between a savings account and a common stock, you can make your own list of advantages and disadvantages after reviewing the lists for the savings account and the common stock. It is interesting to note that, although the behavior of one type of investor in housing, the slumlord, and the behavior of another type of investor in housing, the suburban homeowner, are different in many respects, they can both be explained in terms of present value as it relates to sound economic choice.

Why do some landlords "milk" a property by simply collecting rent and letting it deteriorate? Because it is profitable to do so. If you minimize costs, a large proportion of gross income becomes net income—that is, the value of the property declines as relatively high current net income is generated. Since it is the income to be received in the *near* future that is valuable, the avoidance of current costs as the reward for a low resale value in the distant future is a very profitable tradeoff.

If a case can be made for the profitability of letting property deteriorate, why does any utility-maximizing homeowner maintain his property well? There are at least three possible explanations: (1) The consumer does not realize the economic folly of well-maintained property, (2) the consumer derives a great deal of noneconomic income from living in well-maintained property under the approving eye of his neighbors, or (3) the consumer may be surrounded by an environment that causes the value of his property to rise, which means that the expected future value of the property may be quite high; in this case more costs are justified in order to collect it.

The comparison of the slumlord's behavior with the surburban homeowner's behavior in the light of these three points is interesting indeed. Each receives utility from different sources, and each plays the game under different circumstances. The slumlord must make hay now, for the world around his property is falling apart. Tomorrow will surely be worse than today. The suburban homeowner lives in the expectation that his surroundings will make tomorrow better than today. The slumlord gets his utility from rental dollars presently received from a property whose value tends to decline because of its surroundings. The suburban homeowner gets his utility from the personal satisfaction of a nice home for himself and the approval of his neighbors in a locality where the surroundings tend to lift property values—all on top of the rental value of his house for pure housing. Each plays the game according to the source of his utility and the things from which he gets utility. Each is perhaps pursuing a good strategy, given the things that give him utility and the conditions under which the game is played.

▶ EDUCATION ◀

Education qualifies as an investment. It entails a present cost for a future benefit. In fact, education is very often a very attractive personal investment, since only part of the cost is typically borne by the "investor." The state pays much of the cost if the educational institution in which the student is enrolled is a public school or university; endowment income often pays part of the cost if the educational institution is private. In addition, there are often scholarships available. On the other hand, the cost is still substantial to the individual and, since much of the benefit lies far in the future in the form of higher income over a lifetime, the value of the benefit may be lower than supposed. A little analysis suggests that many students are in educational programs only because they are paying very little of the costs. For many persons, there is very substantial non-economic income accruing to education, both from the process itself and from the end result. There is satisfaction in *getting* educated and in *being* educated.

The analysis that follows is sketchy but deliberately so, since you should by now be familiar with the mechanics of present value. For illustrative purposes, we will assume a standard 4-year college course. The data used, while not unreasonable, are to be considered hypothetical only, and not representative of any particular situation.

The college recruiter announces, "The college graduate earns, on an average, $230,000 more over his lifetime than the noncollege graduate. You, too, can have this fantastic offer for the low, low price of only $2,500 per year at good old Green Pea University." Unfortunately, college recruiters, like other salesmen trying to move their product, do not always tell the whole truth. It may prove to be a good buy—indeed, an outstanding buy—but probably not the fantastic buy it is often assumed to be. There is a natural temptation to multiply the $2,500 per year by 4 years and compare the $10,000 cost with the $230,000 income. This is no more valid than adding apples and kumquats and trying to make sense of the result.

Picking apart the cost is the most difficult. It is obvious that the benefit being bought is what you expect to earn in *addition* to what you would earn otherwise; therefore, the appropriate cost figure is the cost in *addition* to any cost realized if the decision is to *not* go to college. It is difficult to generalize as to what these costs might be, so we will make some rough assumptions. Assume that the $2,500 cost mentioned above breaks down into $1,000 room and board, $1,000 tuition and fees, and $500 miscellaneous (e.g., travel, books, personal effects). How much of this do you count as the cost of education? All of it? Certainly not! The $1,000 tuition and fees is undoubtedly all assignable to the cost of education, but not all the room and board should be charged against your education. After all, you presumably have to eat and sleep whether you go to college or not. Assume that this cost is only one-half attributable to the special circumstances of your education. Also assume that the $500 miscellaneous is one-half attributable to your education. Of the $2,500 "cost," then, only $1,000 + $500 + $250 = $1,750 per year is legitimately the cost of education.

But the $1,750 is only the tip of the iceberg above the water. The major cost is *earnings foregone.* The fact that this item is frequently overlooked does not mean that it is irrelevant. Suppose that you could have earned $5,000 per year if you had taken a job instead of going to college. The full cost then comes to $6,750 per year!

If these costs are discounted at 8 percent, the present value of them for 4 years is

$$\$6,750 \times 3.31 = \$22,342.50$$

If the additional income is to be received over a 50-year period from *beginning* of college (retirement at 68: college entrance at 18), the first 4 years yield no benefit. The benefit will therefore be received in years 5 through 50 or spread over 46 years *after* college completion at the end of 4 years. The average yearly benefit is therefore $5,000. Discounting this to the present at 8 percent yields

$$\$5,000(12.23 - 3.31) = \$5,000 \times 8.92 = \$44,600$$

You would be willing to pay $44,600 but are required to pay only $22,-342.50. A cost of half what you would be willing to pay is probably attractive when compared to other investments, but it is certainly a far cry from the $10,000 to $230,000 comparison that beckoned at the outset. In addition, it is not difficult to see that rather undramatic changes would cause a negative decision on college. A high-cost school, far from home, high interest rates, and an expected failure to be able to earn well soon after graduation can rather easily make college a poor buy on economic grounds. It is not surprising that the outlook for jobs for college graduates and the location of a college profoundly affect any given student's decision to attend school.

In addition, the willingness to pay of $44,600 probably overstates the attractiveness of college on economic grounds, because the highly skilled and professional occupations find their practitioners realizing peak earnings later in their careers than do those in occupations at lower skill levels. This would put a disproportionate share of the college graduate's additional earnings far into the future, which would tend to put the present value below $44,600, a value which was computed on the basis of the assumption that the college graduate's advantage over the nongraduate was uniform through his career.

▶ EVALUATION OF EDUCATION ◀

There are a number of interesting circumstances to be contemplated with regard to investment in education, both from the standpoint of the individual and from the standpoint of society. Education has long been encouraged as one of the best buys available both for society as a whole and for any given individual. It has been argued that progress made by society on any front (and according to any definition of progress) has come only through an educated populace. Although education does not ensure progress, it is indeed probably a necessary ingredient for social and economic progress of any kind. Therefore, our society has attempted to create a stimulus to individuals to undertake this particular form of investment. The primary stimulus has been to make education available at a very attractive price. Education is nearly free to the individual through high school and is typically offered to the individual at a price substantially below cost beyond the high school level via direct government subsidy in the form of state-provided schools or through private contributions to endowment funds and scholarship programs. These programs are frequently supported by private contributors who realize substantial tax savings by doing so. The point is that the emphasis on education comes from a society realizing its importance and taking specific steps to stimulate individuals to avail themselves of it and/or to support it. For society as a whole, investment in education has been extremely productive and society has taken steps to encourage it.

It does not follow, however, that since the cost of most education is paid indirectly through taxes, persons would therefore buy as much education if they paid the full cost directly. Since tax payments are nonvoluntary and subject only to general and long-range control through elected representatives, it is interesting that society should see fit to provide education in this somewhat rigid way rather than relying on purely voluntary purchases. Payment through taxes also allows the "investor" to postpone the cost (to match the deferred benefit) because he will pay more taxes later in life as his income and wealth rise. The total cost to society in resources expended on the same amount of educational effort would be about the same whether each individual paid the full cost directly or whether the cost is borne indirectly through taxes. The explanation of society's choice of the particular way in which this service is provided lies in what we have already discussed—risk and present value. If each individual paid the full cost directly, considerably less education would probably be bought.

If the investor in education is strictly on his own to pay the full costs, the price looks ominous. There are substantial costs and perhaps more risks than commonly supposed. As observed earlier, it is virtually mandatory that good employment opportunities be available immediately upon completion of education—even when education is priced considerably below full cost to the individual—if the education is to be a good buy on economic grounds. If the student pays the full cost, the urgency for immediate employment is all the greater. Added to immediate employment uncertainties is the possibility that certain kinds of job training may become obsolete. Furthermore, the student may not have the ability or maturity to complete an educational program. Although a partially completed educational program does have value, its value is certainly below that of a fully completed program. Thus there are risks to the beginning student, and rather substantial ones at that. Finally, the ability of the typical investor in education to bear these risks is usually very low. The typical college student, for example, has little income-earning ability and even less personal wealth, in which case an economic loss of any kind is a major loss. The prospect of an economic loss of the magnitude of an education investment would be enough to discourage even the most stouthearted.

At the other extreme, there are students who realize costs and risks so low that the "investor" is scarcely motivated to collect the benefit. Some students are fully supported by government and/or parents or other outside sources, even to the extent of a living allowance providing a level of living that would be realized if the student were earning income at employment. This student finds that his education has an opportunity cost of remarkably close to zero. The "Eat, drink, and be merry for tomorrow we eat, drink, and be merry" attitude of some students illustrates something of the special nature of education as an investment. After paying the cost, the buyer has a good deal of choice as to how much he takes for his money! Of course, you can also take less than the amount for which you paid of other goods, too; yet the "overpaying" is sometimes a bit more visible in education than elsewhere. It is certainly not unique. Consumers get less than they pay for—and knowingly so—every day. With regard to education, this is a somewhat formal way of saying, "You get out of it what you put into it." The problem seems to be a matter of motivation. The consumer may get little for his cost because he is ignorant *or* because he is unmotivated to do better or both.

The subject of motivation is a complex one that goes far beyond the scope of this book, but it is interesting to observe that very likely risk and motivation have a connection. The strength of that connection seems to vary from person to person. Some people get motivated only in the face of impending disaster, and others see an essentially riskless benefit as a chance to really make hay while the sun shines.[2] The student who performs badly while enjoying parental support but later returns to school and performs well while paying his own way and supporting a family besides might be viewed as having responded, motivationally, to a changed risk condition. Since his cost has increased substantially, the only way he can justify it is to take a larger benefit. The student is probably also a bit less ignorant of the benefit from education at that point, so he makes a more intelligent purchase—both because he is more knowledgeable and because he is more motivated to purchase as well as he knows how.

The major point discovered here does not relate to education only. We have heretofore implicitly assumed that the consumer is always motivated to do the best he can. It is particularly evident from the behavior of certain students that this assumption is far from universally satisfied. A bit of reflection clearly indicates that people frequently make bad decisions and do so almost knowingly. If there is a risk–motivation relationship, however, there would seem to be an objection from the standpoint of both the individual and society to making education too cheap, just as there would be objection to pricing it to the individual at full cost. Just what proportion of the total cost the individual should pay is a subject of ongoing public policy debate. These are issues that can be discussed further in Part IV. The message to the individual is clear: Take all you can for your cost, no matter how low—or high. Before you object to the almost insulting obviousness of that statement, ask yourself how many students you know who act as though they are unaware of it.

Finally, a major—perhaps *the* major—consideration to the individual in buying education is the noneconomic income. Indeed, the traditional view of education holds that education is not an economic issue in the conventional sense at all. Education is for enrichment, for understanding, for life, for appreciation, and so on, not for employment. If employment opportunities arise, fine, but they are secondary. For better or worse, education in the broadest definition has come to include both the economic and noneconomic dimension. Although we suspect that the primary emphasis for most persons is now on the economic dimension, there are still substantial noneconomic benefits. For whatever reason, most persons find the educational process itself somewhat satisfying. The social conditions within the educational community are quite satisfying to most students. The increased awareness of the world is a noneconomic benefit upon completion of formal education. Any person having the intellectual and risk-bearing ability to pursue the educational program of his choice will probably find his choice dictated by the noneconomic benefits. On purely economic grounds, most persons would find the best buy to be in the area of specific skill acquisition with little or no attention to what are commonly called general education or liberal education requirements.

Although there are noneconomic costs, they are surely minor compared to the noneconomic benefits. Perhaps some anxiety over one's academic performance or success constitutes the major noneconomic cost. You may be able to add others.

SUMMARY

1 • In general, common stocks are a relatively risky investment. Just how risky obviously depends on which common stock you are citing.

2 • The willingness to pay for a common stock is the present value of the estimated dividend payments plus estimated future value.

3 • Fundamentally, the dividend payment and future stock price relate to the ability of the issuing corporation to be profitable.

4 • When there is uncertainty as to future value, a subjective probability of occurrence is assigned to the various possible future values. The relationship among the probabilities reveals your view of the relative likelihood that each future value will be correct.

5 • If all the possible future values are fairly close to the most likely future value, the investment is relatively low risk, particularly if low probabilities are assigned to the most extreme future values. The probabilities must sum to 1.0.

6 • If the investment is relatively low risk, each future value is multiplied by the probability assigned to it and the series is summed. This sum is treated as the equivalent of present value under certainty for decision-making purposes.

7 • If the investment is high risk, it should be excluded from consideration.

8 • What is high or low risk varies from individual to individual and from one point in time to another for any given individual. In general, a high-risk situation is one in which an unfavorable outcome would appreciably restrict your actions in the future. This issue will be discussed in more detail in Chapter 15.

9 • Investment in housing, whether owner occupied or rental property, is subject to analysis in terms of present value the same as any other investment. It is typically somewhat more risky than a savings account but less risky than a common stock. Housing entails future costs as well as future benefits. The present value of the future costs must be subtracted from the present value of the future benefits. The present value of the future benefits (after subtracting costs) is, as always, willingness to pay.

10 • Investment in education is popular. The major cost is usually earnings foregone, not tuition and fees or board and room. Noneconomic income typically constitutes a large part of the benefit. Extremely low pricing of a benefit may destroy the incentive to collect the benefit. This is not unique to education but is occasionally particularly evident in education. Throughout our analysis we have necessarily assumed that the consumer is motivated to do the best he can—that is, to incur the smallest possible cost for any given benefit or to receive the largest possible benefit for any given cost. A consumer may fare badly because he is ignorant but also because he does not care.

study materials

1 • What is a common stock?

2 • Why do corporations sell stocks?

3 • In what two ways is income generated for the stockholder?

4 • Set up an example assuming a price of a stock in 5 years with an assumed expected dividend yield and compute the present value.

5 • Why do "far-off, long-shot" investments have little present value?

6 • Why is it easier and safer to determine a reasonably accurate present value for an established stock rather than a new stock?

7 • What elements make for uncertainty in common stocks?

8 • What is the difference between objective and subjective probability?

9 • How can the *degree* of risk be assessed using the probability framework?

10 • State briefly the five rules of thumb mentioned in the chapter regarding investments and evaluate each. Add others you may have heard and evaluate them.

11 • What additional considerations are there in real estate investment as opposed to stocks?

12 • Evaluate education as an investment.

footnotes

[1] Although the raising of large amounts of capital is the primary justification for the corporate form of business organization, it should not be concluded that the brief discussion of proprietorships and corporations here exhausts the arguments for and against either kind of business organization. There are many other facets of the corporation as a legal device; however, many of them relate to its ability to successfully raise capital and/or to keep large amounts of capital intact.

[2] Winston Churchill might have made an observation on the connection between risk and motivation when he observed that, "There is nothing so stimulating as to be shot at and missed."

appendix
a

PROTECTION AGAINST INFLATION

A more adequate title might be "Protection Against Changing Price Levels," since inflation is only one side of the coin—deflation being the other. But history has seen, and undoubtedly will see again, more inflation than deflation, so we will proceed in terms of inflation. You might suspect that an "implied reversibility" of the procedure for protection against inflation constitutes the protection against deflation. Indeed it is largely so. Look at either side of the coin you like; it is our guess you will feel more comfortable looking at the inflation side since you have seen more of that.

What is inflation and why do you need protection against it? Perhaps no other major economic term is so simply defined: **Inflation** is *a rising general price level.* Similarly, **deflation** is *a declining general price level.* In other words, there is inflation if prices *on the average* are rising. Some prices will rise and some will fall over a given period of time, but overall they will net out to an increase or decrease (or by coincidence, no change). Although most people know that inflation has to do with price increases, they nevertheless are apparently unaware of the disarmingly straightforward definition. Most of the arguments in households, bars, political groups, and even in the press over inflation and whether it exists are really arguments over the *cause* of inflation—that is, why prices are rising—and whether inflation is sufficiently pronounced to be *worthy of concern*—in other words, the rate of price increase that is acceptable. While the determination of a maximum acceptable rate of price increase from a social point of view is difficult and controversial, and while identification of the specific forces behind inflation may be obscure, the fact of whether inflation exists is relatively easy to determine; it is purely a matter of measurement, and after prices are measured, they are either going up or they are not. If they are going up, there is inflation; if they are not going up, there is not inflation. Period. Our concern will be over the implication of rising prices for you as an individual. If people are concerned about inflation, it must have some significance.

Perhaps the chief argument against *inflation* is that it *redistributes real income*. Obviously, then, your protection against inflation is to see to it either that you are *not* in a position to have real income distributed *away* from you, or, better still, that you are in a position so that real income is distributed *toward* you. (For every loser there is a winner: Why settle for a draw?) As anyone who is (or has friends or relatives) on fixed-money incomes well knows, the losers are those who are on fixed-money incomes. The pensioner finds that his money income buys less under higher prices. He has therefore had real income distributed away from him. Working people, who for one reason or another receive money incomes that rise more slowly than prices in general, lose real income. The winners are those who own things whose prices are rising the most rapidly.

In a broad way, protection against inflation is simple: Get out of fixed-dollar positions; get into real goods and services, since it is the prices of these goods and services that are rising! Employed people *generally* manage to hold their own against inflation *over the long run* since it is the prices of what they produce that are rising, which in turn raises the money value of the resources they supply as well. The need for employers who do not produce a specifically salable product, such as government, to remain competitive in labor markets causes gainfully employed people to more or less hold their own against inflation over the long run. To be sure, a great deal of see-saw may take place along the way as every group scrambles to stay ahead of the pack, but employed people are "in real goods and services," and the rising tide of prices *tends* to carry their incomes along with it. The big losers are retired people "in fixed-dollar positions" as well as recipients of public assistance and any other groups whose money incomes rise slowly or not at all in response to rising prices.

At this point it might seem that there is little you can do to protect yourself against inflation. If you are currently employed, your income will tend to jiggle up over time to more or less match the price increases of things you buy; but if you are a pensioner, you are just out of luck. Things are not that grim if you plan ahead, however. Since pensioners are in trouble because prices rise over time (they earned and paid into the pension fund when prices were low and now get too few dollars to keep them afloat), protection against inflation is through your investment program, which ties the present to the future.[1]

In what can you invest that will rise in price over time? Again, get into real goods and services and out of fixed-dollar positions. Probably the

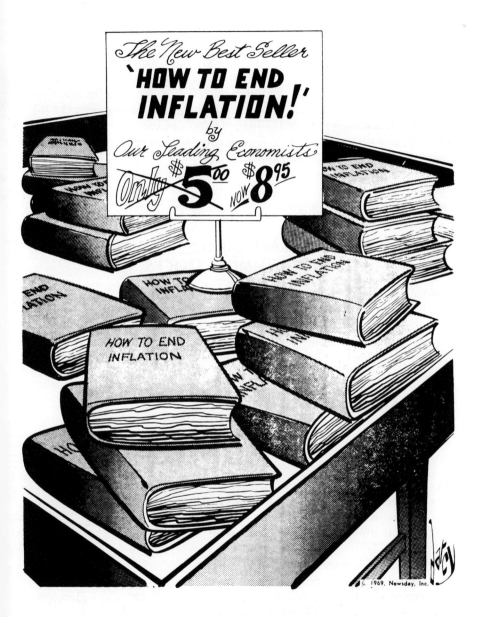

. . . On redistribution of real income through inflation . . .

two major vehicles through which more people will find more protection against inflation over the next 50 years than any others are real estate and common stocks. Probably the two poorest bets for protection against inflation among the popular investment opportunities will be savings accounts and bonds. The reasons are simple: Real estate and common stocks are the only categories of real goods and services, or their direct representation, available in sufficiently large quantities and of sufficient durability to serve as a vehicle for protection from inflation for large numbers of persons. To be sure, any real good has the potential to do the job; the list of inflation hedges is bounded only by the limit of your imagination. People look to such varied sources of protection as ownership of rare stamps and coins, art, antique automobiles, cattle, scotch whisky, frozen pork bellies, and firearms—to cite only a sample of the smorgasbord. But these items are available only in relatively limited quantity, so the majority will look elsewhere.

► REAL ESTATE AND COMMON STOCKS ◄

Let us assume that we are dealing with a very "neat" inflation where the prices of everything move up at exactly the same rate—the prices of everything rise, say, 5 percent per year. How will real estate protect you? Very simply. The price of your real estate (home, lot, farm, apartment building, factory, or whatever) also rises by 5 percent and you stay even with the board.

the XYZ corporation

	AT PRESENT	AFTER 5% INFLATION
(1) Capital supplied by stockholders	$1,000,000	$1,050,000
(2) Number of stockholders (each owning 1 share of stock)	10,000	10,000
(3) Capital supplied by each stockholder [(1) ÷ (2)]	$100	$105
(4) Income generated by the $1,000,000 capital in 1 year (profit after all costs except a return to the $1,000,000)	$100,000	$105,000
(5) Income accruing to each stockholder [(4) ÷ (2)]	$10	$10.50
(6) Rate of return on stockholder capital [(4) ÷ (1) or (5) ÷ (3)]	10%	10%

The argument in favor of common stocks is less obvious and hinges on their nature. The example of the XYZ Corporation will be a convenient starting point. Another column is simply added where all dollar figures are 5 percent higher.

The initial $1,000,000 supplied by the stockholders was converted into plant and equipment or other things used in the business whose dollar price rose along with everything else. Similarly, profits rise by 5 percent, since the prices of what the firm buys as inputs and the price of what the firm sells also rise by 5 percent. Since the value of the company's stock is theoretically the present value of the stream of future profits, the price of the stock can also be expected to rise by 5 percent. Thus everything is shifted upward by 5 percent—including you as a stockholder. *Over the very long run* it is impossible for common stocks *not* to rise in price along with inflation. If they do not, virtually indisputable underlying theories that tie stock value to the company's assets and earnings cannot hold. If you assume that stock prices will not rise with inflation, eventually—after a long period of inflation—you end up with a company producing fantastically high profits from fantastically high priced capital and a very low price on the common stock that says none of it is worth anything at the higher prices! Ridiculous.

Two refinements are in order: One stems from the simplifying assumption that all prices rise in lock-step together; the other from the assumption that human vagaries play no part in stock prices. The net result of these refinements is that common stocks (or anything else for that matter) may not be worth a plugged nickel as an inflation hedge *in the short run*. Indeed, the short run may be distressingly long also. In the late 1960s and early 1970s, stock prices not only failed to rise but, in general, sank. Why? The two refinements explain it. First, since all prices do not rise in lock-step, it is possible for the prices of the things firms buy to rise faster than the prices of things firms sell and for profits to be squeezed, and that's bad for stock prices. But sooner or later a correction must occur that restores profits, or the firms will go out of business. In the long run firms are not going to go out of business on a wholesale basis. (If they do, we are all going back to tents and caves, and inflation will be the least of your problems.)

Second, the role of expectations as a human element must be considered. If everyone is pessimistic and looks at the negative factors but not the positive factors in the always somewhat unclear future, there are going to be more stock sellers than stock buyers, and prices will fall. But pessimism turns to reconciliation, and reconciliation turns to optimism; optimism turns to realism, and realism turns to pessimism. Such is human nature. Over the long run, expectations "average out"; over the long run it is the *trend* and not the *cycle* that is relevant. And the trend of common stock prices in general, in the face of inflation, can be only one way. Up.

EXAMPLE 14A–1

For more than 5 years in the late 1960s and early 1970s stock prices tended to fall for basically the two reasons cited: a profit squeeze due in part to inflation, attempts by government to control it, and public pessimism. First, profits would be low. Then as profits improved, it was a balance-of-payments problem. Then it was Watergate. Then it was high interest rates. Earlier there was disenchantment generally over Vietnam. There were economic distortions from attempted price controls. Events all lined up wrong. If it wasn't one thing, it was another. When things were bad, people said, "Things are bad." When things were good, people said, "Things can only get worse." Indeed, even the fact of inflation itself contributed to uncertainty and pessimism. But, as cited above, these conditions cannot endure indefinitely. Sooner or later unwarranted pessimism turns to unwarranted optimism, and the market makes up for lost time. The point is that "protection-against-inflation" is one thing; "get-rich-quick" is another. People confuse the two. Protection against inflation is a truly long-term proposition. There is no reason to fret over short-term fluctuations. And even 5 years is short-term in this context.

A final word of caution. The foregoing discussion is true of real estate and common stocks *collectively* for an *"average"* person. Some *individuals* will prefer other forms of real goods or their representation. Perhaps you are one of them. Similarly, some *individual* pieces of real estate and common stocks will decline in value no matter how rampant inflation may run. There are always losers. Therefore, you, as an *individual,* may still do badly in either common stocks or real estate. There are no guarantees in the real world. A loss to inflation is better than an even larger loss to inept attempts at protection. Thus you must decide what fits your abilities and temperament. In any event it is useful to know where the most traveled path will necessarily lie. It will be real estate and common stocks.

▶ SAVINGS ACCOUNTS AND BONDS ◀

The reason that savings accounts and bonds do not constitute protection against inflation is that the *maximum* number of dollars you can get from these investments is specified. As inflation occurs, these dollars have less and less purchasing power and you get left behind.

EXAMPLE 14A–2

If you put your money in a 5 percent savings account, the most you can get for $100 after 1 year is $105 (ignoring compounding within the year). If there is 6 percent inflation, it takes $106 next year to buy what $100 did this year. Thus your *real* (as opposed to *money*) rate of return was minus 1 percent; if there is 8 percent inflation, your real rate of return was minus 3 percent; and so on. In other words, your rate of return must equal the inflation rate for you to stay even in purchasing power. There is no tendency for the number of dollars you receive to rise and fall with the inflation rate as in the case of real estate and common stocks. Hence the term, *fixed-dollar* investments.

Bonds are evidence of a loan to a business or a unit of government. As such, they pay a specified rate of return just as a savings account does. If you own a $1,000 bond, you have lent $1,000 to the bond issuer whether it be the U.S. government, General Motors, or some other unit of government or business. The rate of return is the *most* you will get. If the bond issuer falls on hard times, you could get less return and even lose the initial principal. The likelihood of loss depends on the solidness of the bond issuer. U.S. government bonds are considered nearly as safe as savings accounts; bonds issued by Moon Mining may be considerably less safe than the common stock of a more substantial company.[2]

▶ A QUALIFICATION ◀

Although the fundamental nature of real estate and common stocks are such that they provide protection against inflation and the fundamental nature of savings accounts and bonds is such that they do not, the fact remains that there are forces at work which modify the potency of the foregoing arguments. Those forces can be envisioned by assuming an extreme inflation situation. Suppose the inflation rate is, say, 20 percent and the interest rate on savings accounts is 5 percent. Even the dumbest saver soon catches on that he is losing ground. Now if the prices of common stocks are moving up at 20 percent along with inflation, more and more savers are going to switch from savings to stocks, are they not? The greater the inflation rate, the greater the tendency to switch.

Your intuition about supply, demand, and prices tells the rest of the story. The "supply" of savings accounts is down and the "demand" for stocks is up as a result of this switching. The prices of stocks are bid up, so that they become poorer and poorer buys—inflation notwithstanding. Similarly, the reduced supply of savings funds tends to lift the rate of return on savings accounts so that they become better "buys" relative to the stocks. Thus the *fact* of inflation *tends* to wipe out the validity of the arguments for protection against it! This is what is behind the observation that "the inflation rate tends to be built into the interest rate." Other things being equal, the higher the inflation rate, the higher interest rates can be expected to be. If inflation is 10 percent, an interest rate of 10 percent is 0 percent in *real* terms; there is a *real* interest rate only to the extent that the *money* interest rate is above 10 percent. Thus interest rates on fixed-dollar investments—such as savings accounts and bonds—can steer a course independent of the rate of inflation only if the public as a whole is completely stupid. And it is not. Nobody is going to sit around to get hit over the head harder and harder indefinitely if other alternatives are available. Some people are more sensitive and astute than others, but sooner or later everybody catches on if things get bad enough.

In some nations where the rate of inflation is both high and variable, variable interest rates have gone into effect in an attempt to prevent fluctuating inflation rates from wrecking capital markets. Indeed, as the rate of inflation picked up in the early 1970s in this country, there was some discussion of variable interest rates here, and some parts of the capital market did go to them. Under variable interest rates, the rate paid on a loan would vary over the life of the loan according to some index of interest rates in the economy as a whole.

There are two lessons. The first has been outlined: There are fundamental reasons why investment opportunities in common stocks and real estate can be expected to provide protection against inflation for large numbers of people and why savings accounts and bonds will provide less protection; there are also forces at work that make savings accounts and bonds more attractive than you might otherwise expect them to be. The second lesson is broader and relates to general economics: Any time substitutes are considered—such as common stocks and real estate versus savings accounts and bonds as investment opportunities—a certain commonness must apply to all of them. Such is the essence of the definition of substitutes—an element of commonness exists. The forces that affect any member of a set of substitutes necessarily have impact (though possibly indirect) on the other members of the set of substitutes. Thus, although some opportunities for protection against inflation will be better than others, even the poorer ones will necessarily have to provide some protection if they are not to pass out of the picture entirely.

► **PROTECTION AGAINST DEFLATION** ◄

If you are worried that prices are going to go down rather than up, the arguments are reversed. As an instructive exercise you can go back through this appendix and partially rewrite it to show that the fixed-dollar investment—savings accounts and bonds—constitute protection against deflation. If you understand the arguments for protection against inflation, the arguments for protection against deflation are self-evident.

footnotes

[1] It should be mentioned that "cost of living" provisions are being increasingly built into pension programs. The social security system now scales payments upward as compensation for inflation if and when it occurs. Private pension funds will probably move in this direction also in spite of some difficulties. This is simply to say that there are ways of compensating for the redistribution effects of inflation even though they are a bit messy. But these provisions are beyond your specific control and are therefore not discussed further here. Even though you may be offered some protection on a platter, you still want to do the best you can. After all, if inflation redistributes income, perhaps you can come out ahead *because* of inflation rather than settling for staying even.

[2] You should know that this is by no means a complete discussion of bonds, which are a major part of the investment world. There are other factors that can affect your rate of return over any period of time, but they are not closely connected to inflation and are therefore not discussed here. That is, the discussion here assumes that these other factors are neutral so that the *expected* performance of bonds as protection against inflation may be examined.

appendix
b

PRESENT VALUE OF AN INFINITE STREAM OF PAYMENTS

From Table 13–2, the present value of $1,900 per year forever discounted at 6 percent was $1,900 × 16.67 = $31,673.00. Whatever the property is worth at the end of "forever" is zero, since the present value is progressively lower as the time when the future sum is to be collected becomes more distant. Thus the present value of a sum to be collected at "infinity" is theoretically zero. (Surely you will not pay to collect something at the *end* of "forever"!) The present value of the property is then obviously the present value of the stream of payments only. You might therefore view your annual costs as those necessary to keep the property in a condition so as to generate the $1,900 per year forever. If this is your approach, notice that simply dividing the annual payment by the interest rate at which you wish to discount the future yields the correct present value. $1,900/.06 = $31,666.67. The difference between $31,673.00 and $31,666.67 is due to rounding of the factor in the table, which was determined by exactly this same procedure but using $1.00: $1.00/.06 = $16.66 . . . or $16.67. The formula for the present value of an infinite stream of payments may therefore be generalized as

$$\frac{A}{I} = P$$

where A is the annual payment, I is the interest rate, and P is the present value.

This method is simple and useful when it is expected that payments will flow indefinitely and/or where it is expected that the value of the asset generating the income will *not* change. Notice that if it is assumed that the present value of \$31,673.00 will not change, then if the property is sold after, say, 5 years, the income is \$1,900 for 5 years *plus* the present value of \$31,673.00 to be received in 5 years. Using Tables 13–1 and 13–2 gives

$$(\$1{,}900 \times 4.21) + (\$31{,}673.00 \times .7473)$$
$$= \$7{,}999.00 + \$23{,}668.00 = \$31{,}667.00$$

Again, any discrepancy is due to rounding in the factors in the tables.

Although this result may seem surprising, it is the same principle that allowed us to determine the present value of the savings account. In one sense the result is obvious. To get \$4.00 per year from a 4 percent savings account forever, you must commit \$100.00 and leave it there and reclaim it only at the "end of infinity." On the other hand, you can commit the same \$100.00 for 5 years, draw five annual \$4.00 payments, and get your \$100.00 back at the end of 5 years. Since each option costs \$100.00 and relates to the same interest rate, they must be equivalent conditions.

chapter
15

INSURANCE DECISIONS: AVOIDABLE RISK

Risk is an important subject within economics. In the previous chapter risk was encountered as a part of the investment decision. Risk is by no means confined to the investment world. Indeed, risk is always present; it is only the degree to which it is present that varies. In some cases the amount of risk is so small that it can be ignored. The risk associated with the buying of a cabbage would normally fall in this category; but in other cases risk must be taken into account and some specific means of dealing with it must be developed. The assigning of probabilities to various possible future values of an investment constitutes a special mechanism for the handling of moderate amounts of risk in investments. Having done this in the previous chapter, we concluded that a high-risk investment should simply be refused; if losing the game would be disastrous, you should refuse to play even though the chance of losing is relatively small.

This chapter will add an additional dimension to the discussion of risk. We will examine very risky situations where the possibility of a disastrous loss exists; however, rather than concluding, as in the previous chapter, that you must refuse such risky situations, we will consider the possibility that you may be able to "buy your way out of them." That is, for a price, you can hire someone else to bear the risk. As you have probably suspected, this is the essence of insurance. *You might logically ask why the buyer of the high-risk investment did not insure against his loss rather than simply refusing the high-risk investment. The answer is that certain conditions have to be met before insurance is a good buy. In some situations (such as the risky investment) the conditions are so notably* unmet *that insurance would be available only at a prohibitively high price. In other situations (such as loss of investment in housing by fire) the risk of a large loss may still be disastrous; yet, rather than refusing the investment, the risk is avoided by buying insurance against it. The insurance is available at a reasonable cost because the conditions for insurability are so notably* well *met with regard to loss of housing by fire.*

The primary purpose of this chapter is to investigate the conditions for insurability, which will lead to some conclusions for you, the consumer, with regard to whether insurance is a good buy in a particular instance. As a vehicle in this discussion, we will draw upon our previous analyses.

We will first investigate risks at sufficiently low levels so that the risk is generally ignored. Insurance against such low risks is usually a bad buy, although insurance could conceivably be available. The reason it is not available is because there is no demand for it even at a very low cost. These are the risks associated with decisions under what was heretofore called (somewhat erroneously) present certainty. We will consider the risks in buying a cab-

*bage and then in buying an automobile as examples.
We will next investigate the risk associated with what we
called risky investments and inquire as to why insurance is
generally not available against these losses, or, in any event,
would be available only at a prohibitively high cost. The
discussion will evolve toward the identification of four
basic insurance principles. We will note that they are well
met with regard to the risk of loss of housing by fire but
notably unmet with regard to other risks not generally
considered to be insurable.*

*Finally, we will make some general observations about the
typical consumer's need for insurance and the extent to
which that need is or is not met by present insurance programs commonly available.*

▶   INCONSEQUENTIAL RISK   ◀

Let us begin by considering the risks of buying a head of cabbage. Do
you know exactly what the costs and benefits from the decision to have
a head of cabbage will be? Certainly not, although you probably know
quite closely. If you are to make your decision at home as to whether to
have the cabbage or something else, you will very likely be uncertain of
the price of the cabbage. You can make an estimate and make a decision on
that basis. You then go to the store to buy the cabbage and perhaps learn
that the price of cabbage is higher than you thought it would be, so you
decide to return home without any, in which case your prior ignorance
of cabbage prices cost you the disutility of a trip to the store. On the
other hand, you might argue that you know that if you do not buy
cabbage, you will buy some other close substitute (food product) from
the same store, so your trip will not really have been a loss after all. In
other words, you might argue that you know you will select some products at prevailing prices in the store which sells cabbage, so why should
you feel compelled to make a hard and fast decision before getting to
the store? If you like this line of reasoning, then consider the possible
loss accruing to your decision to go to a store which, unknown to you,
is higher priced on the bundle of products you select than some other
stores. To be certain that you are getting the best buy, you might have
to do a good deal of calling or traveling to different stores. But this may

cost you more in time and money than the results can justify. Of course, you can never be *sure* of this unless you actually do it. The existence of uncertainty creates risk of loss in the form of elevated costs or reduced benefits that can never be completely avoided.

Can you be certain of the benefits from the cabbage? After all, you have eaten cabbage before and know your reaction to it. But, remember, you have never eaten *this* head of cabbage, so it may turn out to be bitter, or to be rotten in the center. The universe is rife with variability and uncertainty, and if you have seen one head of cabbage, you definitely have *not* seen them all.

This rather trivial example illustrates a point that is far from trivial. Although many decisions are made under the assumption that costs and benefits are known and certain, actually *the costs and benefits of any action are never certain.* The importance of this observation is tremendous. Obviously, if the costs and/or benefits associated with any decision turn out to be different from predicted, what otherwise would have been a good decision may turn out to be a bad decision. Thus perfect decisions require perfect predictability of costs and benefits. Since perfection is not attainable, you settle for making the best of it. Insurance is a way of making the unpredictable more predictable.

The cabbage example was deliberately chosen because it is trivial. It was designed to illustrate that although you face uncertainty at every turn and would thereby very likely not make the best possible decision, the typical cabbage buyer does not worry very much about the uncertainties, because they are so minor. More formally, the difference in benefit or cost from a bad decision versus a good decision is so minor that it is almost certain that the gain from a better decision would be less than the cost necessary to produce it. Cabbage can probably be bought satisfactorily by picking a random head from a random store. On the average you get a good head for, say, $.40. If you were really unlucky you might get stuck for $.20 more than the cheapest store. Unless you can find the cheapest cabbage for less than $.20 worth of time and effort there is no point in researching the cabbage market. This suggests, accurately, that decision making itself is subject to economic analysis. *Do not incur more costs in the decision-making process itself than the decision is worth.* This explains precisely why the average consumer does not exercise more care in buying cabbage. The uncertainties are minor, so the gain from more care is small relative to the costs of being more careful. The meticulous search through a bin of cabbages undertaken by some shoppers suggests that they either have a very low alternative cost of time or they would be better off spending less time on minor decisions.

Now consider the purchase of an automobile. The typical buyer takes more care in evaluating the uncertainties of cost and benefit from an automobile than from a head of cabbage for the obvious reason that the stakes are higher and he can therefore afford to spend more time and effort sorting the good alternatives from the bad alternatives. You stand to gain, say, $.20 from a good (as opposed to a willy-nilly) cabbage decision but, say, $500 from a good automobile decision. You can therefore afford to spend as much as $.20 to improve your cabbage buying and $500 to improve your automobile buying if necessary. Although there is more to learn about automobiles than about cabbages and the research is therefore more complex, it is certainly more likely that you can make a bigger saving, with the same time and effort, researching automobile alternatives than researching cabbage alternatives. This, of course, explains the typical consumer's care in the buying of automobiles and his nonchalance in the buying of cabbages.

As observed in Chapter 14, the uncertainties of an investment decision may loom large. The price to be paid for an investment is keyed to the future income generated by that investment. The income must be estimated and the estimates are necessarily subject to variability, depending on a number of things that can be scarcely more than guessed at. The estimates are therefore subject to substantial error. Nonetheless, one particular estimate must emerge as your best estimate.

Compare the cabbage, the automobile, and the investment which is represented here by a share of stock. In each case we needed to estimate the present value of the costs and benefits. The alternative that showed the highest benefit to cost ratio was selected in each case as the best alternative based on our estimates. You decide to buy X cabbage from Y store, to buy B automobile from C dealer, and to buy L stock from M broker. You are quite certain that the estimates of cost and benefit upon which the cabbage decision hinged were correct. To the extent that they are incorrect, the errors were of virtually no consequence. In fact, we might say that the estimates were not estimates at all—they were *known,* although this is necessarily somewhat of an overstatement.

Clearly the uncertainties of automobile ownership are more important. Uncertainties as to the length of life of major components such as engine and transmission, the cost of tires, gasoline, and maintenance, and the used car market's view of your car, say, 5 years hence are important; yet estimates of all of these things must be made directly or indirectly in an automobile decision. The best decision that can be made on an automobile is less solid than the best decision that can be made about a cabbage. The figures that go into the estimates are more uncertain for the automobile, and the consequences of being wrong are more severe.

The investment decision, although "best," may be highly uncertain. The present value is tied to future earnings, which must be estimated. Or, even more accurately, present value is tied to future value, which is dependent upon the dividend payment and the future price of the stock. The *immediate* determinant of stock prices is supply and demand for the stock. Demand and hence price rises if the buyers get optimistic about the future price of the stock. Thus, it might be argued, your decision to buy a stock is not based so much on *your* estimate of earnings as on your estimate of *everyone else's* estimates about the stock. These estimates may be founded on rational analytics or on mob psychology. The list of uncertainties in determining stock prices therefore becomes impressive: What will the general economy do? What will this firm do given general economic and industry behavior? And, how do I think that my fellow investors will assess these things? Considering that a firm's fortunes can be affected by such random elements as the domestic tranquility or lack thereof for key personnel, it is perfectly obvious that your best decision may not be very good at all. Furthermore, the unfavorable consequences of bad investment decisions may be enormous. At this point it would be easy to become a cynic and give up trying to make good decisions. But all is not lost. There may be a way of improving on this disagreeable condition. It is inevitable that decisions involving the lapse of time will be shakier than those that do not. To recapitulate:

	CABBAGE	AUTOMOBILE	STOCK
Best possible decision is relatively	good	fair	poor
Consequences of a bad decision likely to be	minor	moderate	major

What a final twist of the sword of fate! The decision that is the hardest to make well is the one that bears the greatest penalty for being wrong and, similarly, the greatest reward for being right! (There ain't no free lunch, revisited.)

▶ SUBSTANTIAL AND UNAVOIDABLE ◀ RISK

We turn now to situations where the risk must definitely be considered because it is substantial. The common stock has been offered as an example. The risk is classified as unavoidable because if you play the game you must accept the risk. Thus **unavoidability of risk** is defined here as *the inability to transfer risk at an acceptable cost;* that is, un-avoidable risk is risk that you *cannot insure against at a price you are willing to pay.* Consider a second example of unavoidable risk.

You are offered $100,000 to go over Niagara Falls in a barrel. This is not your idea of a good time, but then $100,000 is a lot of money. If you survive, you get $100,000. If you do not survive, you get $0. This caper has been performed before, and "barrel technology" is getting better all the time; suppose six of the last eight people to go over the falls have survived. So what is your best estimate of the value of the "investment"? Clearly it appears that you are more likely to get $100,000 than $0—the only two possibilities.

The best estimate of the value of the trip over Niagara Falls can be improved upon by assigning probabilities to the possible outcomes just as the best estimate of stock value was converted to best *adjusted* estimate by assigning probabilities to the possible present values. You get $100,000 if you survive, $0 if you do not; six of the last eight persons to attempt the trip survived. If we accept the experience of the last eight as grounds upon which to establish an objective probability, then we have the situation shown in Table 15–1. The expected value from the trip is

Table 15–1

PAYOFF FROM TRIP OVER NIAGARA FALLS

POSSIBLE VALUES	PROBABILITY	PROBABILITY × VALUE
$100,000	$\frac{6}{8}$ = .75	$75,000
$0	$\frac{2}{8}$ = .25	0
	$\frac{8}{8}$ = 1.00	$75,000

$75,000. That is, if we conceptualize your taking the trip repeatedly, the average payoff would be $75,000.

With the Niagara Falls example under our belt as the ultimate in risky undertakings, we make a definitive though somewhat arbitrary categorization of the riskiness of various kinds of activities and circumstances. Let us agree to acknowledge *moderate possibilities* and *extreme possibilities.* **Moderate Possibilities** are *those events which will* not *substantially reduce the alternatives available to you in the future.* **Extreme Possibilities** are *those events which* will *substantially reduce the alternatives available to you in the future.*

It is clear from these definitions that risk relates the present to the future. The interest rate was cited earlier as connecting the present and the future. It does. And in a very concrete way. Risk does not connect the present and the future quite so specifically. Risk has implications for you as you recognize that events today affect the conditions under which you will operate tomorrow. One of the chief concerns today, with regard to tomorrow, is not what to *do* tomorrow but what the range of *available alternatives* will be tomorrow. Clearly it is desirable to have a wide rather than narrow range of choices available tomorrow. Since the range of choices available tomorrow is influenced in part by events today and since events today are determined in part by the presence of risk, it follows that risk relates to the relationship of the present and the future, albeit in a somewhat subtle way.

Our primary focus here will be on the extreme possibilities. The moderate possibilities are not sufficiently severe to affect what you will be able to do tomorrow. But the loss of a major portion of your investment capital or an "unfavorable outcome" of the trip over Niagara Falls would certainly reduce the alternatives open to you in the future. The loss of one's life might be construed as the ultimate extreme possibility. Death has a way of reducing one's future alternatives rather decisively. In discussing investments, we concluded that extreme possibilities should simply be refused when possible. Do not invest in (what are for you) high-risk ventures, and do not go over Niagara Falls in a barrel if you value the future at all.

► SUBSTANTIAL AND AVOIDABLE ◄ RISK

Some risks are substantial and cannot be avoided by living one's life circumspectly. It is therefore unsatisfactory to announce that substantial risks should be refused. It is not possible, for instance, to refuse the extreme possibility of death. It is not possible to live in an abode without withstanding the risk of loss of possessions by fire or wind. It is not possible to refuse the risk of substantial loss through serious illness. A bit of care may minimize all these risks but will not eliminate them the way the risk from an investment may be eliminated simply by deciding against buying it.

Although certain risks may not be avoided by refusing to confront them, other risks may be avoided through the purchase of *insurance*. Indeed, given our definition of *un*avoidability, **avoidable risks** are *those which are readily insurable*. Certain conditions have to be met before insurance can be attractively priced. To illustrate the insurance principle, we will examine a simple illustration of the insurance principle at work.

We will then analyze the characteristics of the example which make it a good illustration of popular insurance. Finally, we will see that other kinds of losses occur under conditions that are quite different and therefore are not readily insurable.

Consider fire insurance on a house. On the basis of previous experience it is known that, on average, 1 house in 1,000 will burn down each year. Each house is worth $20,000. Therefore, it might be said that 1/1,000 of each house will burn each year; 1/1,000 of $20,000 is $20. Table 15–2 gives the figures involved. The total value of housing is $20 million,

Table 15–2
FIRE INSURANCE

HOUSE	VALUE	PROBABILITY OF FIRE	PROBABILITY × VALUE
1	$ 20,000	1/1,000 = .001	$ 20
2	20,000	.001	20
3	20,000	.001	20
⋮	⋮	⋮	⋮
997	20,000	.001	20
998	20,000	.001	20
999	20,000	.001	20
1,000	20,000	.001	20
	$20,000,000		$20,000

$$\$20,000,000 \times .001 = \$20,000$$

of which $20,000 will be destroyed by fire each year. It might be said that $20 worth of each house burns down each year. In fact, of course, each house either burns down, or it does not. Some unlucky owner will lose $20,000 and everyone else will lose nothing. Thus the "best" estimate of loss from fire is $0, but the extreme possibility is a loss of $20,000. Thus $20 is the best adjusted estimate of each homeowner's loss by fire each year. Each homeowner would therefore apparently be willing to pay up to $20 to avoid the risk of this extreme possibility because, on the average, he will get back $20 per year. This conforms perfectly to the conclusion drawn in the investment chapter: *Risk has disutility.* Through investment, investors demanded additional benefit in the form of interest as reward for bearing risk. Through insurance the consumer is willing to incur cost to rid himself of risk.

Although the extreme possibilities of fire cannot be circumvented in many instances, they can be shifted elsewhere through the payment of a small insurance premium. Having bought the insurance, you know you will "lose" $20 per year. Without the insurance, you may lose $20,000 but much more likely will lose nothing. The insurance is a good buy if you are willing to pay $20 per year to guarantee the future alternatives that $20,000 represent. With no insurance and a fire you lose $20,000, and with it, substantial alternatives in the future, since you are saddled with the consequences of this disaster. You are willing to pay to guarantee these alternatives. Thus insurance may be defined in a somewhat abstruse way as *the purchase of a guarantee of future alternatives.* This definition acknowledges our earlier conclusion that risk involves the relationship between the present and the future. Future alternatives therefore have a "present utility equivalent." You receive satisfaction *now* from knowing that the *future* will offer you latitude of choice. You are willing to pay for these future alternatives, just as you are willing to pay for any other source of utility.

With this simple fire insurance example as background, we offer the following four criteria for insurability:

INSURABLE	UNINSURABLE
1 • Objective probability of loss can be established	1 • Objective probability of loss cannot be established
2 • Many individuals involved	2 • Few individuals involved
3 • Probability of loss very low	3 • Probability of loss relatively high
4 • Loss by an individual independent of the loss by any other individual	4 • Loss by an individual dependent on the loss by another individual

The extent to which these criteria for insurability are met tends to dictate the popularity of the insurance among consumers. The essence of these criteria is the fact that the insured band together and share their collective loss. Each individual is willing to pay his share of the loss to guarantee his future options. As long as these four conditions are met, the insurance program is apt to remain strong and popular. The 1,000 insured homeowners attack their problem as a group. The four conditions of insurability make it possible for them to attack the problem collectively. Examine each point.

1 • An objective probability of loss makes it possible for each home-

owner to know his cost precisely and for the group to assess its individual members that cost.

2 • Obviously, many individuals are needed to adequately diffuse the risk among them.

3 • If the probability of loss is high, insurance is pointless. If the probability of loss is, say, .5, then half the houses, or $10 million worth, burn down every year; on the average, every homeowner loses his $20,000 every other year. He knows his losses are going to be substantial—insured or not. He is just as well off to face the risk on his own. Uncertainty has evolved toward certainty. There are no appreciable future alternatives to be purchased through insurance. If he cannot bear such a large risk, he will have to live in a tent or otherwise circumvent the risk as best he can.

4 • If all the participants in the insurance program suffer losses simultaneously, the group of insured persons is transformed into the same position as the individual consumer prior to buying insurance. For example, if it is assumed that if one house burns down they all burn down, the group of homeowners is no better able to stand the loss of $20 million than each individual was able to stand the loss of $20,000; so, again, the insurance would be pointless. The group has become a straight multiple of the number of individuals in it in every respect.

Let us pursue, for a moment, these insurance principles as they relate to risks of loss from fire, the stock market, and trips over Niagara Falls in a barrel. The reasons for the popularity of insurance against fire but the unavailability of insurance against stock market loss are almost self-evident and hopefully will cause the insurance principles to appear as little more than the obvious.

▶ **FIRE INSURANCE**

Insurance against loss from fire is readily available and carried by nearly everyone. Insurance against loss from fire meets the insurability criteria laid down above admirably. Vast experience is available upon which to determine objective probabilities of loss. Many individuals are involved in the program. The probability of loss is very low. And the probability that any house will burn down has nothing to do with whether or not any other house has burned down. For these reasons, fire insurance is economical and carried by nearly all homeowners in order to avoid the risk of the extreme possibility of his house burning. The popularity of fire insurance attracts and holds individuals in the program, thereby contributing to its continued strength.

▶ NIAGARA-FALLS-IN-A-BARREL INSURANCE

Ignoring for the moment that fact that a loss from a trip over Niagara Falls results in death, suppose that you were contemplating buying insurance to cover the loss from the unsuccessful trips. From Table 15–1 we see that ¾ of the trips pay off at $100,000 and ¼ at $0, for an average of $75,000. What would the insurance premium have to be to bring payoff up to $100,000 for every trip? Obviously, it would have to be $25,000. If the premium is less than $25,000, no one will sell the insurance to you, since the average payout by the insurer to you will be $25,000. If the premium is more than $25,000, you would be better off without insurance. This activity is therefore essentially noninsurable. There are no willing buyers and no willing sellers of insurance. The primary reason for this state of affairs is that you are *alone* in your predicament. The houses were insurable because several individuals were involved. Let us suppose, however, that several individuals were involved in the Niagara Falls venture. Would such activity then be insurable? It is doubtful. The probability of loss is relatively high; therefore, each individual *expects* an insurance payoff periodically. When he *expects* periodic payoffs, his premiums must cover the payoffs as always and the insurance is pointless.[1] However, where the probability of loss is very low, each individual does not really expect a payoff but is willing to pay a very small premium in order to avoid the extreme possibility of a crippling loss. If the loss is routine, you are well aware that its cost will be present on an ongoing basis and you must plan for it as a "cost of doing business," so to speak. Furthermore, if the loss is routine, the amount of that loss is essentially the same whether you insure against it or whether you bear it directly. (It will be shown shortly that the cost of routine losses is actually higher if insured than if uninsured.) In any event you are not purchasing any additional future alternatives via the insurance because you end up with the same costs and benefits, whether you insure or not.

▶ STOCK MARKET INSURANCE

If you can insure against a loss from fire, why not insure against a loss from a drop in stock price? Try finding insurance against stock market losses and see how far you get. If you can understand (as well as sense) why this suggestion is ridiculous, you are well grounded in the principles of insurability. An objective probability based on experience cannot be established. To simply observe that "what goes up eventually comes down" or otherwise point out that certain patterns of gains and losses may exist is far different from specifying precisely the probability that on a given day a given stock will be worth so much. Second, the probability of loss is relatively high. Third, the loss by one person is not independent of the loss of other persons. Obviously, if the holder of a share of stock suffers a downturn in prices, all other holders of that same company's stock also suffer a downturn. Furthermore, there is a substantial tendency for the prices of all stocks to move together in response to general conditions. Thus as one stockholder suffers a loss, there is a great probability that all suffer a loss. Although there are many stockholders participant in the "game," the activity is still noninsurable because they all tend to realize losses and gains together. Houses, on the other hand, do not all tend to burn down at one time. When all stockholders suffer losses, all receive payment from the insurer—frequently and in large amounts. To support such a system, the premium must be frightfully high—so high that each individual is just as well-off to either bear his own risk of loss, or, if he cannot do that, simply refrain from exposing himself to it—that is, head for the savings bank.

When the average insurance holder plans on actually collecting insurance with reasonable frequency, premiums tend to rise to the point where the insurance becomes pointless, the good risk individuals tend to leave the system, and the system ceases to perform its intended purpose and, perhaps, to collapse. There is some indication that hospitalization insurance and auto collision insurance are headed in this direction. It is no coincidence that both systems are in some difficulty and under pressure for reform. Successful reform will undoubtedly carry some incentive or feature to prevent or discourage frequent claims by large numbers of holders.

▶ INSURANCE AGAINST WAR OR WEATHER

Insurance against fire seems very workable. Insurance against stock market losses seems completely unworkable. Insurance against loss from war or weather is available but not, for the most part, widely accepted. An exception is windstorm insurance. Objective probabilities on the occurrence of individual weather events can be established. On the average, once in 25 years it will rain more than, say, 6 inches in 24 hours; once in 50 years it will rain more than 10 inches in 24 hours; once in 10 years it will freeze before September 1 in the fall; and so on. The probability of damaging windstorms can generally be calculated for any area. Windstorm damage (with the possible exception of hurricanes) tends to be fairly localized. Although much damage may occur in a single town, city, or county, the numbers affected are still relatively few compared to the total coverage by a large company or group of companies. It is interesting to note in this regard that small insurance companies that have all their customers in a small area often reinsure themselves with larger companies to minimize the extreme possibility of a windstorm hitting a large number of their customers. Similarly, even large companies may band together to insure against natural disasters. Lloyds of London, the famous insurer against off-beat events, is a consortium of insurers formed to take on risks too great for any single one of them.

If insurance against windstorm is generally available, why is insurance against flood generally not available? A windstorm is a single weather phenomenon and as such may be fairly predictable. A flood is often the combination of a number of weather phenomena and therefore almost impossible to predict. (Flooding that occurs routinely in some locations occurs with a probability of nearly 1.0 in which case no meaningful prediction is involved at all. The losses from flooding are then uninsurable because the expected payoff is large and frequent so the insurance is prohibitively costly.) Rainfall is merely the most conspicuous single, immediate contribution to flooding. If flooding is from snow melt, rainfall need not occur at all. Flooding is often the product of a combination of such things as amount of rainfall, snow, temperature, depth of frost, and the water already in the soil. Although establishing an objective probability on each of these factors individually may be possible, it may also be nearly impossible to establish an objective probability on their occurring in a combination so as to produce a flood. Loss from windstorm is generally unavoidable, or at least less avoidable, than loss from flood. By refraining from engaging in unnecessary activity on floodplains, flood loss can simply be refused. There are other means of protection, such as levees, which may be cheaper than insurance. The resources going into these protective devices are possibly less than the resources lost through flooding. Thus, partly relating to inherent inability to insure against floods and partly due to society's desire to discourage waste of resources, flood insurance is not generally available.

Most insurance policies explicitly exclude coverage of loss due to war. The occurrence of war is very uncertain; and wars affect large numbers of individuals when they do occur, although some insurance policies make exceptions and insure for certain losses that are war connected.

The point of this discussion of insurance as it relates to war and weather is simply to show that these are gray areas as far as the principles of insurability are concerned. With the exception of windstorm insurance, insurance relating to war and weather tends to be expensive and therefore relatively unpopular, even where subsidized by government, as is often the case.

▶ DECISION TO INSURE ◀

You approach the insurance decision the same as any other decision. You consider what you are getting for what you give up—that is, you look at the utility received and the opportunity cost of getting it. An interesting observation can be made by returning to the fire insurance example. Although the example was simplistic, it inadvertently illustrated that perhaps no one should ever insure against anything! The inevitable conclusion would be that the entire insurance industry is supported by consumers making bad decisions. This startling possibility sneaked up on us in all the previous insurance examples. Consider fire insurance.

One $20,000 house in each 1,000 burns down each year. The unlucky homeowner is paid $20,000, which consists of $20 collected from each of the 1,000 homeowners. Alternatively, we concluded earlier, $20 worth of each house may be viewed as burning down each year. That is, the average loss for each homeowner for each year is $20. This is his payment to the one owner whose home actually burns. It is the function of the insurance company to act as the intermediary and collect the $20 from everybody and give it to the one homeowner whose house actually burns down. From the above example, then, if the insurance were to run forever, the expected or average payoff each year to each homeowner would be $20, which is exactly equal to his cost of $20. But, in addition, the cost to the homeowner must include compensation to the resources employed by the insurer who is collecting and redistributing the $20,000. The people who are doing the collecting and redistributing must be paid. Thus each homeowner's cost is slightly over $20 (how much over $20 depends on how efficient the insurance company is) and his expected return for this is exactly $20. *The consumer is thereby assured that in the long run his costs will be greater than his benefits.* It might appear at first that insurance is always a bad buy, and the insurance industry is supported by ignorant consumers; when consumers become more enlightened, insurance salesmen will become extinct. Try the argument as a conversation opener the next time an insurance salesman graces your party. Guaranteed results!

Indeed, it is true that the expected return from *any* insurance must *necessarily* be less than the cost of it by the cost of operating the insurance company. Yet it seems hard to believe that this mammoth industry lives on as a hoax and that virtually every consumer is ignorant or stupid, as evidenced by nearly universal ownership of some insurance. Somewhere there must be a key point overlooked. Certainly. We have encountered the explanation previously but perhaps did not recognize its significance: The explanation lies in *extreme possibilities*. The conclusion that all insurance is a bad buy was based on the assumption that a house burning down was only a moderate possibility and, as such, did not substantially affect the alternatives you would face if it burned. Insuring against *moderate possibilities* means that you will necessarily pay more than you get back—everything on a present basis. Only when the possibilities become extreme and remote does insurance become a good buy, because then you are buying the *preservation of future alternatives,* in addition.[2]

As suggested earlier, it is now abundantly clear that *insurance is protection against the reduction of future alternatives.*

This is certainly a different kind of definition of insurance than is usually offered, but it is a very fundamental kind of definition that conforms to the concept of utility. Certainly the restriction of future alternatives very likely results in a reduction in utility. It is hard to envision how you could be *more* satisfied if your range of choice is *reduced.* The only exception would seem to be possible frustration from the inability to decide among numerous alternatives. But the intelligent consumer knows how to make decisions and is not frustrated by numerous alternatives. The conclusion, therefore, is that numerous alternatives in the future have present utility.

Thus the crux of the insurance decision lies in *what you are willing to pay for the utility gotten from the assurance that future alternatives will not be appreciably reduced.* Two aspects of this statement indicate that decisions to insure or not to insure can vary considerably among individuals: (1) What is an extreme possibility for one person may not be for another, and (2) the preference for future alternatives can vary among individuals.

Consider the difference in what may constitute an extreme possibility for one family but not for another. Mr. and Mrs. W. E. Arepoor with two children and $8,000 in income and $5,000 in net worth live in a $20,000 house. If they lost that house, it would certainly constitute an extreme possibility, since the added burden from which they received nothing would force them into a very narrow channel at a substantial reduction in utility in the future. They would undoubtedly find that insurance was an excellent buy, since it would allow them much greater latitude should their house burn down. However, to Mr. Manybucks, who also lives in a $20,000 house but who has an income of $100,000 a year and a net worth of $5,000,000 (he is a bit eccentric to live in such a cheap house), the loss of $20,000 is only a moderate possibility—it would not reduce his future alternatives any more than the loss of, say, $10 would for the Arepoors. This suggests that perhaps Mr. Manybucks should bear the risk of fire himself and not insure but that the Arepoors definitely should insure. Perhaps. The conclusion is tempered by the observation that, since Mr. Manybucks has so many more dollars, he is probably getting less utility per dollar at the margin and is therefore willing to spend more for a given amount of utility than are the Arepoors. If so, this will tend to make Manybucks more inclined to insure than he would otherwise be. But the central point is intact. What is a good insurance decision for one individual is not necessarily a good decision for another. In addition, simple differences in preference for future alternatives can cause different individuals to approach the insurance question differently.

It is virtually impossible to specify just what you would be willing to pay for insurance in the same way you specified what you would be willing to pay for a consumer durable or service or investment. You cannot really specify willingness to pay because the insurance buys the preservation of future alternatives and you are not always able to know just what they might be. You do know, however, that you do not want them unduly reduced. Although any specific insurance decision is shrouded in vagueness, the recognition of insurance as relating to the preservation of future alternatives is nonetheless a powerful analytical device. You will be able to identify obviously good insurance buys and obviously bad insurance buys and get a fair focus on those insurance questions that are less obvious. It is also possible to see that certain conditions, practices, and trends in the insurance industry may not be very desirable. Since consumers are the ultimate purchasers of insurance, but often at the encouragement of the insurer, it is difficult to assign blame fairly for any possibly undesirable situation. In any event, you should be aware of the issues and act in your own best interest. It is also abundantly clear that reforms within the insurance industry will come about more quickly and decisively if the buyers of insurance understand the issues.

► COMMON PRACTICE VERSUS ◄
DESIRABLE PRACTICE

Certain characteristics of the insurance industry and common practice by the typical consumer make an interesting analysis in light of our major conclusions. Again, they are as follows: (1) Insurance is the purchase of assurance that future alternatives will not be substantially reduced, and (2) when insurance begins to cover what are only moderate possibilities (as opposed to extreme possibilities) for the average consumer, the insurance inevitably becomes a bad buy in that the cost will be more than the expected benefit because money is simply being reshuffled and consumers must bear the cost of reshuffling. There is no offsetting benefit because no extreme possibilities are eliminated.

The implications of the two conclusions are enormous. Consider hospitalization insurance, including major medical coverage. It covers both the moderate possibilities of, say, $300 per year medical costs that a young family might expect, plus the extreme possibility of a crippling bill for $10,000 or more. Conclusion (2) above indicated that that portion of the premium covering the "small" routine bills may be a bad buy. If it takes 10 percent of each insurance premium dollar to cover the cost of operating the company, this "average" family will routinely pay in $300 and get back $270. A family with below average bills is under strong incentive to get out of the program. But the portion of the premium covering the payment of possibly large bills is probably a good buy. These big bills are not routine and would therefore represent a reduction of future alternatives if one were to occur. This should prompt the consumer to consider bearing the risk of the small bills himself and insuring only the big ones. That is, perhaps he should consider the purchase of a policy that does *not* pay the first $100, $200, $500, $1,000, or whatever is a routine amount of bills, but pays everything over that. Such policies are available but relatively uncommon. Normally you must buy the basic policy, which will cover the routine bills (the bad buy) in order to get the major medical coverage (the good buy).

The possibility of not insuring routine medical bills (or any other kind of routine bills for that matter) is particularly attractive to the family with below average bills, since they are paying the way for those with higher bills. This adds to their incentive to leave the program, thereby further raising costs to those remaining and creating an incentive for still others to leave. To make a long story short, insurance that pays for moderate possibilities contains a built-in incentive for the consumers collecting below average benefits to leave the program. Since someone is always below average in claims, there is pressure for a continual exodus, which tends to drive the program out of existence, carrying its desirable as well as undesirable features down the drain together.

Now consider auto collision insurance. A $4,000 loss for many owners is an extreme possibility. If they wrecked their car, it would cramp their style. However, by the time the car is several years old and worth, say, $800, wrecking it would be only a moderate possibility. If so, perhaps collision insurance on an old car is not a good buy; yet many people seem to carry it out of habit. If you can afford to lose $800 without substantially reducing your future alternatives, you should probably bear the risk yourself. If the collision insurance costs $100 per year, then you have to wreck an $800 car on the average of once every 8 years to justify the insurance. Surely you are not *that* careless!

Life insurance is also interesting and complex. You receive present utility from the knowledge that your family may continue its existence in satisfactory economic condition in the event of your death. If you die, their future alternatives would be substantially reduced. How much are you willing to pay now to guarantee a given level of future alternatives for them? Many life insurance salesmen assume that the family necessarily wants to keep its level of future alternatives where they would be if the chief income earner had lived. The opening ploy, "Now here is what your family needs to live as they are living now if you should die," is well known. The built-in assumption is that your family agrees that it wishes to take no reduction in alternatives in the event of your death and is willing to pay what is necessary in order to have them as long as you live. This approach certainly assumes many things about your preference for future alternatives in the event of your death as compared to present alternatives in the event that you do not die. You should evaluate the alternatives for yourself rather than depending on the judgment of someone else, who may have a set of preferences based on his profit and not on your alternatives. If keeping the full range of alternatives open in the event of your death comes at a great expense in present alternatives (because of the very high cost of the insurance), your family may decide that it is willing to accept some reduction in future alternatives in the event of your death as the price of more present alternatives and adjust the amount of life insurance downward accordingly.

In addition, there are a wide variety of types of life insurance. Some protect only the future alternatives and some carry a savings program in addition. A number of alternatives exist which involve various combinations of saving and protection. The evaluation of the costs and benefits of the component parts of life insurance programs can be an interesting but complex undertaking. It can also be worthwhile because the stakes are often high.

SUMMARY

1 • Risk is a fundamental characteristic of a personal economic universe; but in some cases, risk is sufficiently minor to be ignored.

2 • Moderate possibilities are events that result in small routine losses.

3 • Extreme possibilities are events that result in large infrequent losses.

4 • It is generally feasible to insure against losses from extreme possibilities but not against losses from moderate possibilities.

5 • The feasibility of protection against loss from risk through insurance depends on the extent to which four conditions are met: (1) The objective proba-

bility of loss can be established; (2) many individuals are in the same situation; (3) the probability of loss is very low; and (4) the loss by any individual is independent of the loss of any other individual. The greater the extent to which any risk situation conforms to these conditions, the more likely insurance is apt to be a good buy.

6 • Fire insurance against housing loss meets these conditions well and is widely accepted as a good buy.

7 • Insurance against stock market losses is unavailable because these conditions are so notably unmet that no one would buy the insurance at a price at which it could be available.

8 • The key to an insurance decision is the fact that insurance is the guarantee of future alternatives that would be eliminated if a loss were realized. Only extreme possibilities reduce future alternatives. Moderate possibilities reduce only present alternatives.

9 • Insurance against loss from moderate possibilities is necessarily a bad buy because the present expected cost (the premium) is necessarily greater than the present expected benefit (the average payoff) by the amount required to operate the insurer. This would be essentially the purchase of present alternatives, which does not make sense because the present is already here. Why pay for it?

10 • Only if the extreme possibility of an infrequent and major loss exists can insurance be feasible, since a *present* cost higher than the *present* expected benefit will be willingly incurred as the price paid for the preservation of *future* alternatives, which would be reduced by the major loss.

study materials

1 • Explain the concept of insurance as the hiring of someone else to bear risk.

2 • List a number of types of consumer risks that are commonly encountered.

3 • Which risks are consumers prepared to assume individually and which do they try to transfer to someone else? Why?

4 • Name the four criteria for insurability.

5 • What does "objective probability of loss" mean?

6 • Why can a person insure against loss from fire but not against loss from financial ruin in the stock market?

7 • Why is flood insurance generally not available or not very satisfactory?

8 • When should the consumer insure? When not?

9 • What type of hospitalization insurance would probably be considered a good buy and under what circumstances?

10 • Why is collision coverage on an old automobile an unwise consumer decision?

footnotes

[1] A payoff from life insurance is "expected" (everybody dies); yet it is *not* pointless. Life insurance normally contains a savings provision in addition to "protection" against death. Term life insurance, which provides no savings, illustrates the pointlessness of life insurance, too, when a payoff is really expected. Simply, term life insurance is a relatively good buy for a young person in good health in any given year since a payoff is not really expected. But the cost to insure a 99-year-old person is exorbitant since a payoff is likely. Much of the payoff from other types of life insurance upon the death of an older person is really only the return of savings incorporated into the life insurance program.

[2] Insurance is sometimes sold as a purchase of peace of mind. For a strictly rational person in an insurance context, peace of mind is knowing future alternatives are preserved. But worry and peace of mind are not always rationally based. (A bit of irrationality is probably normal.) Therefore, if insurance makes you feel good, it is presumably a good buy on the basis of noneconomic utility acquired, just as any other good or service may be a good or bad buy on other than traditional economic grounds. The issue, as always, is to be aware of what you are getting for your money.

III

PRIVATE
DECISIONS
IN THE
PUBLIC
SECTOR

In Part I we presented several basic economic concepts. The single "product" of the economy, utility, was identified and the basic components of the economy explored. Given that you control some part of the economic system, we then assumed that you want to get as much out of what you control as you can. In Part II we looked at some specific types of situations to see how you can get as much as possible from what you control. We examined in detail several examples of private decisions in the private sector in such categories as consumer services (concert versus movie), consumer nondurables (beef versus pork), consumer durables (the transportation decision), investments (savings accounts, stocks, housing, education), and insurance (the decision on risk-bearing). The consumption decisions were all made under the assumption of present certainty. Investment decisions required that we acknowledge the existence of the future and that we assume that certain risks would have to be borne if you wanted to play the game. Insurance decisions recognized that under certain conditions you could "hire" someone else to bear risk. Thus there are many differences in the consumption decision versus the investment decision versus the insurance decision.

Yet there is another way in which all those decisions are similar. That similarity separates them as a group from the decisions to be investigated here in Part III. The decisions in Part II all involved what we will call a *private cost for a private benefit*. That is, *you*, as an individual, decided whether to have a specific benefit in light of the cost to *you*, as an individual. Not all economic goods are of a nature such that you yourself can make a decision independently of what other members of society decide. Some decisions to "buy" or "not to buy" are collective, or *public*, decisions. Society as a whole decides how much national defense, highways, social services, education, and so on to provide; it is beyond your individual power to decide these issues.

What *is* to be decided? You have control over neither the benefit

from public goods nor over tax policy, which is the foundation stone
that supports the public goods. Is it all that we can do to discuss how
you can be a more effective voice in public policy formation? No; as
a matter of fact, we can be more specific.

What are the conditions facing you over which you have direct
control as you receive benefits from the public sector (government)
and pay costs (taxes) to it? We have already concluded that there is
much over which you have little control. Some public goods such as
national defense are virtually "forced" upon you. You are a consumer of national defense simply by your presence. You may consume or not, as you wish, other goods such as highways, but they are
essentially free goods to you as an *individual* who decides whether
to avail yourself of them or not. Your costs are no higher or lower
according to whether you do or do not use them. Still other goods,
such as postal services, are specifically purchased from the government, in which case your decision to buy is the same as it would be
if you were purchasing from a private business. It seems that with
regard to *benefits* from the public sector there are either no really
interesting decisions to be investigated or they are the same decisions
as private sector decisions, which we have already discussed.

How about the *cost* side? Do you have any control? Are there
any decisions to be made? You have no more control over tax policy
than you have over benefits provided. You are a single voice in the
wind. Nevertheless, there is some room to maneuver on the tax question. Although you have little control over tax *policy,* you are left
some room to exercise choices within the policy framework handed
to you. Thus you have some individual choices to be exercised in
regard to taxes. Hence we have titled Part III *Private Decisions in
the Public Sector.* In particular, we will discuss taxes and what you
can do to minimize them personally. Put simply, the "best buy" in
the public sector is the lowest possible tax bill.[1]

footnote

[1] It must be acknowledged that there are some private decisions in the public
sector with regard to benefits, but they are quite straightforward and not very
interesting. They are mostly a matter of familiarizing yourself with the "free"
benefits that the government offers and of asking yourself whether you may have

been overlooking something. At least in major urban areas, government typically provides an amazing quantity of free or nearly free services. Museums, galleries, parks, concerts, and libraries abound in many metropolitan areas. The entertainment value of city council meetings is frequently considerable. In addition, you reap the satisfaction from doing your civic duty in following council activities and occasionally getting the city fathers back on course. Local politics is truly a "best buy."

chapter
16

THE INCOME
TAX SYSTEM:
MAJOR FEATURES

Taxes are an immense subject. Thousands of units of government, some rather obscure—mosquito control districts, soil conservation districts, airport commissions, etc.—are collecting billions of dollars each year in taxes from a variety of such sources as income, property, sales, and even death. About 25 percent of the economic output of the United States is public goods, which are provided primarily by tax dollars. It is impossible to be part of a modern economy without paying taxes—visible or invisible. In this chapter we will look at that part of the tax system which is the most visible—the federal income tax—in many respects the backbone of the U.S. tax system and that part of the tax system where you probably have the most opportunity to make advantageous personal decisions. Since much of

*what is true of the federal income tax system is also sub-
stantially true of many state income tax systems and to a
lesser extent of other tax systems also, we are simply using
the federal income tax as an example from which to work.*

*We will construct a hypothetical income tax system of our
own creation which happens to possess the same key features as the federal income tax (and most state income
taxes). We do not intend to end up telling you how to fill
out your tax return any more than we intended to tell you
how to buy a used car or open a savings account earlier in
the book. We will continue the "what's really going on
here" approach. We can do that with our own tax system
modeled after the federal system. We do not pretend that
the specific numbers we use are accurate with regard to any
existing tax system; they change from year to year. Therefore, we will limit ourselves to those key features that are
likely to endure and explore how they affect your tax bill.
In the course of the exploration we will call on at least two
old friends,* marginalism *and* time.

*We will look at the operation of a marginal and essentially
progressive tax system and then hinge our discussion on
four key factors under your control which determine your
tax bill: the* size *of your income; the* form *in which you
receive your income; the* time *at which you receive your
income; and* who *receives your income. Our guess is that
the first factor is obvious to you as a determining factor in
your tax bill and that the other three are a puzzle—particularly the last one which suggests you might want someone
else to receive your income.*

*In the next chapter we will look at some specific applica-
tions of these four factors to real-world situations and show
how they may be used in combination to even greater
advantage.*

▶ LEGAL BACKGROUND ◀

The tax system is a legal institution. The law provides for certain things and does not provide for other things. You are expected to avail yourself of the advantages the law allows. Just as the government surely assumes that you are going to seek out the best buy in the private sector, the government assumes that you will seek out the "best buy" in the public sector, which means minimizing your tax bill. The law contains many provisions that grant favorable tax treatment to persons who qualify on one ground or another. Take all you have coming—but no more of course. Don't be bashful about not paying taxes if you don't have to— even if you're a millionaire. If the law doesn't require you to pay taxes, you are under no obligation to do so. If you are in poverty and the law says pay taxes—well—tough! Pay up!

The purpose of the bluntness is to point out what we *are* and *are not* going to talk about here. We *are* going to talk about the personal implications of certain kinds of tax structures; we *are not* going to talk about the *adequacy* of the law. We assume that the law is *given,* and we simply take it and work from there. The law grants concessions to an unbelievable array of conditions. We are not concerned about whether the law is fair; we are only concerned about what it allows, since that is your concern as an individual taxpayer at tax-paying time. Our concern in this book is for the personal point of view.

It is frequently said that the people who have substantial incomes and pay no or little in taxes have found *loopholes*. Almost always this is *not* the case; they have found *gates*. A *loophole* is a means of escape or evasion *unintentionally* left by the makers of the tax system. The better-known means of escape from high taxes such as capital gains, tax free municipal bond interest, and deferred income, for example, are not loopholes at all; they are deliberately provided tax concessions to certain conditions. There is nothing irregular about availing yourself of those provisions if you qualify.

At the risk of getting into the *adequacy* of the law (which we said we would not discuss), it must be said, to address any cynicism that may arise, that most of these provisions were created with good intentions and have considerable substantive basis; they were not created to let the rich escape taxes or to pay off political cronies. On the other hand, this does not mean that tax concessions are without criticism and should not be reviewed. In some cases, the basic philosophy behind a provision is sound but is too liberally applied. It necessarily follows that any tax concession is worth more to someone with a high income than to someone with a low income. If your income is $1,000, it makes little difference in your tax bill how the law looks at your income; if your income is $1 million, it obviously makes a great deal of difference. Since tax concessions necessarily tend to favor the high incomes of the rich, they are apt to be looked at askance by the nonrich. Any merit a tax concession may have on economic grounds has to be balanced against the equity demerits it contains. Much tax reform is validly promoted on just such equity grounds.

One of the more novel ideas for tax reform promoted recently would have replaced practically the whole federal income tax system with approximately the following: Take all your income no matter where it came from; keep, say, $1,000 for yourself and for each person you support; send the government, say, 20 percent of the rest. (The proposal didn't get anywhere; it was too simple.) Some people complained that this proposal would tax the poor at the same rate as the rich. The point, of course, is that the rich now avail themselves of tax concessions in the form of special kinds of nontaxable income, or favorably taxed income so they don't actually pay a whole lot more than that as a group anyway. (Remember that "what is" and "what appears to be" are not always the same.)

In any event, the question of the adequacy of the law is not our concern, though it is a vitally important matter. Our concern is that you make the best deal for yourself under the law. These two issues are separate, since there is no way that paying more taxes than necessary is going to correct inequities in the law. Indeed the opposite might be argued: There is no better incentive to legislators to tighten the tax law than for it to be evident that special provisions are horribly expensive in lost revenue. Many an economics professor (including this one) has argued, without a twinge of conscience, for tax reform which, if enacted, would have cost him dearly on the tax return that he had filled out the night before. They are simply two separate issues.

▶ THE TAX RATE ◀

You have no control over the tax rate, so our interest in the tax rate is only to explain the nature of the rate and the implications for you, the taxpayer. Our discussion will explain the meaning of the statement often given as a summary of the federal income tax: *The federal income tax is marginal and progressive.*

▷ marginal taxes ◁

Focusing on the first part of the tax statement above, we see that the tax rates published by the government to apply to income are *marginal*. Recall from Chapter 9 that the margin is the "edge" and therefore relates to *changes*. Thus the basic tax rate (on ordinary income) is marginal since it applies only to that portion of your income above a certain figure; the government says, "If your income *changes* upward from $X, this is the tax rate that applies to that *additional* income." Assume that the rates in Table 16–1 are in effect. (We will use them for all our problems.) You get

Table 16–1
HYPOTHETICAL TAX TABLE

INCOME	MARGINAL TAX RATE (%)	TAX LIABILITY	TAX AS A % OF INCOME (TAX/INCOME) × (100)
$ 1,000	0	$ 000	0.00
2,000	14	140	7.00
3,000	15	290	9.70
4,000	16	450	11.25
5,000	17	620	12.40
10,000	22	1,720	17.20
20,000	30	4,720	23.60
30,000	38	8,520	28.40
40,000	46	13,120	32.80
50,000	50	18,120	36.24
Over $50,000	50		

a small amount of tax-free income for your personal exemption, and then the marginal rate is scaled upward as income rises. The tax on $2,000 is $140 since $1,000 is not taxed, and the second $1,000 (or marginal $1,000) is taxed at 14 percent. Thus

$$(\$1,000 \times 0\%) + (\$1,000 \times 14\%) = \$0 + \$140 = \$140$$

Similarly, on $3,000 the tax is

$$(\$1,000 \times 0\%) + (\$1,000 \times 14\%) + (\$1,000 \times 15\%)$$
$$= \$0 + \$140 + \$150 = \$290$$

Notice that if you are in the 50 percent tax bracket, you do not pay 50 percent of your income in taxes; 50 percent is the *highest* rate you pay on any *part* of your income. This means that the receiver of a $1 million income gets the first $1,000 free and the next $1,000 taxed at 14 percent, just the same as someone who has no more than $2,000 in total.

▷   average tax rate   ◁

Average tax rates tell whether a tax is *regressive, proportional,* or *progressive*. All taxes are either regressive, proportional, or progressive. A tax is **regressive** if the proportion of income going to taxes *falls* as income rises; it is **proportional** if the proportion of income going to taxes remains *constant* as income rises; it is **progressive** if the proportion of income going to taxes *rises* as income rises.

─────────────────── **EXAMPLE 16–1** ───────────────────

A Regressive Tax

The clearest example of a regressive tax is a lump sum tax. The government levies, say, $1,000 against everybody. Obviously, if your income is $1,000, the tax rate is 100 percent; if your income is $2,000, the tax rate is 50 percent; and so on.

INCOME	TAX	TAX AS A % OF INCOME (TAX/INCOME × 100)
$1,000	$1,000	100
2,000	1,000	50.0
3,000	1,000	33.3
4,000	1,000	25.0

The percentage of income going to taxes is falling as income rises, so the tax is regressive.

─────────────────── **EXAMPLE 16–2** ───────────────────

A Proportional Tax

INCOME	TAX	TAX AS A % OF INCOME (TAX/INCOME × 100)
$1,000	$200	20
2,000	400	20
3,000	600	20
4,000	800	20

The third column simply reproduces the constant 20 percent tax rate. Actually, we knew the tax was necessarily proportional when a flat rate of 20 percent was applied to *all* income.

EXAMPLE 16–3

A Progressive Tax

The federal income tax is progressive over most income levels, but *not* because of the higher *marginal* rate against higher incomes; it is the *average* tax rate that determines progressivity, proportionality, and regressivity. The right-hand columns in Examples 16–1 and 16–2 are *average* tax rates, which tell what proportion of *every* dollar goes for taxes; the *marginal* tax rate tells what proportion of *additional* dollars above a certain level go for taxes. The average rate of 9.7 percent for $3,000 is $290/ $3,000 × 100 = 9.7 percent for example. The right-hand column in Table 16–1 is tax as a percentage of income— the average tax rate. It rises as income rises. The tax is progressive.[1]

But our main concern is not with regressive, proportional, or progressive tax systems. Rather, we want to recognize that the marginal tax rate is one thing and the average tax rate another. Which of the two is of more interest to you? Shouldn't you be more interested in the average tax rate? The average rate tells what proportion of *every* dollar goes to taxes, and you are concerned for *all* your dollars; the last one received and the way it is taxed has no special standing. Or does it? The whole basic message of Chapter 9—on the margin as the place where the action is—applies to taxes also. You want to focus on the margin. When someone says he is in the 30 percent tax bracket, he is talking about the marginal rate, though he may not realize it. Why? Purely because it is, as always, only the margin that is relevant in decision making.

Consider an illustration. Tax management consists of getting your *taxable* income down to some figure below your *actual* income. This is possible, remember, because to you a dollar is a dollar, but to the government for tax purposes the circumstances that generated that dollar and the conditions under which you received it make a difference. You try to cut your *taxable* income without cutting your *actual* income. Thus when you want to know how much a given maneuver will save you in taxes, you need to look at the margin because any *change* in your taxable income will *change* your tax liability by the marginal rate applied to the change.

For example, if you are in the 30 percent bracket and your income rises $1,000, your tax liability rises by $300 ($1,000 × 30%); if you "find" another $1,000 of deductions, your tax liability will fall by $300. It's as simple as that. How much does a *change* in income *change* your tax? That's what interests you and that's a marginal issue.

If the tax rate is marginal and fractional, it is impossible to have less aftertax income by receiving more pretax income.[2] More pretax income will boost your tax liability but always by *less* than the amount of the additional income, thereby leaving additional aftertax income. Even though the extra income puts you in the "next tax bracket," you are still better off receiving the income. If you are at the very top of the 30 percent bracket and receive an additional $1,000, it would be taxable at 38 percent rather than 30 percent; you would owe an additional $380 in taxes instead of the additional $300 you would have owed at 30 percent, leaving $620 after taxes rather than the $700 you would have had if you had not gone to the next bracket.

If the marginal rates were average rates, you could be worse off by receiving more income, since the extra income would change the tax liability on all *previously* received income as well. Assuming that the 30 and 38 percent were average rates, you would owe $6,000 on $20,000 ($20,000 × 30% = $6,000), and the extra $1,000 would give you $21,000 × 38% = $7,980. You got an extra $1,000 in income and owed an extra $1,980 in taxes because the extra income made you liable for another 8 percent (38% − 30%) on the whole initial $20,000, which overbalanced the extra income. Occasionally someone talks as though he does not understand this, although we question whether many people are really spurning additional income because of it. People in high tax brackets may, of course, fail to seek additional income eagerly because, even though they know they would be better off with it than without it, they do not believe they would be *enough* better off to be worth the trouble. This is the *disincentive effect* of taxation.

▶ SIZE OF INCOME ◀

As we look at the four major factors over which you have control and which affect your tax liability, *size* of income is the most obvious. Even the greenest novice with regard to taxes understands that an income tax collects a percentage of income. Thus, other things being equal, the higher your income the higher your tax. Obviously, then, the surest way to get your tax liability down is to have no income. Most of us would consider the "cure" worse than the "disease," and the name of the game is therefore to get the tax liability down *without* lowering your income.

▶ FORM OF INCOME ◀

The *form* in which income is received determines how it is taxed. Each form of income carries a definition of what is included in it. We do not pretend to explain all the different types of income the government may recognize. However, citing some of the major forms will illustrate the importance of this feature of income in determining your tax bill.

Ordinary income is the major category of income, which we will define as that income taxable at the marginal rates in Table 16–1. Other forms of income are essentially modifications of ordinary income. The major part of ordinary income is wages and salaries, although many other sources of incomes are also defined as ordinary income.

Tax-free income is self-explanatory; a tax rate of 0 percent applies to it. The best-known source of tax-free income is interest on state and municipal bonds.[3] The federal government does not tax property of lower units of government on constitutional grounds.[4] Thus the interest on bonds issued by lower units of government is usually not taxable by the federal government. Lest you jump to the conclusion that municipal bonds are therefore a great investment, it must be recognized that the rate of return on these bonds is lower than on comparable quality nonmunicipals precisely because the interest is tax-exempt. The attractiveness of tax-free interest depends on the size of your income—the higher your income, the more it is worth to get tax-free income. We will explore that in Chapter 17.

Certain kinds of income qualify as **capital gains** and are taxed at a favorable rate. For many years capital gains have been taxed at one half the rate on ordinary income up to a maximum tax rate of 25 percent. The rationale for the capital gains provision is that it is an incentive to investment, which contributes to overall economic growth. Without debating the effectiveness of capital gains in this regard, you need to know that the profit you make from holding many kinds of assets for a certain period (at least 6 months presently) is taxable at this favorable rate. Thus if you own a house, stocks, a farm, or whatever for more than 6 months and sell at a profit, the profit is taxed at one half the rate of ordinary income.[5] The judicious handling of your financial affairs can result in realizing as capital gains what would have been ordinary income if you had used less finesse. It has been said that the most widely pursued intellectual activity outside the halls of ivy is the search for means whereby ordinary income may be converted into capital gains.

Income received in kind may be tax-exempt. Income received "in kind" is in the form of goods and services directly, rather than money received, which you would then convert to goods and services. For example, if your employer furnishes a house you are required to occupy as a condition of the employment, the rental value of the house is certainly income to you, but it is not taxable. Similarly, self-sufficiency income (see Chapter 7) is tax-exempt. Certain fringe benefits may also be nontaxable. If you participate in a health-care plan for which your employer pays the cost, you receive value (income), but it is not taxable. In effect, your employer is providing health care directly, just as he might provide housing directly.

▶ TIME OF RECEIPT OF INCOME ◀

When you receive income affects the way it is taxed. In some instances, you may receive income at one time, but for tax purposes the government considers that you receive it at a later time. This may have multiple advantages.

First, if you are confronted with the choice of paying a dollar in taxes now or next year, which should you choose? Obviously, pay later, other things being equal, since you will have had the use of the money in the meantime. You can earn interest on it (or avoid paying interest you otherwise would have paid). Since you may be able to defer your tax payment several years (if not decades), this can be a major attraction.

Second, you may be able to pay your taxes on that income when your additional income from other sources is lower (e.g., after retirement), so that you are taxed at a lower rate than you would have been taxed if you had paid the tax earlier.

Third, very frequently a program that defers income also changes the form of income, so that it is taxed at a lower rate. If you can get all three of these forces working together you may have a very good thing going. Postponed receipt of income often relates to retirement. Since your income normally drops at retirement, you will pay at a lower tax rate on the income you do receive, in addition to which you will have had the money you otherwise would have paid in taxes earning a return for you until you retire. Furthermore, some ordinary income may get converted to a more favorably taxed form of income—usually capital gains—in the process.

Since all this discussion relates the present to the future, it is essentially an investment issue; *tax-deferred annuities* are popular investment vehicles for reaping these advantages. An **annuity** pays a specified amount at specified intervals for a specified length of time. Under a tax-deferred annuity you pay regularly into an investment program—possibly an employer-sponsored program, possibly not—over your productive years. The dollars you pay into the plan are not taxed at the time you pay in; thus

you are able to invest more than you otherwise would be able to invest
if you were investing only aftertax income. You are taxed when the annuity is received (paid back to you) after retirement. You are therefore
taxed *later* than you otherwise would be and you are taxed at a *lower rate*
(assuming your income is lower after retirement). In addition, there is a
chance that some of the receipts from the annuity will qualify as capital
gains, which helps you further.

It may also be possible to defer taxes through certain kinds of self-
employment activities which may be undertaken in addition to other employment you may hold. In Chapter 17 we will illustrate this with an
example in which you buy a small apartment building that allows you to
defer taxes—as well as to avail yourself of other advantages.

► IDENTITY OF RECEIVER ◄
OF INCOME

The size of the tax bite on your income depends on who receives "your"
income. Why would you want anyone else to receive your income? If you
are going to support someone else anyway, it may be advantageous to
channel income to them directly, reducing your tax bill in the process.

It is necessary to view a group of people as a single unit to make sense
of this argument. The group receives a given income and it may be shuffled around among the members of the group in many different ways.
Since you view the *group* as a unit seeking to minimize taxes taken from
any given income, and since the government may look at the members of
the group as *individuals* for purposes of taxation, you have room to maneuver. That is, your view of the interrelationships among the members
of the group and the government's view may not coincide. If they don't,
you are free to abide by the rules based on the government's view, if they
work to your advantage.

Obviously, we are talking about family situations almost exclusively,
although alternative life styles may widen this application. Usually the
receipt of income is concentrated in the hands of one or two persons in the
family. There may be considerable tax advantages to spreading income to
other members of the family, particularly children—although such procedures need to be thought through carefully and may be subject to particularly close scrutiny by the government, since the boundary between legitimate schemes and illegitimate schemes is often a fine line. In other words,
be sure that what you are doing is what it is purported to be and not a
facade for tax evasion. In addition, the opportunities here for the typical
family may be somewhat limited, since the government *does* view the
family as somewhat of a unit even for tax purposes. For example, the gov-

ernment allows husband and wife to file joint income tax returns or separate returns. The government says, "You may be considered a unit for purposes of taxation or not, as you wish." The principle is extended to children by allowing the parents to claim a *personal exemption* for each child: The parents exclude from their taxable income $X for each child. Thus the government recognizes the family as a unit to a point. However, beyond a point the government views the members of the family as individuals and taxes them accordingly. Specifically, if children earn income, they are subject to the same tax law as anyone else and must pay taxes accordingly.

Assuming you are a parent, your children pay taxes the same as anyone else if their income exceeds a certain level. It is to the family's collective advantage to transfer income to them assuming their income is lower than yours! [6] Suppose, for example, that your income is $10,000 and your child earns $1,000 on his own. From Table 16–1, you pay $1,720 in taxes and your child pays nothing. If you can somehow transfer $1,000 of your $10,000 to your child, your taxes will drop by $1,000 × 22 percent, or $220, and your child's will rise by $1,000 × 14 percent, or $140 for a saving between you of $220 − $140 = $80. This works because of the upward scaled marginal tax rate against income and illustrates a basic point.

> In general, anything a group can do to equalize income among the members of the group can be expected to lower the tax liability for the group as a whole.

The opportunities of the typical family to do this may be limited. The most straightforward method would be for the children to become *bona fide* employees in the parent's *bona fide* business. Paying the children for work they might do anyway reduces business profits and therefore reduces the parent's taxable income and increases the child's taxable income. The leveling effect is accomplished. But not a great many parents are self-employed in the kind of business in which the child can become employed.[7] Agriculture may be the notable exception. There may also be opportunities in small, family-owned retail stores. In any event, if your child is working in your business in return for his support, it is possible that you could improve your collective position by hiring the child and having the child pay you for his support.

The *trust* is another means of transferring income to someone else. Suppose that you receive income that you would like to transfer to a child. You do not necessarily want to transfer the income, as such, now, but from your income you are accumulating a nice little bundle of wealth, part of which you know you are eventually going to want to transfer to your shining offspring. So you decide you might as well set some income aside now for that purpose if you can do so to good advantage. You set up a trust (probably from which *you* may *not* withdraw the money) in the name of your child with the condition that the money goes to the child at a specified time or under specified conditions.[8] The income is therefore taxable to the child later and probably at a lower rate.

▶ A PERSPECTIVE ◀

Perhaps the discussion of this chapter seems excessively upper-middle class in its orientation and therefore out of place, since most of you are probably not among the economic elite—or do not consider yourselves so. Several comments are in order.

1 • Admittedly, tax management is irrelevant if you have no income. The higher your income, the more important the subject becomes; however, it is very possible that you should be giving more thought to these matters than you are.

2 • But a more compelling argument for the present relevance of tax questions to you is that most of you will someday be much more affluent than you are now or may even expect to be, based on your current condition and that of your parents. The long-term trend in per capita income will undoubtedly be up and many of you will land higher on the ladder than you expect to; you should be ready for prosperity when it hits. Furthermore . . .

3 • You must remember that it is not intended that you will run right out and set up a trust or buy a bond yielding tax-free interest. The examples of this chapter are popular examples, not recommendations. They are designed to show that who, when, and how income is received makes a tax difference. Finally . . .

4 • "There ain't no free lunch" in the public sector anymore than there is in the private sector. In every instance that we discussed, the tax advantage entailed an additional cost of some kind. To be sure, the cost may be minor compared to the potential benefit, but it is there. For example, the trust requires that you give up control over your income—you can't change your mind in most cases; the tax-free interest on the municipal bond is, of course, tax-free, but it is also a lower amount than taxable bond interest on a pretax basis; the conversion of ordinary income to capital gains requires investment, so you risk the loss of your income; and so on.

Above all, keep your eye on the ball. Tax management is necessary; financially successful people practice it. On the other hand, we suspect that some people fret too much about taxes and, in doing so, follow courses they really should not be following. In other words, don't let tax considerations throw you off the trail by causing you to lose sight of even more important issues. Do not let the favored tax status of a particular source of income lead you to making a bad investment. You do not pay taxes unless you have income. Therefore, the acquisition of income is the *first* priority; the tax status of that income is *secondary*. It is obvious folly to purchase a municipal bond because the interest is tax-free, only to learn that the financial condition of the issuing municipality is so shaky that it cannot pay the interest. You would have been better off buying a first-rate bond paying taxable interest at ordinary income tax rates. This is the point behind the *relative* lack of tax concern by many financially successful people. They spend their time on the more crucial matter of acquiring income. Since tax rates are less than 100 percent, they simply acquire income, pay the taxes, and move on to more income. If your tax bill is high, it probably means you are doing well. As is frequently the case, a middle-of-the-road approach is warranted. Do not let tax questions obscure more important issues. On the other hand, avail yourself of the tax advantages if you can do so with reasonable convenience.

Finally, although you should avail yourself of professional tax advice when you need it, just as you should avail yourself of professional medical advice when you need it, there is no substitute for knowing what is going on yourself. Anyone who thinks he can satisfactorily place his affairs totally in the hands of others is due for a rude awakening. You must be sufficiently knowledgeable to converse intelligently with your advisers —whether tax or medical—in order to get as much from them as they are capable of delivering.

SUMMARY

1 • The law provides favorable tax treatment to persons who qualify under one or more of several special provisions of the tax law.

2 • The federal income tax is *marginal* and *progressive* over most ranges of income.

3 • The significance of the marginal rate is that the first dollars of everyone's income are taxed at the same rate no matter how high or low the income. It also

means that you can never have less aftertax income by receiving more pretax income.

4 • It is the marginal tax rate that is relevant in determining the increase or decrease in your tax liability due to a *change* in income.

5 • A progressive tax levies a higher *average* tax per dollar as income rises. A proportional tax levies a constant *average* tax per dollar as income rises. A regressive tax levies a lower *average* tax per dollar as income rises.

6 • The *size* of your income is the foremost factor that determines the size of your tax liability under any given tax rate structure.

7 • The *form* in which income is received (ordinary, tax-free, capital gains, "in kind," for example) determines the way it is taxed.

8 • *When* you receive income determines the effective tax rate. The present value (cost) of a tax paid later is necessarily less than the value (cost) of the same tax paid now. Tax-deferred annuities are one way to postpone tax payments.

9 • *Who* receives your income influences the taxes levied against it. Income may be transferred through an employee–employer relationship between you and the person you wish to receive the transfer. Trust funds may also be used for this purpose. The marginal tax rate structure causes a leveling of income among members of a group to result in a lower total tax paid by the group.

10 • If you have no income, tax questions are irrelevant; the higher your income, the more important they become. As your income rises in the future, as it almost certainly will, you must develop a feel for tax matters and recognize various types of vehicles for minimizing taxes.

study materials

1 • Name the four key factors under your control which determine your income tax bill.

2 • Contrast the *adequacy* of the (tax) laws against *acceptance* of the law as given and working from there.

3 • In problem 2, under what conditions or circumstances is each point of view valid?

4 • Differentiate between tax loopholes and tax concessions.

5 • Explain the terms *regressive tax, proportional tax,* and *progressive tax.* Set up a simple five-income-level table to illustrate each.

6 • Explain the terms *marginal* and *progressive* as they are used in the statement, "The federal income tax is marginal and progressive."

7 • Following sound tax management principles, why would you want to cut your taxable income without cutting your actual income?

8 • What is a negative income tax?

9 • Explain the difference between the *marginal tax rate* and the *average tax rate.*

10 • Develop ways and means of maintaining your present income or increasing it and yet reducing your tax liability by (1) controlling the *form* of the income and (2) by controlling the *time of receipt* of the income.

footnotes

[1] Although the federal income tax is progressive over most ranges of income, it does turn slightly regressive over a range of middle incomes. Regressivity, or a downturn in average tax rates while the marginal tax rate rises, may seem peculiar; it is possible within limits under certain conditions. Since the *ability to pay* principle of taxation finds wide favor in this country, the tendency of the federal income tax toward regressiveness at income levels that catch many wage and salary earners is frequently considered an undesirable feature of the federal income tax. If all taxes—income, nonincome, federal, state, and local—are added together and expressed as a percent of income, the regressiveness of the total tax structure on middle incomes is slightly more pronounced. One of the arguments in favor of the *negative income tax* (the government pays you instead of your paying it—if you are poor enough) is that it would help eliminate this regressive tilt in the tax structure.

[2] We are assuming that tax rates are also *fractional,* that is, always less than 100 percent. Obviously, if the rate were 110 percent, you would pay all your

additional income in taxes, plus another 10 percent of it taken out of previous income! You would of course avoid additional income in such a situation.

3 As used here, *municipal* refers to all units of government below the state level.

4 This relationship between levels of government shows signs of change. Increasingly, units of government make compensatory payments to one another in lieu of taxes. A federal installation, for example, may pay a local unit of government for police and fire protection, school costs for the children of their employees, and the like. These payments are certainly quasi-taxes and lead to the speculation that sooner or later an attempt to remove the federal tax exemption from municipal bond interest may be successful.

5 Actually, we are talking about *long-term capital gains*. Short-term capital gains are the same as ordinary income for purposes of our simple problem.

6 As mentioned above, it is well to think these schemes through carefully. This income transfer could (but will not necessarily) cause you to lose your child's personal exemption, in which case you would, of course, have to take that into consideration in evaluating the attractiveness of the proposal.

7 Notice we said a *bona fide* business. Hiring your kids to mow your lawn won't do the job. It is not an income-generating activity—as the government defines income. That is why the government may look at your income transfer scheme closely (as it should); is this relationship "real" or is it a coverup? The tax agent wonders, "Does that kid *really* work as the old man says he does?"

8 Perhaps when the child is 18 or 21. The woods are full of (hopefully exaggerated) stories about domineering fathers who set up trusts for their children with conditions such as "payable to my daughter upon graduation from Harvard and marriage to a brown-eyed Swede."

chapter 17

THE INCOME TAX SYSTEM: PERSONAL EXAMPLES

In Chapter 16 we looked at the major income tax issues: the legal background and context of the income tax; its marginal nature; and its progressiveness (or in a few instances, the lack of progressiveness). We also looked at the tax significance of size, form, time of receipt, and identity of receiver of income. We now want to push on to see specifically how you may use these features to your advantage. We will develop an example illustrating the significance of each of the four major factors that affect your tax bill. In some cases, the features can be used in combination.

▶ SIZE OF INCOME ◀

The impact of your income on your tax liability is evident simply by reading Table 16–1. What more need be said?

▶ FORM OF INCOME ◀

Using *ordinary income* as the reference point, we can evaluate the worth of other forms of income by comparison. You frequently need to decide what you are willing to pay for one form of income compared to another, since you have a choice as to the form in which you receive income—particularly investment income.

▷ tax-free income ◁

You are confronted with a decision to buy a municipal bond paying tax-free interest or an industrial bond paying taxable interest. The amount you are willing to pay for each will clearly be different—you are willing to pay more for tax-free income than for taxable income—and the difference in your willingness to pay for the bonds is your willingness to pay for the tax concession. Market conditions reflect the "average" willingness to pay for tax-free income by bond holders, since tax-free interest bonds pay a lower return than taxable interest bonds. The question, of course, is how *your* willingness to pay stacks up against this "average" willingness to pay—that is, are tax-free interest bonds a good buy for *you?*

Suppose that you have decided to buy a bond; it is only a question of whether to buy taxable or tax-free interest bonds. Suppose also that

―――――――――― **EXAMPLE 17–1** ――――――――――

Tax-Free Versus Taxable Interest (Low Income)

	TAX-FREE INTEREST	TAXABLE INTEREST
Price of bond	$1,000	$1,000
Interest received	$1,000 × 5% = $50.00	$1,000 × 7½% = $75.00
Taxes on interest	$50.00 × 0% = $00.00	$75.00 × 17% = $12.75
Aftertax interest	$50.00 − $0 = $50.00	$75.00 − $12.75 = $62.25

You are better off with the taxable interest apparently, because your income is so low that your tax bite is not big enough to bring the aftertax interest from the taxable bond down to the tax-free interest on the municipal bond. The tax concession is worthless to you. Indeed, you would be willing to pay as much as $62.25 − $50.00 = $12.25 for the "privilege" of paying $12.75 in taxes if necessary!

---

the rate of return is 5 percent on tax-free bonds and $7\frac{1}{2}$ percent on taxable bonds. Assume that your income is $4,500 per year.

All this changes when you have a higher income. Suppose that your income is $35,000 a year.

EXAMPLE 17–2

Tax-Free Versus Taxable Interest (High Income)

	TAX-FREE INTEREST	TAXABLE INTEREST
Price of bond	$1,000	$1,000
Interest paid	$1,000 × 5% = $50.00	$1,000 × $7\frac{1}{2}$% = $75.00
Taxes on interest	$50.00 × 0% = $00.00	$75.00 × 46% = $34.50
Aftertax interest	$50.00 − $0 = $50.00	$75.00 − $34.50 = $40.50

Since the tax bite is bigger, you would be willing to pay as much as $50.00 − $40.50 = $9.50 to gain the tax-free interest. Of course, you are not required to pay this—the $9.50 is gravy so to speak—but you would be willing to pay it if necessary. The example simply verifies an earlier observation: Tax concessions are worth more if you have a high income. Appendix A contains a simple method of determining precisely whether or not to go the tax-free route, given available returns from tax-free and taxable sources of income and given your tax bracket.

▷ capital gains ◁

Suppose that long-term capital gains are taxed at one half the rate on ordinary income up to a maximum of 25 percent. For example, if you are taxed 30 percent at the margin on ordinary income, you will pay 15 percent on capital gains. How much more is it worth to receive income as capital gains than as ordinary income? Contrast $1,000 in income taxed at each rate.

EXAMPLE 17–3

Aftertax Income from Ordinary Income and Capital Gains

	ORDINARY INCOME	CAPITAL GAINS
Income	$1,000	$1,000
Tax rate applicable	30%	15%
Tax	$300	$150
Aftertax income	$700	$850

You are $150 better off by receiving income as capital gains ($850 − $700 = $150). You may be faced with choices where you need to know what you would be willing to sacrifice ("pay") in income to have capital gains rather than ordinary income. In this example you would be as well-off with $823.53 of income that is taxable as capital gains as you would be with $1,000 taxable as ordinary income ($1,000 of ordinary income × 70% that you keep is $700; $823.53 of capital gains × 85% that you keep is also $700). Thus $823.53 of capital gains is the equivalent of $1,000 of ordinary income, and you would be willing to "pay" $1,000 − $823.53 = $176.47 to "convert" $1,000 of ordinary income to capital gains. Appendix B shows how you can determine exactly what equivalent ordinary income and capital gains would be for any rates of taxation on ordinary income and capital gains.

If your income, and therefore the tax rate, is higher, the difference between ordinary income and capital gains required to yield the same aftertax income is greater. At a 40 percent tax rate on ordinary income, $750 of income in capital gains is equivalent to $1,000 in ordinary income.

You would be willing to pay (sacrifice) $250 from $1,000
in ordinary income in order to take $750 in capital gains
(40 percent tax from $1,000 leaves $600 after tax; 20 percent tax from $750 also leaves $600). The increase in your
willingness to pay from $176.47 at an ordinary income
rate of 30 percent to $250 at an ordinary income rate of
40 percent is verification of what we have seen before: The
higher your income and therefore the higher the tax rate,
the more valuable is a tax concession.

▷ "in kind" income ◁

"In kind" income is value received directly as goods rather than money.
Some employment yields substantial "in kind" payment. The value of "in
kind" income may or may not be taxable. If your employer furnishes
housing that you are required to live in as a condition of your employment, the rental value of the house is income to you, but it is not taxable.

In a closely related vein, many fringe benefits are not taxable. For
example, a health insurance plan provided by your employer may be nontaxable income. The same is true for payments into some retirement
plans on your behalf.[1] Any nontaxable benefit has a higher taxable equivalent value. If your employer provides $500 in tax-free health insurance,
it is worth more than $500 to you, because if you were to provide it for
yourself, you would need enough more than $500 in income to pay the
taxes and then have $500 left to buy the health insurance. If you were in
a 30% tax bracket, you would need $714.29 in pretax income since
$714.29 × 70% equals $500.00. Thus you would be willing to pay
$214.29, so to speak, to have this benefit on a nontaxable basis. As always,
the tax concession is worth more at higher income and tax levels. If you
are in a 40 percent tax bracket, it would take $833.33 in pretax income to
yield $500.00 aftertax income, in which case the tax concession is worth
$333.33. To generalize, the taxable income equivalent of a tax-free benefit
is

$$\frac{TFB}{(1 - MRT)}$$

where TFB is the value of the tax-free benefit and MRT is the marginal
rate of taxation. Thus

$$\$714.29 = \frac{\$500}{(1 - .30)} = \frac{\$500}{.70}$$

and

$$\$833.33 = \frac{\$500}{(1 - .40)} = \frac{\$500}{.60}$$

▷ self-sufficiency income ◁

Self-sufficiency income is tax-free income. If you make minor repairs to your car rather than hiring it done for $10, you have earned $10 of *after-tax* income. If you are in a 30 percent tax bracket, you would have to earn $14.20 to have $10 left after taxes. Therefore, the repairs were really worth $14.20, since you would have to earn that to have enough left for $10 of repairs. Stated another way, you earned $10 of tax-free income. Notice that this means that as a do-it-yourselfer you can be a little less skillful than the professional who might be hired instead, since you have to earn enough above what the professional earns to pay him *and* the tax on what you pay him. You can afford a few blunders. (A *few,* we said.) Obviously, resource income and noneconomic income are also tax-free.[2]

▶ TIME OF RECEIPT OF INCOME ◀

If income can be received later for tax purposes and therefore taxed later, the effective tax burden is lighter than if you had to pay it now. Just as the present value of future income is lower than the future income itself, a cost (tax in this case) has a lower present value than future value. Therefore, delayed tax payment reduces its burden. The reason is intuitively simple: If you can pay the tax later, you can collect interest on that money in the meantime; therefore, an amount of money *now,* which is *less* than the tax, will grow at compound interest into the amount needed to pay the tax later. The present-value tables of Chapter 13 will be useful here.

Deferred taxation gets interesting when the deferred date is far in the future. Assume that you can defer the tax on $1,000 for 20 years and that you are in the 30 percent tax bracket both now and at the end of 20 years. If you pay the tax now, the present value is $300 ($1,000 × 30%); if you defer the tax 20 years and can realize a 5 percent return compounded annually, it takes only $113.07 now to grow to $300 at 5 percent in 20 years (from Table 13–1, the present value of $1 at 5 percent in 20 years is $.3769; .3769 × $300 = $113.07). It is therefore worth $300 − $113.07 = $186.93 to defer that tax, since you could pay up to $186.93 to defer the tax and be better-off than paying it now. At the higher tax bracket of 40 percent, the present value of $400 of tax in 20 years at 5 percent is. .3769 × $400 = $150.76, so the tax concession is worth

$400.00 − $150.76 = $249.24. Same old story—the higher your tax bracket, the more the tax concession is worth.

Also, of course, if you can earn 8 percent instead of 5 percent on your money, the tax concession is worth more because the present value of the future tax is worth less. In the 30 percent bracket, the present value of $300 in taxes is .2145 × $300 = $64.35, and the deferment is worth $300.00 − $64.35 = $235.65; in the 40 percent bracket, the present value of $400 in taxes is .2145 × $400 = $85.80, and the deferment is worth $400.00 − $85.80 = $314.20.

Now suppose that after 20 years, you retire; your income will drop so that you are in the 15 percent tax bracket. If you are in the 30 percent bracket now, the issue then becomes $300 in taxes now versus $150 in 20 years. Notice that cutting your tax rate in half after 20 years (from 30 to 15 percent) cuts the present value of your tax from $113.07 to $56.54, which is exactly half. However, the fact remains that only a $56.54 *reduction* in the present value of the tax occurs when a $150 reduction in the future tax occurs. It seems that it does not really make much difference now what you expect your tax *rate* to be in the future—if the future is a long way off. This is the same message inherent in the present value tables encountered in Chapter 13—it really doesn't make much difference what happens in the distant future since its present value is very low.

It must be noted that a future reduction in the tax rate makes a great deal of difference if you are talking about the *near* future; however, the interest that can be earned on the taxes saved makes *little* difference on the present value of the taxes. Assume that the future is 1 year hence, that a 5 percent rate of return applies to taxes saved, and that the tax rate is 30 percent now and 1 year later also. The $300 of deferred taxes has a present value of $300 × .9524 = $285.72; at 8 percent they have a present value of $300 × .9259 = $277.77, a reduction of only $285.72 − $277.77 = $7.95. But if the tax rate falls next year to 15 percent, the problem then becomes $300 in taxes now versus the present value of $150 (rather than $300). At 5 percent you get $150 × .9524 = $142.86, so deferring to gain a drop in tax rate is worth $300.00 − $142.86 = $157.14. The lesson is clear and plausible:

> The main advantage of deferred taxes is to be taxed at a lower rate if the future is *near;* the main advantage of deferred taxes is to collect interest on the taxes saved if the future is distant.

Table 17–1 summarizes our computations using time lapses of 1 and 20 years, interest rates of 5 and 8 percent, and marginal tax rates of 30 percent presently and 15 percent in the future.

Table 17–1

THE PRESENT VALUE OF THE TAXES ON $1,000 AT 15% OR 30% TAX RATE, 5% OR 8% INTEREST RATE, AND TO BE PAID 1 YEAR OR 20 YEARS HENCE

	1 YEAR HENCE		20 YEARS HENCE	
	30%	15%	30%	15%
Interest rate				
5%	$285.72	$142.86	$113.07	$56.54
8%	$277.77	$138.89	$ 64.35	$32.17

Tax-deferred annuities are one way of setting aside pretax income to be taxed later. You can invest more dollars than you would be able to if you had to pay tax on them first, now. Many banks, insurance companies, brokerage firms, and so on would be happy to tell you about tax-deferred annuities. Many employers and unions sponsor such programs independently or in connection with their pension program. The law also allows self-employed people to invest pretax dollars with an eye to retirement. As always, the tax consideration is secondary; do not buy an investment simply because the income is tax-deferred. A bad investment is a bad investment without regard to taxes; you are only interested if it is *first* a good investment.

► IDENTITY OF RECEIVER ◄ OF INCOME

If you are a member of a group and are indifferent as to who within the group receives the income, the tax liability of the group can usually be reduced if the income can be more evenly spread among the members of the group. Suppose that you run a small business and that your son, John, works in the business part-time, in return for which you provide his support (food, clothing, housing, etc.). You would probably be better off entering into an employee–employer relationship and having John pay you for his support. Assume that your ordinary income (which includes business profits) is taxed at 30 percent, John works without pay, and you support John in exchange for his working part-time in your business, but no money changes hands. If John has no other income, the following tax changes occur when you put him on the payroll to the extent of $1,000.

Change in your income:	−$1,000 (the $1,000 wages becomes a cost to the business, reducing profits and therefore your taxable income by $1,000)
Change in your tax:	−$1,000 × .30 = −$300
Change in John's income:	+$1,000 (wages)
Change in John's tax:	+$1,000 × 0% = $0
Change in combined tax:	−$300 + $0 = −$300

The mechanics are obvious: Income was transferred out of a high bracket into a low bracket for a net gain to the two parties. Of course, John can pay you back the $1,000 for your support of him if you want to agree to that, in which case the whole operation was a paper transaction yielding $300 to you together; you can split it up any way you want.

The *trust* is another means of income transfer; however, it normally may be transferred only in the future: *you* put the money in *now* and *someone else* takes it out *later*. This has the advantage of not only (probably) transferring funds from a high tax person to a low tax person but also allows investment of pretax dollars as well. If you know that you are going to be transferring property anyway (say, from parent to child), the trust can be a useful and simple device.

▶ **THE BLOCKBUSTER** ◀

As always, in the absence of brute power (and sometimes in the presence of brute power also), the brass ring goes to the ingenious. Any single tax advantage may be a nice tune, but several together can be a beautiful symphony. The extent to which you can avail yourself of multiple advantages, in taxes or elsewhere, is largely dependent on imagination and diligence. (That's why good tax lawyers make big money.) It is also dependent on getting into a situation where there is room to maneuver; there isn't much you can do with a straight paycheck, which is why many average working people get hit fairly hard with taxes. The following example illustrates the possibilities in the use of several tax options simultaneously; we do not say that you cannot do better. On the other hand, for personal reasons you may find the activity in our example to your disliking and not be interested. It is simply an illustration that incorporates the tax advantages of changing the *time* at which income is received, the *form* in which it is received, the *identity* of the receiver, and even the *rate* at which ordinary income is taxed. Specifically, we will defer income (which in turn will defer taxes) until after retirement, so a lower tax rate will apply against the lower postretirement income. In the meantime we will have the money available that otherwise would have gone for taxes. In addition, the postponement of income will allow us to convert it to capital gains; it will therefore be taxed at only one half the lower rate on reduced postretirement ordinary income. Finally, we will transfer some income to a person taxed at a lower rate. As an added bonus, we will pick up some protection against inflation along the way.

Such a package might sound frighteningly complex; it is not. All you need to do is to set up a proper situation and let it work itself out. In fairness, however, it must be noted that our example is a bit more complex than collecting interest on a savings account, but it is well within the reach of an average citizen. It is done every day.

Assume the following plausible situation:

1 • You are 55 years old and will retire in 10 years.

2 • You earn $15,000 per year in wages.

3 • You anticipate that after you retire you will have $4,000 of taxable income.

4 • You have $30,000 in savings that earns 5 percent interest that can be converted to cash conveniently.

5 • You have a 16-year-old son. (For those of you who object that most 55-year-old men do not have 16-year-old sons, throw him out; he's not crucial to the example. But if you do have a 16-year-old son, he may be worth something in taxes.)

6 • Furthermore, you are in good health and expect to be buying growth stocks when you are 90 years old; so you are planning ahead.

What course over the next 20 years will help you taxwise? One answer: Buy a small apartment building and sell it after you retire. (Why do you think real estate gets shuffled from hand to hand? People make money at it.)

To analyze the situation, compute the present value of your aftertax income the next 20 years with and without the apartment building. Although some of our assumptions are a bit antiseptic (income constant at $15,000 for 10 years, for example), they contribute to the simplicity of the problem but do not greatly distort the results.

The present value of your aftertax income for the next 10 years as a wage earner without the apartment building and then for 10 years as a retiree capitalized at 5 percent (using Tables 13–2 and 16–1) is

$$[(\$15,000 - \$3,220 \text{ taxes}) \times 7.72]$$
$$+ \ [(\$4,000 - \$450 \text{ taxes}) \times (12.46 - 7.72)]$$
$$= (\$11,780 \times 7.72) + (\$3,550 \times 4.74)$$
$$= \$90,041.60 + \$16,827.00 = \$107,768.60$$

That is, if you could earn 5 percent compounded annually on your money and did not have to pay taxes, you would be as well-off receiving $107,-768.60 now as receiving $15,000 per year for 10 years and then $4,000 per year for the next 10 years, all taxable at ordinary income rates.

We now compute the present value of the 20-year package that includes the apartment building. We first compute the profit from your self-employment—you have gone into business for yourself on the side—to see how this modifies your taxable income. Suppose that you pay $100,-000 for your (used) apartment building, which contains 10 rental units. You put up $20,000 and borrow the other $80,000 at 8 percent interest. You depreciate the building over a 20-year period; that is, for record-keeping purposes, it declines in value at $100,000 ÷ 20 years = $5,000 per year. (This does not necessarily reflect its true market value.) You rent each unit for $150 per month. Your income is $150 × 10 units, or $1,500 per month, and $1,500 × 12 months = $18,000 per year.

On the expense side, you have $80,000 × .08 = $6,400 interest and $5,000 per year in depreciation. You and your son decide that since this is something of a family venture anyway, you might as well hire him as maintenance man to the extent of $1,000 per year, and he can then pay some of his own expenses you would otherwise pay. To get on with the illustration, assume that all other expenses (insurance, upkeep, utilities, hired management if any, etc.) come to $7,600 per year. In summary, then,

GROSS INCOME	EXPENSES	
$150 per month per unit ×	Interest $80,000 × 8%	= $ 6,400
10 units × 12 months =	Depreciation $100,000/20 years	= $ 5,000
$18,000 per year	Maintenance (son)	= $ 1,000
	Miscellaneous	= $ 7,600
	Total	$20,000

Net income = $18,000 − $20,000 = −$2,000 per year

Beautiful! It loses money! This cuts your taxable income by $2,000 for a tax saving of $2,000 × 30% (the marginal rate of taxation on the last

$2,000 of a $15,000 income) = $600 per year. Thus your taxable income over the next 10 years with the apartment building is $13,000 per year, and your aftertax income is

$$13,000 - \$2,620 \text{ in taxes} = \$10,380$$

Your postretirement income will be higher in the year you sell the apartment building. Suppose that you sell it immediately upon retirement. Your income in that year is the $4,000 postretirement income you would normally receive, plus the profit from the sale of the apartment building. Assume that through good upkeep and inflation you will sell it for what you paid for it, $100,000. It is worth $50,000 on your books because you depreciated it at $5,000 per year for 10 years to ($100,000 cost − $50,000 depreciation) equal $50,000 remaining value. When you sell for $100,000, you have a $50,000 profit to add to income, but only half of it is taxable because it is capital gains.[3] Thus in the first year after retirement your taxable income is $4,000 + $25,000 = $29,000 from the sale of the apartment building. Your taxes in that year are $8,140 from Table 16–1, so aftertax income is

$$29,000 - \$8,140 \text{ taxes} = \$20,860$$

plus the tax-free one half of the capital gains, which is

$$20,860 + \$25,000 = \$45,860$$

To summarize, the next 20 years *including* the apartment building yields $10,380 aftertax income in years 1 through 10, $45,860 aftertax income in year 11, and $3,550 aftertax income in years 12 through 20, the same as without the apartment building.

The present value of the aftertax income package with the apartment building is

Year 1–10	Year 11	Years 12–20

($10,380 × 7.72) + ($45,860 × .5848[4]) + [$3,550 × (12.46 − 8.30)]
= $80,133.60 + $26,818.93 + $14,768.00 = $121,720.53

The present value of the income stream *as reported for tax purposes* is therefore $121,720.53 with the apartment building and $107,768.60 without the apartment building.

It appears that you would be willing to pay $121,720.53 − $107,768.60 = $13,951.93 for the apartment building opportunity, if necessary, rather than go without it. The apartment building will make you the equivalent of $13,951.93 better off now.

But there is more! For tax purposes you are pulling $5,000 per year out of your taxable income in depreciation. This is actual money taken in, and you can spend it or earn interest on it. After all, you are collecting $18,000 per year in rent and actually paying out only interest ($6,400), maintenance ($1,000 to your son, who is a member of the family), and miscellaneous ($7,600), the total of which = $15,000. Your cash position is therefore $18,000 − $15,000 expenses = $3,000. In addition, you will actually have the $2,000 loss charged against your nonapartment income to spend—you actually received that $2,000 in salary—so the $3,000 + $2,000 = $5,000 depreciation, a noncash cost. Therefore, as you "receive" the $5,000 depreciation each year, you can put it out at interest.[5] The question is: What is the present value of $5,000 per year for 10 years (using the same 5 percent rate as on the other income)? It is $5,000 × 7.72 = $38,600.00. The present value of the package of income including the apartment building is therefore

$$\$38,600.00 + \$121,720.53 = \$160,320.53$$

The difference in the values of the apartment package and the non-apartment package is therefore

$$\$160,320.53 - \$107,768.60 = \$52,551.93$$

For those of you who were wondering what you were going to use to pay off the principal on the $80,000 loan on the building that loses $2,000 per year, you now have the answer—cash flow.

The decision therefore becomes: Will you take $52,551.93 *now,* provided you could earn 5 percent interest on it, to undertake whatever hassle all this may entail over the next 10 years? Before you conclude that anyone in his right mind would undertake it, you must recognize a few things.

1 • **This is a rigged example—not false, just rigged.**

Our example is designed to show what can be done—not to show the wildest possible gain or loss, but to show how the mechanisms work. At the same time that we warn you that it may not all work out this well, it must be said that it may work out better. The magnitudes are not unreasonable. But you do have to pull it off. It is a business venture—albeit a simple one—and it will take some manage-ment; in the final instance you are responsible for it. The general attractiveness may well hinge on what you can get for the $7,600 miscellaneous expenses. If this will get you the services of a good reliable management company to keep the books and to operate the building full of nice, neat tenants of long tenancy, the package is probably a dream. However, if you will have to get new tenants yourself frequently because of high turnover, collect the delinquent rent, keep the books, pay the bills, and take care of the burst plumbing in the middle of the night, in addition to the $7,600 for still other operating costs, you may think twice—particularly at 55 years of age. Obviously, "It all depends. . . ." Some people get noneconomic income from these kinds of ventures; others avoid them like the plague. But there are opportunities; people are doing it every day.

2 • **A key component of the package is depreciation.**

The opportunities for tax management stem from the possibility of reporting income for tax purposes that is different from the dollars you actually receive. Depreciation is a noncash cost that reduces taxable income below the number of dollars you actually get. Furthermore, notice that for depreciation to do you the most good, you must *not* be *actually experiencing* the depreciation. (We assumed that you could actually sell the building for what you paid for it. Many properties have been sold for more than was paid for them as you are undoubtedly aware; others *actually* depreciate very rapidly.) It is the disparity between what is really happening and what you can say is happening on paper that helps you. Since depreciation is a noncash cost, you have some latitude here. You begin to see why depreciation policy is a major concern to large property owners and why the Internal Revenue Service will get agitated if you push it too hard. Check with them before you buy to see what they will allow.

3 • **The attractiveness of the project is dependent on the interest rate used to determine its present value.**

In this illustration the apartment building option would be worth $52,551.93 if you could earn 5 percent on that money for the next 10 years. That is, you would be willing to pay as much as $52,551.93 to avail yourself of this opportunity if there were not other costs involved (economic and noneconomic), and you could earn 5 percent on that money. (In reality, of course, you do not have to pay anything in cash for the option; this figure is only a means of evaluating the attractiveness of the offer against the extra bother it entails.)

Notice what a change in interest rate does to the attractiveness of the offer. If you have opportunity to earn 8 percent on whatever money you have, the present value of your income without the apartment building for the next 20 years becomes

($15,000 − $3,220 taxes) × 6.71] + [($4,000 − $450 taxes)
      × (9.82 − 6.71)] = ($11,780.00 × 6.71) + ($3,550 × 3.11)
                       = $79,043.80 + $11,040.50 = $90,084.30

The present value of your income for the same period with the apartment building becomes (paralleling the computation on page 352):

($10,380.00 × 6.71) + ($45,860.00 × .4288)
        + [$3,550 × (9.82 − 7.14)] = $69,649.80 + $19,664.77
                                   + $9,514.00 = $98,828.57

Then we add the present value of the depreciation at 8 percent:

($5,000 × 6.71) + $97,828.57 = $33,550.00 + $97,828.57
                             = $131,378.57

The difference in present values between the two income packages at 8 percent is $131,378.57 − $90,084.30 = $41,294.27, compared to the $52,551.93 difference in present value between the same two packages at 5 percent.

Are you surprised that the project is less attractive at a high rate of interest than at a low rate of interest? You shouldn't be. Remember that the interest rate you use to determine present value is a statement of your alternatives (opportunity cost). An opportunity to earn 8 percent is a better alternative than an opportunity to earn 5 percent; therefore, *this* project, and the extra income *it* will generate, is more attractive when you can only get 5 percent elsewhere. Remember that present value is willingness to pay. You are certainly willing to pay more for *this* alternative if you can take the same money elsewhere and get only 5 percent than if you can 8 percent. Deferred income is always worth less, presently, at high interest rates than at low interest rates because you are all the more anxious to have the money now. Since the apartment building is supposed to defer income for a tax advantage, it is not surprising that the high interest rate cancels part of the tax advantage from the deferred income.

4 • **There are many other provisions in the tax law and refinements to the example from a business standpoint that affect the outcome of the example.**

Since this is intended to be a basic illustration of simultaneous use of multiple tax and investment principles, it cannot be exhaustive. However there is at least one other set of possibilities that sweeten the project further; they relate to the conditions under which your building is sold. It is possible, if you wait to sell until 3 or 4 years after you retire, that you will qualify for *income averaging,* which will substantially reduce the tax bite on the profit from the sale (which is $8,140 in this example). If your income is abnormally high in any one year, you are allowed, in effect, to spread it over more years and pay tax on that basis. Since your postretirement income is very low, an income spurt from the sale of the building can be spread to other years at a considerable tax saving because the lower income is taxed at a lower rate.

Another way of accomplishing essentially the same tax saving is to receive payment for the sale of the building over more than 1 year, thereby putting more of the income into lower tax brackets. Which is best? Read the tax booklets, or see a lawyer; better still, do both.

Also, after you (and your wife) are 65, you will receive an extra personal exemption each—not a big deal, but it is worth more when your income (and therefore marginal tax rate) is high than when it is low. This is further incentive to postpone income until after retirement.

▶ EVALUATION ◀

At the outset of this example we sought to incorporate multiple tax savings into a single illustration by changing the *time* at which income was received, the *form* of receipt, the *identity* of the receiver, and the *rate* at which ordinary income was taxed. Can we partition the example into component parts so that we can see what each of these provisions provides in a tax gain or other form of gain? To a degree. However, we will not be able to do so completely because there is interaction between some of the provisions.

▷ Step I

We said earlier that the presence of the 16-year-old son was not a big issue. Check it out. Assuming that the son has no other income and that the first $1,000 is tax-free, paying the son simply allows the family another $1,000 of tax-free income. If the son drops out of the picture, one of two things happens: Dad does the work himself and his income is $1,000 higher (he no longer has that expense). It is taxable at 30 percent; *his* aftertax income is $300 lower because when the son was paid, he got to "keep" the $300 in "taxes." Thus from the *family* point of view employment of the son was worth, in present values at 5 percent (from Table 13–2), $300 × 7.72 = $2,316.00. Throwing the son out therefore reduces the present value of the apartment building package to $50,235.93 ($52,551.93 − $2,316.00 = $50,235.93). As we said, he's not crucial, but if a little paper shuffling will bring in some extra cash, you might as well do it. Of course, by the time the 10 years is up, the son will probably not be in a position to pick up $1,000 in tax-free income (he will be 26); so if the integrity of the example had depended on it, we would have been in trouble. Perhaps you have a needy nephew you can hire when your son leaves.

If you hire an outsider to work in your son's place (rather than do the work yourself) you will be $700 worse off per year: $1,000 wages goes outside the family, so your income is $1,000 lower— which cuts $300 from your current taxes (at a 30 percent tax rate), leaving you $700 worse off. (The government in effect pays $300 of the wages.) The present value of the $700 for 10 years is $700 × 7.72 = $5,404.00. Still not a tremendously significant reduction in present value when you consider that you transfer work outside the family in exchange for it.

▷ **Step II**

We can also compute precisely what the transformation of ordinary income to capital gains is worth simply by recomputing year 11 income as ordinary income. If the entire $50,000 profit on the sale is taxable in year 11, your income in that year is $54,000 (including the normal $4,000 postretirement income). The tax on it is $20,120 (from Table 16–1), leaving $33,880.00 aftertax income. The present value of it is $33,880.00 × .5848 = $19,813.24. With capital gains, year 11 income at 5 percent was worth $26,818.93. The difference between $26,818.93 and $19,813.24, or $7,005.69, is what the capital gains provision is worth. If this seems a surprisingly small amount, it is because your capital gain "windfall" is so far in the future that its present value is quite low.

The initial present value of the apartment building as an income producer was $52,551.93. We attributed $2,316.00 of that to income transfer to your son or other family member and $7,005.69 to capital gains. This still leaves $43,230.24 unaccounted for.

▷ **Step III**

Although it does not relate directly to taxes, we determined that the $5,000 per year in cash flow from depreciation was worth $38,600.00. In a sense, depreciation is deferred income for tax purposes—you get dollars in years 1 through 10, but you do not settle up your taxes until year 11.

Thus we allocate the gain of $52,547.34 from the building approximately as follows:

$38,600.00	Depreciation (income transfer to other *time* periods)
$ 7,005.69	Capital Gains (a change in the *form* of income)
$ 2,316.00	Transfer (a change in the *identity of income receiver*)
$ 4,630.24	Miscellaneous "interactions"
$52,551.93	Total gain from the apartment building (present value)

Actually there are some interactions in at least the first two items also—they are not "pure" figures. If you want to analyze the problem further, be our guest. Even such a rough analysis as this, however, is useful in identifying what is *really* important. Obviously the depreciation item is the backbone of the gain. It is interesting that this is true only partially because of tax considerations. The real significance of the result is the support of the earlier observation that overzealous tax planning can cause disastrous oversight of other more important matters. The real reason depreciation dominates the problem is because it generates dollars *now*—not later.[6] Beyond this, of course, tax planning is important but not sufficiently so to prompt you to buy an otherwise bad investment that does not generate income. First things first.

Finally, the protection against inflation stems from the ownership of real property, which may rise in value as prices rise. This is frequently a major reason why *actual* dollar depreciation is less than *accounting* depreciation.

SUMMARY

1 • Your tax bill can be altered by altering the *size* of your income, the *form* of your income, the *time of receipt* of your income, and the *identity of the receiver* of your income.

2 • Certain types of income are *tax-free*—most notably, the interest on the bonds of states and their political subdivisions. Like all tax concessions, tax-free income is worth more to high-income persons than to low-income persons.

3 • Many incomes from property, tangible and intangible, qualify as capital gains that are taxed at one half the rate on ordinary income.

4 • Income received as goods and services as such ("in kind") is often tax-free. In addition, goods and services produced by yourself, for yourself (self-sufficiency income), are also tax-free.

5 • Any deferred tax is preferable to a tax payable presently because the present value of the tax is less than the tax itself. It may be possible to actually receive income now for some "spending" purposes but to defer it for tax purposes and therefore to defer the tax.

6 • Deferring income for tax purposes until after retirement is often particularly attractive because post-retirement income is usually lower so the deferred income is therefore taxed at a lower rate.

7 • For purposes of receipt of income, you may be indifferent as to whether you or another member of your group or family receives income; the government may *not* be indifferent, however. That is, you see your group as a unit and the government sees a series of individuals for tax purposes. This allows the group to reshuffle income within itself for possible tax advantages.

8 • Many opportunities exist that allow use of several tax advantages simultaneously. Most of these are business opportunities of one sort or another; the straight salary check offers little opportunity for maneuvering.

study materials

1 • What should one consider when assessing tax-free municipal bonds and taxable industrial bonds?

2 • Why are interest rates on municipal bonds lower than on industrial bonds?

3 • Explain what constitutes long-term capital gains. Give examples.

4 • What is "in-kind" income? Give examples.

5 • Under what circumstances can taxes be deferred?

6 • What are the advantages of deferred taxes?

7 • Make up an example that illustrates the simultaneous use of multiple tax and investment principles.

8 • Name as many ways with examples as you can think of to vary income so as to minimize the tax liability.

9 • Assume two individuals: One has regular income only from wages, and the other has regular income from wages plus rental real estate. Which of the two has more options available to modify his tax liability, and why?

10 • Why in the example used in the chapter was the project less attractive when a higher rate of interest was considered than when a lower rate of interest was considered?

footnotes

[1] In general, the test that determines the taxability of employer-provided benefits is whether the cost is paid from money *withheld* from your compensation: If the benefit is paid from withheld funds, it is taxable; if not paid from withheld funds, it is not taxable. Thus, for example, the employee's half of social security taxes are taxable income to the employee; the employer's half are not taxable income to the employee. This distinction may not make a lot of sense economically but that's another issue.

[2] The story of the tycoon who was chided by his neighbor for cleaning out his own eave troughs comes to mind. Neighbor: "Things really tough, eh, Charlie, when you have to clean out your own eave troughs?" Tycoon: "Look, in my tax bracket I have to earn $100 to hire a high school kid to do it; for $100 I will do it myself."

[3] Earlier we said that capital gains were taxable at one half the rate on ordinary income—for example, 30 percent on ordinary income, 15 percent on capital gains. Now we are saying that capital gains are taxable at ordinary income rates but that only one half the income is taxed: 30 percent of all your income if it is ordinary income; 30 percent of one half your income if it is in the form of capital gains, for example. It all comes out the same. The latter expression was more convenient in this example. To illustrate,

$$30\% \text{ of } \$1,000 = \$300 \text{ tax} \quad \text{(Ordinary income)}$$
$$\left.\begin{array}{l} 15\% \text{ of } \$1,000 = \$150 \text{ tax} \\ 30\% \text{ of } \quad \$500 = \$150 \text{ tax} \end{array}\right\} \text{(Capital gains)}$$

[4] $.5790 is the present value of $1 to be received in 11 years at 5 percent. The eleventh-year figure alone is a lump sum, so Table 13–1 applies. Since the eleventh year does not appear in the table, we computed it from what is in the table. Recall that the present value of a lump sum is the reciprocal of the future value. Taking year 1 as a reference point, the *present* value of $1 to be received in 10 years at 5 percent (from Table 13–1) is $.6139; the *future* value of $1 now to be received in 10 years at 5 percent is

$$\$1.629 \text{ (from Table 12–1)}; \ 1/\$1.629 = \$.6139$$

The *future* value of $1 in 11 years at 5 percent will be what it is worth in 10 years ($1.629) plus 5 percent of that, or

$$\$1.629 \times 1.05 = \$1.710$$

The present value of $1 to be received in 11 years at 5 percent is therefore

$$\frac{1}{\$1.710} = \$.5848.$$

[5] The money that depreciation makes available is an example of what is sometimes called *cash flow*. A business may generate spendable money (cash flow) in addition to profits. Depreciation is a source of additional cash. It is money set aside (in an accounting sense) to replace the depreciating property when it is worn out. In reality, of course, property is not replaced piecemeal; until it is actually replaced, depreciation charges are a source of cash.

Lest depreciation sound like gimmickry to favor businesses taxwise, remember that you did not reduce your income by $100,000 in the year you bought the building because it was going to be "used up" over 20 years; the cost was therefore spread over 20 years as depreciation. The only gimmickry is the extent to which *accounting* depreciation may be greater than *actual* depreciation. Accounting depreciation can frequently be accelerated from actual depreciation, which is an attractive business situation and one we are using in this illustration.

[6] Recall that in Chapter 14 we concluded that slumlords made good money by letting property deteriorate because keeping expenses down generated money *now*, which was more attractive than incurring costs in the present to maintain the value of the property for the future, which had a low value (benefit). We seem to have gotten some reinforcement of that conclusion when we see how very dominant depreciation is in this problem.

appendix
a

EQUALITY OF TAX-FREE
AND TAXABLE INCOME

The basic investment-tax question "Should you seek tax-free income or not?" may be asked in any of three different ways, which stem from knowledge (or an estimate) of (1) the rate of return generated by the tax-free source of income contemplated, (2) the rate of return generated by the taxable source of income contemplated, and (3) your marginal tax rate. How can you decide whether to go the taxable or tax-free route? The three different ways of asking the same question are:

A • Given the rates of return from taxable and tax-free income sources, is your tax bracket high enough so that you should take the tax-free income?

B • Given your tax bracket and the rate of return on taxable income sources, is the rate of return on tax-free income sources high enough so that you should go to tax-free income?

C • Given your tax bracket and the rate of return on tax-free income sources, is the rate of return on taxable income sources high enough so that you should go the taxable route?

These are three versions of the core question "Do you go the taxable or the tax-free route given any set of conditions consisting of (1) a taxable rate of return, (2) a tax-free rate of return, and (3) a marginal rate of taxation?" Typically you know all three values, but you have to establish a criterion for evaluating them that will allow a decision.

In more formal terms, you have three variables: the taxable rate of return; the tax-free rate of return; and the marginal tax rate. Each of the three questions really asks you to plug in values for two of the variables to solve for the value of the third variable, which you then compare to its known or estimated value. You make a decision on the basis of the comparison.

To solve the problem, identify the circumstances under which you would be indifferent to a choice between the taxable and tax-free income sources. You are indifferent when they both yield the *same* return *after taxes*. Thus what marginal tax rate and rates of return from tax-free and taxable income sources will give

(1) Aftertax income from taxable sources
$$= \text{Aftertax income from tax-free sources?}$$

Or, abbreviating,

(2) $$ATI_t = ATI_{tf}$$

Taking ATI_t,

(3) $$ATI_t = BTI_t - Tx$$

where BTI_t is taxable income before taxes and Tx is taxes paid on that income.

(4) $$Tx = (BTI_t)(MRT)$$

where MRT is the marginal rate of taxation, and

(5) $$BTI_t = (R_t)(P_t)$$

where R_t is the rate of return from the taxable income source and P_t is the principal on which the rate is paid. Substituting (5) into (4),

(6) $$Tx = [(R_t)(P_t)](MRT)$$

Substituting (6) and (5) into (3) yields

(7) $$ATI_t = [(R_t)(P_t)] - [(R_t)(P_t)](MRT) = [(R_t)(P_t)](1 - MRT).$$

With regard to ATI_{tf} from (2), it is noted that $ATI_{tf} = BTI_{tf}$ by definition. BTI_{tf} is given by

(8) $$BTI_{tf} = (R_{tf})(P_{tf})$$

where R_{tf} is the rate of return from the tax-free income source and P_{tf}

is the principal on which the rate is paid. Substituting (8) and (7) into (2) gives

(9) $$[(R_t)(P_t)](1 - MRT) = (R_{tf})(P_{tf})$$

Since the equal income $(ATI_t = ATI_{tf})$ must be generated from equal resources (principal) if the problem is to be meaningful, it turns out that $P_{tf} = P_t = P$, so each side can be divided by P and the P_{tf} and P_t disappear from the equation; (9) then becomes

(10) $$R_t(1 - MRT) = R_{tf}$$

You now have one equation and three unknowns, which can be juggled algebraically to solve for any unknown if the other two are known. Question (A) is answered by $MRT = 1 - (R_{tf}/R_t)$; question (B) is answered by $R_{tf} = R_t(1 - MRT)$; and question (C) is answered by $R_t = R_{tf}/(1 - MRT)$.

To take question (A), if $R_{tf} = 5$ percent and $R_t = 7\frac{1}{2}$ percent, a $MRT = 1 - (5/7\frac{1}{2}) = 1 - .66 = .33$ causes you to be indifferent to a choice between taxable and tax-free income sources. If your income is high enough so that you are taxed above 33 percent at the margin, you prefer the tax-free source; if your income is low enough so that you are taxed at less than 33 percent at the margin, you prefer the taxable source.

To take question (B) and to use different numbers as an illustration, if the taxable return available is 9 percent and your marginal rate of taxation is 25 percent, you are indifferent between taxable and nontaxable sources if $R_{tf} = .09(1 - .25) = .09(.75) = .0675$ or $6\frac{3}{4}$ percent. If the tax-free return is above $6\frac{3}{4}$ percent, you prefer it; if the tax-free return is below $6\frac{3}{4}$ percent, you prefer the taxable source.

appendix
b

EQUALITY OF CAPITAL GAINS AND ORDINARY INCOME

You can easily determine how much income as capital gains is equivalent to a given amount of income as ordinary income by stating your indifference to the equality of the amounts from each source *after taxes*. The procedure is analogous to determining whether to choose the taxable or tax-free source of income. Indeed, Appendix A is really a special case of this appendix.

(1) $$ATI_{oi} = ATI_{cg}$$

where ATI_{oi} is aftertax income from ordinary income and ATI_{cg} is aftertax income from capital gains.

(2) $$ATI_{oi} = BTI_{oi} - Tx_{oi}$$

where BTI_{oi} is beforetax income from ordinary income and Tx_{oi} is the taxes on the ordinary income.

(3) $$Tx_{oi} = (BTI_{oi})(MRT_{oi})$$

where MRT_{oi} is the marginal rate of taxation on ordinary income. Similarly, for capital gains,

(4) $$ATI_{cg} = BTI_{cg} - Tx_{cg}$$

(5) $$Tx_{cg} = (BTI_{cg})(MRT_{cg})$$

Substituting (3) into (2) and (5) into (4) gives

(6) $ATI_{oi} = BTI_{oi} - [(BTI_{oi})(MRT_{oi})] = BTI_{oi}(1 - MRT_{oi})$

and

(7) $ATI_{cg} = BTI_{cg} - [(BTI_{cg})(MRT_{cg})] - BTI_{cg}(1 - MRT_{cg})$

Substituting (6) and (7) into (1) gives

(8) $(BTI_{oi})(1 - MRT_{oi}) = (BTI_{cg})(1 - MRT_{cg})$

but $MRT_{cg} = \frac{1}{2} MRT_{oi}$, so (8) can be rewritten

(9) $(BTI_{oi})(1 - MRT_{oi}) = (BTI_{cg})(1 - \frac{1}{2}MRT_{oi})$

Solving for BTI_{cg},

(10) $$BTI_{cg} = BTI_{oi}\frac{1 - MRT_{oi}}{1 - \frac{1}{2}MRT_{oi}}$$

Using data from Example 18–3 in the text,

$$BTI_{cg} = \$1,000$$

$$\$1,000\,\frac{(1 - .30)}{(1 - .15)} = \$1,000\,\frac{.70}{.85} = \$1,000 \times .82353 = \$823.53$$

If you have a choice between $1,000 in ordinary income and *more* than $823.53 as capital gains, take the capital gains; if you have a choice between $1,000 in ordinary income and *less* than $823.53 in capital gains, take the ordinary income. In more general terms, at tax rates on ordinary income and capital gains of 30 and 15 percent, $.82 in capital gains is as good as $1.00 in ordinary income.

The solution can be easily generalized to include any tax rate relationship between capital gains and ordinary income. For example, if the rate of tax on ordinary income were 40 percent and the rate on capital gains 30 percent, the statement between Equations (8) and (9) would become $MRT_{cg} = \frac{3}{4} MRT_{oi}$, since the coefficient of MRT_{oi} is the ratio MRT_{cg}/MRT_{oi}. You plug in the values of the tax rates and proceed to (10), which becomes

$$BRT_{cg} = BRT_{oi}\frac{(1 - MRT_{oi})}{(1 - \frac{3}{4}MRT_{oi})}$$

in this case, since the capital gains tax rate is $\frac{3}{4}$ of the ordinary income tax rate.

IV

PUBLIC DECISIONS IN THE PUBLIC SECTOR

In Part I and particularly in Part II we looked at decisions in which you enjoyed a specific, personal (private) gain (benefit) for a specific, personal (private) loss (cost). In Part III we looked at decisions in which you enjoyed a general gain as a member of society in exchange for a specific personal loss in the form of a tax payment. In Part IV we will look at decisions in which both the gain and the loss are general; they redound to other members of society as well as to you. Your loss and gain is not exclusively your own doing. You must become part of society as a whole in order to enjoy certain kinds of benefits and to incur the costs necessary to have them.

This is the realm of public policy decisions in the economic arena. The decision is not private, but public. Society as a whole decides. Your personal role in this is as a member of society who has the opportunity to influence other members of society; it is the group decision in a grandiose setting. (See the Appendix of Chapter 3, "Collective Decisions.") Your economic role in these decisions is to identify and decide on the merits of the various alternatives; how much you want to persuade others of the merits of your analysis by getting out your soapbox, writing your elected representatives, and so on is another matter. Our concern here is primarily for the economic issues that relate to your decisions on economic public affairs.

We really seem to be saying that to be a constructive influence in the modern economic world you need to know some economics. Alas, it is true. But don't be tempted, therefore, to turn over economic affairs to economists! An economist may be able to tell you what *will* happen if we do certain things, but he has no more business than any other citizen telling you what *should* happen. This is the old issue of *economic analysis* (what will happen) versus *economic policy* (what should happen). There is no reason why an economist's preferences should carry more weight than your preferences. Unfortunately, economists' preferences are apt to prevail over noneconomists' preferences. The saving grace is that different economists have different preferences just as different noneconomists have different preferences among themselves, so some balance is provided within the economics profession.

Why do economists tend to play a disproportionately important role in determining public economic policy? Why do a few key economists tend to have large followings of disciples? It is certainly *not* because economists have the divine right to determine public policy. Very frequently it *is* because noneconomists offer half-baked proposals that don't hang together; they will not take us where we want to go.[1] Thus the citizen's role in public economic affairs is dependent on a fuller appreciation of underlying economic conditions and relationships. This is the essence of the argument for economics as a part of general, or liberal, education. Put simply: You can't tell what you want unless you know what you have to give up to get it, and you can't tell what you have to give up to get it unless you understand some economics.

Unfortunately, economics in the public sector is a little more complicated and more subject to judgment than in the private sector. In the private sector, your personal viewpoint is all there is to it. In the public sector you are more apt to get involved with long-range considerations with "secondary feedbacks" (what I do now affects you tomorrow, which in turn affects me day-after-tomorrow, etc.). In addition, you may deliberately reduce your own welfare to enhance someone else's, depending on your philosophical outlook toward your fellow man. Many people favor income redistribution schemes that work to their personal economic disadvantage—and they favor them *knowing* that they work to their immediate disadvantage—on philosophical grounds. This would seem to be a matter of giving up personal economic income to gain personal noneconomic income—the satisfaction of doing the "right thing."

Thus economic decisions in the public sector, like economic decisions in the private sector, require an understanding of the issues. As always, the central issue is what is lost (cost) for what is gained (benefit). The difference between private and public sector decisions is that the costs and benefits may be a bit more elusive and indefinite in the public sector.

In Chapter 18 we will look at the need for public economic decisions. Why don't we have an exclusively private economy? In Chapter 19 we will look at some specific private decisions that have significant public dimensions. In Chapter 20 we will look at decisions wherein the private dimension is virtually nonexistent; the decision is almost totally a public policy decision that has no immediate bearing on you directly but affects you only as a member of society.

footnote

[1] Before you charge that some economists' proposals don't hang together too well either, consider the possibility that "it doesn't make sense" is often a euphemism for "I don't want to do that." Most often, disagreement among economists is due to disagreement over what each is *willing* to give up to get something else; more frequently, disagreement among noneconomists is due to ignorance over what *must* be given up to get something else.

chapter
18

PUBLIC ECONOMIC ACTIVITY

Through Part II, we implicitly assumed that all goods were private goods; goods were sold by private parties to private parties. Even in Part III, although we assumed that you were paying taxes to the government, the discussion had a private focus—what could you do to lower your tax bill personally. We now want to look at the case for direct action by the public (society as a whole), through government, in the economic arena.

We will begin by defining public goods and private goods. Then we will look at the competitive market system—what it is, what it does, and the conditions necessary for it to exist—as the backbone of the (private) U.S. economic system. Although the competitive market system is hard to find today in the United States in a pure form, it is relevant because in many respects public economic activity is designed to produce the result that would be realized if a competitive market economy did exist. That is, market economics is frequently a norm to which we aspire. It is therefore important to understand something about competitive market economics even though the subject may seem quaint in a modern industrialized world.

We will see that in certain instances the competitive market system cannot work because of what we will call an identification problem. *In other instances it does not work because of an* externality problem. *Finally, we will observe that the identification problem is something of a special case of the externality problem. They are treated separately because the solution of the identification problem requires stronger medicine than the solution of other externality problems. But all solutions call for action by the public, which means that you must understand the issues to act as an intelligent citizen in a democratic system that will be formulating these solutions to economic problems.*

▶ PRIVATE VERSUS PUBLIC GOODS ◀

Since we profess to have been talking about private goods and now proclaim our intent to talk about public goods, what do we mean by each? **Public** (with regard to *goods*) means society as a whole—as represented by government. **Private** is everything else. That is, anything not public is private. *Private* is sometimes divided into personal, corporate, and nonprofit. The **private sector** is run by individuals and households acting on their own behalf (personal), by boards of directors and managers running business corporations (corporate), and by boards of directors and administrators running churchs, charitable foundations, professional associations, and so on (nonprofit). The **public sector** is run by government. Our focus heretofore has been on private sector transactions between individuals (households) and business. Households are the buyers in the case of consumer goods; households are the sellers in the case of factors of production.

　　Public goods are *goods that are provided by government for society*

as a whole (for reasons we will investigate). These goods are not transmitted to consumers through markets but are rather simply made available for anyone's benefit who is inclined to avail himself of them. This
would include such things as national defense, social services, and most
highways. They are free to the individual user. (Obviously they are not
free to society as a whole.) Public goods normally must be provided by
the public sector, since there are no private buyers, in the traditional
sense, to reimburse the private suppliers of the goods for the resources
they used up in providing the goods. No private business will produce
things for general consumption; private businesses produce things to sell
to specific buyers. Thus the public provides goods for public consumption. No market transaction occurs as the goods pass to the hands of the
final user. Of course, many public goods are produced by the private
sector, which "sells" the goods to the government, which in turn makes
them available to the public. Highways, for example, are typically constructed by private contractors and "sold" to the government, which
makes them available to the public at no direct charge. The government
itself, however, typically *maintains* highways, although there would seem
to be no reason why it could not contract this function to the private
sector as well. The government itself provides national defense but buys
most of the mechanical inputs and supplies from the private sector. Thus,
the test of a good's "publicness" is not who produced it but whether or
not it is sold, as such, to the final user.[1]

Private goods are necessarily, then, *goods that are sold, specifically,
to the final user.* Most private goods are provided by the private sector;
however, government can also produce and sell private goods. The municipal power plant, the sewer system, or the water works that charges
users the full cost of the system's operation according to usage is an example of the public sector supplying private goods.

As a background, we will consider the competitive market system
and its merits as a supplier of private goods as the point of departure into
the realm of public goods.

▶   COMPETITIVE MARKET ECONOMICS   ◀

The merits (and demerits) of the competitive market system can be
demonstrated with graphs and equations in formal terms, but we will
settle for an explanation.

How shall *competitive market economics* be defined? We have disposed of *economics* earlier in the book. Let us focus on *competitive* and
market.

Ignoring **competitive** for the moment and taking **market** first, we define it in a somewhat abstruse, but revealing, way as *the sphere through*

which price making influences work. The market is the arena wherein buyers and sellers settle on a price (terms of exchange). Notice that the definition has no geographical dimension. A market is not necessarily a place. The market may consist of a telephone network rather than a physical location. What *is* necessary is that there be good communication between buyers and sellers. The notion of a market as a physical location is probably a holdover from the days when communication meant a face-to-face encounter. All that is required for prices to be established is that buyers and sellers be able to communicate with one another. Whatever events influence price are relevant to that market.

For example, what happens in Los Angeles may influence the price of aeronautical engineers (their wages) in New York. If so, New York and Los Angeles are part of the same market for aeronautical engineers. However, what happens in Los Angeles probably has no effect on the price of bread in New York. If so, New York and Los Angeles are *not* part of the same market for bread. The reason is simple: It is economically feasible to move aeronautical engineers from Los Angeles to New York; it is not economically feasible to haul bread from Los Angeles to New York. Stated another way, an increase in the demand for aeronautical engineers in New York will tend to draw engineers from Los Angeles to New York; an increase in the demand for bread in New York will *not* tend to draw bread from Los Angeles to New York. Of course, it must be recognized that an increase in the price of flour can cause the price of bread to rise in both New York and Los Angeles at the same time, but that does not make them part of the same market. It simply says that they are both subject to the same outside influences.

Competition refers to a specific set of market conditions under which prices are determined. A full-blown definition of competition has a number of facets, which, taken collectively, boil down to this: **Competition** exists if *no one buyer or seller is able to influence the market price by his own personal actions.* Under competition, you are a drop in the bucket: You are a *small* supplier if a seller, a *small* demander if you are a buyer. You are not a big enough part of the picture to alter price by changing the amount you buy or sell.

Notice that in some respects this definition is opposite from everyday usage. You and a business rival across the street may say that you compete with one another. Actually you are *rivals* rather than competitors. Your ability to personally identify your "competitor" is evidence in itself that your situation is not very competitive. It may be bloody; but it is not competitive. This illustrates one of the virtues of competitive market systems: They are impersonal; they do not play favorites. There are *many* buyers and sellers, no one of whom is personally visible because each is "small." The price-making forces pervade the atmosphere as the collective result of many buyers and sellers interacting with one another. Nobody calls the shots. A price evolves. "Take it or leave it" is the message to all *individual* buyers and sellers.

The corn market is quite competitive. There are a great many sellers and rather numerous buyers also. Each corn farmer competes intensely with all other corn farmers; he does so by trying to grow corn more cheaply, which means "two blades of grass where one grew before"; this tends to increase the quantity and lower the price of corn, which in turn tends to drive his neighbors out of business, unless they, too, can grow corn more cheaply. But it is all very impersonal. It is curious that "competing" neighbors are frequently brought to cooperation (to get their costs down—to be even more efficient) by the economic chastisement of competition. It is impersonal because there are so many corn growers (i.e., each corn grower is so "small") that there is no single identifiable culprit who is growing more corn more cheaply and thereby causing the price to fall—or be lower than it otherwise would be.

Some observations about the illustration point up the social merits of competition.

EXAMPLE 18–1

Suppose that you are willing to pay $1.00 for a widget but that a seller is willing to sell for $.75. How is it that a business that is presumably trying to maximize profit is willing to sell for less than you are willing to pay? It seems that there is $1.00 − $.75 = $.25 up for grabs. You, of course, would be very willing to pay $.75, which is $.25 less than the $1.00 maximum you are willing to pay, and the business would certainly be very willing to sell for $1.00, which is $.25 more than the $.75 minimum at which it is willing to sell. Who is going to get the $.25 which seems to be floating around loose? The answer—as so often—is, "It depends."

Let us suppose that there is only one seller of widgets (no competition) but many buyers willing to pay $1.00. The seller will "charge what the traffic will bear" if he is trying to maximize profits. But the fact that he was willing to sell for $.75 means that he could do so and still stay in business—that is, continue to supply you with widgets. If there is nothing to prevent it, other firms can be expected to get into the widget business to get a chunk of the gravy.

GRIN AND BEAR IT   BY LICHTY

"...And in spite of record harvests food prices are still up!...
I say what's the use of the law of supply and
demand if it isn't being enforced?"

But how do you enforce a set of impersonal forces, Senator?

GRIN AND BEAR IT by George Lichty.
Courtesy of Publishers-Hall Syndicate.

As they do, they can be expected to shave their prices below $1.00 to take part of the market away from the existing
widget producer. In any event, the extra widgets coming
from the new widget makers will tend to depress the price
to, say, $.90, whereupon each widget sells for $.15 above
the minimum price at which the widget makers would be
willing to sell. Notice that each firm is, in a sense, still
charging what the traffic will bear, but the traffic will bear
much less when there are more sellers. More sellers keep

appearing on the scene until the price of widgets finally
falls to $.75—the minimum at which the firms are willing
to sell.

Some of the virtues of competition can be gleaned from this example.

1 • **Prices tend to gravitate to the lowest level at which producers are
willing to sell rather than to the highest level at which consumers
are willing to buy; prices continue to drop until they are just high
enough to hold the factors of production in that use.**

If prices are lower, firms find the industry unprofitable and tend to
leave; if prices are higher, firms find the industry attractively profitable and tend to enter. This results in the lowest possible price at
which a good can be made available, and you may take it or leave
it, depending on the amount of utility you get from it. If you take it,
you are assured that you are getting it at the lowest possible price.

2 • **If there is any "gravy" to be had, the consumers rather than the producers get it.**

This is a direct result of—if indeed, not another way of stating—
that prices tend to gravitate to the lowest possible price rather than
the highest possible price. *A competitive system therefore maximizes
consumer surplus and minimizes producer surplus,* where consumer
surplus is defined as the amount by which consumers get goods at
less than they would have been willing to pay and producer surplus
is defined as the amount by which producers get returns *greater* than
they would be willing to accept. Producers end up with little or no
more than the minimum they are willing to accept, but consumers
end up with less cost than they would have been willing to bear.

3 • **As a direct outgrowth of this, the foundation for the observation
that "competitive market economics is consumer oriented" is evident: The consumer gets the best of it; the producer gets enough to
stay alive and no more.**

The rationale is that everyone is a consumer but everyone is not a
profit receiver. Therefore, any "excess profits" should go to the consumers in the form of lower prices.

4 • **A competitive market economic system is impersonal.**

Prices are accepted as given; that is, you observe what various prices
are and you can buy or not buy, sell or not sell, at that price since
no one buyer or seller can personally influence those prices. It must
be quickly emphasized that this is true only if there is competition.

If competition is weak or absent, price can be influenced by an individual in the market to his own advantage. This was clear at the outset of the example where the lone seller was able to charge a higher price when he was the only seller than he was able to charge after competition came onto the scene.[2]

Thus the "redeeming social value" of competitive markets is that they result in the most goods at the lowest possible price to whomever wants to buy. They beget efficiency; they are fair.

▶ THE CASE FOR PUBLIC GOODS ◀

If competitive markets are so wonderful, why do we have public goods at all, which obviously are not transmitted to the user through markets— competitive or otherwise? Very simply, because goods must possess certain properties to be transmitted through markets, and not all goods possess those properties.

▷ the identification problem ◁

Some goods possess disagreeable properties (from a market point of view) which make it inconvenient or impossible to transmit them through markets. What property *must* a good have to be transmitted through a market? The **identification problem** is that *certain goods do not come in measurable units.* If you are unable to buy or sell a certain number of units at a certain price, you are out of luck as far as the market is concerned. You cannot provide this good through the market channel. The good must be provided in a more general way.

National defense has no units in which it can be sold to those who wish to buy. Of course, you could buy and hire the wherewithal via which you could defend yourself—tanks, guns, soldiers, supplies—in which case you have identifiable units of defense as measured by inputs. But you cannot acquire these identifiable units of defense in sufficiently *small* units to be practical. The nature of many "goods" is such that there is insufficient divisibility to provide identifiable units of the size you are willing and able to buy as an individual.

Many other public goods display the same troublesome properties— police and fire protection, highways, social services, and so on. Furthermore, if you are contemplating providing these services through the private sector operating for a profit, you encounter other troubles. Do you want a profit-maximizing firm fighting a war for you? Can a profit-maximizing firm undertake poor relief? Not directly, certainly. It might

be possible, however, for the government to contract some of these services to the private sector to perform while the government foots the bill.
This is the typical pattern in highway construction. The end product
(highway) is a public good, but it is constructed by the private sector
rather than by the government itself. This has always been the pattern in
highways, whereas in education and social services the government has
typically provided the service directly—although there is no reason why
it must. Indeed, there has been some timid experimentation contracting
school operation to the private sector. However, no matter how provided,
they are still public goods unless the full cost of them is charged to the
user.

We could charge drivers for the use of highways. We do this with
toll roads, but the mechanics would get messy if we did so on city streets.
A tollbooth on every corner? Obviously, it is much cheaper to provide
them as a public good and let those who want to drive on them do so.
Of course, those who don't drive get stuck with part of the cost in taxes,
resulting in some inequity. But on the other hand, the financing of much
highway construction is from taxes collected on gasoline, which tends to
eliminate that inequity. Nothing is totally clear in these matters.

Problems of inequity (among other things) cause us to tend to prefer
the private-good approach if the good is capable of transmission through
markets. Those who want to buy do so and pay the cost of their benefit;
those who do not want to buy refrain from doing so and bear no cost.
Some goods, however, cannot be provided this way. This much is abundantly clear: There is more than one way of going about things; a wide
variety of combined public and private approaches in providing goods
are available.

▷ the externality problem ◁

An **externality** is a *cost or benefit to another person from your action.*
Competitive markets must operate without the presence of externalities
if they are to function efficiently and fairly, as suggested earlier. Our previous example assumed that there were *no* externalities. It was assumed
that the cost you pay is the *total* cost and the benefit you receive is the
total benefit. For example, if you decide to buy a carton of milk, the
cost to *you* represents the *total* cost to *society* (loss of resources) of providing it, and the satisfaction from drinking it is the *total* benefit to
society from it. All costs and benefits to society are *internal* to you, the
decision maker, as a specific member of society. Frequently, however, your
action causes *others* to be worse off (external costs) or better off (external
benefits).

If all costs and benefits are internal, society's welfare is maximized as each individual member of society maximizes his personal welfare. That is, society is the direct sum of its parts.

If some costs and benefits are external, the market will not allocate resources to end products efficiently and fairly. For example, your neighbor likes a $1,000 sound system that will knock the paint off the walls with no distortion. His willingness to pay for it is such that it is a good buy at $1,000, so he purchases it. The market will allocate enough resources to these sound systems to satisfy the people who want to buy them at the price at which they can be made available. Those who want to buy do; those who don't want to buy don't. Everything is lovely. Society is allocating just the right amount of resources to this use through its competitive market system to maximize its welfare, given other possible uses for those same resources *if* there are no externalities.

Suppose, however, that you hate loud music—especially the kind your neighbor plays. You get disutility from it; you would be willing to pay to *avoid* his sound system—in other words, there is a negative externality. Obviously, the two of you together would be willing to pay *less* than your neighbor alone, and the two of you together would be less inclined to buy than your neighbor alone. Thus if negative externalities exist, competitive market systems will overallocate resources to that use, since the cost to the buyer is less than the full cost (or viewed from the other side of the coin, the benefit is not as great as the buyer's benefit alone).

Similarly, if there are positive externalities, the market system will underallocate to those uses that are the source of the positive externalities. To revamp the previous example, suppose that your neighbor is on the verge of buying his sound system but does not get quite enough satisfaction from it to prompt him to buy. Unbeknown to him, you are in the same situation, for we are now assuming that you, too, have your neighbor's taste in music. Neither of you alone will buy, but the two of you would buy if you could share the cost between you. Conditions call for a sound system to be allocated to you and your neighbor together, but as long as each of you must bear the full cost alone, neither of you will buy and no sound system will be allocated to either of you.

The externality problem is big and growing. The pollution problem is a matter of externalities where costs are not borne by the polluters but are borne by society as a whole. As the world gets more populated and wealthier, the externality problem grows. The closer together we get, the more externalities are apt to exist. Unfortunately, they tend to be more negative than positive. Anytime your preferences are different from your neighbor's, a negative externality is apt to arise. Increased wealth as well as increased population puts us closer together. A wealthy person takes up more "room" than a poor person, since the rich man's big house, car, boat, and snowmobile create additional costs, some of which are foisted onto society as a whole in air, water, and noise pollution.

Physical closeness also aggravates the problem. Your decision to throw your garbage out the window has no effect on your neighbor if he lives 10 miles away. However, if he lives 10 feet away, your slovenly existence affects him negatively. The two of you together would be happy to pay to dispose of the garbage, but the decision is in your hands alone and you have a stunted sense of smell. Your neighbor is powerless in a market economy to do anything about it, short of disposing of your garbage himself.

This example illustrates one of the roles of government in such a situation. You undoubtedly were saying, "But throwing garbage out the window is against the law." Aha, yes! And why is it against the law? Because the law is one of the mechanisms that can be used to correct externalities and make the market system work better than it otherwise would. Another means of correction for the externality would be for the government to take over garbage collection itself, in which case garbage collection would become a public good on the grounds that the whole neighborhood benefits; so the whole neighborhood—that is, the government—will bear the cost.

Much more could be said on this subject, and we will explore it further in later chapters. For the time being, we will settle for the observation that the solutions of the externality problem are necessarily public policy issues, since government action of some kind is required either in the form of pressure on the externality-creating parties or by taking over the externality-creating function itself in such a way as to eliminate the externalities.[3]

▷ the identification problem ◁
as an externality

We suggested earlier that the identification problem might be viewed as a particular kind of externality. Indeed. The reason the unit of good cannot be identified is because it is almost totally external to the buyer! You are buying something so general that the benefits accrue to everybody around you; the benefit is so insignificantly internal it never occurs to you to buy it on your own.

Consider national defense. The only way you could really buy national defense for yourself would be to buy enough so that the benefit would spill over to, perhaps, several million other people. The benefit is

almost exclusively external—so much so that the prospect of paying this
total cost for the small portion of the benefit you would receive never
even crosses your mind. It's ridiculous, you say. Of course. So the only
feasible way of providing this good is for society to provide it collectively
as a public good.

SUMMARY

1 • Public goods are goods supplied by the government
for society as a whole without any market transaction—national defense, most streets and highways,
many social services, and education at least through
high school.

2 • Private goods are goods sold by one party to another
through markets according to the amount the buyer
and seller wish to transfer at a mutually agreeable
price.

3 • The public sector (government) produces some
goods that are really private goods—postal services,
for example, since the senders of letters could pay
the full cost of mailing letters just as the eaters of
apples pay the full cost of the apples.

4 • Competitive market economics is the backbone of
the U.S. economic system—if not as an operation, as
a norm.

5 • A market is a set of price-making influences at work.

6 • Competition exists if no one buyer or seller can influence price by his own actions.

7 • A competitive market is therefore one in which
prices are determined by a set of impersonal forces.

8 • Competitive market prices are the lowest that can
prevail consistent with continued supply of the
product at that price. The sellers just break even.
The consumers get the best of it.

9 • Markets cannot transmit some goods, such as national defense, where no unit of the "good" exists
that is small enough so that an individual buyer is
interested in buying (the identification problem).

These goods, then, are necessarily public goods—
they are supplied by society as a whole for society as
a whole.

10 • A *competitive market system* allocates resources to
various goods so that each individual maximizing
his welfare results in society maximizing its welfare.
There are no externalities.

11 • Externalities are either

   a. Negative externalities—there is disutility (cost)
   to other people in addition to those paid by the
   buyer of the product, or

   b. Positive externalities—there is utility (benefit) to
   other people in addition to those realized by the
   buyer of the product.

12 • If there are positive externalities, the market system
will underallocate resources to the externality-generating use; if there are negative externalities, the
market system will overallocate resources to the
externality-generating use.

13 • The externality problem grows as we get closer together—in a physical sense by populating the earth
more heavily and/or in an economic sense by becoming wealthier.

14 • The ways in which the externality problem may be
corrected, and hence the market system made to
work better, will be explored in Chapters 19 and 20.
For now, we recognize that all solutions required
some kind of public (government) action.

study materials

1 • Explain what is meant by each of the following. Use examples.

   a. Private decisions in the private sector.

   b. Private decisions in the public sector.

   c. Public decisions in the public sector.

2 • Distinguish between the public sector and the private sector.

3 • Define and give examples of public goods; private goods.

4 • Give examples of goods or services that are partly public and partly private, and explain why.

5 • What is meant by consumer surplus? Producer surplus?

6 • Define competition (in the economic sense). Explain how a competitive economic system functions.

7 • Explain why the "identification problem" calls for public goods.

8 • What is an externality? A negative externality? A positive externality? Give examples of each.

9 • Why are externalities more of a problem today than they were 100 years ago?

10 • Explain why, in a market system, an underallocation of resources tends to occur when there are positive externalities. An overallocation when there are negative externalities.

footnotes

[1] Some authors seem to define public goods as all goods *produced* by the public sector. For reasons that will unfold as we go along, we think that such a definition is not very useful. We prefer to view the public–private good distinction according to whether the final user pays the cost of the good directly himself.

[2] The importance of the impersonality of competitive markets must not be underestimated. For example, in the summer of 1973, there was a critical shortage of soybeans in the United States and in the rest of the world. Prices skyrocketed. The U.S. government, under pressure to "do something about inflation," rationed our remaining supply to foreign buyers. The Japanese, a large and valued customer for our soybeans, were furious. They did not object to paying prices several times as high as a year earlier, but they resented a specific edict telling them how many they could have. High prices were "just one of those things." Export controls were "discriminatory." The U.S. government thereupon swore off export controls.

[3] To avoid possible confusion later, let us agree to define the competitive market system by the absence of externalities, as discussed here. A *market* system (as opposed to a *competitive* market system) may include externalities.

chapter
19

PUBLIC POLICY
AND THE
PRIVATE DECISION

Having laid the groundwork for public decisions in Chapter 18 by suggesting that it is impossible to live in a modern industrialized world without your actions frequently resulting in costs or benefits to your neighbors as well as to yourself—either individual neighbors or the neighborhood (society)—we will now look at some specific instances where your actions may result in externalities. We will consider some means whereby the externalities may be internalized, if that is desirable, or whereby the externalities may be perpetuated, if that seems to be desirable.

We will look at the public policy issues of driving without insurance and of providing free—or heavily subsidized—education. In the first instance the externality would seem

*to be negative; in the second instance it would seem to be
positive. What are the issues?*

▶ REVIEW AND ASSUMPTIONS ◀

Before we begin, let us reinforce the foundations. You may disagree with
the foundations, although we think that they probably represent mainstream thought in the United States. Whether that is an accurate assumption is really beside the point; all we need is a set of reference points.
Indeed, a useful exercise might be to change the underlying assumptions
and rework the examples. Much of the disagreement over public policy is
disagreement over the ground rules and goals that society ought to seek.
More of the disagreement, however, is probably due to ignorance about
what is *really* happening compared to what appears to be happening. In
any event, assume:

1 • We desire, as much as possible, the end result that the competitive
    market system would produce if it were in operation. This means
    a. That each person should pay the *full* cost of his actions—that is,
       everything that is lost or given up to get something for *you* is lost
       by *you* personally (there are no negative externalities).
    b. That each person should receive the *full* benefit of his actions—
       that is, everything that is gained in exchange for what is given up
       by *you* is gained by *you* personally (there are no positive externali-
       ties).
2 • Furthermore, we are interested in getting as large a benefit for as
    small a cost as possible—that is, we are interested in efficiency since
    resources are scarce.
3 • The competitive market system produces the efficiency condition in
    (2) both for every individual member of society and for society as a
    whole.

As you undoubtedly recognize, this is a reiteration of the competitive
market system, discussed in Chapter 18. Fine. It must be squarely before
us if we are to see where we are going.

Most U.S. citizens more or less apparently accept these conditions
because, in the first place, efficiency is important—we know we cannot
have everything and so must conserve. We go around suggesting that it is
"unethical," "un-American," "immoral," "anti-social," and so on to be
wasteful. (Clean up your plate; there are starving children in China.)

Curiously, none of these terms are really appropriate. (Waste is uneconomical.) It is difficult to see how the uneaten food on the child's plate will get to the Chinese mouth. But we believe that we ought to have a built-in bias for efficiency, even if the reasons for it and the evidences of it in specific instances are a bit strained. Even fruitless attempts at personal efficiency seem to constitute something of a vicarious penance; frugality is good for the soul. (Many continuing "wastes" such as big cars, for example, are wastes due to the failure of the market system to work properly—the owners do not pay the full costs of their cars; or, in other instances, "waste" is simply a nasty word thrown at the owners of big cars by other members of society who get less utility from big cars than from other things. In other words, calling something "wasteful" may be only name-calling. If you and I happen to like different things, it does not mean that either is necessarily wasteful. We are wasteful only if we use up more resources than necessary to get what we have or are not really getting what we want from the resources used up.)

Second, it appears that we favor the competitive market system in the absence of externalities because it conforms to our individualized outlook. Each person does his own thing.

Thus, although our discussion of the competitive market system is less than complete (there are other criticisms), it does seem to be a key foundation stone of the U.S. economy; it frequently serves as a norm or standard as government determines the direction of its economic influence. We will accept the competitive market's virtues of *efficiency* and *individual fairness* as goals toward which we aspire in evaluating public policy.

▶ DRIVING WITHOUT INSURANCE ◀

What is the cost of driving a car? Gasoline, oil, tires, maintenance, wear and tear (depreciation), interest on the capital tied up in it, and the like. Insurance? Maybe; maybe not. Really? Actually, you cannot answer the opening question (What is the cost of driving a car?) because it is ambiguous. "What is *your* cost of driving *your* car?" is one question; "What is *your share* of society's driving cost?" is another. The answers to the two questions are the same only if there are no externalities. First, we will consider the total "driving bill" (cost that society must bear to have the utility from this activity), and then we will see how it may be split up among individual drivers.

Society's cost of driving is, simply, all the resources lost in the process —gasoline, oil, tires, depreciation, and interest on equipment and roadways, *plus* the cost of resources destroyed by motorists ricocheting their cars off one another, signs, utility poles, crash barriers, bridge abutments, and so on. Insurance, of course, is not an issue for society as a whole, because all insurance does is shift the cost of hitting things around to parties other than those who do the hitting in any specific instance. For society as a whole, the loss is the things that are hit plus the lost productivity of persons who are put out of commission.[1]

What *is* your share of this cost and what *should* be your share of the cost? Your share of the cost *is* probably as little as you can make it be. Does this mean driving without insurance? Maybe; maybe not. If you are essentially broke anyway, you would probably find it advantageous to drive without insurance. If you hit someone (your fault) resulting in a $50,000 loss to the other person—tough. It is part of society's driving bill which you cause but which you will not pay; you will foist it off onto the person you hit. There is a $50,000 externality. The person you hit can sue you, but he can't get milk out of a financial turnip. If you have the $50,000, however, there is a very real possibility that the $50,000 will become an internal cost to you, in which case you will want to consider insurance.

In either case—insurance or no insurance—the cost of driving is the same; the only difference is how it is distributed.

What is your stance on the public policy question of mandatory auto insurance if you believe in competitive market economics? Clearly, the driver who causes the damage ought to pay for it, in which case each driver is required to carry insurance or otherwise demonstrate ability to pay for damage he is likely to cause. Most drivers choose to carry the insurance. The possibility of a large financially crippling loss exists, but with a low probability; so the insurance is a good buy (see Chapter 15). In any event, the innocent bystander or other driver is protected from having driving costs unfairly dumped in his lap at the same time that your car is dumped in his lap.

▶ **NO-FAULT INSURANCE** ◀

The merits (or lack thereof) of no-fault insurance are an interesting corollary to the foregoing discussion. How does it stack up against competitive market economic principles? As you probably know, no-fault insurance requires each party to an accident to have his expenses paid by his insurance company in contrast to "fault" insurance where the insurer of the driver who is at fault pays the expenses of both drivers.[2]

Curiously, no-fault insurance seems to run contrary to the fairness principle of competitive market economics but in accord with the efficiency principle. If your premiums under "fault" insurance are based partly on the number of accidents you have caused, no-fault insurance is particularly contrary to the fairness principle. The fairness principle says that those who create the costs should pay for them. An insurance premium based on your accident record therefore makes sense.

The arguments in favor of no-fault are essentially efficiency arguments. There is waste in establishing fault which employs platoons of attorneys stumbling over one another trying to determine what really happened at the same time other attorneys may be trying to obscure what really happened. The whole process uses up vast quantities of resources. We could save those resources (the accident-investigating attorneys could do something useful like digging ditches) if we just let everybody's own insurance company pay his own damages and forget about who was to blame.

The choice is clear: Do you prefer fairness or efficiency? The choice gets complicated when you begin to ask *how much* fairness we want to lose in exchange for *how much* efficiency from no-fault. It is difficult to measure (or at least to predict) efficiency in this instance and even more difficult, if not impossible, to measure fairness in *any* instance. Hence the controversy. Further complicating the matter is the possibility that if the efficiency gains are great enough, even those who are treated relatively less fair under no-fault may nonetheless end up better off than they are now. We are not saying that that is the case, only that it is a possibility.

For example, under no-fault, even though you were *not* at fault, your insurance company would pay, thereby tending to make your premiums higher relative to the fault(y) driver than they would be under "fault" insurance, where your company could get off the hook by establishing the fault of the other driver and forcing his company to pay. As we said, no-fault is less fair. *But* offsetting this is the possibility that it might be cheaper for your company to pay the claim and be done with it than to prove the fault of the other driver. If so, the gains in efficiency could cause your premiums to drop from what they are now, even with your good driving record. The person with the bad driving record would find his premiums dropping by an even larger relative amount. Thus you both come out ahead, but you with the good driving record probably feel that you deserve the biggest gain from the increased efficiency. You won't get it of course; the person with the bad driving record will get it. So you stick to your guns; no-fault is less fair—especially less fair to you as a good driver. But to oppose it is to cut off your nose to spite your face.

So how would it all come out if we really went to no-fault on a wholesale basis? Nobody knows for sure. If we did know, the arguments would be all over. The current tilt of the public toward no-fault suggests that the public is at least suspicious that the efficiency gains from no-fault would outweigh the fairness losses. Or perhaps the public has little confidence that present legal procedures establish fault accurately and so there are few fairness losses to be realized. Or, possibly, the public just does not value fairness highly compared to efficiency. In any event, it is easy to see why no-fault insurance, like so many other public issues, is controversial.[3]

► A RETURN TO INCOME ◄
DISTRIBUTION

The competitive market system, which requires each person to pay according to the costs he generates (no negative externalities), is really nothing more than a reencounter of the central principle of the income distribution mechanism discussed in Chapter 7, and particularly in the appendix to that chapter. Recall that a competitive market system distributes income to persons according to the productivity of each person—as opposed to need or custom or any other criterion: He who makes the biggest contribution to the pie shall be served the biggest piece in the end. You, as an individual, determine your income according to how much you produce. The individualistic outlook of the income distribution system is evident. Our concern over negative externalities is essentially the other side of the income distribution coin. Notice the symmetry:

1 • *Income distribution point of view:* Every individual should receive the full benefit of what he produces—that is, there should be no positive externalities.

2 • *Negative externality point of view:* Every individual should pay the full cost of what he destroys—that is, there should be no negative externalities.

The two statements say essentially the same thing because income and cost are different by the direction of flow: Income is inflow; cost is outflow. Cost without any attendant benefit is waste. Thus waste is negative income. Therefore, it follows that paying for what you waste (no negative externalities foisted onto others) is nothing more than a negative version of enjoying what you create (no positive externalities snatched from you by others). The controlling principle applies no matter which way the flow. Income distribution is income distribution, positive or negative. Individualism reigns in either case.

► TO SCHOOL OR NOT TO SCHOOL ◄

One of the more significant personal decisions made by most people is whether to continue a formal education beyond high school. We are moving in the direction of lifelong education of one sort or another, which diminishes the once-and-for-all nature of the immediate post-high school education decision. Nevertheless, it is not an easy matter for most people to return to full-time school later in life. So completion of high school still represents a major fork in life's road. The decision to continue in school is certainly a private decision, since you evaluate the costs and benefits to you personally. Yet the public dimension of that decision is enormous: You are probably able to attend school at a private cost to you considerably below the total cost with the difference made up by the public; there may be benefits from education to society as a whole beyond those collected by you personally. The public therefore has a considerable stake in your private decision and can, by altering public policy, alter the attractiveness of the private option to pursue education. What are the issues that must be considered to produce the "right" amount of education? Why should the public subsidize education? Why not charge the student the full price?

We looked at an education example in Chapter 14 but from a purely private point of view. If we pursue that same general type of example into the realm of public policy, some interesting things emerge. We will not use specific real-world dollar figures. Perhaps you could work out a parallel illustration for yourself, comparing figures for earnings forgone while acquiring an education with the expected lifetime earnings of people with various levels of education as supplied by your college's job placement and student recruitment people. These figures are available and will undoubtedly be more up-to-date than the ones we would be able to use in such an example. So we will proceed on a slightly more general level that can be accepted as plausible simply through observation of the real world.

Everyone is well aware that the public provides schooling at a private cost less than total cost. The private cost of education is very low through high school. The public pays the bill, and the earnings forgone by the student are negligible. Beyond high school the public pays a substantial portion of the cost, but the private costs also become significant. The proportion of the cost of operation of the post-high school educational system borne by the student as a private cost varies widely from school to school within the system. Some states provide "free" post-high school education, and a few private schools charge tuition to cover nearly all costs. Thus the *private* cost of post-high school education may range from 0 to 100 percent *of the cost of the operation of the school.* Suppose that the average post-high school student pays 20 to 25 percent *of the cost of the operation of the school.*

But that is only the tip of the iceberg. More than half the private cost of a typical post-high school education is *earnings* forgone. That cost is, as far as we know, always borne by the student. (We know of full tuition, fees, and board and room scholarships; we do *not* know of full tuition, fees, board and room, *and* earnings forgone scholarships. If we accept for working purposes that more than 50 percent of the cost of post-high school education is earnings forgone and the typical student pays 20 to 25 percent of direct school costs [i.e., he pays 20 to 25 percent of the other (less than) 50 percent], the average post-high school student "pays," say, 70 percent of his total educational costs. The public picks up the rest.

What proportion of educational costs *should* the student pay? Competitive market economic principles say that the student should pay *all* his costs if he personally receives *all* the benefits; the student should pay proportionately less of the costs if the proportion of benefits from education accruing to society as a whole rises. *Fairness* requires payment by the benefit receiver: If there are no positive externalities, the student pays the full cost; if there are positive externalities, the student pays in proportion to the share of the total benefit he receives personally. Efficiency also requires that the student pay according to benefit received, since students will decide to buy education after comparing private cost and private benefit. If there are additional external benefits, society will want more resources allocated to education than the students will buy, hence the justification of the public subsidy. Therefore, if the average student currently pays about 70 percent of his higher education costs, the student realizes personally about 70 percent of the benefit, and 30 percent of the benefit is as an externality to society as a whole *if* we are on the beam of the competitive market system.

The crucial question, of course, is: What proportion of the benefits from education *are* external to the student? We cannot answer the question because many of the benefits are difficult to measure: We *can* mull over the issues. In doing so we will divide education into two parts: through high school; post-high school.

▷ **elementary and secondary** ◁
education

As suggested earlier, elementary and secondary education are normally available at a private cost of close to zero. According to competitive market economic principles, the total benefit of elementary and secondary education is to society as a whole, and none of the benefit is to the student. Ridiculous! What rationale can be offered for free elementary and secondary education?

The overriding rationale seems to be that society simply does not intend that competitive market economic principles should apply here.

There is more to life than economics. Every individual is entitled to certain "inalienable rights" (benefits?). Certain constitutional guarantees are not subject to economic analysis. Your simple being as an individual entitles you to certain things. Economics is not the highest order. Now, to be sure, education is not one of those constitutional guarantees as is free speech, for example. But society is inclined to view education in a similar way. We are not interested in debating the merits of that view, since it is not really an economic question. It does, however, seem to make some sense to provide free minimum education to all persons on the grounds that many individual rights are not very meaningful in the absence of any education. However, the quantity of education that constitutes a minimum entitlement is open to question, and it is not reasonable to assume that all education occurs in schools. To get on with the economics we will accept the noneconomic rationale for free education through high school.

Neverthless, we can look, in the beginning, at the economics of elementary and secondary as well as post-high school education. Education provides private and public benefits. Furthermore, the private benefits may be divided into what we will call *producer benefits* and *consumer benefits*. Although the public benefits might also be so divided, there is little point in doing so. *Producer benefits* are *those fruits of education that accrue to you as a factor of production* and therefore can be converted to money income—the skills that allow you to hold a higher paying job for instance. *Consumer benefits* are *those fruits of education that accrue to you directly as a consumer,* such as the ability to appreciate life more fully because of your expanded background. The difficulty of measuring the value of education is that it is normally only the *private producer benefits* that can be measured with satisfactory accuracy. The higher lifetime income to the educated person is normally only the higher income from private producer benefits. Placing a value on consumer benefits is difficult because many of them are in the form of noneconomic income (see Chapter 7). What is it worth, for example, to more fully appreciate the arts? Placing a value on public benefits is also difficult, although some of the benefits may be measured. However, are you prepared to say what it is worth to you to have an educated neighbor versus an uneducated one, other things being equal? The externality can be very difficult to measure. The only thing we can say with certainty is that any "hard" dollar figure on the value of education is an understatement of total benefits from it.

How much education is warranted for society to commit the necessary resources? To get at the answer, it will be useful to ask two questions: Are the *producer benefits* subject to the law of diminishing marginal productivity, which says that *additional* units of a variable input added to the production process bring forth smaller *additional* increases in output as the quantity of variable input increases? (See Chapter 7.) Are the *consumer benefits* subject to the law of diminishing marginal utility, which says that *additional* units of a good acquired by a consumer provide less *additional* utility per unit as the consumer acquires more units of consumer good? (See Chapter 9.) There would seem to be no reason to suppose that these laws would *not* apply.

If, for example, the law of diminishing marginal productivity did *not* apply, it would follow that $5,000 spent teaching a graduate engineer a specialty would increase his income just as much as $5,000 spent teaching him basic reading, writing, and mathematical skills. It is unlikely that an engineering specialty, for example, will increase one's income as much as basic literacy will increase income—assuming the same number of educational dollars are spent for each. If basic skills are worth more, the law of diminishing marginal productivity seems to apply to education. Most research results bear this out: Elementary school is a better buy for society than secondary school; secondary school is a better buy for society than higher education. Thus the most interesting public decisions are in the realm of higher education, since it is here that society has to decide where to stop spending. The return from expenditures for elementary and secondary education are the most apt to be above the returns that we could get for the same expenditure elsewhere in the economy. Higher education is the poorest buy (though nonetheless a very *good* buy in most instances). The question remains: Given the probable operation of the law of diminishing marginal productivity and the law of diminishing marginal utility and the *public* benefits that flow from education, how far should society "push" higher education by making it available at a private cost below its total cost? That is, given the other opportunities society has to invest its capital, how many resources should it commit to education? If there were no external benefits, perhaps the market would decide adequately. Since there obviously are external benefits, society has to make a conscious decision as such.

▷ higher education ◁

If we accept "free" education through high school on the basis of the noneconomic right of each individual to a minimum of education and on the public benefits it produces, we then have to determine what we believe constitutes an equitable split of the cost of higher education between an individual student and society. We saw in Chapter 14, using hypothetical but plausible data and including only private costs and producer benefits, that a traditional four-year college education was perhaps not the fabulous buy it is often considered to be. The two things that cut its value dramatically were two things that are apt to be over-looked: (1) The cost of a college education is really quite high, consider-ing the rather substantial earnings that must be forgone; and (2) the benefit flows forth over a lifetime and thus the present value of much of that benefit is very low. This example, however, is inadequate for our purposes here in two respects: (1) It did not consider the consumption benefits from higher education; and (2) it did not consider the external benefits from higher education.

We have confessed that we cannot determine an equitable private–public cost split because we cannot adequately measure either the con-sumption benefits or the external benefits. We can, however, make some observations which hint that competitive market economic principles are subtly at work, albeit imperfectly, as a guiding hand to students' private decisions and to policy makers' public decisions.

1 • If we accept the probable operation of the laws of diminishing mar-ginal productivity and diminishing marginal utility as applying to college education, we can see that as it is provided in greater quan-tity, it will tend to become less attractive both to the student as a private decision maker and to the public as it determines policy. We see signs that it is indeed so. The Carnegie Commission on Higher Education reports that

> *higher education may be reaching a ceiling in the amount of money it can expect from society—it used about 1% of GNP (Gross Na-tional Product) in 1960 and is using about 2.5% now, and no other segment of society more than doubled its take of GNP during that short period of time. A resistance point may have been reached.*[4]

Enrollments more than doubled during this period. The marginal product per dollar spent on education surely must have been lower at the end of the decade of the 1960s than at the beginning relative to other public and private investment opportunities. The tendency for college enrollments to drop in the early 1970s suggests that in-creasing numbers of students were finding college a poor buy and were spending their dollars in other markets. Similarly, the public's tendency to restrict the growth of educational institutions from the rate of expansion of the 1960s, even in the face of more favorable state finances in the early 1970s than in most of the 1960s, suggests that society as a whole also increasingly questioned whether the quantity of educational services had expanded to the point where investment elsewhere was more attractive. Other factors such as student unrest may have caused the public and many students to disfavor education; but it then must be asked whether disrespect and destruction were only part of a normal change in behavior toward something that had become less valuable.

None of this says that investment in education is too high or too low. It only suggests that if the law of diminishing marginal productivity applies to the producer benefits from a college education and the law of diminishing marginal utility applies to the consumer benefits from a college education, there is an inevitable point, as the educational sector expands relative to the rest of the economy, at which further investment is no longer as attractive as it was earlier. The rapid expansion in education in the 1960s clearly could not go on forever for very fundamental economic reasons.

As a corollary, it is interesting to note that for many years in the 1950s and 1960s, school-bond proposals met with much public favor. The rate of passage was very high. Voting down a school-bond proposal was tantamount to giving public notice that your community didn't have its collective head screwed on straight—don't you know education does wonderful things? Not surprisingly, there came a point when most communities had their new schools and attempts at further expansion in the physical plant met resistance. The rate of rejection of school-bond proposals rose sharply in the late 1960s and early 1970s.

2 • If we accept the hypothesis of Theodore W. Schultz that one of the functions of higher education is to *discover* talent as well as to develop it, we can justify some "overspending" on higher education.[5] That is, we should let students into school at a very low private cost the first few years, so students and society alike can find out who can absorb the higher education. After that has been determined, the private costs of education should be scaled upward sharply. This suggests a two- or three-tiered fee system with very low fees for beginning students and relatively high fees for graduate and professional students. Some schools are moving in this direction.

If we accept the law of diminishing marginal utility as applying to the external benefits from education, it would seem that elementary and secondary school are the best buy for the public and justify the largest subsidy. The higher up the educational scale, the more likely specialized training is apt to be reflected in higher earnings of the student. There would seem to be quite a good case for charging the lawyer, doctor, engineer, accountant, and the like nearly the full cost of his *professional* education. The exception to this justification is perhaps the highly trained scientist who is doing basic research that may result in enormous social benefits in the form of some historic discovery; often the value of that discovery is scarcely reflected in his income at all—very possibly because it was not valuable until after his death. The liberal arts student who comes off the educational assembly line a delightful person and a good citizen but a drag on the job market should have his education heavily subsidized, since a larger proportion of his benefits (compared to the professional student) are external to him. Society needs only to answer the impossible question of how many such people it can justify producing.

3 • The Schultz hypothesis on the *discovery* of talent as an educational function prompts further observation on uncertainty, or risk, as a cost (see Chapter 15). Uncertainty is a cost since some things will necessarily turn out wrong. You will occasionally have zigged when you should have zagged. You will have less benefit for the cost than you would have had if you had put your eggs in the right basket.

There is uncertainty as to which students have talent, and there is a cost associated with determining who they are. If we assume that the only way to know for sure who is talented is to let everyone in and see who cuts the mustard, society and some individual students will have sent some resources down the drain with those students who do not make it. If we take the opposite approach and keep all the "uncertain" students out, we will lose the public and private benefits we might have had from letting those in who would have succeeded. Either way you can't win—there is a cost to the uncertainty. The question, as always is: Who should bear it? Is it a public or private cost? Schultz's interesting thoughts on this frustrating question are in the appendix to this chapter. He concludes, "Here we have one of the unsolved problems in planning and financing higher education." [6]

Notice further that if a student faces great uncertainty as to whether he can succeed academically and whether he can get a good job upon graduation, he is less inclined to go to college, as he is required to pay a higher proportion of his total costs as private costs. This simply restates: Uncertainty is a cost. If that cost is added to all other costs, obviously college looks less attractive.

So what can be concluded about an equitable private–public cost split? Very little. Two respected sources offer different recommendations. The Carnegie Commission on Higher Education likes it the way it is.

> No precise—or even imprecise—methods exist to assess the individual and societal benefits as against the private and the public costs. It is our judgment, however, that the proportion of total economic costs now borne privately (about two-thirds) as against the proportion of total economic costs now borne publicly (about one-

'No—I Have a Ph.D. in Aerodynamics'

. . . On the cost of educational uncertainty . . .

Editorial cartoon by Don Hesse. Copyright, St. Louis Globe Democrat.
Reprinted with permission of Los Angeles Times Syndicate.

third) is generally reasonable. We note that for one item—additional earned income by college graduates—about two-thirds is kept privately and about one-third is taken publicly in the form of taxes. We also note that this two-thirds to one-third distribution of total economic costs has been a relatively stable relationship for a substantial period of time (although the internal components of each share have changed—for example, the private share is now more heavily composed of forgone income and less of tuition charges).

We see no strong reason to change this distribution in any revolutionary fashion either in the direction of full costs privately borne or full costs publicly borne, although there are forceful advocates for fundamental change in each of these directions. In the absence of stronger proof than we have seen or stronger arguments than we have heard, we accept the current distribution of burden as generally reasonable.

Bowen and Servelle (1972, Sec. 9) have recently reached much the same conclusion: that it is reasonable to have about a two-thirds private and one-third public sharing of total economic costs.

We define private costs for these purposes as those borne by the family unit (parents and students), and public costs as those borne by governmental agencies and philanthropy. The former

> *might alternatively be called* personal *and the latter* nonpersonal
> *costs. Philanthropy, of course, is a different phenomenon than direct
> governmental support, although about one-half of philanthropy
> consists of taxes forgone by public bodies.* Governmental costs *are
> those borne by federal, state, and local governments.*[7]

The Committee for Economic Development, however, takes the position that college students should pay a higher proportion of their college education as private costs.

> *We believe that tuition charges at many colleges and universities are unjustifiably low. We recommend an increase in tuitions and fees, as needed, until they approximate 50 percent of instructional costs (defined to include a reasonable allowance for replacement of facilities) within the next five years. For two-year community colleges and technical colleges, we recommend that the increase be phased over ten years.*[8]

In addition, the CED recommended an expanded program of loans and grants to students so as not to exclude lower income students from the educational system. Although this recommendation may have been in tune with the tone of the early 1970s when the public benefits from education were viewed with an extra measure of skepticism, the CED's evidence based on competitive market economic principles, to which the CED is a well-known subscriber, seems to be no better than anyone else's.

SUMMARY

1 • Competitive markets find favor because they tend to conserve resources (they are efficient) and require each person to pay the full cost of his benefits (they are fair).

2 • Driving without insurance results in external costs to other persons; therefore, mandatory insurance is more in accord with competitive market economics than allowing drivers on the road without insurance.

3 • No-fault insurance is apparently less fair and more efficient than "fault" insurance; however, the efficiency gains can work to offset the fairness losses. Conceivably the efficiency gains could be great enough to cause even those treated less fairly under

no-fault to be better off than under "fault" insurance.

4 • An attitude of disfavor toward negative externalities
is essentially a negative view of the income distribution principle, which states that each person receives
income according to productivity—which requires
an absence of positive externalities.

5 • Education yields private and public benefits.

6 • Private (and public) benefits from education are
either *producer benefits,* which appear as increased
money income, or *consumer benefits,* which result in
enhanced enjoyment directly.

7 • The *producer benefits* of education are apparently
subject to the *law of diminishing marginal productivity;* the *consumer benefits* are apparently subject
to the *law of diminishing marginal utility.* Therefore, the more education, the less valuable are additional units to private parties and public alike.

8 • Society apparently believes that a minimum education is a personal entitlement on noneconomic
grounds (through high school?).

9 • Competitive market conditions require that a student pay that proportion of the costs of education
that are private benefits.

10 • Although the typical college student pays about 70
percent of the cost of education (including earnings
forgone), it is impossible to determine whether this
division of cost is really equitable, because it is impossible to put a reliable value on either the *private
consumer benefits* or *the public benefit.*

study materials

1 • Discuss the term *wasteful* in the following contexts: economic name-
calling; noneconomic name-calling.

2 • Considering auto insurance only from the private viewpoint, why
and how might a "poor" person view it very differently from a
"rich" person?

3 • What is "no-fault" auto insurance?

4 • Why does "no-fault" auto insurance appear to run contrary to competitive market economics on the fairness principle? How and why may it be in accord with the efficiency principle?

5 • Why should the public subsidize education?

6 • How does the law of diminishing marginal utility relate to the idea that elementary school education is a better buy for society than secondary school education and secondary school education a better buy than higher education?

7 • Explain the Schultz hypothesis regarding the functions of higher education. Do you agree? How could it be applied in a practical way if you agree? How differently should higher education proceed if you disagree?

8 • Defend or criticize the proposition that the full cost of formal education through college should be borne publicly.

9 • Defend or criticize the proposition that the full cost of formal education through high school should be borne publicly; that the full cost of formal higher education should be borne privately.

10 • Explain the formal educational system now employed in the United States in terms of who bears the cost and why (public versus private cost division).

footnotes

[1] Nothing so demonstrates economic ignorance as the comment—when a ship sinks, an airliner is blown up, or a large building burns down: "Well, it was probably insured." So what? If you are not directly connected with either the company that owned the destroyed property or the insurance company that paid the claim, what difference does it make to you whether it was insured or not? In either case you are a member of society, which is poorer by the amount of the loss.

[2] There are many versions of no-fault insurance. Our discussion proceeds in terms of a rather "pure" no-fault concept.

[3] This discussion does not pretend to cover all the issues of no-fault insurance. We have ignored, for example, the whole question of whether the absence of fault will make the average driver more careless, thereby wiping out much—or all—or conceivably more than all—of the efficiency gains to be realized from the elimination of litigation. Our discussion implicitly assumes that there are no differences between fault and no-fault other than those things specifically mentioned.

[4] Carnegie Commission on Higher Education, *The More Effective Use of Resources* (New York: McGraw-Hill Book Company, June 1972), pp. 2–3.

[5] Theodore W. Schultz, *Investment in Human Capital* (New York: The Free Press, 1971), pp. 163–65.

[6] Schultz, *Investment in Human Capital,* p. 187.

[7] Carnegie Commission on Higher Education, *Higher Education: Who Pays? Who Benefits: Who Should Pay?* (New York: McGraw-Hill Book Company, June 1973), p. 3.

[8] Committee for Economic Development, *The Management and Financing of Colleges,* Oct. 1973, p. 25.

appendix

ON THE PUBLIC AND PRIVATE BENEFITS OF EDUCATION

Following are some of Theodore W. Schultz's thoughts on the social (public) benefits from education.[1]

ON RECKONING SOCIAL BENEFITS (LOSSES)

When this box is opened, we are in trouble, for there is so little agreement on what it contains. It is hard to distinguish between fact and fiction because the task of specifying and measuring these benefits has been grossly neglected. No wonder that claims and counterclaims are the order of the day. Most of us have a vested interest in higher education, which is hard on objectivity. We are prone to lay claim to most of the advance in knowledge from which the social benefits are undoubtedly large. University research and instruction are, as a rule, joint products; at the doctoral level, graduate instruction and research are highly complementary. Are there identifiable social benefits from instruction that do not accrue to the college student from his private investment in education? It is plausible that having neighbors who are educated gives a family with such neighbors some positive satisfactions. It is also plausible that having co-workers who are educated is a source of additional satisfactions. It has been argued that parts of our public administration—namely, individuals coping with our "income tax forms"— give rise to an administrative social benefit. But it is also plausible that the private benefits of education accruing to college students leave some other persons worse off. It is argued that some elementary school teachers *favor* the children from homes with (college) educated parents and that this favoritism leaves other children worse off. It is also alleged that in buying and selling homes some educated families act to exclude uneducated families from acquiring property (homes) in their particular neighborhood.

But it is all too convenient to engage in double counting. Education, no doubt, increases the mobility of a labor force, but the benefits in moving to take advantage of better job opportunities are predominantly, if not wholly, private benefits. Educated labor has access to more of the relevant economic information than uneducated labor; but here too the benefits from this advantage presumably accrue to the persons who have the education. The cultural component embodied in higher education is the source of another benefit which invites double counting. There is also a tendency to claim that higher education makes for better citizens and for a better political democracy. It could be, but our belief with respect to these benefits is a matter of faith. It is not obvious that the political self-interest of college graduates results either in more responsible citizenship or in a more perfect government than the self-interest, say, of high school graduates.

To the extent that there are benefits that accrue to persons other than to the student acquiring the education, there could be underinvestment in higher education, regardless of how efficient students are privately in their investment in education. But there is an important set here that does not qualify; namely, those benefits accruing to the student that make the private investment at least as good as investment in terms of the rate of return as that to alternative investment opportunities. Under these circumstances, presumably, privately efficient investment by students would suffice to bring forth the required education and assure whatever benefits might accrue to others, as was true in investing in physical capital in the case of Henry Ford and his very profitable Model T.

Suppose, however, that there are some potential college students who would not benefit enough privately to warrant the investment privately and that there were some social benefits that were sufficient when added to the benefits accruing to the student privately to raise the (social) rate of return sufficiently to make it a good investment by the standard set by the priorities of the relative rates of return to alternative investment opportunities—then, under these circumstances, some underinvestment in higher education at the margin would be implied.

It follows, of course, that if there were no such social benefits, this bit of economic logic would be wholly empty. Thus we are back to a question of fact; namely, are there any such benefits that can be identified and that are subject to measurement?

ON THE SOCIAL BENEFITS OF HIGHER EDUCATION

In producing these education services, the required organizational changes pertaining to incentives and information are not easy to determine. Consider the problem that arises in planning and financing these components so that public and social bodies would become efficient in allocating investment resources for these purposes. What are the pertinent educational activities that render social benefits? University research is in substantial part one of them. So is a part of the activity pertaining to the discovery of talent. Let me elaborate briefly on why this may be true. My conception of the cost and returns pertaining to the *discovery of talent* could qualify here. There are many colleges that admit at least two freshmen for every one who will survive to graduation. If these colleges charged full costs, I would assume that this ratio of entering freshmen to graduating seniors would decline sharply. Presently, that half of the entering freshmen who discover that they lack the capabilities and motivation to complete college drop out and enter the labor market, benefiting sufficiently from the year or more they spent in college to have made their private investment in that amount of college work a good investment privately, although when the subsidy entering into their instruction is taken into account, it was all told a poor investment. But suppose now that out of the entering freshmen who would not have sought admission at full costs, there were a substantial number of students (say, a tenth of the seniors who complete college) who did not know they had the necessary capabilities. These discovered students could (should) pay full cost; but they would not have become college educated had it not been for the extra cost of the discovery process. It would be a matter for public policy to decide whether this extra cost was worthwhile. A part of instruction may also belong here; but the instruction that accrues wholly to the benefit of students is excluded. It must be admitted that it is exceedingly difficult to specify the particular types of information and the nature of the incentives that would prove strong and clear in attaining these purposes. Here we have one of the unsolved problems in planning and financing higher education.

footnote

[1] Theodore W. Schultz, *Investment in Human Capital* (New York: The Free Press, 1971), pp. 182–87 (selected sections).

chapter
20

PUBLIC DECISIONS
IN THE
PUBLIC SECTOR

In the previous chapter, we looked at situations where the decision was of considerable private interest to you but where there were substantial public costs or benefits. We used auto insurance and education as examples. You not only had to decide what to do as a private decision but you were also obligated to form an opinion on public policy.

In this chapter we will look at questions that are almost totally public policy questions. We will use pollution control and watershed management as examples. The issues are the same as in the public aspects of the questions in the last chapter: If we accept the validity of competitive market principles, we evaluate public economic policy in terms of overall efficiency and fairness.

*In each of the two examples in this chapter—pollution
control and watershed management—we will determine
whether we believe that the proposed program represents
the most efficient use of resources and investigate some of
the fairness questions that inevitably arise.*

▶ POLLUTION CONTROL ◀

The competitive market system requires each purchaser of a product to
pay the full value of the resources used to produce it. That's why the
competitive market system is fair and efficient; if *you* want a product, *you*
withstand the resource loss necessary to get it. The money prices of the
resources and products reflect (1) the value society places on those resources and products, and (2) society's ability to convert the resources to
products: The lower the value society places on the products, the lower
the value society places on the resources, the lower the prices on the products; the higher the ability to convert resources to products (efficiency in
production through technology), the lower the prices on the products.
The absence of externalities means that your decision to buy or not buy
a product leaves no one else worse off nor better off.

It is clear that the existence of a pollution problem is in itself evidence that competitive market economic principles are not operating.
Pollution is a negative externality; the polluters are not paying for the
resource "destroyed" by reducing its quality through pollution. Oddly,
pollution problems may be identified—and therefore pollution may be
defined—in terms of *complaint;* if no one squawks, there is no pollution
in an economic sense. The complaint comes when the complainer's resource is destroyed by someone else who makes no compensating payment
for it. If no one feels unfairly treated, apparently nothing is being destroyed without a compensating reward. Therefore, if no one complains
(nor is inclined to complain), there is no pollution.[1]

Consider air pollution. If gases and particulates are given off into
the air in sufficiently small quantity so that no layman can detect them
or so that there are no long-term identifiable adverse health effects, there
would seem to be no pollution in economic terms. No one feels any loss,
even though a scientist may be able to detect technical pollution by
analyzing the air. If there is a readily identifiable loss of utility from
reduced air quality, there is pollution if the owners of the air are not paid
for the loss of this resource. The "owners of the air"? Ah, yes—there is

"DETERGENT, DEODORANT, DRAIN CLEANER, SCOURING POWDER.... MY, THEY MUST BE VERY NEAT UP THERE."

Fastidiousness as a negative externality.

the problem and the reason the pollution exists in the first place: Air is a free public good.

Why do firms and individuals (who are the biggest polluters) use resources they do not pay for and thereby shift the cost to others? Simply, because they can get away with it. "Isn't that scummy," you say. Not at all! The efficiency of the competitive market system requires that everyone use as few resources as possible to produce any given end result. In money terms this means keeping money costs down, which, of course, means not paying for anything you don't have to pay for. In order for a payment to be made for a good or resource, it must exist as an identifiable unit specifically controlled by some individual seller. Does air meet the test? It exists in identifiable units (cubic feet or weight) but it is a bit academic to talk about selling units of air because the buyer can have it free; there is no way to exclude the nonbuyers from using it also, so obviously no one is interested in buying it. The prospective "buyers" all prefer free air as a cheaper substitute. And the efficient firm or individual necessarily always uses the cheapest source.[2]

We now see that most of the criticism of polluters is misdirected. Polluters are looking at the world from a private point of view, which is what competitive market principles asks them to do. The valid criticism relating to the pollution problem is of the public that lets the polluters get away with it. Remember, we concluded earlier that what you *are* able to do and what you *should be able* to do are not necessarily the same. The public always sets the rules of the game. The players are expected to do the best they can under the rules. If the game is unfair, it doesn't necessarily mean the rules are being broken; it may mean that the rules are badly conceived and need to be changed.

We also see now that public policy is an integral part of competitive market economics and the operation of the private sector. The belief that government necessarily conflicts with private enterprise is erroneous. To be sure, a government saying to a polluter, "You must stop," is a conflict with a private firm or individual, but the purpose of, and preference for, competitive market economics is a social purpose and preference—it results in what we believe are fair and efficient end results. And a private sector operating in a public policy vacuum will not necessarily produce those desired end results. Therefore your thoughts and opinions on matters of economic public policy are an integral part of your personal economic life.

Since no individual *private* unit (firm or person) owns air—that is, can sell air by enforcing payment for it—apparently society as a whole "owns" the air; since it is a free good, one person has as much rightful claim to it as another. That's why its destruction through pollution brings crys of anguish from those who end up losing utility (real income) to those who gain from air pollution by having the pollution-creating product or service at less than its full cost. The complainer is paying part of someone else's cost. The chief economic objection to pollution is that it results in arbitrary real-income redistribution. This should come as no surprise when we consider the tie between income distribution and externalities developed in Chapter 19. Pollution creates an income distribution pattern quite contrary to competitive market principles. This is the fairness issue. What can be done about it?

From the efficiency point of view of society as a whole, the lack of

payment for air results in the overallocation of air to the production of
other goods, since its private cost is less than its apparent real value;
society is using up more air than it really wants to. What can be done
about it?

Happily, the correction of either the efficiency or the fairness question tends also to correct the other at the same time. Any solution clearly
requires public action; the problem exists because it slips through the
many fingers of the private sector. The general nature of any acceptable
solution is simple and obvious: Increase the cost of air to those who are
using it so that they will be required to bear the full cost of their activity,
which will solve the *unfair income distribution problem;* increase the
cost of air to those who are using it so that they will use it more sparingly,
which will solve the *efficiency problem.* Notice that both solutions start
with "increase the cost of air to those who are using it." As we said, the
solutions to the two facets of the pollution problem tend to come simultaneously. The only issue is to pick which solution is best—again, according to efficiency and fairness standards. How imaginative are you?

▷ legal prohibition ◁

One of the more straightforward solutions to the pollution problem is to
simply pass a law setting maximum emission standards on factories,
homes, autos, and so on. The legal approach snaps things into conformity
with competitive market economic principles quite nicely. The prohibition of pollution will either force the polluters out of business, thereby
depriving the users of the polluter's "underpriced" products and reducing
their real income relative to the nonusers of the polluter's products; or,
if it is feasible, the polluter may undertake extra costs of production in
the form of pollution control devices, thereby raising the cost of products
—which will also result in a correction of the income distribution inequity. In either case the users of the polluter's products are made worse
off than they were and the nonusers are made better off than they were,
thereby bringing about the desired real-income distribution correction.

▷ the license to pollute ◁

Or the polluters may be fined. If the fine is very high, it is a means of
enforcing a legal prohibition. If the fine is lower, the polluter may elect
to pay it repeatedly as a more attractive alternative to installing pollution
control equipment. The fine becomes a cost of doing business—a license
to pollute—raising the cost and therefore the price of the polluter's products to more nearly their full value. The adequacy of this approach

would seem to depend on what is done with the proceeds from the fines. If the proceeds from the fines are used for public services that would be provided anyway for those suffering from the pollution, the fines result in lower taxes than the pollution sufferers would otherwise pay, and the fines become essentially a compensatory payment in the form of a tax reduction to the pollution sufferers for the loss of utility from their resource. However, if the fine proceeds are used for public services that benefit mostly the polluters, they accomplish nothing. If the fine proceeds are used for public services for a third group—different from either the polluters or the "pollutees"—only half the problem is solved so to speak. Those using the polluters' products find income distributed away from them as desired, but the pollution sufferers get no gain. The gain goes to the third group, who get a windfall, which is just as inequitable as the "windfall" previously enjoyed by the users of the polluters' underpriced products. Nothing has really been accomplished: The fairness problem has not really been even half solved; it was merely hauled to another location and unloaded there.

▷ the side payment ◁

Occasionally a pollution problem may exist where the external cost of pollution is borne by another private party(s) rather than by the public as a whole. If so, the injured party can be compensated by a payment from the polluter. (Actually, the license to pollute is a side payment to the public.)

Suppose that there are two users of a river—one upstream from the other. The upstream user is a polluter. The downstream user has to clean up the water before he can use it. Costs are therefore shifted from the upstream user to the downstream user and hence to the final user of his products. A side payment could be required from the upstream user to the downstream user to compensate the downstream user for putting the water back into usable condition or for the extra cost of "working around" the polluted water. If the upstream user could clean up the water for less cost than the side payment, he would elect to do that and the downstream user would get clean water; if the upstream user could *not* clean up the water for less than the side payment required, he would make the payment to the downstream user, and the downstream user would make the correction in the water. Thus the cost of the pollution is borne by the polluter; the actual correction of the pollution is done by either the upstream user or the downstream user, depending on who can do it more cheaply.

▷ public cleanup ◁

In some (probably rare) cases, direct cleanup of the environment at public expense might be warranted. If the polluters are producing goods exclusively for the use of the people who are suffering the pollution, the same people who are suffering the cost of pollution are those who are getting products underpriced by the amount of the pollution. The losers are also the gainers. If they would prefer to have a cleaner environment, they could just as well go ahead and clean it up at public expense. Taxes would go up; they would have less of other things after paying the higher taxes. On the other hand, they could require the polluter to clean up at his expense; they would have less of other things after paying the cost of the cleanup in elevated prices for the polluter's products. Either way, the public comes out the same. The choice would seem to hinge on who could do it more cheaply—the government or the polluter. The problem, of course, is that underpriced products from polluters normally go largely to people who are not suffering the pollution, in which case this solution is not legitimate.

We might look at the pollution control issue in terms of *willingness to pay* versus *market prices,* as developed as a decision mechanism in Chapter 9. The best buy was that good where willingness to pay exceeded market price by the greatest margin. Could a public policy maker ask himself what the public would be willing to pay for pollution control? Willingness to pay makes an interesting handle to the problem. Suppose that there is a proposal to require spending $10 million on environmental cleanup for a city of 100,000 people. As a public policy maker, are you in favor of it? You note that the proposed cost comes to $10,000,000/100,000 = $100 per resident. Suppose also that you believe the average resident would be willing to pay $1.50 for what costs him $1.00 in that good *he values least* (the one he would give up first) from among those goods he is *now buying.* In order for the pollution cleanup expenditure to be feasible, you would have to believe that the average resident of the city would be willing to pay at least $150 for this benefit since he is now getting $1\frac{1}{2}$ times as much benefit as he is willing to pay for at the margin (willingness to pay/market price = $1.50/1.00 = $1\frac{1}{2}$ for the least valued good). For the proposed expenditure on the environment to be feasible, the payoff per dollar would have to be at least as great. Therefore on a per person basis, the project is feasible only if (willingness to pay/market price $\geq$ $150/$100 $\geq$ $1\frac{1}{2}$). Many a public policy maker has pondered essentially this question (although we have no idea in just what form), sitting in a traffic jam going to or from work or gazing out the window of the commuter train. Although there are no hard answers, such a framework for evaluation of public projects may be able to distinguish sure winners from sure losers.

The greatest difficulty with implementation of any of these pollution remedies is to determine how far to push them. What standard should be set? How much is clean air, water, and the like worth? These are the questions debated every day in the public media. It is generally accepted that absolute preservation of the environment is not worth the price— which presumably would require the extinction of mankind. How do we determine the value of the environment? The answer is no more concrete than the determination of the right amount of education. But we can discuss the issues.

It will be useful to look at the pollution question from a slightly different point of view. Asking what it will cost to preserve the environment is the same as asking what it will cost to *produce* a clean environment, since the preservation entails extra costs of one kind or another. The pollution control device on the car or factory uses up more of some resources to produce (preserve) other resources. If we make a good decision, we value that which we produce (preserve) more than that which we give up to get it. Thus we can view pollution control as a production problem where the product produced is an increase in the quality of the environment. What is the cost of the production of clean air, for example? Is it a relatively efficient or inefficient process? Does the cost of production vary according to whether we produce a lot or a little? These are standard production questions. The answers determine the optimum (efficient from the standpoint of satisfying society's desires) quantity of resources to be devoted to pollution control.

Standard production relationships would seem to apply here. They suggest that the cleaner the environment, the more costly it is to clean it up still further. Consider the *law of diminishing marginal productivity* as it relates to environmental cleanup. (See Chapter 19 and the appendix to Chapter 7.) The inputs to the production of a clean environment are (1) the dirty environment, and (2) all other devices and methods used to clean it up and the resources it takes to provide them. The dirty environment is the fixed input; the methods and devices to clean it up are the variable inputs. The law of diminishing marginal productivity says that we should expect to find the variable inputs less effective in getting more output from the fixed input as we get more and more output from the fixed input. That is, the dirty environment yields up a big improvement fairly easily, but if you want to go the last inch to perfection, that will be expensive.[3]

So the question remains: How far should we push toward a clean environment? We only know that the further we go, the more expensive it will get. Although this may seem obvious, both extreme camps of the environmental issue act as though they don't know it.

Like other products, a clean environment is subject to *diminishing marginal utility*. The more (less) we have, the less (more) we value additional amounts. If the environment is taken in comparison to all economic goods, it is not surprising that as more economic goods became available and caused the environment to deteriorate, the clamor over the environment grew, because there was a relative "shortage" of it. Neither is it surprising that, when the energy crisis hit, that environmental concern tailed off a bit (suddenly, the Alaskan pipeline didn't look so bad), since we could see that we were not quite as long on economic goods as we had thought; we became more willing to "spend" a bit more environment to have the economic goods.

We still cannot determine the right environmental program: We can only anticipate which way we can expect public preference to move under certain kinds of economic developments and therefore which way public policy should move. If we continue to get wealthier in terms of economic goods, it seems clear that we will want to spend more and more to preserve environmental quality. The only reading policy makers can get is to listen to the clamor level and try to steer a middle course. Although this is not a very tasteful guideline, it is what we must rely on in the political process—and public policy is the result of a political process. Further confusing public policy issues is the tendency for the complainers to inaccurately assess the costs of what they are asking for. Therefore, the public policy makers have to try to distinguish between what people *say* they want and what they *really* want.[4]

▶ WATERSHED MANAGEMENT ◀

Let us turn to public goods of a slightly different nature. In pollution control we were preserving the environment, which was very difficult to value in money terms. Other public undertakings may be beyond the ability of private enterprise to undertake but we may nevertheless be able to put a fairly accurate money value on them. For example, a watershed management project may create value in the form of recreational opportunities, electrical power production, increased farm crop production from improved conservation practices and irrigation, and reduced losses from flooding. Suppose that the proposed public project is a dam and reservoir on a river with an educational program to induce landowners around the reservoir to engage in better conservation practices to keep the reservoir from filling up with silt. All the benefits—recreation, electrical power, farm crop production, and decreased flooding—may be private and we can therefore put a value on them. It is easy to establish values by observing what the products and services sell for. Nevertheless, the core of the multifaceted project—dam, reservoir, and educational program—are public goods. No firm could conveniently build a dam and recover the cost by selling its various benefits to all the various users.

Projects of this type can be evaluated by comparing their estimated benefit with estimated cost. The cost of construction and operation of the project is estimated on the one hand and the value it induces is tallied up on the other. Most of that value will come from expansion in the private sector surrounding the dam and reservoir. But since it would not have come to pass without the dam and reservoir, that increase in value is attributable to the project and is its payoff. Because most of the benefits come, finally, through private sector markets, we can price them more accurately than the benefits from pollution control, which tend to be a public consumer good that never passes through a market and is therefore very difficult to value accurately.

The method of analysis used here is, as you might suspect, called *benefit–cost analysis*.[5] We use it for at least four reasons: (1) It is essentially the application to public decisions of the principles we developed earlier in the book to facilitate private decisions—willingness to pay versus market price was a statement of benefit versus cost; (2) benefit–cost analysis is actually used to determine the feasibility of many public projects; (3) it is sound as an economic principle; and (4) it is treacherous territory in practice—it is easy to be lied to. It is no coincidence that "rivers and harbors" is a part of the public domain where benefit–cost analysis is very applicable and that "rivers and harbors" is also acknowledged to be a very large pork barrel: Most anything can be made to look good on paper if the reader is not too astute. (Having just said (1) that benefit–cost analysis was the foundation for much of the early part of the book, and (2) that it is subject to manipulation by an author, we hasten to restore your confidence by saying that the real difficulties with benefit–cost analysis are as it relates to application in the public—not private—sector.)

Let us proceed with a hypothetical illustration. We warn you in advance that we are going to be "friendly" to the project to the extent of introducing some plausible "errors." That is, we want to make the project look attractive. Then we will alter things step by step to finally produce a more realistic—and less "friendly"—conclusion.

First, the costs. Suppose that it will cost $200 million to construct the necessary facilities and that it will cost $2 million per year to operate them (e.g., upkeep). Also assume that the facilities can be expected to last 50 years. All this was fairly easy to determine; we called up the engineers and asked what it would take to pull it off. (If you think that cost overruns on public projects are evidence that costs are *not* easy to determine, remember that everything is relative; wait until you see the difficulties with the benefits! "Errors" may be due to a lack of desire to tell the truth as well as to estimating difficulties.)

And now the benefits.

▶ Analysis 20–1

Suppose that the annual value of the benefits is as follows:

	AVERAGE ANNUAL BENEFIT	
Electrical power	$ 3,000,000	
Recreational services	2,000,000	
Farm crop production	1,500,000	
Flood damage reduction	500,000	
New jobs	3,000,000	(300 jobs at $10,000 each)
Total primary benefits	$10,000,000	
Secondary benefits	30,000,000	(3 times the primary benefits)
Total benefits	$40,000,000	

Primary benefits are those that come directly from the project itself. **Secondary benefits** are those that flow from the primary benefits and are therefore secondary to the project—they are one step removed. For example, if the project creates a job in power production, that employee spends his income, thereby creating jobs in all those industries where he spends (e.g., groceries, education, recreation, and automobiles). In turn, tertiary (third-level) benefits are created, although we have called all nonprimary benefits secondary. Each person who gets income saves part and spends the rest. Thus each round of spending finds a smaller amount of spending, because each round is reduced by some saving. In our example we have assumed that each primary dollar results in $3 of secondary benefits, hence secondary benefits are 3 times the primary benefits.

These benefits are going to flow forth for 50 years, the life of the project, so we compute their present value at, say, 5 percent, which we believe will be the going interest rate at which money can be obtained for such a project. From Table 13–2, the factor for 5 percent and 50 years is 18.26, so the present value of the income stream generated is

$$\$40,000,000 \times 18.26 = \$730,400,000$$

The present value of the costs is $200 million construction costs, which will be incurred now, plus $2 million annual operating costs for 50 years, or

$200,000,000 + ($2,000,000 × 18.26)
$$= \$200,000,000 + \$36,520,000 = \$236,520,000$$

Given a 5 percent opportunity cost of capital, this project has a benefit–cost ratio of

$$\frac{\$730,400,000}{\$236,520,000} = 3.09$$

We get back $3.09 for every $1 spent. When do we start construction?

▶   **Analysis 20–2**

But wait, take another look at those benefits. The $3 million in jobs is being counted twice! For example, if $3 million is the value of the output of electrical power, the $3 million received by the power company already covers the *jobs* in power production because the power company obviously pays its employees out of its receipts from the sale of power. Thus we are counting both input (jobs) and output (power). But the input is part of the output, so we are double-counting. The value of the jobs is scattered through the value of the benefits.

{   **Lesson: Avoid double-counting.**   }

Revamping the benefits to avoid double-counting, we throw out the jobs and drop the secondary benefits accordingly, because the secondary benefits depend on the primary benefits.

	AVERAGE ANNUAL BENEFIT	
Electrical power	$ 3,000,000	
Recreational services	2,000,000	
Farm crop production	1,500,000	
Flood damage reduction	500,000	
New jobs		
Total primary benefits	$ 7,000,000	
Secondary benefits	21,000,000	(3 times the primary benefits)
Total benefits	$28,000,000	

Now the present value of the benefits is

$$\$28,000,000 \times 18.26 = \$511,280,000$$

and the benefit–cost ratio drops to

$$\$511,280,000/\$236,520,000 = 2.16$$

Still very good.

▶ ## Analysis 20–3

But wait. Take still another look at those benefits. The $3 million in jobs is still buried in the value of the output of the project-related activities. Are we still counting something we should not be? Very possibly. Remember, we are totaling up the *increase* in value to economic society attributable to the *increase* in costs from the project. If the 300 jobs are going to *increase* value produced by $3 million, then it appears that we are assuming that these 300 workers were all unemployed and are therefore available at an opportunity cost of zero! That may be true, of course; but on the other hand, suppose that they were previously employed. If they are going to come to work in these project-related activities, they have to be enticed there by higher wages than they earn now, because they are going to be more productive. Suppose that they all left $8,000 jobs to take the $10,000 jobs. In that case the project is adding $2,000 per job—not $10,000. Thus 300 jobs × $2,000 per job = $600,000. This is a little more realistic as the *increased* value attributable to the project; that is, there is an $8,000 cost required to get this $10,000 benefit.

} **Lesson: Count all costs.** {

Revamping the benefits to wring out costs that, in a sense, were called benefits, we get

	AVERAGE ANNUAL BENEFIT	
Electrical power	$3,000,000	
Recreational services	2,000,000	
Farm crop production	1,500,000	
Flood damage reduction	500,000	
Less losses elsewhere	−2,400,000	(300 jobs × $8,000 loss from alternative present employment)
Total primary benefits	$ 4,600,000	
Secondary benefits	13,800,000	(3 times the primary benefits)
Total benefits	$18,400,000	

The secondary benefits fall further as the result of this assumption about employment, because when the workers left the $8,000 jobs there were *secondary losses* of 3 × $8,000 = $24,000 per worker at that point—for the same reasons that there are *secondary benefits* from this project.[6]

The present value is now

$$\$18,400,000 \times 18.26 = \$335,984,000$$

and the benefit–cost ratio falls to

$$\$335,984,000/\$236,520,000 = 1.42$$

▶ Analysis 20–4

But wait. Take yet a third look at the benefits. Is it possible that some of these benefits would come to pass without the project? Possibly. It depends on how honestly they were calculated. For example, suppose that the estimate of farm crop production was determined by projecting an upward trend in yields and adding to that the increase from irrigation and conservation practices. The general upward trend is not attributable to the project. That is, perhaps the $1.5 million was determined from what the value of farm crop production would be over time with the project in place. That is not legitimate because time alone (or more accurately, nonproject forces over time alone) would increase the value of farm crop production. The proper figure is, as always, the amount by which the value of farm crop production is *higher due to the project* than it *otherwise* would be. Perhaps some recreational development would also have occurred anyway, in which case recreational benefits are overstated also. If so, the project looks less attractive, of course. All of which brings us to another observation.

}   **Lesson: Count only *marginal* benefits.**   {

If some of the benefits would have occurred anyway, the benefit–cost ratio is somewhere below 1.42.

▶ Analysis 20–5

In addition, we have rolled merrily along assuming that 5 percent is the proper rate of capitalization. This implies that capital can be obtained for 5 percent—meaning that it can produce a 5 percent return elsewhere in the economy under comparable risk conditions. But suppose that 5 percent is too low; perhaps capital will be worth more than that over the next 50 years. Assume an opportunity cost of capital of 8 percent. If we rework the previous illustrations at 8 percent, the project looks less attractive as you would expect. If capital can command 8 percent elsewhere, obviously committing capital to this use for this particular set of benefits is less attractive than if capital can get only 5 percent elsewhere.

Table 20–1 shows that the benefit–cost ratios are lower if capitalized at a higher rate (8 instead of 5 percent). Since cost, including capital as expressed in the capitalization rate, is a statement of the value of these resources *elsewhere* in the economy and benefits are an expression of the desirability of the return that these resources can generate in *this* use, a benefit–cost ratio above 1.00 says that we have a feasible project from a public policy point of view. A benefit–cost ratio of less than 1.00 says the costs are greater than the benefits, in which case the resources should be used elsewhere and the project is therefore economically unfeasible.

In reality, a benefit-cost ratio close to 1.00 is borderline, unless the benefits are computed conservatively and the costs liberally. Therein, as we have seen, lies the hooker. Since both benefits and costs are subject to a large estimation error, the competence and motivation of the estimator is a significant consideration.

} **Lesson: "Price" capital accurately.** {

▶ **Analysis 20–6**

There may be still more difficulties. For example, we said that there would be $3 million of electrical power produced per year. Did the cost figures we gave you include the cost of construction of the actual power plant or were our costs only the costs necessary to make the water available—the dam and reservoir? We were a little vague on that point, weren't we? The context would suggest that perhaps the costs we gave you were the *public* costs only. It might also be reasonable to suppose that some private corporation is going to build the power plant in proximity to the project but that the cost of that construction will be *private* cost. If so, we must add that private cost to the public cost, since it will take that total block of resources to generate the $3 million of power per year.

Table 20–1

PRESENT VALUES OF COSTS AND BENEFITS AND BENEFIT–COST RATIOS AT 5% AND 8%

	CAPITALIZATION RATE	
	5%	8%
Present value of costs	$200,000,000 + ($2,000,000 × 18.26) = $200,000,000 + $36,520,000 = $236,520,000	$200,000,000 + ($2,000,000 × 12.23) = $200,000,000 + $24,460,000 = $224,460,000
Present value of benefits		
Analysis 20–1	$40,000,000 × 18.26 = $730,400,000	$40,000,000 × 12.23 = $489,200,000
Analysis 20–2	$28,000,000 × 18.26 = $511,280,000	$28,000,000 × 12.23 = $342,440,000
Analysis 20–3	$18,400,000 × 18.26 = $335,984,000	$18,400,000 × 12.23 = $225,032,000
Analysis 20–4	Analysis 20–4 shows the difference in present value at 5% and 8%	
Analysis 20–5	Less than $335,984,000	Less than $225,032,000
Benefit–cost ratios		
Analysis 20–1	$\dfrac{\$730,400,000}{\$236,520,000} = 3.09$	$\dfrac{\$489,200,000}{\$224,460,000} = 2.18$
Analysis 20–2	$\dfrac{\$511,280,000}{\$236,520,000} = 2.16$	$\dfrac{\$342,440,000}{\$224,460,000} = 1.53$
Analysis 20–3	$\dfrac{\$335,984,000}{\$236,520,000} = 1.42$	$\dfrac{\$225,032,000}{\$224,460,000} = 1.00$
Analysis 20–4	Analysis 20–4 shows the difference in benefit–cost ratios at 5% and 8%	
Analysis 20–5	Less than 1.42	Less than 1.00

}   **Lesson (relearned): Count all costs—public and private.**   {

It is easy to see with this highly simplified illustration that it is not too difficult to take the analysis where you want it to go if you think your reader is not very sophisticated. "Optimistic" estimates of benefits and costs, capitalizing at a low rate of interest, double-counting benefits and omitting costs, are all fairly easy to do. Even if you are suspicious that the project promoter has an interest on one side or the other, it is frequently difficult to argue the other side persuasively because you are dealing with estimates of benefits, costs, and interest rates over a long period of time; although it may be argued your opponent's figures are subject to "evaluation," you may be hard-pressed to show that yours are any better. Our example has suggested that benefits are frequently overstated and costs understated.

So how should benefit–cost analysis be viewed and used? With respect and caution—but not with disdain. We present a sketch of it here to suggest that the *principle* behind it is economically impeccable and that it rightfully constitutes the basis for evaluation of much public economic activity. Anything can be misused, however, and benefit–cost analysis is particularly subject to abuse. You, as a private citizen making decisions on public issues, must be aware of that.

SUMMARY

1 • If we subscribe to competitive market economic principles, we evaluate public policy decisions according to *fairness* and *efficiency*.

2 • Pollution is a *negative externality*.

3 • Pollution is *unfair* because cost is usually borne by people who do not get the offsetting benefit.

4 • Pollution is *inefficient* because a resource is "overused" in the absence of specific controls by anyone who could extract a payment for it—which would elevate its cost to the user of the resource and thereby prompt the user to use the resource more sparingly.

5 • No specific party is able to sell the resources being polluted (the environment) because it is a free public good. Therein lies the problem. It is outside the net of the competitive market system.

6 • Polluters may be required by law to stop polluting, in which case the polluters and the users of the polluter's products bear the cost.

7 • A "license to pollute" is a compensating payment to the public for its loss of utility from pollution.

8 • If a private party is injured by pollution, the compensating payment (side payment) may be made directly to the private party.

9 • Ever higher levels of environmental quality come at ever higher costs because the "production" of a clean environment seems to be subject to the law of diminishing marginal productivity; ever higher levels of environmental quality are worth ever less because environmental quality seems to be subject to the law of diminishing utility, as are economic goods at whose sacrifice environmental quality comes. Therefore, as we "produce" more environment, it becomes more costly and less valuable. In private goods the market tells us when to stop producing: We have no similar mechanism for the environment.

10 • Benefit–cost analysis can be used to evaluate the economic feasibility of public projects where the cost and benefits can be estimated with adequate accuracy.

11 • If the present value of the benefits exceeds the present value of the costs, the benefit–cost ratio will be greater than 1.00, and the project is feasible.

12 • The benefit–cost ratio is usually quite sensitive to the interest rate on which present values are computed. Thus what you think capital is going to be worth over the future is central in determining the economic feasibility of many public projects. This is to be expected, since many public projects require enormous amounts of capital.

13 • In addition, an accurate benefit–cost ratio may be difficult to establish because costs and benefits may be far-reaching and hard to value accurately.

14 • Benefit–cost analysis is impeccable as an economic

foundation for evaluating public projects, but its implementation is subject to manipulation. Costs or benefits may be estimated particularly liberally or conservatively; capitalization rates may be selected to make a project look good or bad; costs and benefits may be double-counted or overlooked; benefits may be included that would have happened even in the absence of the project. Thus benefit–cost analysis is a good tool, but it must be carefully and conscientiously used.

study materials

1 • In the absence of significant private dimensions, why are public policy questions perhaps more related to efficiency than to fairness?

2 • Explain the concept that in the competitive market system the purchaser pays the full cost and receives the full benefit.

3 • Explain the concept that in economic terms pollution occurs only when someone complains or is inclined to complain.

4 • How does pollution result in an arbitrary real-income redistribution?

5 • Explain the statement: "Users of goods and services produced by polluters get underpriced goods."

6 • Considering only the private issues, does anyone benefit from pollution? Is anyone hurt by pollution? How?

7 • What economic principle explains, at least in part, the reason(s) for greater concern for the environment occurring at a time of very high level of production of goods and services.

8 • Explain the statement that "complaints are to politics what prices are to economics."

9 • Why is benefit–cost analysis difficult and suspect, especially when considering public goods and services and public policy?

10 • Which is more difficult to assess, benefit or cost? Why?

footnotes

[1] This definition of pollution is more economic than technical. Technically, there may be pollution if there is any man-made change in the environment.

Economically, there is pollution only if altering the environment makes a difference to someone. If it makes no difference to anyone, the resource had no value
and destroying it through "pollution" entailed no loss of utility to anyone, in
which case there was, in fact, no pollution at all—from an economic point of
view.

2 *Compressed* air is sold, of course. But it is not really the air that is being sold
but rather the changed form of its existence. That is, the compression service is
what is really being sold. The buyer is forced to pay for that because the compression service is not a free good, so it will not be available without a payment.

3 Most of the ring in the bathtub comes off easy: If you want to remove the
last trace, it comes off hard. Never thought of it as a production problem, did
you?

4 It is fun, and maybe even instructive, to make comparisons between our economic system and political system.

   Economic System: In the private sector, consisting of a market economy,
individuals register their desires by buying or not buying and selling or not
selling. Out of this comes a set of equilibrium prices and the economic system
responds to changes in them. In an analogous vein . . .

   Political System: In the public sector, consisting of a political system, individuals register their desires by complaining or not complaining on either side
of all issues. Out of this comes a set of equilibrium complaints and the political
system responds to changes in them.

   Thus complaints are to politics somewhat as prices are to economics. If the
complaints go up, something is becoming more valuable relative to other things.
Perhaps someone can develop a "complaint index" that is as reliable as prices.
In the meantime, it is easy to see why we prefer the impersonal reliableness of
markets as the allocator of those goods which markets can handle—private goods.
In public goods, we have to settle for second best. (Notice that the articulate
complainer is to politics what the careful shopper is to economics; each gets more
for his time and money.)

5 Frequently called cost–benefit analysis. It makes no difference whether the
method is called benefit–cost or cost–benefit. It all comes out the same. It is
probably a bit easier to see the meaning in benefit–cost form.

6 It is now easy to see that a public project can much more easily be justified
if it will *increase* employment than if it will simply shift employment from one
place or activity to another. This undoubtedly comes as no great surprise—the
public project as an aid to a depressed area is a case in point—but the formal
explanation of that justification is now before us.

ANNOTATED BIBLIOGRAPHY

The basic purpose of our book is to "get your thinking straightened out"; it is not to "tell you which brand of cheese is the best buy." (That depends on what kind of cheese you like and only you can answer that.) But after grasping the principles of personal economic behavior you will indeed need to know how to proceed in the market-place and where to go for assistance in implementing your chosen course. In addition, you may want to pursue questions and issues of economics and related disciplines further. Therefore, we are offering the following sources for your consideration.

There is no problem finding information; the problem is culling the wheat and the chaff from a quantity of material that would choke a hippopotamus. At the risk of errors of omission we believe that the references cited here are worthy on one or more of the following grounds.

1 • The reference is an excellent source of sources. There is no way we can list all the useful references on buying a car for example, but we can offer you sources that do list other sources by title, author, and/or subject.

2 • The reference is particularly strong in a specific area not otherwise populated by good references.

3 • The reference is widely accepted and respected by persons knowledgeable in the subject.

4 • The reference has withstood the test of time.

5 • The reference picks up and develops the thread spun in this book.

It is our intention to keep our list relatively short given the range of subjects covered. It is not the final answer to your questions; it is the portal through which you will find your answers. The references cite other sources that you may wish to follow. In each instance, brief comment explains the particular strength of the source. Generally, the references are written for laymen—but for serious laymen. If you are genuinely interested in learning the particulars of a subject, you will find most of the references understandable without extensive background and, hopefully, even enjoyable.

▶   PART I   ◀

▶   VALUES AND ECONOMICS

Boulding, Kenneth E. **Beyond Economics: Essays on Society, Religion and Ethics.** Ann Arbor, Mich.: The University of Michigan Press, 1968.

Boulding, Kenneth E. **Economics as a Science.** New York: McGraw-Hill Book Company, 1970.

No discussion relating economics to its noneconomic foundations is complete without the articulate wisdom and insight of Kenneth Boulding, an economist whose contributions in philosophy, mathematics, and the social sciences place him among the world's leading contemporary intellectuals. He always has something to say to everyone—professional and neophyte alike; he is delightful.

Economics as a Science is a collection of seven essays, entitled (1) Economics as a Social Science; (2) Economics as an Ecological Science; (3) Economics as a Behavioral Science; (4) Economics as a Political Science; (5) Economics as a Mathematical Science; (6) Economics as a Moral Science; and (7) Economics and the Future of Man.

Beyond Economics covers a broad range of subjects, but Part III, entitled "Religion and Ethics," is probably of the most interest to anyone exploring economic behavior as it stems from values.

Hammer, Louis Z. **Value and Man.** New York: McGraw-Hill Book Company, 1966.

This book of readings in philosophy is for the student who is interested in probing as deeply as possible into the foundations of value and therefore of consumer choice. The selections are written by leading thinkers throughout history, and many (if not all) of the selections have played a significant part in the history of man. Although the book has no particular economics orientation, at least four of the authors—David Hume, John Locke, John Stuart Mill, and Friedrich Engels—figure prominently in the development of economic thought.

Hook, Sidney, ed. **Human Values and Economic Policy: A Symposium.** New York: New York University Press, 1967.

The essays in this book relate more narrowly to economic values and public policy than the essays in *Value and Man,* which are broader ranging. Nevertheless, it is clear in this book also that economic choices are based on noneconomic values. The public policy orientation of the book makes it a good springboard for the discussion of public policy in Part IV of our book.

Rath, Louis E., Merrill Harmin, and Sidney B. Simon. **Values and Teaching.** Columbus, Ohio: Charles E. Merrill Publishing Company, 1966.

This book on values is of considerable interest to the general reader despite the educational orientation suggested by the title. It is of considerable aid to insight into oneself and is interesting reading besides. It has an extensive bibliography of other sources on value formation.

▶ **PSYCHOLOGY AND ECONOMICS**

Holloway, Robert J., Robert A. Mittelstaedt, and M. Venkatesan. **Consumer Behavior: Contemporary Research in Action.**
Boston: Houghton Mifflin Company, 1971.

As explained in the appendix to Chapter 2, this reference offers insight into consumer behavior from a marketing point of view, although
it is written at a higher level than our book.

Katona, George. **Psychological Analysis of Economic Behavior.** New York: McGraw-Hill Book Company, 1951.

Katona, George. **The Powerful Consumer.** New York: Mc-
Graw-Hill Book Company, 1960.

Katona, George, Burkhard Strumpel, and Ernest Zahn. **Aspirations and Affluence.** New York: McGraw-Hill Book Company,
1971.

As pointed out in the appendix to Chapter 2, George Katona is the
best-known of those who would bridge the gap between psychology and
economics. The three works listed, which relate economic behavior to psychological and sociological influences and span a period of 20 years,
cover a great deal of territory but nevertheless constitute only a few of
the books that this productive scholar has published during this period of
time.

Markin, Rom J. **The Psychology of Consumer Behavior.** Englewood Cliffs, N.J.: Prentice-Hall, Inc., 1969.

Although this book is written from a marketing–management approach to consumers, the explanations of consumer reaction and motivation can be a considerable stimulus to the development of your own maturity as a consumer.

▶ **GENERAL ECONOMICS TEXTS**

McConnell, Campbell R. **Economics,** 5th ed. New York: Mc-
Graw-Hill Book Company, 1972.

Samuelson, Paul A. **Economics,** 9th ed. New York: McGraw-
Hill Book Company, 1973.

Spencer, Milton H. **Contemporary Economics.** New York: Worth Publishers, Inc., 1971.

These are three of the more popular, "traditional," beginning economics texts. Many of the concepts and approaches to personal economics we use in our book are, of course, applicable to a wider variety of situations and can be developed in more formal terms. These books (along with many others) do just that, as well as *many* things in addition. Samuelson's book is undoubtedly the most widely read economics text ever written; if you can explain everything in it, you are a *very* decent general economist. (The same may be said for the other two books.) McConnell's *Economics,* which appeared a few years after Samuelson's is written on a slightly lower level, covers a more restricted range of subject matter, and is less detailed; it, too, has been a very popular text. Spencer's is a new book that has gained quick acceptance with its more topical, current-events approach. In addition to photographs and biographical sketches of leading economic thinkers, it contains a dictionary of economic terms and concepts.

Heyne, Paul T. **The Economic Way of Thinking.** Chicago: Science Research Associates, Inc., 1973.

Rogers, Augustus J., III. **Choice: An Introduction to Economics.** Englewood Cliffs, N.J.: Prentice-Hall, Inc., 1971.

Rogers, Augustus J., III. **Goods and Not So Goods: Consumer Economics for the '70s.** Hinsdale, Ill.: The Dryden Press, Inc., 1972.

Sanborn, Henry N. **What, How, For Whom: The Decisions of Economic Organization.** Baltimore: Cotter-Barnard Company, 1972.

These paperbacks are representative of books that have recently appeared on the scene for beginning economics students. They include many of the fundamental concepts covered in such traditional texts as McConnell, Samuelson, and Spencer. However, the coverage is much less extensive and often less intensive as well. They are invariably less formal in style and tend to be written at a lower level than the traditional, beginning economics texts.

▶ **DECISION AND STRATEGY**

McDonald, John. **Strategy in Poker, Business and War.** New York: W. W. Norton & Company, Inc., 1950.

With only slight exaggeration, it might be said that there is little
in life that is not akin to poker, business, and war. Certainly a book that
purports to develop a strategy to cover all three situations must be considered when our concern is for decisions that lead to a goal—in other
words, strategy. The book is short, humorous, plainly written, and laced
with illustrative cartoons. But basically it is sound stuff and provides insight into modern decision-making techniques and mechanisms.

Parkinson, C. Northcote. **Parkinson's Law and Other Studies
in Administration.** Boston: Houghton Mifflin Company, 1957.

Although Professor Parkinson's message is not as directly personal
as ours, he does deal, in his delightfully humorous way, with human
behavior and decision—both private and public. From his keen insight
have come such modern classics as (1) the amount of work expands to fill
the time allotted to it, and (2) the amount of care and time given to a
decision tends to be inversely proportional to the amount of money
involved. If you can see yourself in his writings (as you almost surely
will), you will be the better-off for it and will have been entertained in
the process.

▶ PART II ◀

▶   GENERAL CONSUMER ECONOMICS

Burk, Marguerite. **Consumption Economics: A Multidisciplinary Approach.** New York: John Wiley & Sons, Inc., 1968.

This work provides a good overview of consumption economics as a
discipline from a variety of standpoints. With the exception of certain
sections the book is comprehensible to the layman. It contains excellent
references and is recommended browsing for anyone interested in pursuing consumption economics as an academic specialty. You should be
forewarned, however, that consumption economics as an academic discipline looks somewhat different from consumer economics approached
from a purely personal point of view.

Gordon, Leland J., and Stewart M. Lee. **Economics for Consumers,** 6th ed. New York: Van Nostrand Reinhold Company,
1972.

Troelstrup, Arch W. **The Consumer in American Society: Personal and Family Finance,** 4th ed. New York: McGraw-Hill Book Company, 1970.

Warmke, Roman F., Eugene D. Wyllie, W. Harmon Wilson, and Elvin S. Eyster. **Consumer Economic Problems,** 8th ed. Cincinnati, Ohio: Southwestern Publishing Company, 1973.

These are three of the more popular textbooks in the field of consumer economics as it has existed for the past several years. They are generally of a how-to-do-it nature and cover a wide range of subjects, such as budgeting, money management and use of credit, "buymanship," housing, insurance, health care, investment, and taxes, in addition to consumer protection legislation. The breadth of their subject necessarily limits their penetration. They are particularly useful as an avenue to other sources on a wide variety of consumer subjects.

Fitzsimmons, Cleo, and Flora Williams. **The Family Economy: Nature and Management of Resources.** Ann Arbor, Mich.: Edwards Brothers, Inc., 1973.

This is the only beginning consumer economics book we have seen that makes a serious attempt to treat consumption activity in its economic context (as economics is traditionally defined). The book describes a broad spectrum of basic economic terms and concepts and develops the area of family consumption from that context. It also discusses specific household management topics.

Niss, James J. **Consumer Economics.** Englewood Cliffs, N.J.: Prentice-Hall, Inc., 1974.

This relatively short paperback covers the application and execution of many of the choices that consumers face. There are chapters on budgeting, consumer credit, housing, occupational choice, insurance, and investment. There is also an explanation of certain consumer goods prices as they relate to cost of production in the business sector.

▶ GENERAL PERIODICALS

Business Week (weekly magazine).

Forbes (biweekly magazine).

Fortune (monthly magazine).

These are the three most popular business magazines; they are useful in keeping abreast of economic affairs as they relate to your personal life.

Forbes, with its numerous short features about individual firms and business leaders and through its regular investment columns written by respected financial analysts, is probably the most useful from the stance of an individual investor. *Business Week* tends to emphasize and analyze overall business and economic conditions more than the other two. *Fortune* leans more toward feature-length stories on persons, firms, and industries and probably has the most journalistic flair of the three.

Changing Times (monthly magazine).

Changing Times is one of the most popular magazines available to the householder interested in stretching the dollar. It covers a wide range of consumer and money management subjects with its short, how-to-do-it articles. As it is written for mass circulation through subscription, it is geared to those with no background in the formalities of consumer or personal economics, though with a slight emphasis on topics of interest to the upper-middle class. It is published by the Kiplinger organization, a long-established advisory service.

Consumer Reports (monthly magazine).

A valuable source for the comparison shopper, particularly in the field of consumer durables. It is published by the Consumers' Union, which tests products, reports test results, formally rates products, and discusses products in detail in light of the test results and the opinions of the testers—all by brand name. Each issue contains a cumulative index for the preceding 12 months, so that you can locate a product in which you are interested in an earlier issue. There is also an annual *Buying Guide,* a compendium of results of tests and reports on products.

The Wall Street Journal (daily newspaper).

This daily newspaper (published every day the financial markets are open) is the most widely read financial paper in the United States. It has the second largest circulation of *any* daily U.S. newspaper. It contains a vast quantity of market reports plus news stories relevant to the business and economic world. It is considered a high-quality paper journalistically. It is "must" reading for any serious investor.

▶ **BUDGETING AND MANAGEMENT**

Mumey, Glen A. **Personal Economic Planning.** New York: Holt, Rinehart and Winston, Inc., 1972.

This book is basically an elaboration of our material on investment and insurance. It develops personal accounting as a planning tool and proceeds to personal financial management. Good practical questions and problems included.

▶ **INVESTMENT**

Graham, Benjamin. **The Intelligent Investor,** revised 4th edition. New York: Harper & Row, 1973.

Graham, Benjamin and Charles McGolrick. **The Interpretation of Financial Statements,** second revision. New York: Harper & Row, 1964.

These two little books by "the father of fundamental analysis" are very useful to the layman who wishes to become a serious investor in stocks and bonds. They are nontechnical and provide an excellent foundation for the determination of the fundamental quality and value of securities and for the development of various kinds of investment programs. Their origins in earlier editions go back 30 years—a testimony to the quality of these works.

Keltner, Chester W. **How To Make Money in Commodities.** Kansas City: Keltner Statistical Service, 1960.

By far the quickest way to get rich is in commodities—corn, wheat, soybeans, soybean oil, cattle, hogs, pork bellies, plywood, lumber, silver, copper, frozen orange juice concentrate, cocoa, coffee, and foreign currency, to name a few. Since there "ain't no free lunch," it should be obvious that commodities are also by far the quickest way to get poor. Gains or losses of 100 percent in a few days are common. (It has been said that a commodity trader who dies wealthy, dies before his time.)

You buy or sell commodity "futures," depending on whether you think the price of the commodity is going up or down. These markets are big and important and growing in importance, but, oddly, little understood by the public. The value of the volume of commodities traded is very large—of the same order of magnitude as the value of

common stocks traded. The markets serve a necessary economic function
—the transfer of the risk of a price change in the commodity. Since these
markets are not widely followed by the public, it might be assumed that
they are the exclusive domain of the obscure big-time professional. Not
so. It is curious that although these markets are admirably suited to the
small investor—but the small investor who likes lots of action of course—
the small investors are largely ignorant of them. If you see yourself as a
potential lover of action, you will find this book's pedantic title indicative
of a feet-on-the-ground approach. It is published by one of the most
respected operators in the field and covers all aspects of the subject from
a practical point of view, including the basic function of the markets,
where you fit into the picture, limitation of risk, trading strategies and
how they would have worked out at various points in market history.
The discussion is from the standpoint of grains (corn, wheat, soybeans,
etc.), but the message is applicable across the board.

> Loeb, Gerald M. **The Battle for Investment Survival.** New
> York: Simon and Schuster, Inc., 1965.

Gerald Loeb, stockbroker, financial analyst, columnist, and successful
investor, sometimes referred to as the "Dean of Wall Street," relates his
thoughts on investing, based on nearly 50 years of experience. First published in 1935, this little book, written in a totally nontechnical style, is
still cited by some very knowledgeable people in the financial world as
one of the most useful books in the field. Because it has been around so
long, your library may have a musty copy (although it has been updated
several times). No matter. The message of the early version is nearly
as good as the last. Some references to tax law, for example, will be out
of date, but such particulars are not the meat of the book. Indeed, since
investments markets are human institutions, a little imagination reveals
that there is much useful advice about life in general scattered along the
way. Perhaps the title *The Battle for Survival* (omitting *Investment*)
would be apt; investing is merely a special case of general survival.
    There are many popular books of the how-I-made-a-million-without-
really-trying type which are entertaining reading but provide no (or incorrect) understanding of the basic issues in successful investing.

> Loeb, Gerald M. **The Battle for Stock Market Profits.** New
> York: Simon and Schuster, Inc., 1971.

Although similar in style and tone to *The Battle for Investment
Survival,* this book is more recent and oriented more directly to the stock
market. Nonetheless there is a lot of good advice that is applicable beyond

the stock market if you but recognize it. The first two paragraphs from the Foreword (p. 11) set the tone.

> *The first part of this book concerns the use of my Checklist to give you the essential facts needed for making an investment decision. This is followed by a practical discussion of my concepts for successful investing and recommended courses of action based on the facts developed in the Checklist. It is the kind of action and investment philosophy that is not based, as I once facetiously remarked, on the way it's taught at Harvard Business School.*
>
> *Every investor has the problem of how to get the most out of his investments. Many read books on the subject and study in other ways, but in the end are confronted with the practical problem of what to do.*

Semenow, Robert W. **Questions and Answers on Real Estate,** 7th ed. Englewood Cliffs, N.J.: Prentice-Hall, Inc., 1972.

Just what the title says it is, the book is sometimes cited as the "Bible of Real Estate." The author is both academician and practitioner, knowledgeable in economics, business, and law. The book contains illustrative cases, a glossary of real estate terms, many test questions at the end of each section, and many arithmetic problems relating to real estate. The short section on valuation and appraisal is especially useful to the prospective real estate investor.

▶ **INSURANCE**

Bickelhaupt, David L., and John H. Magee. **General Insurance,** 8th ed. Homewood, Ill.: Richard D. Irwin, Inc., 1970.

This book, currently in its eighth edition, is one of the *Irwin Series in Insurance and Economic Security,* which consists of about 30 volumes on insurance and related topics. Needless to say, somewhere in the *Series* your question will be answered. This book, *General Insurance,* is somewhat of an overview. It does not tell you which is the best insurance buy, but it will familiarize you with the basic features of different kinds of policies and will provide some guidelines as to what kind of insurance coverage you might need.

Denenberg, Herbert S., R. Eilers, G. Hoffman, C. Kline, J. Melone, and H. Snyder. **Risk and Insurance.** Englewood Cliffs, N.J.: Prentice-Hall, Inc., 1964.

The preface (p. vii) suggests an approach to insurance in harmony with the approach here in our book but at a more specific level.

> *The purpose of this book is to provide a beginning text with an approach substantially different from anything previously available. It must be stated at the outset, however, that the traditional textbooks have well served the insurance industry and insurance education. All of the authors of this volume have both learned their insurance and taught their students from these traditionally oriented insurance texts. Our debt to their authors is indeed great. And yet, from our experience as students and teachers, we have slowly become aware of certain inadequacies in their presentation. First, they tend to describe specific insurance contracts in great detail while they neglect the fundamental principles of risk and insurance. Second, they have been written primarily from the viewpoint of the insurance industry rather than the consumer.*
>
> *In contrast, our approach has been guided by three specific objectives. First, we have attempted to integrate the subject of risk and its treatment with other fields of learning. We firmly believe that for the beginning student it is desirable to emphasize the interlacing of knowledge, rather than its separation. By so doing we hope that those students who already have a particular interest in other fields will also become interested in risk and insurance.*

Part Four, which discusses personal property and liability risks may be of the most direct interest.

The **Shoppers' Guide** series.

The Insurance Department of the State of Pennsylvania has produced a series of shoppers' guides on the purchase of insurance and related subjects. The pamphlets compare cost of insurance by company name. The series represents a breakthrough of consumerism in insurance. The *Guides* came into existence under the tenure of Herbert S. Denenberg as Pennsylvania Insurance Commissioner. Denenberg is a man of impeccable academic credentials who, at one time, occupied the Henry J. Loman chair at the Wharton School of Finance and Commerce. The chair was endowed with $500,000 from the insurance industry—an investment it surely, at times, has regretted. The *Guides* have become immensely popular and may be ordered from the Pennsylvania Insurance Department, Harrisburg. Although they focus on the companies doing business in Pennsylvania, they are very applicable throughout the United States. Very practical. A request to the Pennsylvania Insurance Department for all the items in the series produced the following blizzard of booklets and pamphlets.

Insurance

- *A Shopper's Guide to Financially Strong Insurance Companies*
- *A Shopper's Guide to Life Insurance*
- *A Shopper's Guide to Term Life Insurance*
- *A Shopper's Guide to Straight Life Insurance*
- *A Shopper's Guide to Pennsylvania Automobile Insurance*
- *A Shopper's Guide to Insurance on Mobile Homes (Pennsylvania)*
- *A Motorist's Guide Through No Fault*

Health Care

- *A Shopper's Guide to Hospitals in the Philadelphia Area*
- *A Shopper's Guide to Surgery*
- *A Shopper's Guide to Dentistry*
- *Citizens' Bill of Hospital Rights*

Miscellaneous

- *Citizens' Bill of Rights and Consumers' Guide to Nuclear Power*

▶ **BIBLIOGRAPHIC SOURCES**

American Council on Consumer Interests Newsletter

The ACCI publishes a four-page newsletter nine times a year which is very useful in keeping abreast of current developments in the field of consumer economics, including references and protective actions by agencies. Although the *Newsletter* is apparently aimed primarily at teachers as a source of current information, there would seem to be no reason why anyone interested could not pay the modest membership fee and receive the newsletter.

Consumer Product Information Coordinating Center. **Consumer Product Information.** Washington, D.C.: Government Printing Office.

This booklet, published quarterly, lists U.S. government publications of interest to the consumer. Most of the items are free or very modestly priced. The booklet is free from Consumer Product Information, Washington, D.C. 20407. Ask to be put on the mailing list.

Office of Consumer Affairs and the New York Public Library. **Consumer Education Bibliography.** Washington, D.C.: Government Printing Office.

This bibliography is designed chiefly as a teacher's aid in the identification of over 4,000 books, pamphlets, articles, and audiovisual aids relating to consumer education, but the consumer may also find things of interest in it. It contains a list of university and business sources of information, of state consumer protection agencies, and a section on children as consumers.

▶ PART III ◀

Internal Revenue Service. **Your Federal Income Tax: For Individuals** (annual ed.). Washington, D.C.: Government Printing Office.

This is the "master" income tax booklet; the various flyers and pamphlets on specific tax topics are frequently reprints or virtual reprints from this book. It is designed to enable the individual taxpayer to complete his own tax returns. It also tells you what documents to send for if you need more elaborate information. Very few people will need more than is in this book. It contains illustrative tax forms (completed) and is very well indexed. Most taxpayers would find browsing through it to be time well spent. It is available at a nominal cost from any Internal Revenue office or from the Superintendent of Documents, Government Printing Office, Washington, D.C. 20402.

Selected U.S. Government Publications. Washington, D.C.: Government Printing Office.

This free biweekly booklet lists a selected variety of government publications that might be of interest to a wide variety of people. It contains a short statement of the content of each publication listed. Ask to be put on the mailing list if you are interested: Superintendent of Documents; ATTN: "S.L." Mail List; Washington, D.C. 20402.

Social Security Administration. **Social Security Programs in the United States** (revised periodically). Washington, D.C.: Government Printing Office.

This is the "master" booklet that explains the particulars of the Old-Age, Survivors, Disability, and Health Insurance (OASDHI) System, commonly called the social security system. It is what is otherwise available in an armful of pamphlets. It gives a brief history and rationale of the system, how it relates to other public assistance programs, how it relates to some private pension programs, and how to determine your benefits.

Social security is undoubtedly a larger factor in personal finance and planning than most people probably realize, and it is growing. Many people would find that their single largest asset is their social security account. Familiarity with the system is essential to plan effectively for the future. This booklet is available free from any social security office or for a nominal fee from the Superintendent of Documents, Government Printing Office, Washington, D.C. 20402.

▶ PART IV ◀

▶ EDUCATION

Carnegie Commission on Higher Education. **Higher Education: Who Pays? Who Benefits? Who Should Pay?** New York: McGraw-Hill Book Company, June 1973.

Carnegie Commission on Higher Education. **The More Effective Use of Resources.** New York: McGraw-Hill Book Company, June 1972.

Committee for Economic Development. **The Management and Financing of Colleges.** October 1973.

As indicated in the text, these references deal specifically with the subject of higher education, and particularly with the public–private benefit–cost relationship. Since both the Carnegie Commission and the CED are reputable agencies and have had significant impact on education and/or economic policy at one time or another, their views are worthy of acquaintance if not agreement.

Schultz, Theodore W. **Investment in Human Capital.** New York: The Free Press, 1971.

Although other economists have done a great deal of work on the economics of education, this book draws on many years of work by a pioneer in the field, is readable, and is amply documented, thereby providing leads to other sources.

▶ **GENERAL PUBLIC POLICY**

Caudill, Harry M. **Night Comes to the Cumberlands: A Biography of a Depressed Area.** Boston: Atlantic Monthly Press, 1963.

This account of the plight of the coal mining country of eastern Kentucky is as much or more history as it is economics. Although the finer points of benefit–cost, externalities, and competitive markets are not in the forefront, it is clear that these are the principles in terms of which the economic problems of this area (and many others) are explained and in terms of which they will be solved if, indeed, they are to be solved. It is clear that the problems of externalities reach not only from individual to individual at one point in time but across time from generation to generation.

Council on Environmental Quality. **Environmental Quality** (annual report beginning 1970). Washington, D.C.: Government Printing Office.

This is very possibly the best source of information on environmental matters as an initial reference. It summarizes state and federal activities and provides references to specific topics within the field. It contains summaries of many studies, one of which is cited next.

Council on Environmental Quality. **The Economic Impact of Pollution Control: A Summary of Recent Studies.** Prepared for the Department of Commerce and Environmental Protection Agency. Washington, D.C.: Government Printing Office, March 1972.

This report is a series of studies of costs of pollution cleanup to given standards in 11 industries plus the general impact on the economy as a whole. It is a good illustration of the real-world consideration of the magnitude and distribution of the cost of cleanup. The studies were done by several private consulting firms.

Garvey, Gerald. **Energy, Ecology, Economy.** New York: W. W. Norton & Company, Inc., 1972.

Ginsberg, Helen. **Poverty, Economics and Society.** Boston: Little, Brown and Company, 1972.

Grieson, Ronald E. **Urban Economics: Readings and Analysis.** Boston: Little, Brown and Company, 1973.

These three paperbacks are representative of material available in essay or readings form that discuss and evaluate current public policy issues. Although not always at the forefront, it is clear that the unifying thread is that which we have presented here: Is it fair? Is it efficient? If not, what should be done about it?

Harrington, Michael. **The Other America: Poverty in the United States,** rev. ed. Baltimore: Penguin Books, Inc., 1969.

This account of poverty in America is similar in nature, for our purposes, to *Night Comes to the Cumberlands,* but it gives broader coverage to the *general* issues of income distribution and the issues of choice, personal and public, that relate to it.

INDEX